The Metamorphosis of *Tianxian pei*

The Metamorphosis of *Tianxian pei*

Local Opera under the Revolution (1949–1956)

Wilt L. Idema

The Chinese University Press

The Metamorphosis of* Tianxian pei*:
Local Opera under the Revolution (1949–1956)
By Wilt L. Idema

ISBN: 978-962-996-593-8

The Chinese University Press
The Chinese University of Hong Kong
Sha Tin, N.T., Hong Kong
Fax: +852 2603 7355
E-mail: cup@cuhk.edu.hk
Website: www.chineseupress.com

Printed in Hong Kong

Contents

Preface

This volume originated as a sequel to my 2009 work on Dong Yong, *Filial Piety and Its Divine Rewards*. Once I started looking into the modern stage adaptations of the legend of Dong Yong's meeting with an immortal, I was amazed by the number of available scripts, especially of the Huangmei Opera version of *Tianxian pei* (Married to a Heavenly Immortal). These scripts allowed me to follow in great detail the transformation of the play in the early years of the People's Republic of China (PRC). The subsequent national and international success of the cinematic adaptation of the play had resulted in a considerable number of writings by the involved scriptwriters, actors, and directors that make it clear that the rewritten opera required a complete rethinking of both its staging and its performance. Together with the writings by contemporary critics, these works inform us, in great detail, about many of the issues involved in the refashioning of local opera in order to meet the requirements of the Communist Party's vision of China's socialist modernization in the early years of the People's Republic. This is a subject that is only now beginning to attract a growing number of scholars.

While I was pleasantly surprised by the number and the quality of writings about the play by those who were involved in its rewriting and performing, to my surprise I also noticed how little attention the play or the movie *Married to a Heavenly Immortal*, despite the immense popularity in China, received in Western scholarship on China. Bringing together issues about the modern rejection of traditional morality, the reform of traditional opera in modern times, and the cruelty of the Revolution toward its own ardent supporters, *Married to a Heavenly Immortal* offers a unique window on the cultural history of China in the twentieth century.

Following a general introduction, this book consists of two parts. In the first part I present a detailed study of the process of revision of *Married to a Heavenly Immortal* in the early 1950s, followed by full translations of both the traditional Huangmei Opera play and a representative edition of the revised play to allow the reader to evaluate both the nature and extent of the changes in the revision (some readers may prefer to read the translated plays before they turn to the account of the process of revision). The second part presents a selection of contemporary articles by scriptwriters, directors, performers, and critics. These allow a detailed understanding of the meanings attached to many of these transformations and at the same time introduce a number of the technical and artistic issues in the performance, as perceived by those most directly involved.

By now almost everyone who was directly involved in the revision of *Married to a Heavenly Immortal* and its performance in the 1950s has passed away, and I have made no attempt to track down the few survivors and interview them. Confronted by the richness of the materials that are readily available in print, I also have not engaged in local archival research. Fortunately, many of the participants in the revision of *Married to a Heavenly Immortal* have been very open in some of the articles they wrote near the end of their lives. One important document that could have resurfaced from archival research, however, would be Sang Hu's original script for the cinematic adaptation. It is not known whether this original script survives, and if so, where it might be found.

An obvious defect of this study is my neglect of the musical aspects of the play. All contemporary observers, even the most critical, praise the appeal of its melodies. Unfortunately, I am completely unqualified to discuss this aspect of Huangmei Opera.

Wilt L. Idema
Leiden, January 2014

Acknowledgments

During my last several years teaching at Harvard I co-taught, with my colleague David Der-wei Wang, a so-called "core class" entitled "Old Tales for New Times: The Appropriation of Folktales in Modern and Contemporary China." In this class we looked both at the development of each of the Four Great Folktales in premodern times and at the ways in which these same stories have been reinterpreted and adapted by modern and contemporary Chinese intellectuals, novelists, playwrights, and film makers. While co-teaching this class with David, I learned much about the intricacies involved in the rise and fall in popularity of each of the stories against the backdrop of the changing political and cultural environments in twentieth-century China. If David had not happily agreed to co-teach the course, I never would have been able to write this book.

As in my other books on traditional Chinese folktales and genres of narrative ballads and prosimetric literature, the core of this book consists of translations. All translations are my own, with the exception of Qiao Zhiliang's "Memories of Directing *Married to a Heavenly Immortal*," which was translated by Tarryn Li-min Chun. Tarryn also helped me with many terminological questions related to modern theatrical jargon. My translation of Shi Hui, "Notes about Directing *Married to a Heavenly Immortal*" was earlier published in *The Opera Quarterly* 26, nos. 2–3 (2010), a special issue dedicated to Chinese opera movies and edited by Paola Iovene and Judith Zeitlin, from whose editorial interventions I greatly benefited.

As I became fascinated by the many incarnations of *Married to a Heavenly Immortal*, I discussed the topic with my Harvard colleagues at the time, many of whom provided useful pointers. Here I would like to mention in particular Eileen Chow, who patiently answered my ignorant questions about Chinese film. During my visits back to Leiden, Anne Sytske Keijser did the same. As always, the staff at the Harvard-Yenching Library at Harvard and the staff of the East Asian Library at Leiden University went out of their way to help me locate relevant materials. My graduate student Sun Xiaosu, who turned out to be much more effective than I am in locating materials on the Web, was also of great assistance.

Of the many other people who assisted me in my research at one moment or another I can only mention a few. Professor Zhao Shanlin kindly introduced me to his colleague Professor Li Yizhong, who answered my questions about his father's original script for the movie. Frank Kouwenhoven introduced me to Professor Lam Ching Wah, who answered my repeated questions about Huangmei Opera in the 1950s. Professor Xu Lan gave me a copy of her copy of the 1954 text of the revised version of the play. Tina Mai Chen and Li Jie both quickly replied to my questions about the importation of Eastern Bloc fairy-tale movies into China in the early 1950s.

In 1970 I spent the summer in Hong Kong at the Universities Service Centre pouring over newspaper clippings from the Union Research Institute about the reform of professional storytelling in the PRC in the early 1950s. Following my return to the Netherlands later that year, an unexpected twist in my career soon steered my research interests away from modern and contemporary China. While researching the transformations of *Married to a Heavenly Immortal* in the early years of the PRC, I was very much aware that I had come full circle but was straying beyond my comfort zone. I would not have been able to complete this project without the assistance of the persons and institutes listed above, as well as many others, and hereby want to express my heartfelt thanks to all of them, named or unnamed. Needless to say, all remaining errors on the following pages are my own.

Wilt L. Idema
Leiden, January 2014

I. Introduction: The Legend, the Play, and the Movie

Following the Communist conquest of the Chinese mainland and the establishment of the People's Republic of China (PRC) in 1949, the Chinese movie industry (studios, distribution, and cinemas) was quickly nationalized.[1] Like all other media, film was expected to serve the Revolution. As a result, the majority of movies produced in the 1950s celebrated China's struggle for national independence against foreign foes and inside China the struggle of the laboring masses against their masters. Against this background, the blockbuster success in 1956 and thereafter of the 1955 movie *Married to a Heavenly Immortal* (*Tianxianpei* 天仙配; released as *The Marriage of the Fairy Princess*, but also referred to as *The Heavenly Match* or *The Fairy Couple*) is even more remarkable. The movie was based on the legend of the filial son Dong Yong 董永. But filial piety (*xiao* 孝), the foundational value of traditional Chinese society, by this time had already been decried for almost half a century as the source of all of China's trials and tribulations. Moreover, the movie, closely based on the Huangmei 黃梅 Opera play of the same title, and starring the Huangmei Opera performers Yan Fengying 嚴鳳英 (1930–1968) and Wang Shaofang 王少舫 (1920–1986), was not an example of the realistic staging preferred by socialist realism—the Soviet-inspired dominant doctrine in the arts. From the very beginning, both its scriptwriter Sang Hu 桑弧 (1916–2004) and its director Shi Hui 石揮 (1915–1957) conceived of the movie as "a fairy-tale film with song and dance."

The Huangmei Opera play *Married to a Heavenly Immortal* was a great success at the East China Theater Festival of October 1954.[2] At that time Huangmei Opera was not a prestigious form of traditional opera. Rather, it was only a minor form of local opera that was hardly known outside its area of distribution in and around Anqing in Anhui province. The movie was not only extremely popular with audiences throughout the PRC, but also throughout the Sinophone world outside of the PRC, where its impact on the movie industry may have been even greater than it was in the PRC itself. *Married to a Heavenly Immortal* inspired the Hong Kong and Taiwan movie industries to produce many Huangmei Opera–style musicals, the most famous of which was the Shaw Brothers' 1963 production *Love Eterne*, an adaptation of the popular legend of Liang Shanbo 梁山伯 and Zhu Yingtai 祝英台. Due to *Married to a Heavenly Immortal*, Huangmei Opera became popular throughout China and transformed Yan Fengying and Wang Shaofang into instant celebrities. But Director Shi Hui committed suicide in 1957 after becoming a victim of the anti-rightist movement, and leading lady Yan Fengying committed suicide in 1968, a victim of the Cultural Revolution, when the movie was attacked as "a great poisonous weed." To this day, the authorship of the play on which the movie is based continues to be a matter of controversy.

The fate of *Married to a Heavenly Immortal* provides a unique window on the history of Chinese theater and cinema in the early years of the PRC. The many versions of the script allow us to follow development of the play in the context of the rapidly changing cultural and ideological climate. Statements by scriptwriters and critics provide us with a detailed picture of their ideological and artistic concerns, and statements by directors and actors allow us an inside view of how theater professionals adapted their performances to the needs of the times.

The Legend of Dong Yong

The origin of the legend of Dong Yong can be traced back to the second century AD.[3] On stone carvings from this period Dong Yong is depicted as a filial son, concerned about the well-being of his ailing father. Pictorial sources from a somewhat later date show Dong Yong seeing off an Immortal Maiden who returns to heaven after helping him to pay off his debts. In the early third century the famous poet Cao Zhi 曹植 (192–232) provided a summary account of the legend of Dong Yong in one of his poems. These lines may be rendered as follows:

> When Dong Yong's family fell on hard times,
> In his father's old age, all money was exhausted.
> He took out a loan in order to provide for him,
> And hired himself out so as to buy delicacies.
> When creditors arrived at his gate in numbers,
> He was at a loss as to how to send them off, but
> Heaven's God was moved by his utmost virtue,
> And a divine maiden worked the loom for him.[4]

Brief prose accounts of the legend are found in collections of biographical sketches of filial sons, a genre that flourished in the fourth to sixth centuries, and in collections of miracle tales of the same period. In these slightly later versions, after Dong Yong sold himself into slavery for three years in order to provide his father with a decent funeral, the divine maiden is sent down from heaven to become Dong Yong's wife for one hundred days to help him quickly pay off his debts.

In late imperial China anyone with only a smattering of literacy knew the legend from the account in the *Twenty-four Exemplars of Filial Piety* (*Ershisi xiao* 二十四孝). This book, intended for young children, provided a short prose version, followed by a four-line poem for easy memorization; the text itself was accompanied by a full-page illustration. The currently available version of the *Twenty-Four Exemplars of Filial Piety* was edited during the Yuan dynasty (1260–1368), but comparable collections may have been circulating from as early as the tenth century. The book is still widely available (also on the Web and in a large variety of adaptations into modern Chinese). Its account of the legend reads as follows:

Selling One's Body to Bury One's Father

> Dong Yong of the Han was so poor that when his father died he sold his body into servitude and buried him with borrowed money. When he set out to repay his debt through labor, he met a woman while on the road. She offered to become his wife, and together they arrived at his master's house. The latter ordered her to weave three hundred bolts of double-threaded silk and then they could return home. She completed the task within one month. While on the way back home, when they arrived at the spot where they had met in the shade of a scholartree,[5] she said goodbye to Yong and disappeared.
>
> To bury his father he needed to borrow money;
> Out on the road he ran into an immortal beauty.
> Weaving silk she paid off his debt to his master;
> His filial piety managed to move Heaven above![6]

Because of her weaving skills, Dong Yong's miracle-working companion was eventually identified as Weaving Maiden.[7] Weaving Maiden is the Chinese name of Vega (in Lyra), who is, according to Chinese lore, the wife of Buffalo Boy, the Chinese name of Altair. Because following their marriage the couple neglected the duties implied by their names, the Heavenly Emperor placed them on opposite banks of the Heavenly River (the Milky Way), allowing them only one meeting each year on the night of the seventh of the Seventh Month, when magpies form a bridge for them across the Heavenly River. In late imperial times, however, Dong Yong's companion was often called Seventh Sister and was identified as the youngest of the seven daughters of the Jade Emperor, the eldest of whom was said to be married to Buffalo Boy. In some versions of the legend, in yet another attempt to remove the suggestion of infidelity on the part of Weaving Maiden, Dong Yong is described as an incarnation of Buffalo Boy.[8]

The legend of Dong Yong was also adapted as ballads and plays. The earliest ballad on Dong Yong, a long poem in lines of seven syllables, was found at Dunhuang among a huge pile of manuscripts that had been stashed away in a side chamber of a grotto temple and bricked up shortly after 1000 AD. In this ballad Dong Yong and the Immortal Maiden have a son, who was born following the Immortal Maiden's return to heaven. When the son, who is raised by his father, becomes aware of the identity of his mother, he requests help from a diviner to find her. After he finds his mother, she becomes furious at the diviner and gives her son presents that destroy the diviner's means of preternatural knowledge. In some later versions of the narrative, these presents also eventually turn against the son. The earliest known stage version of the legend may date from the thirteen or fourteenth century. Onstage, two scenes were very popular: first, while on his way to his master, the meeting of very virtuous Dong Yong with the Immortal Maiden who boldly proposes marriage; and second, the parting scene when, following completion of his shortened period of servitude, the Immortal Maiden informs Dong Yong that she will leave him then and there. Although the legend of Dong Yong was originally associated with Shandong, later versions moved the action to Xiaogan in Hubei.[9]

In the complete version of the play as a *chuanqi* 傳奇 the son and daughter of Dong Yong's owner, now surnamed Fu 傅, were also assigned major roles. The son of Old Master Fu is a lecher who tries to rape the Immortal Maiden but he is swiftly punished by her magic; the daughter of old Master Fu studies weaving with the Immortal Maiden, marries Dong Yong following her departure for heaven, and raises the child of Dong Yong and the Immortal Maiden as her own. This *chuanqi* circulated under a number of titles beginning in the sixteenth century. It has not been preserved in its entirety, but we do have a detailed summary which dates to the eighteenth century:

Dong Yong, whose style is Yannian 延年, hails from Dong's Scholartree Village of Danyang County in Runzhou. His mother had died during his infancy. His father had been a transportation commissioner, but eventually he returned home and passed away. Because Dong Yong is too poor to provide his father with a proper funeral, he sells himself to the prefectural magistrate Fu Hua 傅華 as a bonded laborer. [Fu] Hua is living in his home village in retirement; he loves to do good works and pities [Dong] Yong because he is so filial, so he provides him with all of his needs, whereupon [Dong] Yong returns home with the money. Because of his filial behavior the Astral God of Great White[10] reports [Dong] Yong to the Emperor Above, who ascertains that Seventh Sister, the Weaving Maiden, has a karmic affinity with [Dong] Yong, so he orders her to go down to the mortal world for one hundred days to help him repay his debt. When [Dong] Yong is on his way to Fu [Hua] he meets the Immortal Maiden in the shade of a scholartree. She lies to [Dong] Yong and tells him that she has lost her husband and wants to become his wife because she is destitute. [Dong] Yong adamantly refuses, but the Star of Great White transforms himself into an old man who strongly urges [Dong] Yong to comply with her request; he also makes the scholartree answer his question and act as their matchmaker. So [Dong] Yong believes the match is heavenly ordained and they go to Fu [Hua] as a couple.

The Immortal Maiden claims that she can weave ten bolts of brocade in a single day and night. Fu [Hua] does not believe her, but gives her an extra supply of thread to try her out. Because the other Immortal Maidens help her to weave, the ten bolts of brocade are finished by dawn, and their dazzling colors are greatly admired by Fu [Hua], who now treats [Dong] Yong as a guest. Fu [Hua]'s daughter Saijin 賽金 becomes the Immortal Maiden's best friend, but Fu [Hua]'s son is a mean knave who tries to seduce the Immortal Maiden, whereupon she slaps him in the face.

When the period of one hundred days is up, the Immortal Maiden and [Dong] Yong take their leave of Fu [Hua]. She tells [Dong] Yong to present the dragon-phoenix brocade she has woven to the court, informing him that this will make his career and provide him with fame. She also shows him the poem in the brocade, saying, "Your marriage with Fu [Hua]'s daughter will originate with this." Thereupon she disappears on a cloud. [Dong] Yong informs Fu [Hua] what has happened and Fu [Hua] realizes that this miracle was due to his filial piety, so he gives his daughter to [Dong] Yong to be his wife.

> When [Dong] Yong takes the brocade to the imperial palace, by edict he is elevated to the rank of Top-of-the-List[11] for Presenting Treasure. When he parades through the streets [of the capital], the Immortal Maiden, after handing him a son, immediately disappears. [Dong] Yong names his son Si 祀, and gives him the adult name Zhongshu 仲舒. When the boy grows up, he is exceptionally intelligent. Because on one occasion people make fun of him for having no mother, Si visits [the famous diviner] Yan Junping 嚴君平. Junping tells him to go to Great White Mountain on the seventh night of the Seventh Month: "Wait until seven maidens pass, and then the seventh person, who is dressed in yellow, is your mother!"
>
> When he does as he was told, he indeed meets his mother. Giving him three gourds, she says: "Two of these are for you and your father, and one is for Junping." After Si returns home, he gives one gourd to Junping. Suddenly flames burst forth from the gourd and burn all his secret books on Yin and Yang. This is because she was angry with him for having divulged the secrets of heaven.[12]

This play, which seems to have circulated widely (under a variety of titles), exerted a major influence on the ballads and operas of the Qing dynasty (1644–1911) and thereafter. In some of the late ballads and operas the story ends with Dong Yong presenting to the Throne the brocade woven by the Immortal Maiden and receiving a high title as a reward. Other versions include a more or less detailed account of the search by Dong Yong's son for his birth mother, their reunion, and its consequences. The stage version that was popular in Huangmei Opera in the late nineteenth and early twentieth centuries and that is translated in this volume, belongs to the former category. By that time, the play was popular enough to have been published in two woodblock editions.[13]

In imperial China filial piety was considered a foundational value that provided the basis for an orderly society. The May Fourth Movement of the 1920s, however, witnessed an all-out attack on filial piety, which was deemed to be the root of everything that was wrong with China.[14] Such attacks were directed in particular at the traditional family system, which, the reformers and revolutionaries claimed, demanded unquestioning obedience by the younger generations to the elder generations, and denied personal happiness for the sake of family welfare and prosperity.[15] An endless stream of short stories, novels, plays, and movies revealed how young people in the "old society" were not allowed to follow their hearts because their callow parents were motivated by financial concerns in arranging their marriages. The struggle for "free love" (the freedom to choose one's own marriage partner) was a major theme in the modern literature of the 1920s and 1930s.[16] But the struggle that freed young men and women from the shackles of the patriarchal family and turned them into individuals also made them available for mobilization by the political parties and their state-building projects.[17] All modernizing movements in twentieth-century China supported "free love" and a reformed marriage law. One of the first major campaigns in the PRC of the early 1950s was the campaign to reform marriage. Marxist ideologues consistently hailed the desire of young people to be able to decide on their own marriage partners as a progressive force in history. Once the traditional marriage system was thoroughly discredited, filial piety, as the natural affection of children for their parents, made a modest comeback. However, it would never regain its position as a foundational value. As such, it was replaced by class struggle and nationalism.

Huangmei Opera

With the exception of several small skits, all forms of traditional Chinese theater are opera, that is, the action onstage is almost continually accompanied by orchestral music and the actors frequently move back and forth from prose dialogue to arias. The main difference between the Western and Chinese traditions of musical theater is that in the Western tradition new music is composed for each new play (with the result that operas and musicals are associated with their composers and only rarely with their text writers), whereas in the Chinese tradition the writers of new plays compose their songs to preexisting tunes (with the result that in China individual operas are associated with their authors). Therefore, in terms of the Western operatic tradition, all Chinese operas are ballad-operas.[18] Moreover, in the Chinese tradition operatic genres are distinguished on the basis of their body of music. For instance, *zaju* 雜劇, which originated in North China in the thirteenth century and flourished until the middle of the fifteenth century, made use of a maximum of four hundred melodies from that area. *Xiwen* 戲文 and its successor *chuanqi*, which arose in the Jiangnan area, made use of several hundred different melodies from that area. Each melody had its own metrical schema, specifying the number of lines and the length of each line. The writing of arias for *zaju* and *chuanqi* required considerable literary skills, and both genres were eventually established as minor genres of elite literature.

Zaju disappeared from the stage after the sixteenth century, whereas *chuanqi* continued to be widely performed in a wide variety of styles until well into the eighteenth century. The most prestigious of these local styles was *Kunqu* 崑曲, which was associated with the economic and cultural center of Suzhou and spread from there. Because *chuanqi* were very long, one might choose between a performance of the entire play (which could take up to two days), a performance of the main play (providing a selection of the major scenes), or a performance of selected highlights. In due time, such highlights (*zhezixi* 折子戲) might develop into more or less independent plays, which could survive onstage even after the original *chuanqi* was lost. By the early twentieth century, the *Kunqu* repertoire had been basically reduced to such highlights.[19]

There also existed genres of drama that for their songs relied on verse in seven-syllable lines, which could be easily memorized and, if need be, improvised by the actors. Moreover, every couplet was sung to the same basic melody (*banqiang* 板腔; melody matrix), which would, however, be varied according to the character, occasion, and mood. Combinations of specific basic melodies and local dialects resulted in a bewildering variety of regional genres of local opera.[20] Modern handbooks list up to four hundred genres of regional opera, but because these genres enjoyed little or no literary prestige they underwent constant development; as old genres faded away, new genres were constantly emerging well into the twentieth century. These regional operas probably have histories at least as long as those of *zaju* and *chuanqi*, but they only became popular beginning in the eighteenth century when they were dubbed *luantan* 亂彈 (cacophony) by disapproving drama critics. The best-known representative of these many genres of regional opera is Peking Opera, which features not one basic melody but two (*xipi* 西皮 and *erhuang* 二黃), and also includes a number of songs borrowed from *chuanqi* (as performed in the *Kunqu* style) and other sources. As soon as Peking Opera was established as the major form of theater in the capital at the end of the nineteenth century, it was also performed in other cities, such as Shanghai.

Huangmei Opera was a regional genre of opera that was popular in the Anqing countryside beginning in the late eighteenth century. At that time, it was known by many different names (the name Huangmei Opera was adopted as late as 1953). Its basic melody is known as Huangmeidiao 黃梅調 (Huangmei tune), named after the city of Huangmei in easternmost Hubei. Huangmei is presumed to be the place of origin of this basic melody. Various local traditions attempt to explain how it moved from eastern Hubei to the neighboring province. Originally, the repertoire of Huangmei Opera consisted only of simple skits, but by the middle of the nineteenth century performers of Huangmei Opera started to add full-length plays to their repertoire. *Married to a Heavenly Immortal* is one of these "thirty-six big plays."[21] As the genre developed its repertoire of plays, it also enriched its repertoire of tunes.[22] In the early decades of the twentieth century Huangmei Opera slowly acquired an urban audience, and beginning in 1926 it was also performed in the city of Anqing itself. This probably had as much to do with the ongoing urbanization and the migration of farmers to the cities and towns during that time as with the changes in the stagecraft and repertoire of Huangmei Opera.[23]

The accompanying orchestra in Huangmei Opera originally consisted of only a drum and gongs. String instruments were added at a relatively late date in the 1940s, when Huangmei Opera was performed by fully professional troupes. The basic way to perform the "Main Tune" of Huangmei Opera is called "level verse" (*pingci* 平詞). To express anxiety and agitation, the Main Tune may be performed at a quicker tempo, which is referred to as an "eight-beat." An even quicker performance is referred to as a "fired-up manner" (*huogong* 火工). The "tune of the immortals" is, as the name suggests, used when the gods and immortals enter onstage, whereas the "underworld tune" is used when the ghosts make an appearance or in scenes of impending doom and desperation. The "colorful tune" was originally the tune of a lively local four-line folksong. For special purposes other melodies could be used, such as the "Five Watches Tune," which was popular all over China in many variations. Further musical variety was achieved by duets (the "paired beat"), choral singing, and choral refrains.[24]

Although regional genres are distinguished by a basic melody and dialect, they share their stagecraft and repertoire with other genres. Huangmei Opera is no exception. The traditional version of *Married to a Heavenly Immortal* is clearly derived from the sixteenth-century *chuanqi* as it was performed locally in the *Qingyang* 青陽 style. As Huangmei Opera continued to develop in the first half of the twentieth century it freely borrowed from the stagecraft of other genres, such as Peking Opera. This process of borrowing was accelerated after 1949 in the context of the theater reform of the early 1950s.

Theater Reform

China's reformers and revolutionaries in the first half of the twentieth century shared a strong belief in the power of the theater to shape the audience's way of thinking.[25] Beginning in the very first years of the twentieth century new plays were composed to spread the gospel of nationalism and feminism.

Initially, the genres used for these purposes were still traditional genres, but soon Western-style "spoken drama" (*huaju* 話劇) became the preferred medium. Chinese students in the West and Japan in the early decades of the twentieth century encountered Western drama during the heyday of the social problem plays, best represented by Ibsen and Shaw. Such plays were performed on a box stage in a realistic, even naturalistic, manner. Although this type of drama enjoyed modest success among educated audiences in the major coastal cities in the 1920s and 1930s, it hardly appealed to larger audiences and could in no way compete in popularity with the many genres of regional opera that flourished during this period. These decades also witnessed efforts by Qi Rushan 齊如山 (1877–1962) and Mei Lanfang 梅蘭芳 (1894–1961) to enhance the status of Peking Opera by positioning it as China's "national theater" (*guoju* 國劇), which in every aspect was the counter image of Western-style "spoken drama." While doing so, they also attempted to raise the status of Peking Opera from a form of low-class entertainment with strong links to prostitution and religion (superstition in the eyes of modern intellectuals) to an art on the same level as painting or calligraphy.[26]

Although some theater activists continued to call for the use of traditional genres to spread a modern message among the masses throughout this period, their impact was limited. This changed, however, with the outbreak of the Anti-Japanese War in 1937. After China's coastal cities were occupied by Japanese troops, the Chinese government moved inland, as did many universities. In order to appeal to a largely rural and uneducated audience, Nationalists and Communists alike turned to traditional regional genres of opera to spread their respective messages.[27] Many rousing plays on ancient heroes fighting barbarian invaders needed little revision to stimulate patriotism, and plays featuring young women eloping with their lovers were reinterpreted as expressions of the perennial desire of young men and women in traditional society for "free love" (that is, the freedom to choose one own marriage partner, without parental interference). Whereas many modern intellectuals had earlier been very negative about traditional Chinese drama, which in their opinion taught the old values of filial piety, female chastity, personal loyalty, and subservience, they now acquired a more positive attitude, not so much envisioning the abolition of traditional opera but rather its reform. They maintained that traditional drama should be allowed to exist as long as it shed its backward (or, according to Marxist terminology, "feudal") repertoire and practices and wholeheartedly served the modernizing agenda of the nation-state.[28]

Once the PRC was established, the new authorities undertook the self-imposed task of theater reform as soon as circumstances allowed. The Bureau for the Reform of Traditional Opera was headed by activist and playwright Tian Han 田漢 (1898–1968).[29] Subsequent to a national conference on the reform of traditional theater in November 1950, a "Directive Concerning Work on the Reform of Traditional Theater" was promulgated on May 5, 1951. And following a Beijing theater festival, which showcased new and revised plays from all over China in a variety of genres, in the fall of 1952 the cultural czar of the moment, Zhou Yang 周揚 (1908–1989), declared:

> We advocate the reform and development of our national drama in accordance with the people's best interest. We are determined to do away with that part of China's dramatic heritage which is reactionary, poisonous and harmful, but to preserve and develop all that is progressive, healthy and beneficial to the people. … We encourage technical brilliance in artistic creation, because such technical brilliance is the result of long and hard work on the part of artists to present life truthfully. But we are opposed to technique which is formalistic, affected, lifeless.[30]

In this speech Zhou Yang also gave the final word on a debate that had been raging throughout the preceding two years (1950 and 1951) on the proper use of myths and folktales, as well as historical subject matter, in new and revised operas.[31] Facing pressures to make their work serve politics, many playwrights turned well-known stories into direct illustrations of contemporary government policies and had their historical or mythical characters voice political slogans of the day, a tendency that later would be characterized as "anti-historicism." Tian Han's second-in-command, Yang Shaoxuan 楊紹萱 (1893–1971),[32] who himself had written a play on the legend of Buffalo Boy and Weaving Maiden and argued that such subjects could be arbitrarily adapted to comment on contemporary issues, became the whipping boy when Zhou Yang sided with those who had argued that one should not stray too far from the original plot and characterization and should pay attention to the historical circumstances of the original event:

> Whether it is a question of giving expression to modern or ancient life, the highest principle in art is truthfulness. Historical truth allows of no distortion, no concealment or whitewashing. However, those who oppose historical truthfulness, like Comrade Yang Shao-hsuan, seem incapable of understanding this fundamental principle.… They fail to grasp the fact that attempts to describe historical figures as if they possessed a modern

> working-class ideology are something quite different from viewing history and writing about it in the light of modern working-class ideology.[33]

Reacting against Yang's claim that "myth" (*shenhua* 神話) was only a matter of form and had nothing to do with content, Zhou distinguished between myths and folktales on the one hand and superstitious tales on the other hand in the following terms:

> A great many folk stories take a positive attitude towards the world and are impregnated with popular character, whereas superstition is always negative and generally serves the interests of the ruling class. … Folk tales often depict man as unyielding before fate and finally triumphing over it in the world of imagination; superstition, on the contrary, preaches fatalism and retribution. … Consequently, mythology always encourages man to break away from his enslavement and seek after the life of a real man, while superstition aims at making him a willing slave glorying in his bondage.[34]

In this way Zhou Yang set clear guidelines for those who were revising traditional plays, especially plays on legendary topics. In view of these guidelines it should come as no surprise that all who were involved in the later revision of *Married to a Heavenly Immortal* would stress that Dong Yong's fate corresponded to historical fact and that the tale of Dong Yong and Seventh Sister was a "myth" and not an expression of superstition. In my translations of these statements I have, however, preferred to render *shenhua* as "fairy tale" as that term seems to better fit the character of the tale.[35]

The theater-reform campaign was only one of the many campaigns conducted in the early years of the People's Republic. Like the other campaigns, this campaign aimed to reform the theatrical institutions and people and to impose Party control.[36] In the following years theaters were nationalized and private companies were increasingly replaced by state-run companies.[37] Although actors may have enjoyed a higher status as state employees, they lost much control over their own performances, as these were now expected to be based on written-out scripts and to be supervised by a director.[38] The repertoire of each genre of regional theater, beginning with Peking Opera, was collected and scrutinized to determine which plays would be forbidden, which could be retained with some changes, and which were basically acceptable. Plays that showed resistance to foreign aggression and class oppression, that propagated love for the motherland, for freedom, and for labor, or that displayed the good qualities of the people could be retained, but any play that gave expression to the "feudal slave morality" or propagated primitive, violent, or lascivious behavior was to be rejected.[39] Long training sessions were organized in which actors, playwrights, and managers studied Marxism with Party cadres and engaged in the practical details of the reform. National and regional festivals were organized in various regions and organizations showcased the results of these activities.[40] But even if politics were clearly in command, we would be belittling the theater-reform movement if we only focused on its political and ideological aspects. The theater reform also aimed to do away with all "backward" aspects of traditional theater, to ennoble it, and to make it more beautiful than ever.

The Revision of *Married to a Heavenly Immortal*

Huangmei Opera was not represented at the Beijing theater festival of 1952. In the years immediately following the establishment of the PRC Huangmei Opera was a local phenomenon limited to Anqing, and its surrounding countryside. In Anqing two major companies performed both traditional plays and new works. But the systematic reform of traditional theater impacted Anhui, and Zeng Xisheng 曾希聖 (1904–1968), who served as Party secretary of Anhui province from 1952 to 1962,[41] played an active role in the reorganization and rewriting of Huangmei Opera. In 1952 a major training session was organized in the provincial capital of Hefei. This session, bringing together actors and actresses, managers and cadres from all over the province, lasted for forty-seven days. The Huangmei Opera plays performed during this session created quite a stir, even attracting the attention of some influential figures in Shanghai. This resulted in an invitation to have Huangmei Opera performed in Shanghai later that year. The Anhui provincial authorities thereupon organized a work group in Anqing to prepare for this event. One of the plays that was revised in this context was the scene "Meeting on the Road" (*Luyu* 路遇) from *Married to a Heavenly Immortal*. In this scene Seventh Sister who has descended to the mortal world, shows up in front of Dong Yong when he is on his way to the house of Landlord Fu and she eventually forces the unwilling Dong Yong to marry her. The social status of Dong Yong was changed from that of a student to that of a poor peasant, and the Immortal Maiden joins him not because she has been ordered to do so by the Heavenly Emperor in order to reward Dong Yong for his conspicuous display of filial piety, but because she had fallen in love with the honest and sincere young peasant who was down on his luck. The rich man who provided

Dong Yong with the money for his father's burial was now characterized as a rapacious landlord.[42] This scene was performed to great acclaim in Shanghai in November 1952. On that occasion the role of Dong Yong was played by Wang Shaofang, whereas the role of Seventh Sister was performed by the young actress Pan Jingli 潘璟琍 (1936–1988). Another piece that was performed on this occasion was a little skit entitled *Collecting Pig Fodder* (*Da zhucao* 打豬草),[43] starring the actress Yan Fengying.[44] When in April 1953 the Anhui provincial authorities established the Anhui Provincial Huangmei Opera Company in Hefei, Yan Fengying was one of the first performers to be reassigned from Anqing to Hefei. Other Huangmei Opera actors such as Wang Shaofang performed for the Chinese troops in Korea during the same year.[45]

The success of this revision of "Meeting on the Road" in Shanghai and elsewhere may well have inspired Lu Hongfei 陸洪非 (Hong Fei 洪非, 1924–2007) in the next year to prepare a revision of the complete text of *Married to a Heavenly Immortal*. Lu Hongfei based his revision on the oral version provided by the veteran actor Hu Yuting 胡玉庭 (1898–1958).[46] The initial reaction of Lu's superiors to his script was dismissive (after three months their only reaction was "This lacks a theme!" [*meiyou zhuti* 沒有主題]),[47] but the play was performed to great acclaim in August and September 1953 in Anqing[48] and was selected by the Anhui authorities as one of their submissions to the East China Theater Festival of October 1954 (September 25 to November 2), again in Shanghai. In order to make the best showing possible the Anhui Provincial Huangmei Opera Company was strengthened by many of the finest Huangmei Opera performers, including Wang Shaofang. Direction of the play was entrusted to Li Liping 李力平 (1919–2002) and Qiao Zhiliang 喬志良 (1921–2005). This in itself was a major innovation as in the past traditional plays had been performed without a specialized director.[49] Li Liping had a theatrical background in modern "spoken drama" and his presence initially met with quite some opposition from the performers. In a short article in his memory Li Liping is credited in particular for challenging Yan Fengying to rethink her character as a peasant girl once she descended to earth and to adapt her performance according to this analysis.[50] Qiao Zhiliang hailed from Nanjing and had been trained as a Peking Opera actor. His career up to the early 1950s had taken him to the major cities in southern China during the Anti-Japanese War and the Civil War. During his wartime engagement in Chongqing he met his future wife Liu Huixian 劉慧嫻, and slightly later at Nanwenquan the couple had made the acquaintance of the famous popular novelist Zhang Henshui 張恨水 and his wife. In 1952 Qiao Zhiliang participated in the summer training session in Hefei and thereafter changed from actor to director. He and his wife played a major role in the transmission of Peking Opera performance techniques to Huangmei Opera performers.[51] At the same time, specialists like Shi Bailin 時白林 (b. 1927) and Wang Zhaoqian 王兆乾 (1928–2006) developed and codified the music of Huangmei Opera.[52] When *Married to a Heavenly Immortal* was eventually performed in Shanghai, it met with a huge success. The performance was rated as excellent, and both of its leading performers, Yan Fengying and Wang Shaofang, received a first prize for their acting. The script, direction, and music also received first prizes. As a result, *Married to a Heavenly Immortal* was selected as one of the reformed operas to be made into a movie.

The pre-1949 *Married to a Heavenly Immortal* told the story of the filial son Dong Yong. The available printed editions of the pre-1949 version of the play begin with a scene in which Dong Yong unsuccessfully tries to borrow some money from his aunt and uncle, leaving him no recourse when his father dies but to rely on his own strength by selling his body into servitude. The plays ends with a number of scenes in which Dong Yong travels to the capital and presents the silk woven by Seventh Sister to the emperor, whereupon he receives a high position, Seventh Sister brings him his son, and he marries the daughter of his former owner. The play shows the progression of a son who loses his father and becomes an orphan to a son who becomes a father himself and also achieves everything a man might desire in traditional society. In between these opening scenes and the concluding scenes the play contains extended descriptions of the Immortal Maidens watching the mortal world,[53] the meeting of Dong Yong and Seventh Sister while he is traveling to the mansion of his owner, their arrival at the mansion, the weaving of the brocade, and their parting after they leave the mansion when the ordained one hundred days of their marriage are over. Remarkably, the printed versions jump from the weaving of the ten bolts of silk to the departure of Dong Yong and Seventh Sister from the Fu Mansion.

In the version dictated by Hu Yuting, which is based on the play as performed in the 1940s, the scene of the night-long weaving is followed by scenes in which the immortal sisters measure the silk before they depart, Seventh Sister hands the silk to Dong Yong, and Dong Yong presents it to Old Master Fu. Old Master Fu then burns the contract by which Dong Yong sold himself into servitude and proceeds to adopt Dong Yong and Seventh Sister as his own children. Subsequently there follows a scene in which Young

Master Fu tries to seduce Seventh Sister, but he is frightened into virtue by Seventh Sister who calls down from heaven the Lord of Thunder and Mother of Lightning. Eventually, Old Master Fu sends Dong Yong and his wife home when his one hundred days of servitude are over, but before doing so he treats Dong Yong to a parting meal and provides him with travel money. It is clear that the printed versions of the traditional play are also based on such a story, because by the time Dong Yong and Seventh Sister are on the way to his old home, they describe Old Master Fu as their adoptive father and they are loath to depart. As Hu Yuting's version is based on the performances, it tends to provide a somewhat fuller dialogue. It also does not shirk from adding supernatural elements. We already mentioned the role of the Lord of Thunder and Mother of Lightning. When, earlier in the play, Dong Yong is writing his sales contract, four gods are present onstage to hail his filial piety. Of course, after 1949 such elements would be condemned as expressions of "feudal superstition."

In the revised version of *Married to a Heavenly Immortal* "The feudal superstition of 'Dong Yong moving Heaven by his filial piety' was dumped"—the word "filial piety" is barely mentioned at all in the printed editions of 1954 and 1955, and it is completely avoided in later versions (for instance in the 1979 edition). The play was turned into not only an illustration of class struggle in the old society, but also a model of young people's struggle for free love and its unavoidably tragic outcome in the old society. The popular nature of the play is stressed by stating that the play was based on the text as orally transmitted by the actor Hu Yuting, but it is obvious that Lu Hongfei and his predecessors also had access to the printed version of the old play.[54] Although most articles devoted to the revision of *Married to a Heavenly Immortal* stress the ideologically inspired changes to the plot and the characterizations, more recent scholarship draws attention to the artistic nature of the changes in terms of characterization, plot and language, and stagecraft. The main characters in the play acquire a more clearly defined individuality, and the plot is more focused on limiting the action to a few major scenes. The tragic nature of the separation after one hundred days is no longer undercut by the later happy ending. In the process of revision, the language of the play acquires a more literary character without, however, losing its directness and ease. All of these elements are combined to enhance the play's appeal outside of its original rural audience.[55]

Married to a Heavenly Immortal as performed in Shanghai in 1954 omitted the opening scenes of the old play (in which Dong Yong tries to borrow money from relatives) as these could be read as portraying a lack of solidarity among the poor, but it still began with the scene of Dong Yong (now a poor peasant rather than a student) selling himself into servitude[56] and, echoing the political climate of the time, it depicted the landlord class in the blackest of terms.[57] The play then has Seventh Sister leave heaven on her own authority once she falls in love with Dong Yong, and it continues with her seduction of Dong Yong, their arrival at the mansion of his owner, and the weaving of the brocade. The Jade Emperor, who ordered Seventh Sister to descend to earth, is now only a threatening presence, and the role of the Astral Lord of Great White is eliminated as his functions are taken over by the God of the Soil. The ideology of class struggle made it impossible to retain the scene of Old Master Fu adopting the couple. But even though Young Master Fu is still depicted as lusting after Seventh Sister, the scene in which he tries to seduce her but ends up groping his own sister is deleted, most likely because such folksy bawdiness was offensive to the puritanical mindset of the times. Also, instead of a scene in which Dong Yong and Seventh Sister tearfully leave their good patron, we now encounter a scene in which Seventh Sister outwits the rapacious landlord who tries every trick in the book to force his serfs to remain (and to enslave them for the rest of their lives). In the long final scene Seventh Sister has every intention of sharing with Dong Yong the simple life of a peasant, but she is called back to heaven by her father who threatens to kill Dong Yong if she does not obey, leaving her no option but to bid farewell to her husband.

The version of the revised play that was printed in 1955 omits the opening scene in which Dong Yong sells himself,[58] as it, like the movie, begins with Seventh Sister's elopement from heaven. Because the emphasis of the play has shifted even more to the theme of the struggle of young people for free love, the negative characterization of the landlord class is somewhat toned down (in the 1954 version Old Master Fu is contemplating sending Dong Yong to his death in order to obtain the lifelong service of Seventh Sister, but we do not encounter this scheme in the 1955 version), whereas the marital affection between the young couple, looking forward to the birth of their baby, is very much stressed. This time Lu Hongfei makes a considerable effort to individualize the characterization of the immortal sisters (for instance, the shy and anxious Second Sister versus the experienced and supportive Third Sister).[59] Although the movie drastically shortened the arias, this script greatly expanded the arias and also enhanced their literary tone by removing some unhappy similes.

The revision of plays may well have been easier in the case of a genre of traditional opera like Huangmei Opera which by the late 1930s had only just begun to be performed on urban stages. The involved actors and actresses, whose status had been changed from riffraff at the margins of society to state employees, were probably only too eager to cooperate, and there was no established community of experts and aficionados who might have wanted to decry the changes as ill-advised and contrary to the nature of the genre. Be that as it may, Lu Hongfei and his successors managed to turn an exemplary tale of filial piety into an exemplary tale of the struggle for free love while retaining most of the scenes that must have made the play a success onstage.

The version of the revised play as published in 1955 certainly was not the definitive version. The script continued to be adapted and edited, even though the changes thereafter were less drastic. The success of the movie resulted in adaptations of the stage version, and the adapted version was criticized by high-ranking cultural bureaucrats when the play was performed in Beijing in the fall of 1956, resulting in yet further rewritings.[60] In the version of the play that was printed in 1979, for instance, the major change is that Dong Yong is not informed that Seventh Sister is pregnant on the eve of the couple's departure from the Fu Mansion; he discovers that his wife is expecting during a rest on their way back after they have left the mansion. This later version of the play takes care to tie up some loose ends in the plot that remained in the earlier versions. It reveals the continuing influence of the movie on the stage versions when, near the end of the final scene, a divine warrior appears onstage to summon Seventh Sister back to heaven, unlike in the earlier versions in which a disembodied backstage voice suffices.[61]

The Movie

The earliest Chinese attempts at producing movies took place in Beijing in the early years of the twentieth century, but we have to wait until the 1920s for the development of lively film production. Most of the studios at that time were located in Shanghai, which would continue to be the center of China's film production during the following several decades. As in the case of many other national film industries, fledgling companies, in order to be assured of sympathetic audiences, often tried to play it safe by adapting well-known and popular local stories. Stories that were most widely known were traditional operas. One of the earliest successful opera adaptations was the 1927 version of the famous love story *The Western Wing* (*Xixiang ji* 西廂記).[62] In due time these "operatic films" (*xiqu pian* 戲曲片) became an established genre in Chinese movie making.[63] Such operatic films include both documentary registrations of stage performances and movie adaptations of operas. As in the case of Hollywood adaptations of Broadway musicals or Italian operas, in the latter case the "operatic film" requires a reinvention of the action as a movie. This reinvention tends to be even more drastic in the Chinese case. Whereas traditional opera was and is performed on a bare stage (with the use of no, or only minimal, scenery), the movie adaptations are set in realistic indoor and outside settings. Although the acting, dialogue, and arias may retain many of the features of the stage performance, in movies they are performed in fully realized sets. This not only creates certain limitations, but it also allows for many new possibilities of expression—scenes which once could only be evoked in words can now be visualized.

One of the phenomena accompanying the reform of traditional opera in the early 1950s was the production of many operatic films. The majority of these were simple recordings of stage performances, but some were inventive adaptations. The most successful of these was *Liang Shanbo and Zhu Yingtai* (*Liang Shanbo yu Zhu Yingtai* 梁山伯與祝英台), a 1954 adaptation of the Shaoxing Opera (*Yueju*) version of the famous love story between the young student Liang Shanbo and Zhu Yingtai, a girl who dons male dress in order to pursue a higher education at an academy outside of her home.[64] Like Huangmei Opera, Shaoxing Opera (*Yueju*) was a very new genre of traditional opera. Performed by all-female troupes, it became popular in Shanghai in the late 1930s.[65] A revised version of the Shaoxing Opera *Liang Shanbo and Zhu Yingtai* was performed to great acclaim at the 1952 theater festival in Beijing.[66] The cinematic adaptation of the play has the distinction of being the first full-length color movie shot in China by Chinese. It was directed by Sang Hu (1916–2004), a successful director in the 1940s who had studied color movies in Moscow in the early 1950s. Sang Hu had also produced the script for *Liang Shanbo and Zhu Yingtai*.[67]

Married to a Heavenly Immortal, starring Yan Fengying and Wang Shaofang, was shot in black and white by the Shanghai Film Studio.[68] The project was entrusted to Shi Hui and Sang Hu, both of whom had ample experience as director and scriptwriter.[69] The director Shi Hui had been a highly popular *huaju* and movie actor in Shanghai in the 1940s, and he went on to direct a number of notable films during the first years of the PRC.[70] From the very beginning Shi Hui's intention was to reinvent the play as a movie.[71] This ambition was shared by Sang Hu, who signed for the script of *Married to a Heavenly Immortal*. Sang Hu stated in 1956: "*Married to a Heavenly Immortal* is a fairy tale. That is why a movie provides even greater possibilities to use various means for its enrichment. From the very beginning we decided to treat the movie as a fairy tale with song and dance and not in the manner of a documentary registration of a stage performance."[72] One of their most drastic changes was to drop the original opening scene where Dong Yong sells his body and to replace it with a cloudscape, moving on to the heavenly palaces and focusing on Seventh Sister who longs for love in the mortal world.[73]

Sang Hu based his movie script on the play script as prepared by Lu Hongfei,[74] but he and his colleagues apparently believed that they were working on the "folk version" and Lu's name was not listed in the credits.[75] Sang Hu basically kept to the plot of Lu's script, but the limited length of the movie, as compared to that of the play, forced him to cut much of the dialogue (and accompanying action). Sang Hu also edited the arias, rearranging many of the lines (by his own account he reduced the songs from 468 lines to 278 lines).[76] Because he dropped the opening scene of Dong Yong selling himself into servitude he tried to stress the moral character of Dong Yong in "Meeting on the Road" by emphasizing his concern for the well-being of Seventh Sister if she were to follow him to the Fu Mansion. He also turned the character of Fu Guanbao 傅官保, the son of Old Master Fu, into that of Zhao Gui 趙貴, Old Master Fu's old and obsequious majordomo.[77] The movie broke up many of the long scenes of the play by cutting to scenes elsewhere in the cosmos or in the same house. Whereas the 1954 version of the play in the scene of the Immortal Maidens observing the world below eliminated the entrances onstage of the fisherman, woodcutter, farmer, and student, and the bridal procession, the movie once again showed these figures through the use of wide angle shots. And when Seventh Sister and the other Immortal Maidens are busily weaving throughout the night, Dong Yong is now shown pushing the mill[78] in a detail added to the movie to stress the relentless exploitation of farmhands by landlords.[79] The movie also freely made use of special effects, for instance in the scenes set in heaven, in the episode of the speaking scholartree, and in the final scene when a divine warrior appears to transmit the orders of the Jade Emperor, whereas in the play a backstage voice had sufficed.[80] The melodious nature of Huangmei Opera music was stressed by eliminating the drum.[81]

Operatic movies are rarely discussed in Western studies of PRC movies from the 1949–1966 period, and if they are discussed at all, attention tends to be focused on either *Liang Shanbo and Zhu Yingtai* or *Fifteen Strings of Cash* (*Shiwu guan* 十五貫), an adaptation of a revived *Kunqu* play that was also released in 1956.[82] If *Married to a Heavenly Immortal* is mentioned at all, the information may be misleading, for instance when (perhaps inadvertently) it is suggested that the movie was a success primarily outside of the PRC.[83] But even though *Married to a Heavenly Immortal* may not have been a highly innovative film, its lack of conspicuous political propaganda must have been very welcome to PRC audiences at the time. Yan Fengying was endearing as the vivacious and forward Seventh Sister, and Wang Shaofang put in a creditable performance of the "honest and sincere" (*laoshi* 老實) Dong Yong.[84] The relative newness of Huangmei Opera also meant that its acting style had not yet acquired the elaborate codification one encounters in some other genres, thus making their acting far more natural than that in, for instance, Peking Opera. The sudden tragic outcome of the love story must have aroused great sympathy. The music and songs appealed to audiences throughout the Chinese world.[85] The aria sung by Seventh Sister and Dong Yong when they leave the Fu Mansion at the end of his term of servitude and set out for their own cottage to spend a happy life together is a popular song to this very day.[86]

The movie *Married to a Heavenly Immortal* was released in February 1956. By the summer of 1958 the movie had been seen by more than 140,000,000 people in the PRC, many of whom saw it multiple times.[87] The movie established the nationwide popularity of Huangmei Opera and overnight turned Yan Fengying and Wang Shaofang into national stars. To understand this spectacular success one must keep in mind that the only foreign films that were shown in China at the time were movies from the Soviet Union and its allies that were characterized by the same heavy-handed political propaganda as the overwhelming majority of films that were produced in the PRC during these years.

The Stars

Despite the contributions by Lu Hongfei, Qiao Zhiliang, Shi Bailin, Sang Hu, Shi Hui, and many others, one of the most important factors in the conspicuous success of both the play and the movie among Communist cadres and audiences at large must have been the seductive charm of Huangmei Opera music and the extraordinary talent of the play's leading actress Yan Fengying.[88]

Yan Fengying was born in Anqing as Yan Hongliu 嚴鴻六, but grew up in the Tongcheng countryside during the Anti-Japanese War where she picked up many local songs. Her father also taught her to sing Peking Opera. From the age of 12 she began to sing Huangmei Opera, and at the age of 15, following her first public performance, she ran away from home to avoid drastic punishment by the village elders and joined a professional Huangmei Opera company. A smart learner, she distinguished herself by her personal charm, acting technique, supple voice, and extensive memory.

Yan Fengying became quite a sensation in Anqing in 1946, but her fame brought her to the attention of unsavory elements. At one point a local militia commander installed her in his home as a concubine, but she could not stand the abuse of the other women in his household and was released when she tried to commit suicide by hanging herself. Later, she was abducted by a local crime boss. This time she was released after she tried to commit suicide by swallowing a golden ring. In the unsettled times of the late 1940s she eventually moved to Nanjing, where she joined a Peking Opera troupe and survived by doing all kinds of odd jobs. She returned to Anqing in 1951, participated in the Anhui provincial training session in 1952, and was assigned to the newly founded Anhui Provincial Huangmei Opera Company in 1953.[89]

Yan Fengying's co-star Wang Shaofang hailed from Nanjing. From a family of strolling players, he was originally trained as a Peking Opera actor, first performing onstage at the age of 9. While spending time in Anqing, he also learned to sing Huangmei tunes, but it was not until 1950 that he became a full-time Huangmei Opera actor. His cooperation with Yan Fengying began in 1954, when he was transferred to the Anhui Provincial Huangmei Opera Company.[90] In a discussion of the acting styles of Yan Fengying and Wang Shaofang, Li Liping concludes that Yan Fengying's strength was her identification with her characters, whereas Wang Shaofang's strength was his technique.

The Aftermath

Due to the huge success of the movie *Married to a Heavenly Immortal* Huangmei Opera immediately became popular all over China. Huangmei Opera companies from Anhui toured throughout the country[91] and many places outside of the province established their own Huangmei Opera troupes. A handful of ambitious bureaucrats, a small band of enthusiastic young cultural cadres, and a generation of gifted performers almost overnight succeeded in developing a new genre of traditional Chinese opera that met the needs of the times. Even though in many respects the new genre was created by a small group of ideologically inspired composers, playwrights, and actors, it could also be touted as popular and traditional as it drew on older and rural subjects and tunes. In contrast with other forms of reformed traditional opera,

Huangmei Opera was not tainted by associations with the old elite (as was the case for *Kunqu* and Peking Opera) or with bourgeois commercialism (as was the case for Shanghai's Shaoxing Opera). Nor was Huangmei Opera disqualified by a conspicuous pre-Liberation relation to local religion ("feudal superstition" in the terminology of the time) or to male and female prostitution. And whereas some other genres of reformed traditional opera did not appeal to a national audience due to their complicated music or regional dialects, Huangmei Opera was performed in a language close to the national standard and the arias were sung to simple melodies that could easily catch on. In addition, the increasingly beautiful costumes and gorgeous stage scenery, as well as the absence of open political indoctrination in the plays on premodern topics, resulted in the massive appeal of the genre in Chinese communities both inside and outside of the PRC.[92]

The success of *Married to a Heavenly Immortal* as a movie stimulated the production of other Huangmei Opera movies in the years between 1959 and 1963. Yan Fengying and Wang Shaofang costarred once again in *The Female Prince-Consort* (*Nü fuma* 女駙馬) in 1959. The play on which this movie is based was a reworking of a traditional script by Wang Zhaoqian that had been further revised by Lu Hongfei, and became one of the most popular Huangmei Operas of all time.[93] In 1963 Yan Fengying and Wang Shaofang played the leading roles in *Buffalo Boy and Weaving Maiden* (*Niulang zhinü* 牛郎織女), a PRC-Hong Kong coproduction. Another 1963 PRC-Hong Kong coproduction was *The Shady Scholartree* (*Huaiyin ji* 槐陰記), a wide-screen color remake of *Married to a Heavenly Immortal*, now performed by a younger cast.[94] But Hong Kong and Taiwan movie makers had earlier already started to make their own Huangmei-style musicals. This culminated in the Shaw Brothers' 1963 production of *Love Eterne*, an adaptation of the legend of Liang Shanbo and Zhu Yingtai. In 1963 the Shaw Brothers also produced their own remake of *Married to a Heavenly Immortal* as *Seventh Sister* (*Qixiannü* 七仙女; released as *A Maid from Heaven*).[95]

But the very success of *Married to a Heavenly Immortal* seems to have worked as a curse for those closely involved in the production of the play and the movie. The first political victims were the directors. Li Liping was classified as a rightist and sent down for reeducation through labor in 1957, and was fully rehabilitated only in 1978. Shi Hui's fate was even more dramatic. His next project was a poorly conceived and poorly executed disaster movie. During the period of political relaxation in late 1956, known as the Hundred Flowers Campaign, perhaps emboldened by the spectacular success of

Married to a Heavenly Immortal, he was one of the first to speak out pulicly against the tight political control in the film industry,[96] only to become a victim of the anti-rightist movement of 1957. However, he refused to appear for criticism sessions, and when at the end of that year he disappeared, it was rumored that he had fled to Hong Kong to resume his acting career under an assumed name. A year later it was revealed that he had committed suicide by drowning himself.[97] Li Liping and Shi Hui were not the only people connected to *Married to a Heavenly Immortal* to run into trouble in 1957; Wang Zhaoqian was also classified as a "Rightist."

Yan Fengying and Wang Shaofang continued to perform in many highly successful plays and movies for the next ten years. Yan Fengying, in particular, who had married in 1956, received many awards and was appointed to a variety of (mostly honorary) positions. She faced some criticism in 1957–1958 but survived that period without a major impact on her career. However, along with practically everyone else who had been active in the production and performance of Huangmei Opera, she became a target of criticism during the Cultural Revolution (1966–1976). As a diva and darling of the Party and the government establishment, she was even more harshly "struggled against," and she eventually committed suicide in 1968. She could have been saved, but she was denied timely medical care.[98] Needless to say, *Marriage to a Heavenly Immortal* was condemned as a "poisonous weed" during these years and became the object of a province-wide criticism campaign in Anhui in 1970, when Wang Shaofang and Lu Hongfei were paraded out as "living targets" at each criticism session. This judgment on *Marriage to a Heavenly Immortal* was reversed after the Cultural Revolution in 1978, and the movie was released once again.[99] Many sequels have now appeared in which Dong Yong and Seventh Sister are eventually reunited. A statue of Yan Fengying in her role of Seventh Sister has been erected in Hefei, probably China's first public monument in memory of an actress.[100] The reputation of Yan Fengying continued to grow over the last decades as she became the subject of many books and biopics. In 2010 the story of her life was adopted as a Huangmei Opera entitled *Yan Fengying*. Wang Shaofang was also starring again in his great roles, but his reputation was tarnished by persistent allegations that his statements against Yan Fengying in the early days of the Cultural Revolution were the cause of her death ("Dong Yong killed Seventh Sister!").

Sang Hu, though never admitted as a member of the Communist Party, continued to thrive throughout the troubled decades of the 1960s, 1970s, and beyond, despite the political changes during those years. He went on to script and/or direct a number of important movies before 1966, including China's first 3D movie. He did not escape criticism during the early years of the Cultural Revolution, but he was one of the earliest directors to shoot movies again in the later years of the Cultural Revolution. For instance, in 1972 he directed the movie version of the ballet adaptation of *White-Haired Girl*. He went on to garner prizes for the movies he directed during the reform period of the early 1980s.[101]

Throughout his life Lu Hongfei claimed authorship of the revised version of *Married to a Heavenly Immortal*, but as late as 2000 others were contesting the extent of his contribution to the revision of the play and putting forward names of other people who had made contributions as large as, or even larger than, those of Lu. Lu retained the services of a lawyer, who advised him not to go to court but to publish "the facts," which then called forth tongue-in-cheek support and partial rebuttals by some of the persons involved in the revision of the play in the early 1950s, when no one could have yet foreseen the spectacular success that the play and movie would eventually enjoy.

Of course, these questions of authorship involve more than issues of personal pride. The sons of Yan Fengying went to court in 2005 to claim their mother's (and therefore their) ownership of her personal rendition of the tunes in the film version of *Marriage to a Heavenly Immortal*, seeking part of the profits from the release of *Marriage to a Heavenly Immortal* on DVD.[102]

* * *

In recent years the story of Dong Yong and Seventh Sister has repeatedly been adapted for television as multi-episode dramas. As before, these adaptations tend to focus more on Seventh Sister than on Dong Yong.[103] But filial piety, once vilified as the root of China's backwardness, is now once again hailed as a positive value as the Chinese government attempts to construct a harmonious society within the borders of the PRC and to present China's culture to the outside world through its Confucius Institutes.[104] In recent years, the *Twenty-Four Exemplars of Filial Piety* has been repeatedly reprinted in the PRC.

Epilogue

In 1997 the well-known female novelist Wang Anyi 王安憶 (b. 1954) wrote a short story entitled *Married to a Heavenly Immortal* (*Tianxian pei*).[105] The story is set in a remote post-Cultural Revolution mountain village. When a young man who had hoped to leave the village and pursue a career elsewhere is killed in an accident while digging a well, the village head comforts the boy's parents by arranging a "ghost marriage" between the young man and a female soldier in the People's Liberation Army who had died during the Civil War of 1945–1949 and had been buried by the villagers. But soon afterwards representatives of the central authorities, urged on by the female soldier's former lover, now a high-level retired officer, demand the restitution of her bones so that she may be reburied and honored as a martyr of the Revolution. And so the short-lived "marriage" of the village boy trapped in his situation and the rich girl who ran away from home in order to join the Revolution comes to an end. The story may be read in many ways, but it is almost certainly also intended as a fable about the often violent and tragic history of China in the twentieth century, highlighting the short-lived alliance between the Communist Party and the peasant masses and the Party's betrayal of the countryside in the decades following the Cultural Revolution.[106]

II. Rewriting the Play

Adaptation and Rewriting in Traditional Drama

Adaptation and rewriting is as old as playwriting itself. Censors, lovers of literature, and literary scholars may be obsessed by the exact wording of a playwright's work, but in the theater the text of a play is only a script, one of the many elements that go into a stage performance. As such, the script must be adapted to the concrete circumstances of each individual performance—actors, venue, occasion, and audience. In fact, professional actors can do very well without a written-out text, as is revealed by the historical experiences of Italian *commedia dell'arte*, American vaudeville, and many varieties of Chinese local theater. Scripts are only needed when the plays defy the actors' power of memory and improvisational talent, that is, when the plays are new or very long and complicated. And even then playwrights may not take the trouble to write out conventional routines. But also when detailed scripts have been developed in close cooperation between playwright(s) and actors, the plays will never be the same in performance as they continue to be adapted and rewritten. It is usually very difficult to trace the day-to-day changes of a play in performance. For the centuries before the invention of film and video we can only follow the development of changes when new versions of old plays were written down. Those texts, however, often provide us with a very haphazard and incomplete record of the process of adaptation and rewriting.

Only a minority of Chinese plays present an original story because most of them are based on legends and tales that circulated in written or oral form for centuries before they were adapted for the stage. The texts of some of the earliest Chinese dramas are already rewritings of plays that had long been popular onstage, thus showing that any new version must be appreciated on its own terms and may well be better than the original that inspired it.[1] This applies not only to the *zaju* of the 1250–1450 period, but also to early southern plays. Gao Ming 高明 (ca. 1307–ca. 1371), the author of *The Lute* (*Pipa ji* 琵琶記), presents his play as an improved version of a popular play, which, according to him, slandered the protagonists and did not sufficiently emphasize filial piety and loyalty.[2] Whereas the protagonist of the story in earlier versions had been a scoundrel who, upon passing the examinations, abandoned his parents and wife to enjoy a life of luxury as the husband of the prime minister's daughter, Gao Ming made every effort to portray him as the embodiment of loyalty and filial piety, always obedient to his father and the emperor. Zhong Sicheng's 鍾嗣成 (1279–1360) *Record of Ghosts* (*Lugui bu* 錄鬼簿), the earliest preserved catalogue of *zaju*, notes in the entries for some titles that they are a "second version," thus a rewriting of an earlier play. In the case of *zaju*, in which only one actor or actress was allowed to sing, one motivation for such a rewriting often was the desire to change the singing role from male to female or vice versa.[3] Another motivation was the desire to "overturn the case" (*fan'an* 翻案), that is, to provide a well-known story with a new and unexpected ending.[4] During this earliest period of written drama in China, we also already find examples in which plays are adapted from one genre to another, as a number of early southern plays were composed on the basis of pre-existing *zaju*. Even if the basic plot remained the same, such cross-genre adaptations entailed major changes as the single *zaju* protagonist was replaced by a pair of protagonists in a southern play, often turning stories of one-sided passion into tales of mutual love.[5]

Whereas the majority of adaptations and rewritings are due to the desire for novelty on the part of actors and playwrights, other rewritings are imposed from above. When *zaju* were adopted as court drama by the Ming dynasty, government decrees soon prohibited the portrayal of emperors and sages onstage. This meant that plays that featured emperors among their characters either could not be performed or had to be more or less extensively rewritten.[6] As plays had to be submitted to palace censors before performance, we also find that for the first time the full texts of the plays were written out, including all conventional routines, lame jokes, and repetitions. It also is clear that such ideologically imposed rewritings went much further than the removal of emperors from stage, as passages containing strong social criticism tended to be toned down considerably in the palace manuscripts. In many cases one can also detect an attempt to enhance the moral stature of the protagonist.[7] Despite the general nature of government decrees, however, it is not quite clear how effective these decrees were outside of the palace and the capitals. It also should be noted that some changes were due to the nature of the palace companies and changing theatrical fashions. Whereas most theatrical companies of the Yuan dynasty probably were very small, only comprising a single star, the palace companies were much larger, resulting in a tendency to reduce the number of arias for the lead singer and to expand the text for the other characters in the play. And whereas the Yuan and early Ming had been fascinated by the mimed performance of horse riding, the later Ming loved the mimed performance of boat trips. Although these rewritings were still closely connected to performance, the play texts were subjected to a different kind of rewriting as drama also became popular reading materials and slowly acquired a certain degree of literary standing during the last century of the Ming dynasty. When Zang Maoxun 臧懋循 (d. 1621) published his one hundred *zaju* anthology entitled *A Selection of Yuan Plays* (*Yuanqu xuan* 元曲選), he edited the included plays with a reading audience of Jiangnan literati in mind; as a result, his changes affected both the form and the content of the selected plays, thus also affecting both the wording and the message.[8]

Southern plays too were often printed during the last century of the Ming and were edited after each new printing. As southern plays were widely performed during that period, many of these changes reflected changes in performance practice. One of the most important areas of change was the development of regional musical styles, which affected the way the arias were sung. Even when by the end of the sixteenth century *chuanqi* were written by well-established literati with a strongly developed sense of authorship, fellow-playwrights in other locations did not hesitate to adapt plays from elsewhere to local performance styles. The most famous case here is Tang Xianzu's 湯顯祖 (1550–1616) *Peony Pavilion* (*Mudan ting* 牡丹亭). Tang hailed from Jiangxi province and most likely had written his very long play (fifty-five scenes) with the music of his home province in mind. When his play became popular in Suzhou, however, local playwrights such as Zang Maoxun and Feng Menglong 馮夢龍 (1574–1646), despite outspoken protests by Tang Xianzu, quickly published shorter versions that were more suitable to the local *Kunqu* 崑曲 style of singing. When in the eighteenth and nineteenth centuries only selected scenes (*zhezi xi* 折子戲) of *Peony Pavilion* were performed, the process of adaptation and rewriting continued, but this time most of the changes were due to the actors and actresses.[9] But once *chuanqi* plays were printed in larger numbers and became popular reading materials from the late sixteenth century onward, their texts were adapted to the taste of their elite audiences.[10] While Mao Jin's 毛晉 (1599–1659) *Sixty Plays* (*Liushi zhong qu* 六十種曲) provided Qing dynasty readers with readable editions of a large selection of *chuanqi*, the ongoing changes in the performance of the *zhezi xi* during the seventeenth and eighteenth centuries were reflected in the aria anthologies of the late Ming as well as in Qian Decang's 錢德蒼 *A Cloak of Patchworked White Fur* (*Zhui baiqiu* 綴白裘) of 1770–1777, a large anthology of selected scenes as they were popularly performed. Alongside selected scenes from *chuanqi*, the latter work also contained examples of various genres of regional drama. During the Qianlong period (1736–1795), when some of the imperial palaces were provided with large three-tiered stages that allowed for elaborate scenery and special effects, a number of large adaptations of popular story cycles, each in 240 scenes and requiring ten days for a full performance, were composed, largely by cannibalizing earlier plays on these materials, to make full use of the special possibilities for pageantry provided by these stages (and the large number of actors available at court).[11]

The eighteenth century also saw the emergence of many genres of regional opera. Many of these genres originated from small skits. A number of these skits had an erotic character as they focused on the attraction between the sexes. Musically, almost all genres of regional theater were very simple. Whereas *chuanqi* playwrights could choose from over three hundred melodies for their arias, most forms of regional theater during their earliest phase of development relied on a single matrix melody, good for singing two lines of seven-syllable verse. Variation was achieved by speeding up or slowing down the tempo, abandoning a fixed meter, or turning the melody upside down. As genres of regional drama developed, they might incorporate a second matrix melody and a number of individual melodies. Their heavy reliance on the seven-syllable line (and its extension, the ten-syllable line) meant that when these genres of regional theater began to incorporate the stories of longer plays in their repertoires, often on the basis of *chuanqi*, the arias had to be adapted extensively.[12] As most texts of the many kinds of regional theater were orally-transmitted creations by actors, this quite often meant that the arias were composed in a much simpler register of language. At the same time, the plots of these longer plays might be further extended or drastically condensed depending on local conditions and preferences. On closer inspection, many plays that nowadays are considered staples of the traditional repertoire turn out to be relatively new additions or rewritings. Traditional Chinese theater on the eve of the twentieth century did not consist of a clearly demarcated number of genres of regional opera, each with its own stable repertoire. Rather, ranging from court to countryside, it offered a bewildering variety of genres, each at a different stage of development and each with an ever-changing repertoire as the actors freely borrowed plots and ideas, and arias and costumes, from one another. The tradition was alive and kicking and therefore never the same. Actually, some of the most popular genres of regional theater came into their own only over the course of the twentieth century.

At every stage in the development of premodern Chinese theater concerned intellectuals tried to use drama to reach large audiences with their message. Religious drama such as the Mulian 目連 plays were sponsored by local communities because their extensive stories of sin and salvation also showcased models of virtuous behavior and their posthumous rewards together with gruesome examples of crime and punishment.[13] Confucian intellectuals of the early Ming tried to outdo Gao Ming's *The Lute* by writing plays that offered perfect exemplars of every Confucian virtue, and some of these plays enjoyed a considerable popularity for quite a while.[14] Other playwrights in late imperial times might have wanted to teach a more limited lesson. For instance, one nineteenth-century playwright wrote a play to warn of the consequences of slaughtering buffalo and eating beef.[15] Many traditional plays had a moral message for the simple reason that interesting conflicts are often moral conflicts, ranging from conflicts of good against bad to conflicts that demand a choice between equally valid values. In premodern times, such moral conflicts were of course expressed in the moral vocabulary at hand, that is, the moral language of Confucianism.

Traditional Drama in Modern China

Concerned intellectuals had ever more recourse to drama in the final years of the Qing. Modernizing intellectuals such as Liang Qichao 梁啟超 (1873–1929) and Chen Duxiu 陳獨秀 (1879–1942) were convinced that the great mass of the population had been inculcated with traditional (and in their eyes backward) ideas by the vernacular novel and stage, but that the novel and theater also were the most effective means to make them aware of China's situation and to confront them with new values and ideas. These modernizing intellectuals were strengthened in this conviction by their belief that the novel and theater had been instrumental in bringing about the revolutionary changes in recent European history.[16] While many of the *zaju* and *chuanqi* penned by modernizing intellectuals in the last years of the Qing had novel, occasionally even foreign, subjects, other plays provided revisions of old and well-known stories, but infusing them with new values and ideas. One example of the latter is the story of Mulan 木蘭, the girl who dresses up as a man to join the army when her father is called up for service but is too old to serve. The story of Mulan was first adapted for the stage in the late sixteenth century by the maverick poet and playwright Xu Wei 徐渭 (1521–1593), who was primarily interested in Mulan's cross-dressing.[17] An eighteenth-century *chuanqi* adaptation by a Manchu prince portrayed Mulan as the embodiment of both filial piety and loyalty. However, in an anonymous two-act Peking Opera script that was published in 1903 filial piety is replaced by feminism and loyalty to a single ruler or dynasty is replaced by patriotism, i.e., loyalty to one's nation and race. And whereas in earlier versions the ethnic identity of

Mulan is often obscure and her loyalty is directed to a non-Han dynasty such as the Northern Wei, the author of this little play strengthened its nationalistic message by making Mulan unmistakably Chinese, moving the action to the Han dynasty and having her fight the invading Xiongnu from the north (Manchus? Russians? Japanese?) and chasing them into the Northern Ice Sea.[18] The nationalism of the final years of the Qing not only resonated with intellectuals, but also with some actors and theater managers in Shanghai and elsewhere, resulting in the performance of hundreds of new plays on topics of contemporary interest, including plays performed in contemporary dress.[19]

Modernizing intellectuals soon abandoned the modernization of traditional theater[20] in favor of "modern" forms of theater such as "civilized drama" (*wenmingxi* 文明戲) and "spoken drama" (*huaju*), believing that these genres that relied primarily on spoken dialogue and realistic action were better suited to deal with the urgent issues of modern society.[21] Whereas *wenmingxi* was primarily improvisational, *huaju*, inspired by Ibsen and Shaw, strongly emphasized the primacy of the playwright's text.[22] In the process, China also became acquainted with the notion of the director and his personal interpretation of the text in the performance under his control. In traditional Chinese theater overall direction of a performance was usually entrusted to the most prestigious senior actor onstage. Because such senior actors performed their signature plays time and again, over time they imbued these plays with their own interpretations. The absence of a director was increasingly seen by modernizing and revolutionary intellectuals as one obvious sign of the backwardness of traditional Chinese theater, and after 1949 all government-run traditional theater companies were assigned directors.[23] But even if the majority of modernizing intellectuals in the early decades following the Revolution of 1911 turned their attention to *huaju*, this did not mean that traditional theater remained the same. With the rapid urbanization of China in the twentieth century, commercial theater became an increasingly important venue for performance. During the first half of the twentieth century the traditional teahouse theater was almost completely replaced in the big cities such as Shanghai and Beijing by Western-style proscenium theaters, in which the actors and the audience were clearly separated from one another. With the introduction of Western-style theaters also came changes in lighting and scenery, and the orchestra was moved from the stage to the wings. Furthermore, whereas the old-style teahouse theaters were open almost all day for continuous shows, now the preferred format was a show of two to three hours, good for one evening's entertainment. A new contractual system, easy communications (steamboats, trains, and planes), and the illustrated press allowed some of the leading actors (and increasingly also actresses) to develop into national stars. All of these changes had a far-reaching influence on all aspects of performance and resulted in the constant adaptation and rewriting of plays. These changes continued to be felt throughout the twentieth century, independent of the political regime.[24]

Whereas the majority of modernizing intellectuals embraced *huaju*, other equally modernizing intellectuals tried to turn Peking Opera into a "national opera" (*guoju* 國劇) that in all respects would be the very opposite of Western-style spoken drama: if *huaju* was realistic in its action, *guoju* would be symbolic; if *huaju* wanted to imitate drab everyday life onstage, *guoju* would make everything more beautiful; and if *huaju* was limited to prose dialogues, in *guoju* every sound would be song and every movement would be dance. This *guoju* movement was part of a larger movement throughout the country to change the nature of drama and theater from vulgar entertainment to art and to change the status of actors from low-class entertainers to artists. The leading ideologue of the *guoju* movement was Qi Rushan 齊如山 (1876–1962), who had spent a considerable period of time in France from 1903 to 1908. His extensive writings on Peking Opera had a formative impact on scholarship on the esthetics of Peking Opera, even though his name could not be mentioned in mainland China for a long time after 1949.[25] Qi Rushan also adapted many plays for Mei Lanfang 梅蘭芳 (1894–1961), the most famous female impersonator of his day. These plays were designed to showcase the characteristics of *guoju* as in contrast to those of *huaju*. Mei Lanfang became the embodiment of the new status of traditional theater, and Mei's own status as an artist was confirmed by the spectacular success of his trips abroad (to Japan in 1919 and 1924, to the United States in 1930, and to the Soviet Union in 1935).[26]

The Chinese Communist Party and Theater Reform

Whereas Qi Rushan and Mei Lanfang created the esthetics of modern Peking Opera, other groups continued to look into the possibility of utilizing traditional forms of theater to reach the rural population with a message of national mobilization and modernization. The organization that eventually would be the most effective in this respect was the Chinese Communist Party (CCP) after it was forced to abandon its urban bases and retreat into the deep countryside. What distinguished the rewriting of plays in the Communist areas (and after 1949 throughout mainland China) from earlier attempts at rewriting was not the desire to modernize traditional theater by infusing it with a new message, but the strict control imposed from above and the desire not only to rewrite the content but also to reeducate the actors and to reform all aspects of the organization of the theater. It should be pointed out, however, that the CCP developed its policy of theatrical reform only by trial and error. During the years of the Jiangxi Soviet (1929–1934) the Communists easily adapted traditional folksong tunes into new songs, but drama during this period was still dominated by simple forms of *huaju*, such as "living newspapers." Local initiatives to infuse the local form of regional drama with new content were ignored by CCP dramatists.[27] This changed after the Long March of 1934–1935, when the CCP moved to Yan'an. But as an increasing number of urban intellectuals moved to Yan'an in the late 1930s and early 1940s, the gulf between intellectuals and local professional and amateur artists widened once again.[28] In order to address this issue, the CCP eventually developed a policy that required that intellectuals first learn from the masses before becoming their teachers. This policy found its canonical expression in Mao Zedong's *Talks at the Yan'an Forum on Literature and Art* of 1942, which became the basic guideline for cultural policy in the PRC for decades to come. Mao insisted on the primacy of the new, Marxist, revolutionary message but called for adaptation of traditional forms to facilitate propaganda among workers, peasants, and soldiers.

The most successful result of this policy in the field of drama was the "new Yangge movement." Yangge 秧歌 (rice-sprout songs, that is, songs sung while transplanting rice-seedlings) in the context of the northern Shaanxi countryside referred primarily to large and complicated group dances that were performed in many villages on the occasion of the Lantern Festival in the middle of the First Month of the lunar calendar. Such dances were often accompanied by little skits featuring clowns performing various village characters, such as amorous young girls and equally amorous young men engaging in suggestive banter and gesture.[29] In many of the rewritten Yangge skits produced in the Yan'an area these young lovers were replaced by husband and wife couples engaged in productive activities such as clearing virgin soil. In order to further enhance the dignity of these peasant characters and their productive labor, the village characters were no longer played by clowns, even though playwrights tried their best to provide some humor so as not to lose the interest of the audience.[30] We encounter the same desire to enhance the dignity of workers and peasants by changing their role category and by downplaying explicit erotic materials in the rewritings of full-length plays after 1949.

The new Yangge plays featured conspicuously in the Yan'an New Year celebrations of 1943 and were greatly popularized thereafter, including the first several years of the People's Republic of China (PRC). But as the People's Liberation Army (PLA) moved into the southern provinces the cultural cadres soon discovered that the local populations far preferred their own local forms of drama. The amateur troupes that were widely established in southern provinces such as Anhui were therefore allowed, or even encouraged, to use local tunes and local dialects as long as the message in their plays served the mass movement of the moment, such as the land reform movement or the marriage reform movement. Following the disruptions of the War of Resistance and the Civil War, southern Anhui witnessed a remarkable resurgence of Huangmei Opera in the countryside between 1949 and 1953. Local communities were stimulated to compose new plays based on local events (such as the crimes of local landlords or especially vicious mothers-in-law) or to adapt old plays to the new circumstances. One successful example of such an adaption involved a play in which a young man who wants to take revenge on a local bully is no longer instructed in martial arts by an immortal but is contacted by an underground member of the CCP and joins the PLA. These amateur troupes also often provided safe haven for professional actors who had lost their jobs.[31] The contribution of these village theatricals to the revolutionary movement strongly boosted Party and government support for regional opera during the theater-reform movement after 1949. In the famous "Directive on Theater Reform" of May 5, 1951 (to be discussed in more detail below) support for regional opera and popular skits is described as follows:

> Regional opera and especially popular skits (*minjian xiaoxi* 民間小戲) are relatively simple and lively in form and easily reflect contemporary life. They are also easily accepted by the masses, so we have to place special emphasis [on these genres]. As of now the work of theater reform in every locality has to take the theatrical genre that has the greatest influence on the local masses as its major object of reform and development. Therefore, people have to widely collect, record, and print old and new scripts of regional operas and popular skits to provide materials for study and revision. If circumstances allow, each year a national competitive festival should be organized to showcase the results of the reform of each genre and to honor the most excellent works and performances so as to provide guidance for further development.[32]

Despite such strong government support for regional opera and local skits, many intellectuals and cultural cadres continued to look down on these vulgar genres, believing that all opera should aspire to the excellence of Peking Opera.

Drama reform in Yan'an was not at all limited to small skits, local genres, and village amateurs. Other efforts included the composition of new Peking Operas on themes from *Water Margin* (*Shuihu zhuan* 水滸傳). All episodes from this novel on the adventures of "righteous bandits" had been widely popular onstage all over China for centuries. The CCP now interpreted the novel as an epic about peasant rebellion, and the activities of its heroes were regarded as a foreshadow of the CCP's own armed struggle. The most successful of these new Peking Operas was *Driven to Join the Liangshan Rebels* (*Bishang Liangshan* 逼上梁山) by Yang Shaoxuan and others.[33] This opera, which teaches that in a corrupt society even the most loyal supporters of the government are forced to join the revolution, was praised by Mao Zedong in a letter dated January 9, 1944 ("You have restored history to its true face, and you have given the old traditional theater a new beginning. … What you have begun is an epoch-making beginning of revolutionizing old traditional theater").[34] Such high praise must have enhanced the confidence of playwrights and directors in Yan'an to believe that it was indeed possible to rewrite the traditional repertoire of various kinds of regional theater. In yet another development, Yan'an also witnessed the creation of *The White-Haired Girl* (*Baimaonü* 白毛女). The story of this opera is reportedly based on a local event in northern Hebei and its music was composed on the basis of local folk tunes. Telling the story of a peasant girl who flees a brutal landlord and whose hair turns white as she hides in a cave, and who survives by stealing the offerings in a local temple until she is saved by the PLA, this opera was by all accounts extremely popular. If the success of *The White-Haired Girl* held a lesson for the many musicians involved in the adaptation and rewriting of items in the traditional repertoire of their local genre of regional drama, it must have been that not only the stories but also the tunes were highly malleable as they adapted their plays to a new format.

The rewriting of traditional stories for regional theater was also attempted outside the Yan'an area by some leftist dramatists.[35] Ouyang Yuqian 歐陽予倩 (1889–1962), who combined a long career as actor, playwright, and director, not only wrote the script for the hugely successful 1939 movie adaptation of the story of Mulan which made her an icon of patriotism, but also, after he moved from Shanghai to Guilin, adapted the story for *Guiju* 桂劇.[36] Tian Han 田漢, a playwright, filmmaker, and songwriter who was obsessed by the legend of the White Snake throughout his life, started to work on a Peking Opera version of the legend, which would undergo many revisions before reaching its final shape in the first years of the PRC.[37] In the traditional versions of the legend of the White Snake, the snake takes on a human shape out of love for a poor drug-shop assistant (Xu Xian 許仙) from Hangzhou whom she marries; although she makes him rich, she also causes him numerous troubles as her wealth is acquired by theft. Despite her great magical powers, she is eventually incarcerated below the Thunder Peak Pagoda (on the banks of Hangzhou's West Lake) by a holy monk who in this way saves her husband from desire. In his early years Tian Han had been fascinated by the White Snake's demonic aspects and had regarded her as a Chinese embodiment of the *femme fatale*, but now he did away with the supernatural elements in the story that could reflect negatively on his female protagonist and turned her into a woman fighting for free love who is liberated from imprisonment when the masses rise up in rebellion and topple the Thunder Peak Pagoda. After 1949 Tian Han was appointed director of the Bureau for Theater Reform in the Ministry of Culture and was in charge of working out the details of government policies on theater reform.

Despite the relative success of the theater-reform movement in Yan'an and elsewhere, the CCP's initial theater policy upon entering the big cities in northern China in the late 1940s, apart from sponsoring Yangge and *The White Haired Girl*, was primarily one of censorship and prohibition when confronted with the rich repertoires of the theatrical genres that dominated urban stages. Local cadres were often far more drastic in their prohibitions than the central authorities, who were tempted to compile an extensive list of prohibited titles, but eventually settled for a short list of twenty-six banned plays (temporarily recalled in 1957, but officially recalled only in 2007), on the understanding that local authorities could outlaw more titles on the basis of analogy (or, preferably, by convincing local theater managers and actors of the negative characteristics of the plays so they would on their own decide whether or not to perform them). Whatever the nature of the censorship, however, these actions by local governments and cadres resulted in an acute shortage in many places of plays that could be staged. The central government tried to remedy the confusion and chaos by a producing number of publications that spelled out in more detail which traditional plays were permissible, which plays were in need of adaptation and rewriting, and which plays should be banned all together.[38]

The most important of these documents was the May 5, 1951 "Directive on Theater Reform" ("Guanyu xiqu gaige gongzuo de zhishi" 關於戲曲改革工作的指示), issued by Premier Zhou Enlai,[39] which called for the reform of the repertoire, the re-education of actors, and the reorganization of troupe management. Three of the six paragraphs in this document are dedicated to ideological revisions of the repertoire. "Plays," the directive states, "should take the glorification of the people's new patriotism and the encouragement of the people's heroism in the revolutionary struggle and their productive labor as their main task." Local authorities who were called upon to play a positive role in the reform of the repertoire were told: "The current work on theater reform has to concentrate its efforts on inspection of the most widely distributed old plays and make the necessary and fitting corrections of their defective contents and defective performance methods. … When revising old plays one must be careful not to violate the true facts of history and their effectiveness in educating the people." From other documents it is clear that the traditional repertoire was primarily seen as entertainment for a decadent urban leisure class and therefore only a small number of plays was expected to be acceptable without any changes; many plays had to be condemned outright; and others perhaps could be salvaged by revision. The process of revision was envisioned as a collective process, and at each stage the results had to be submitted to the judgment of a supervisory committee.[40] Three types of revision were envisioned: a mild revision ("brushing away the dust"), a thorough-going revision ("eradicating the weeds and keeping the essence"), and an all-out revision ("extracting the embryo and changing the bones"). *Married to a Heavenly Immortal* was eventually submitted to a "thorough-going revision."

To evaluate the results of this revision process the central government organized national and regional theater festivals. Local theater companies were invited to cities such as Peking and Shanghai to showcase their old plays that had been adapted to the new times. The first of these large meetings was convened in Peking in the fall of 1952. The purpose of this activity was of course that theater companies all over China would learn from one another's experiences as well as from the directives that their experiments elicited from the leading cultural cadres who attended the performances. Huangmei Opera was not represented at the 1952 Peking Theater Convention, but comparable genres were represented, for instance Flower Drum Theater (*Huaguxi* 花鼓戲) from Hunan, which presented *Liu Hai Cuts Wood* (*Liu Hai kanqiao* 劉海砍樵). This little play, based on a much longer traditional play on the relation between a woodcutter and a demonic fox, made their relation into one of pure love; the role category of the woodcutter was changed from a clown (*chou* 丑) to a *sheng* 生, a role-type which traditionally specialized in performing upper-class young men; and the beauty of the woodcutter's labor was emphasized by changing his movements into dance. The play had already been highly praised by Minister of Culture Zhou Yang in the summer of 1952, and, not surprisingly, it won a prize at the 1952 Peking Theater Festival.[41] Huangmei Opera was invited to Shanghai to perform in the fall of 1952. There "Meeting on the Road" ("Luyu" 路遇), a rewritten scene from *Married to a Heavenly Immortal*, was performed together with revised versions of some small Huangmei Opera skits. In general, the revisions followed models that could be deduced from the new Yangge plays and the honored plays performed in Peking.[42]

The revision of traditional plays and the composition of a large number of new plays, often based on traditional stories from history and folklore that tried to meet the demand that art should serve politics, resulted in a 1951 debate on the extent to which plays set in the past could depart from the historical truth. Should such plays reflect the Party's understanding of history or could figures from a mythical or historical past become spokespersons for current Party and government policy (such as the Resist America, Support Korea campaign)? One topic that enjoyed considerable popularity in 1949, 1950, and 1951 was the Buffalo Boy and Weaving Maiden fairy tale. In modern China this fairy tale had circulated in many forms. In its most common form the male protagonist is a poor peasant who is cheated out of his inheritance by his elder brother at the instigation of his evil sister-in-law; when the two brothers divide their parents' possessions, the younger brother only gets the family's old buffalo and cart. But because he treats the buffalo well, the animal tells him how he can obtain a wife. If he steals the clothes of Weaving Maiden when she and her sisters are taking a bath, he will be able to force her to marry him. This takes place and the couple have children, but eventually Weaving Maiden finds her gown, puts it on again, and flees back to heaven. When Buffalo Boy pursues her, he and Weaving Maiden become stars on opposite sides of the Celestial River (the Milky Way) and are allowed to see each other only once a year, in the night of the seventh day of the Seventh Lunar Month, when magpies form a bridge for them across the waves. Derk Bodde saw a performance of a rewritten version of the play on August 1, 1949 in Tianjin, in which the final scene where the Jade Emperor allows the lovers to meet once a year was dropped "to combat superstition."[43] In a Daoqi Opera 倒七戲 adaptation of the legend performed at Wuhu, however, the play ended with Buffalo Boy and Weaving Maiden joining forces to fight the Jade Emperor and the Queen Mother, waving the Party flag with hammer and sickle while shouting "Down with imperialism!" An even more conspicuous modernization of this fairy tale (in which the buffalo symbolizes a tractor) was apparently performed in Wuxi.[44]

When these blatantly anachronistic adaptations were criticized, they were defended by Yang Shaoxuan. Yang Shaoxuan, who served as one of the deputy directors of the Bureau for Theater Reform under Tian Han, had not only composed yet another play based on an episode from *Water Margin* and a play based on the story of the *Foolish Old Man Who Removed the Mountains* (*Yugong yishan* 愚公移山),[45] but also had produced his own version of the Buffalo Boy and Weaving Maiden fairy tale entitled *A New Account of the Celestial River* (*Xin tianhe ji* 新天河記). This play was performed in Beijing in August 1951. One of the conspicuous features of this adaptation was the marriage of the buffalo and the cart because "the buffalo is a means of production, and the cart is an instrument of labor." Yang's critics faulted him for having his buffalo quote, "Eyes askance, I cast a cold glance at the thousand pointing fingers/ but bowing my head I gladly agree an ox for the children to be," a couplet by the famous modern writer Lu Xun 魯迅 (1881–1936).[46] Further criticisms concerned his introduction of hawks (as symbols of warmongers) and doves (as symbols of peace). Yang's play ends with the following lines:

> Buffalo Boy herds his buffalo on the mountain slopes;
> Weaving Maiden works the loom with nimble hands:
> She weaves the web of heaven as well as the net of earth
> And so captures the hawks and obtains peace for all!

This was considered too direct a reference to the contemporary campaign to Resist America, Aid Korea, and Safeguard World Peace.[47] But what must have sealed Yang Shaoxuan's downfall, however, most likely was not his eagerness to adapt old tales to new times but his strident and stubborn defense of his own style of writing even after criticisms had started to appear.[48] As we saw in the Introduction,[49] at the 1952 Peking Theater Festival Zhou Yang eventually condemned this ample use of blatant anachronisms and reiterated that historical events and characters should reflect historical truths (as understood by the Chinese Communist Party). Such a condemnation of this quite recent adaptation of the fairy tale of Buffalo Boy and Weaving Maiden[50] must have been a major warning for anyone attempting an adaptation of the very similar legend of Dong Yong and Seventh Sister. We will see that in his various publications on his revision of *Married to a Heavenly Immortal* Lu Hongfei always stresses that the fate of Dong Yong as an indentured servant or slave corresponds to the stage of economic development during the Eastern Han dynasty (25–220), and that the myth of Dong Yong and Seventh Sister is a truthful reflection of the ideals and hopes of the peasant masses in feudal China. Others expressed admiration of Lu Hongfei's extensive use of documentation for his revision.

The First Rewriting of *Married to a Heavenly Immortal*

The tale of the filial son Dong Yong, who sells himself into slavery for three years in order to be able to provide his father with a decent funeral and his encounter with a heavenly immortal who with her weaving skills helps him to pay off his debts within three months, enjoyed wide popularity from early on. Whether we characterize the tale as a myth or a fairy tale, it belongs to that large body of folktales that "make themselves particularly available for continuous re-creation and rewriting … because of their essential abstraction from a specific context."[51] From a narrative ballad discovered among the Dunhuang manuscripts we know that by the tenth century at the latest the story had been expanded to include the detail that the Immortal Maiden is pregnant when she returns to heaven after one hundred days and she later delivers a son to Dong Yong. The boy wants to meet his birth mother when he grows up and succeeds in doing so, but with terrible consequences for the soothsayer who betrays the secret of how the boy can find of his mother.[52] During the Yuan, Ming, and Qing dynasties the story was adapted for the stage in many theatrical genres, but none of these adaptations has been preserved in its entirety; only isolated songs and individual scenes from the period up to the early years of the twentieth century still exist. Our earliest evidence of a dramatic adaptation is a set of songs, preserved in a sixteenth-century source, that probably makes up the arias in the second act of an otherwise unrecorded *zaju* devoted to the tale of Dong Yong. The arias are written in the voice of Dong Yong, who, after he has just buried his mother (sic!), is on his way to the house of the landlord. Still overcome by grief, he is suddenly accosted by a pretty young girl who wants to accompany him. Dong Yong tries every argument to dissuade her from this preposterous idea, but she adamantly insists and eventually he allows her to come along.[53] Because these arias derive from a *zaju* we only hear the voice of Dong Yong, and we have no idea how aggressively the Immortal Maiden pursues her objectives. Later examples of amorous young maidens forcing themselves on timid lovers, which were quite popular as skits in many parts of China, suggest that such scenes could be played with very broad, and at times bawdy, humor. We do not know which other scenes were included in this *zaju* (did the couple's son already make his entrance?), but the fact that it is this set of songs that has been preserved probably means that from its very beginning the "Meeting on the Road" scene was a stage favorite.

By the time of the Ming dynasty the tale of Dong Yong had been adapted as a *chuanqi* which circulated under a number of titles. No complete copy of the play has been preserved, but some scenes are included in anthologies of drama arias and scenes from the earliest years of the seventeenth century. We know that this version also included the adventures of the couple's son, as one anthology includes a scene entitled "On the Streets of the Capital the Immortal Maiden Brings [Dong Yong] his Son" (*Xianji tianjie songzi* 仙姬天街送子). Another anthology includes a simple version of the scene corresponding to "Meeting on the Road." By far the most popular scene in the play, however, was the scene of the couple's tearful parting at the end of one hundred days, which is found in no less than seven anthologies.[54] As might be expected of a *chuanqi*, Dong Yong and the Immortal Maiden have now been recast as a loving couple, and since the role of Dong Yong is performed by a *sheng*, his status is raised to that of an impoverished student. But when Dong Yong and the Immoral Maiden leave the landlord's mansion, Dong Yong is not yet aware of their impending separation; the poignancy of the scene is achieved as the Immortal Maiden tries, through various suggestions, to alert him to the fact that she must return to heaven.[55] If the attraction of "Meeting on the Road" has always been its humor, the attraction of this scene must have been its combination of dramatic irony and pathetic display of emotion—the latter greatly facilitated by the sentimental music of southern drama and its ample store of images for feelings of loss and separation.

As is clear from the summary of the contents of the Ming *chuanqi* play in the *Comprehensive Catalogue with Content Abstracts of the Sea of Songs* (*Quhai zongmu tiyao* 曲海總目提要), as quoted in full in the Introduction to this volume, the greater length and larger cast of a *chuanqi* in comparison with a *zaju* resulted in a much more complicated plot than in any earlier known versions of the tale. Dong Yong and the Immortal Maiden are now adopted by the landlord who wants his daughter to study weaving with the Immortal Maiden. The landlord's son is, as so often is the case, depicted as a lecherous playboy. He tries to seduce the Immortal Maiden; in order to do so, he attempts to have Dong Yong killed by ordering him to cut trees on a bandit-infested mountain. But Dong Yong is saved due to the intervention of the bandit chief, who turns out to be an old friend.[56] A *chuanqi* play needs a happy ending, so the daughter of the landlord marries Dong Yong after the Immortal Maiden has left, and this woman becomes a dutiful mother to the son of Dong Yong and the Immortal Maiden. Dong Yong, moreover, receives a high title from the emperor and his son is able to meet his birth mother. Although the full text of the Ming *chuanqi* was lost, the full play remained in the repertoire of many genres of regional theater,[57] including some local genres of *Qingyang*-style theater in Anhui and Jiangxi until the middle of the twentieth century. But the Hukou Gaoqiang 湖口高腔 version was lost during the Cultural Revolution, with the exception of three scenes, including "The Edict Issued at Magpie Bridge," "Meeting in the Shade of the Scholartree," and "Separating at the Scholartree."[58] In the case of the Yuexi Gaoqiang 岳西高腔 version, only three scenes have been preserved, including "Meeting in the Shade of the Scholartree," "Starting on the Job and Weaving the Silk," and "The Separation and Return to Heaven." Ban Youshu 班友書 stresses the extent to which the first of these developed the scene of "Meeting on the Road" not only by greatly increasing the characters' dialogue, but also by adding the character of the old man (a manifestation of the Astral Lord of Great White, The Metal Star [the planet Venus], a common character in traditional Chinese folk literature), and adding many twists and turns to the plot. Ban Youshu also states that the traditional version of "Meeting on the Road" in Huangmei Opera was copied, lock, stock, and barrel, from the *Qingyang* version.[59]

After 1949 Chinese critics stressed time and again that Dong Yong originally was a poor peasant who had been brutally exploited by the landlord class, and that therefore the traditional version as it finally took shape in the Ming *chuanqi* play (and the many prosimetric versions that followed its plot) that made Dong Yong a student and Master Fu 傅 a kind benefactor was a distortion of the original story by the ruling classes. Lu Hongfei, in particular, made great efforts to assert that the tale of Dong Yong was based on historical fact with respect to the economic situation during the Eastern Han dynasty (25–220).[60] One may well question that assertion. The version of the tale of Dong Yong, which apparently was very much on the mind of Lu Hongfei, is the one that is found in the *Twenty-four Exemplars of Filial Piety*, but this is a very late version of the story, as are all the pious reiterations of this account that are encountered in local gazetteers, such as the Xiaogan gazetteer.[61] But it should be stressed that even if tales of filial sons ended up as primers during late imperial China, their origins were very much an elite tradition.[62] Moreover, the earliest pictorial representation of the tale (of AD 151 at the famous Wu Liang Shrine) shows a filial Dong Yong who takes his elderly father with him in a carriage when he goes out to the fields.[63] Cao Zhi's Dong Yong hires himself out for money and indebts himself, but this occurs during his father's lifetime. It is difficult to imagine that a starving peasant could allow himself the luxury of providing his father with his own carriage, and one may also wonder to what extent members of the Six Dynasties elite would have been impressed by a poor peasant indebting himself, even if to the extent of selling himself into servitude. Unfortunately, that must have been an all-too-common occurrence. In fact, the character of the filial son Dong Yong most likely derives from the life story of Dong Yong, the Marquis of Gaochang. This Dong Yong was a great-grandson of a certain Dong Zhong 董忠 who was ennobled as marquis of Gaochang in 66 BCE. His son and grandson inherited the title, but the latter was deprived of his rank in 1 CE. His son Dong Yong, however, established such a virtuous reputation that he was reinstated as marquis of Gaochang in 26 by the first emperor of the Eastern Han dynasty.[64] If Dong Yong indeed belonged to this rarefied elite, his actions would have been extremely exceptional for a member of his class. It also would make it understandable why another member of that same class would want to help him out by providing him with a loan. Because Master Fu states explicitly in many versions of the story that he will not insist on repayment, Dong Yong's action to follow up on his contract becomes even more exceptional. For traditional readers Dong Yong's exceptional filial piety is demonstrated by his self-sacrificing decision, despite his status, to sell himself into servitude and to follow up on the obligations of his contract regardless of the kindness of his fellow elite. As such, the tale of Dong Yong in the Ming and Qing dynasties has its own internal logic.

The traditional story of Dong Yong is a tale of conspicuous filial piety and its divine rewards. Whereas other traditional stories may be easily reinterpreted as tales of patriotic fervor and/or the struggle for free love,[65] the traditional story of Dong Yong does not invite such a reinterpretation. Like the other poster boys of filial piety, Dong Yong was shunned by the modernizing and revolutionary dramatists of the first fifty years of the twentieth century. It is difficult to imagine how the story could have been successfully adapted after 1949 as long as the filial son Dong Yong remained the central character. It is quite amazing that the story was selected for revision at all. Once it was selected for revision, however, the major innovation likely was not the change in Dong Yong's social status from student to peasant, but the shift in focus from Dong Yong to Seventh Sister, who becomes a rebellious daughter and loving wife and who sheds all traces of her obedience and high status to become a vivacious and inventive peasant girl.

Although the revisers of the traditional *Married to a Heavenly Immortal* stress their originality in making this change, it should be pointed out that traditional plays and ballads did provide models of divine maidens who leave heaven on their own initiative to join the (poor but deserving) men of their choice. One example of such a divine maiden is the daughter of the God of Mt. Hua, Huayue Sanniang 華岳三娘, who descends to the mortal world and forces the student Liu Xiang 劉向 to marry her. After she gives birth to the boy Chenxiang 沉香, she is discovered by her brother Erlang 二郎, who has her imprisoned beneath a mountain. She is later freed by her son after he becomes an accomplished Daoist magician.[66] But whereas traditional authors interpreted Huayue Sanniang's actions as an expression of sinful lust, the modern rewriters of *Married to a Heavenly immortal* saw Seventh Sister's actions motivated by pure love. And whereas Huayue Sanniang is imprisoned by patriarchal authority as punishment for her transgression, Seventh Sister, who in the traditional version of the play is sent to earth as a punishment, now experiences the loveless realm of heaven as a prison and yearns to escape.[67]

Yet another example of a divine maiden who descends to earth to find love is Seventh Sister's elder sister Zhang Sijie 張四姐 (Fourth Sister). Zhang Sijie's lover and husband Cui Wenrui 崔文瑞 is a filial son, in this case one who is so impoverished that he supports his mother by begging.[68] Zhang Sijie will revive the family's fortune once she has been accepted as daughter-in-law. She also fiercely fights to protect her lover. By using her martial and magical skills she not only defeats all mortal troops sent against her, but also all celestial commanders.[69] But whereas Seventh Sister, in both the traditional and revised versions of *Married to a Heavenly Immortal*, knows some magic tricks, even her weaving skills are too limited to deliver on her promise to the landlord and she has to call on her sisters for help. In addition, Seventh Sister exhibits none of the martial skills that distinguish heroines such as Zhang Sijie and the White Snake. While the White Snake is eventually imprisoned below Thunder Peak Pagoda, Zhang Sijie will only submit to her father's authority once she is allowed to bring her husband and her mother-in-law with her to heaven. Seventh Sister endears herself to her audience because, despite her divine background, she has to rely on her own wit. This of course is a characteristic which is also already quite prominent in the traditional versions of *Married to a Heavenly Immortal*.

In the March 17, 2000 issue of the *Xin'an wanbao* 新安晚報 a certain Chen Rongsheng 陳榮升 claimed that Wang Zhaoqian, not Lu Hongfei, was the author of the modern revised version of *Married to a Heavenly Immortal*. This provoked a strong reaction from Lu Hongfei who insisted on his authorship and called on some of his colleagues from the early 1950s to confirm his claim.[70] Lu may well have felt entitled to assert his authorship of the play because he had been severely "struggled against" during the Cultural Revolution for his part in revising and staging the play. In the summer of 1970 together with Wang Shaofang he had served as a "living target" in a province-wide criticism campaign against the "great poisonous weed" of *Married to a*

Heavenly Immortal.[71] The issue of the authorship of the revised version of the play at least on two occasions was the subject of a more or less official inquiry, once following the success of the 1955 movie (which made no reference at all to Lu's contribution)[72] and once in 1963, and in each case Lu was vindicated.[73] Lu's article and the reactions it engendered provide us with a rather detailed description of the various stages in the revision of *Married to a Heavenly Immortal.* This is useful as the actual process of rewriting plays during the early 1950s is difficult to reconstruct because of the ideologically-required emphasis at the time on collective endeavors.

Writing in 2000 in reaction to the above-mentioned article by Lu Hongfei, Ban Youshu provides us with a rather detailed description of the earliest steps, all of which took place in Anqing, in the revision of the Huangmei Opera version of *Married to a Heavenly Immortal.* Following Liberation, Anqing had reestablished itself as the center of professional Huangmei Opera. The stage was dominated by two commercial companies, Minzhong 民眾 (The Masses) to which Wang Shaofang belonged, and Shengli 勝利 (Victory) to which Yan Fengying belonged.[74] At the end of the summer of 1951, shortly following the publication of the May 5 "Directive on Theater Reform," two young cadres, Ban Youshu and Wang Shengwei 王聖偉, were assigned to work on drama reform, and they shared a room with Lu Hongfei who was assigned to the Bureau of Culture. As their first assignment, Ban and Wang were given the task of revising *Married to a Heavenly Immortal* (as well as *Liang Shanbo and Zhu Yingtai*). The selection of this title most likely was not due to its "progressive content" but due to the political directive that mandated first focusing on the revision of popular titles in popular genres. At the end of September Ban Youshu, according to his own much later statement, presented the following four principles about the first play to a small work group consisting of himself, Wang, Lu, and their superior Liu Fangsong 劉芳松:

1. This is a fairy-tale (myth) play; it does not propagate superstition;
2. That Seventh Immortal Sister, disobeying her father, descends to earth to marry Dong Yong reflects the struggle of women in the old society to have the right to choose their own marriage partners, and thus the play has an anti-feudal, positive meaning;
3. Dong Yong is a poor farm laborer, not a student (*xiucai* 秀才). That by selling himself to bury his father he moved the Emperor of Heaven was originally a primitive way of thinking of the laboring people, but it was used by feudal rulers as an instrument to propagate filial piety;

4. The happy life that Dong Yong and Seventh Immortal Sister pursue is an expression of the laboring people's ideal life of "the husband plows and his wife spins" in the small farm economy, and its final result cannot but be a tragedy.[75]

As none of his colleagues, according to Ban, voiced any objections to these principles, he proceeded to revise the play and by November had completed a first draft. He summarized his changes under the following four headings:

1. Doing away with "Student Dong" and returning [to Dong Yong] his status as a member of the laboring people;
2. Applying "destructive" surgery to the original text, that is to say, "cutting of the head and removing the tail" by removing the beginning scenes of the father's illness, the borrowing of money, and the sale of the body, as well as the ending scenes of becoming son-in-law at the Fu Mansion, becoming the Top-of-the-List for Presenting Treasure, and delivering the son, and by doing away with the episodes in the middle such as the attempted seduction, the becoming of good friends with Landlord Fu, and the acts of kindness by Landlord Fu;
3. Preliminarily establishing the skeleton of the entire play as consisting of the seven scenes—"Leaving the Hovel," "Magpie Bridge," "Meeting on the Road," "Starting Out on the Job," "Weaving Silk," "Completing the Job," and "The Separation."
4. Treatment of the arias and dialogue based on the fact that there was no need for major action beyond appropriately removing the dross and maintaining the essence, doing away with all superfluous verbiage, and maintaining as much as possible the original linguistic characteristics of the play as a popular play and shortening the text in a few places.[76]

Ban claimed that he had been able to work so quickly because "Meeting on the Road" and "Separation" were already well developed and complete in the manuscript that had been put at his disposal. As an example of his own changes to the text, he quotes the ending of "Meeting on the Road." In the manuscript provided to him, the last six lines of the scene, sung by Dong Yong and Seventh Sister, read as follows:

> Leading my wife by the hand I go to the Fu Mansion;
> Together the two of us proceed to Fu Family Bay.
> In the mountains the birds sing their songs,
> While in the streams the fishes frolic about.
> With small steps of her golden lotuses my wife can only walk slowly,
> But earlier than expected we have arrived at Fu Family Bay.

Ban turned this into a duet:

SEVENTH SISTER. The birds in the trees sing as happy as can be.

DONG YONG. The flowers along the road show their smiles.

SEVENTH SISTER. My husband goes to the Fu Mansion as a laborer.

DONG YONG. Over there my wife will wash clothes and starch shirts.

SEVENTH SISTER. The three years of long labor will be easily finished.

DONG YONG. Husband and wife will together go home as a couple.

SEVENTH SISTER. You will plant the fields while I will weave cloth.

DONG YONG. And as a loving couple we will stay together forever.[77]

It should be noted that in the process Ban also changed the Immortal Maiden from a dainty damsel with bound feet into a working woman. But even though Ban completed a full revision of the play, for the time being no attempts were made to have it performed.

When by the end of 1952 the Anqing city government selected Huangmei Opera plays to be performed in Shanghai in the fall of that year, "Meeting on the Road" was included in the program. The roles of Dong Yong and Seventh Sister were to be performed by Wang Shaofang and Pan Jingli,[78] and Zheng Lisong 鄭立松 (1928–) assisted as director. Wang Zhaoqian 王兆乾 (1928–2006), who had been with the army up to that time, was brought in to serve as musical consultant as he had worked on Huangmei Opera music. According to Wang Zhaoqian writing in 2000, the 1952 performance was based on Ban Youshu's revised version of "Meeting on the Road," which established a solid basis for all later adaptations. Wang adds that he included Ban's text in his *Huangmeixi yinyue* of 1953 (published in 1957).[79] Also writing in 2000, however, Zheng Lisong, in his reminiscences of his role in the revision of *Married to a Heavenly Immortal*, provides a rather different account of what happened in 1952. He mentions that Ban provided him with his draft revision of the play, but then states that at the time he did not have an opportunity to study it and that, almost fifty years later, he could not remember how Ban had revised this scene.[80] Zheng claims that it was based on the initiative of the actress Pan Jingli that the character of Seventh Sister was changed from a maiden who meekly accepts her punishment into a rebel who leaves the celestial realm on her own initiative. According to Zheng, in the traditional version of "Meeting on the Road," upon entering Seventh Sister sings only the following four-line aria:

> My father in his Western Heaven has issued a decree,
> Ordering me to descend to earth and marry Dong Yong.
> For a hundred days we'll share the gauze bed-curtains as husband and wife,
> And at the end of that term I'll return to my position and ascend to heaven.[81]

According to Zheng, Pan Jingli changed this to:

> Riding on my cloud I leave the realm of the immortals, leave the realm of the immortals,
> And drifting along I descend to the lower world of dust.
> As I walk on, I arrive quicker than expected in Danyang,
> I see him as he moves a rock to block the door of his hovel.
> With a pack on his back and his umbrella—what's going on?
> I lower my cloud and am filled with sympathy,
> So let me ask the local God of the Soil.[82]

Zheng claims that in one stroke the fatalism[83] in the original play was thus done away with. But even though the song indeed drops any mention of the order of the Jade Emperor, its language actually very much resembles that of the corresponding song in the woodblock edition of the play,[84] and this also applies to the ensuing dialogue between Seventh Sister and the local God of the Soil. The song as quoted by Zheng is found in the text printed by Wang Zhaoqian, so perhaps the actors found time to consult Ban's revised version even if Zheng did not. Zheng also claims that it was he and his colleagues who decided to change the status of Dong Yong from a student into a poor peasant, and that Wang Shaofang created a costume appropriate to Dong Yong's new status.[85] As peasants were traditionally performed by clowns and never were given a leading role as a lover in a "big play," this required considerable creativity and invention on the part of Wang. When interviewed in 1956 in *Chinese Cinema*

(*Zhongguo dianying* 中國電影), Wang said that he had adapted not only the costume but also the way of walking and the way of speaking of his character based on the behavior of peasant friends from his youth.[86] It is not clear, however, to what extent Pan Jingli already took on the character of a village girl as Yan Fengying later did. If we follow Zheng's account we therefore would have to conclude that the principal changes in the reconceptualization of *Married to a Heavenly Immortal* were due not to Ban Youshu, but to the group he worked with in 1952. More modestly, his claim may perhaps be that whatever thoughts were aired about a revision before 1952, it was in the fall of 1952 that such changes were tried out for the first time onstage, and with considerable success.[87]

In contrast to the available traditional versions of the play (see below), the text of "Meeting on the Road" as printed by Wang Zhaoqian does not start with the entrance of Seventh Sister, but rather with the entrance of Dong Yong who, as he is blocking the entrance of his house with rocks, laments his fortune as an indentured servant—Seventh Sister only enters the scene after Dong Yong has left the stage.

(Dong Yong *sings backstage to a weeping beat.*)

Father, oh father!

(Dong Yong *enters and sings in level verse.*)

Alas, my father has passed away,
But I lacked the money to buy a coffin to bury the old man.
At a loss what to do I had no option but to offer myself for sale,
To sell my body as an indentured servant bound to suffer pain.
Here I arrive in front of his tablet and kneel down on the floor.
My dear departed father, please listen carefully to my reasons:
Father, when you were still alive, you have told me, your son,
Told me never be an indentured servant bound to suffer pain!
It's not the case that I have forgotten your words of advice,
But how can one dredge the full moon from the stream?
Now I have said goodbye, I'll get my pack and umbrella.

(Dong Yong *gathers rocks to brick up the gate of his house.*)

I carry rocks in my hands to close up this poor cottage.
Suppressing tears of sadness I set out on the distant road,
Not knowing at all on which day I will come back here.

(Dong Yong *exits.*)[88]

This opening of the scene is not encountered in the 1954 version of the revised *Married to a Heavenly Immortal* (printed for the East China Theater Festival), but it reappears in the version printed in 1955 with a completely different text. In the 1955 version Dong Yong sings the song lamenting his fate as he leaves his own house to go to the the Fu Family Mansion before a drawn curtain, providing the stage hands with an opportunity to change the scenery from Magpie Bridge to the road by the old scholartree. In the 1954 version of the play Dong Yong sings his song lamenting his fate after Seventh Sister has entered the stage, sung her opening song, and engaged in a short dialogue with the God of the Soil. Even though the stage directions or the words of the song do not specify that Dong Yong is a peasant, that would have been immediately clear in the 1952 performance by his costume, and all references in the traditional versions of the scene to Dong Yong's study of the Classics and his status as a student have been carefully removed from the text as printed by Wang Zhaoqian. But even though Ban Youshu and Zheng Lisong both state that in 1952 the roles of the local God of the Soil and the Old Man (the manifestation of the Astral Lord of Great White) were fused, the text as printed by Wang Zhaoqian still keeps these two roles separate.

Following the great success of the Huangmei Opera performances in Shanghai in late 1952 the Anhui authorities in April 1953 established the Anhui Provincial Huangmei Opera Company in Hefei. Many of the leading actors and actresses in Anqing were included in this new ensemble, and Qiao Zhiliang and Lu Hongfei were reassigned from Anqing to Hefei. Inspired by the success of "Meeting on the Road," Lu Hongfei now set out to produce his rewriting of *Married to a Heavenly Immortal*, and he presented a draft to his superiors.[89] In the summer of 1953, Ban Youshu claims, Lu returned to Anqing to borrow Ban's draft, and the two of them discussed the ending of the play. Lu Hongfei preferred to end the play with the happy scene of the Immortal Maiden presenting Dong Yong with his son, but Ban claims that he maintained that the theater reform required a more drastic rewriting.[90] In October of 1953 the new Anhui Provincial Huangmei Opera Company performed *Married to a Heavenly Immortal*, as revised by Lu Hongfei and directed by Li Liping and Qiao Zhiliang, in Anqing. During a roundtable discussion following this performance, Lu Hongfei declared, again according to Ban Youshu, that his stage version had been produced on the basis of the original draft of Ban's revised version.[91] It comes as no surprise then that Ban Youshu does not consider Lu Hongfei as the single author of the modern version of *Married to a Heavenly Immortal*.[92] Ban credits Lu with major changes to the "Magpie Bridge" scene, but he places an even greater emphasis on director Qiao Zhiliang's revision of this scene because it was Qiao's contribution to do away with the parade of the fisherman, woodcutter, farmer, and student, and to bring down the Seven Immortal Sisters from their chairs and to have them mime the labor of the fisherman, woodcutter, farmer, and student in their dances, borrowing the dance movements from Peking Opera and *Kunqu*.[93] To add insult to injury, Ban further stresses the importance of the changes later made to Lu Hongfei's text by Jin Zhi 金芝.[94]

The Second Rewriting of *Married to a Heavenly Immortal*

Ban Youshu mentions that he was provided with a manuscript of *Married to a Heavenly Immortal* but he does not provide any details. In his spring 2000 article on his involvement in the rewriting of *Married to a Heavenly Immortal* Lu Hongfei provides more information. Lu recounts that he participated in the 1952 Anhui province summer training session for actors, and, subsequently, directed the training session for actors in the Anqing region. One of the topics discussed during this session was the distinction between "myth" (fairy tale) and "superstition" in traditional plays. In order to facilitate the discussion following a performance of *Married to a Heavenly Immortal*, Lu claims, he asked for the stage version of the play as dictated by the veteran actor Hu Yuting and he also bought a copy of the woodblock edition of the play put out by the Kunji shuju in Anqing.[95] Even though Lu does not explicitly state it, he creates the impression that his rewriting was directly based on these two texts.

The woodblock edition of the play was reprinted by Du Yingtao in his *Dong Yong Chenxiang heji* of 1957,[96] and a full translation of this text is included in this volume. In this edition the play is divided into three parts. The first part, "Dong Yong Sells his Body" (*Dong Yong maishen* 董永賣身), shows the filial Dong Yong, an impoverished student, taking care of his father and selling himself into servitude upon his father's death; when the Seven Heavenly Sisters observe the world below and the youngest of them is aroused by the sights and sounds of a wedding procession,[97] the Jade Emperor orders her to descend to earth and assist Dong Yong for one hundred days. The second part, "Married to a Heavenly Immortal" (*Tianxian pei*), starts with the long and elaborate scene of "Meeting on the Road" and proceeds to the couple's arrival at the Fu Mansion, where that night the Immortal Maiden weaves ten bolts of silk with the aid of her sisters. The third and final part of the printed version of the play, "The Separation from Dong Yong" (*Dong lang fenbie* 董郎分別) starts when Dong Yong and Seventh Sister have already left the Fu Mansion and are on their way to his home. After a long and complicated dialogue Seventh

Sister finally discloses to Dong Yong that she is a heavenly immortal. When she leaves for her celestial abode, Dong Yong returns to the Fu Mansion, and in a quick succession of short scenes the landlord (who already earlier has adopted him) now sends him with the celestial silk woven by the Immortal Maiden to the capital, where Dong Yong receives the title of Top-of-the-List for the Presentation of Treasure from a grateful emperor. While he parades through the streets of the capital Seventh Sister appears to him and hands him their son. When Dong Yong returns to the Fu family, he marries the landlord's daughter, who is charged to be a good mother to the baby. As will be obvious from this summary, the printed text of the play leaves a considerable gap between the first night after the couple's arrival at the Fu Mansion and their departure one hundred days later.

It may well be that the original publisher of the woodblock edition decided to omit those scenes that culminate in the attempts by Landlord Fu's foolish son to seduce Seventh Sister as too obscene: the boy ends up by groping his sister. But on the stage those scenes were not omitted as is clear from the text dictated by Hu Yuting 胡玉庭.[98] In that text, following a full night of weaving through all five watches the sisters complete the weaving of ten bolts of silk. When Dong Yong and Seventh Sister present the silk to Master Fu, he adopts them as his son and daughter. He orders his daughter to study weaving with Seventh Sister and he orders his son to study the books with Dong Yong. But when Dong Yong and the young master have retired to his study, the latter complains of a stomach ache, leaves Dong Yong, and goes upstairs to his sister's room. Whenever he tries to get his hands on Seventh Sister, however, she switches places with the landlord's daughter. Eventually she calls down the thunder gods to give him a good scare. The scene then moves to the day of departure, when Master Fu sees Dong Yong off as he intends to go home with Seventh Sister.[99] In order to make up for the gap in the woodblock edition of the play, this volume includes a translation of these scenes from Hu Yuting's stage version. Apart from these scenes that are lacking in the woodblock edition, the stage version and the woodblock edition are largely identical, even though the wording of the songs varies considerably from time to time. One major difference is found when, following his father's death, Dong Yong decides to sell himself in order to provide for his father's funeral. As he prepares to write a poster offering himself for sale, the four gods for the recording of virtuous deeds appear onstage. Witnessing this act, they decide to report his exemplary filial piety to the Jade Emperor. The presence onstage of these four gods at this moment underscores the importance of Dong Yong's act. Also, when Seventh Sister is about to leave Dong Yong and return to heaven, she is summoned by a backstage voice. This is not included in the printed edition. Perhaps the most convincing explanation of the differences between the woodblock edition and Hu Yuting's stage version (including the appearance of the thunder gods and their pyrotechnics) is that Hu's version reflects slightly later stage practices when *Married to a Heavenly Immortal* was performed in the urban theaters of Anqing.

Lu Hongfei worked on his rewriting of the play during the first half of 1953. Even if his rewriting was not based directly on Ban Youshu's draft, it closely conformed to the principles outlined by Ban. Like Ban, Lu shortened the play by omitting the opening and closing scenes of the traditional play. Both changed the status of Dong Yong from student to peasant and both stressed Seventh Sister's initiative in running away from heaven. In the complete texts of the revised plays as we have them from 1954 onward, considerable space is devoted to describing the mutual attachment of the young couple, who embody the new Marriage Law ideal of partners who have freely chosen each other on the basis of love, without any ulterior motivation. In the 1954 version of the revised play the mutual love between husband and wife is especially highlighted in the first part of "Completing the Job." Whereas in the traditional play a grateful Dong Yong and an equally grateful Seventh Sister were incorporated into the landlord's family, they are now shown living apart from the landlord's family. When Dong Yong returns home after a long day of back-breaking toil he is tenderly welcomed by his affectionate wife, who heats some water so he can take a bath. When it turns out Dong Yong has brought some dates for her (given to him by a fellow peasant), Seventh Sister whispers in his ear that she is pregnant and then she tells him that the next day will be the final day of his servitude so they should prepare to depart. In the 1955 version of the revised play the importance of the episode is further underscored by expanding "Eating Dates" into a separate scene.[100]

Whereas in the traditional play an unhappy Seventh Sister was only too aware that she had to abandon Dong Yong after the couple left Master Fu's house because her one hundred days on earth had come to an end,[101] the final scene of the 1954 version of the revised play opens with a song in which Seventh Sister looks forward with eager anticipation to a happy life with Dong Yong:

SEVENTH SISTER (*sings*).

> The sun rises on eastern hills, then travels toward the west:
> Husband and wife have survived the full one hundred days.
> On this day today I follow Dong Yong back to his old home:
> The love and affection of husband and wife a joy without end.

> Today the hundred days' period has come to an end and we, husband and wife, are returning home. This makes one so happy! Just now Dong Yong went ahead to the village in front to say goodbye to a peasant who was a good friend, and he will wait for me on the road ahead; I will make sure to catch up with him, so we can go home together.

(*Sings.*)

> Today as we were going home I am in blessed circumstances;
> There's a happy smile on my face as my heart is filled with joy.
> Once when our little boy will have been born,
> And with his two little eyes will smile at us,
> Dong Yong will be filled with joy, and I'll be filled with joy,
> And everyone will praise us as a fine couple and a fine pair.
> Pregnant as I am, here on the main road
> I hurry to catch up with Dong Yong so we may go home together.[102]

This song is immediately followed by a roll of the celestial drum and a voice from heaven that orders her to return to heaven and threatens to kill Dong Yong if she does not obey. Then, in a long aria Seventh Sister bitterly complains about her father's cruelty, but eventually decides that she has no option but to obey and return to heaven in order to save Dong Yong's life. This means that in the revised version Seventh Sister's decision to return to heaven is inspired by her love for Dong Yong, whereas in the traditional version it is partly inspired by fear for her own life. In the 1954 version of the revised play this emotional aria runs to twenty lines, but in the 1955 version the aria is more than doubled in length. In order to emphasize the pressure that Seven Sister is facing, in the revised versions the Jade Emperor's order is twice repeated later in the scene.[103]

While no fellow peasants appear onstage in either the traditional or the revised versions, the revised play now contains a number of passages in praise of the solidarity and cooperation among the downtrodden, for instance the gift of some dates by a fellow peasant mentioned above. Master Fu, the couple's benefactor in the traditional play, has now been recast as an evil and rapacious landlord who works his slaves to the bone.[104] The role of Young Master Fu, however, is very much simplified. In Lu's version he is reduced to a foolish side-kick of his father. The most drastic rewriting in Lu's version occurs in "Starting Out on the Job" and "Completing the Job." When in the latter scene Master Fu tries to exploit Dong Yong to the maximum, he finds his plots foiled by Seventh Sister and he has to allow the couple to depart. Master Fu's offer to adopt the couple is now ridiculed as a ploy to extend Dong Yong's contract. Young Master Fu's attempts to seduce Seventh Sister fell victim to the increasing prudery on the PRC stage—at one point the revised version contained a scene entitled "Embroidery," which was most likely devoted to this episode and designed to further blacken the image of the ruling class, but this scene was dropped before the play reached Shanghai. Of course, one may also imagine that the purpose of the scene focusing on Seventh Sister teaching her skills to the landlord's daughter was to highlight the productive capabilities of peasant women.[105]

The revised play was first performed in October 1953 in Anqing ("with the unstinting assistance" of Ban Youshu, according to Lu), and Ban Youshu published a short but very positive evaluation of the revised version in the provincial newspaper, the *Anhui Daily* (*Anhui ribao* 安徽日報).[106] As preparations proceeded throughout 1954 for the fall 1954 performance of the play at the Shanghai East China Theater Festival,[107] many small changes continued to be made, but it is difficult to gauge the extent of these changes as our earliest text of the revised play dates from the fall of 1954.[108] One point that continued to be discussed was the ending. Whereas Ban Youshu claims that it was Lu Hongfei who wanted to provide the play with a happy ending, Lu claims that his colleagues insisted on a happy ending as that would better satisfy the demands of the audience. Lu claims that Yan Fengying suggested to bring the all-powerful Monkey King Sun Wukong 孫悟空 onstage at the end of the play to come to the aid of Dong Yong and Seventh Sister.[109] Lu himself wrote two happy ending scenes in which Seventh Sister hands Dong Yong his son (one scene in which a rebellious Seventh Sister descends to earth with her son to join her husband, and one scene in which she brings Dong Yong his son in a dream), but such a happy ending was dropped on the eve of their departure for Shanghai.[110] Zheng Lisong claims credit for suggesting that the play open with "Magpie Bridge," and not with "Departing from Home and Blocking the Gate" (*Biejia mayao* 別家碼窯), a long and depressing 20-minute scene, in which only Wang Shaofang is onstage in the role of Dong Yong who is narrating his background (even though the printed text of the 1954 stage version still opens with the scene in which Dong Yong sells himself into servitude following the death of his father).[111]

The revised text with an ideological message as required by the times was only one aspect that made for the play's success. New content and new stages required a new style of performance. We are very lucky to have two interviews, published in 1956 when the Anhui Provincial Huangmei Opera Company performed in Beijing, in which Yan Fengying and Wang Shaofang tell in considerable detail how they had to re-envision their roles—from their costumes to their tiniest gestures. Yan Fengying stresses how she learned to "analyze" her character onstage and to "identify" with her character and Wang Shaofang stresses how his performance of the poor Dong Yong was based on his memories of peasant friends during his early years as a young strolling player.

Especially important of course was the role of the directors. *Married to a Heavenly Immortal* had not one but two directors, Li Liping and Qiao Zhiliang. The former had a background in modern "spoken drama," while the latter was an experienced Peking Opera actor. Both have left us reminiscences that complement each other quite well. Li Liping wrote one short factual article in 1981 (translated in this volume) in which he details the three different stages in the production of the play,[112] but he is far more forthcoming in a 2000 article written on the occasion of the seventieth birthday of Yan Fengying.[113] It is clear from this latter article that Li initially had a hard time being accepted by the actors and actresses, many of whom were confident that their set ways of performing were perfect, and they called him a "theoretical director who could talk but not act." One of the confrontations concerned a little detail in Yan Fengying's performance in "Meeting on the Road." Seventh Sister successfully blocks Dong Yong's road twice, but her third attempt fails. Ashamed, she is at a loss as to what to do, but she also wants to see how Dong Yong reacts, so she "peeks" at him from behind the wide sleeve of one arm that she has picked up with her other hand. When Li Liping criticized this as a traditional gesture of a high-born young lady taking a peek at a handsome student and therefore not suitable to the context, she asked him to show her how she should do it. He refused, telling her that the gestures had to be designed by the performers themselves, so she complained to the other actors and the authorities about Li's "rudeness," but after thinking about it, she returned a few days later to show her solution. Having failed to block Dong Yong's way a third time, she quickly steps back, covers her face with both hands, and observes Dong Yong through her fingers. Li Liping highlights this as the moment when Yan Fengying discovered the key to her portrayal of Seventh Sister as a peasant girl, which gave her confidence to draw more on her own experience rather than to rely on existing conventions.

When Qiao Zhiliang was interviewed shortly before his death, he discussed at great length his conception of each scene as part of the whole. As his area of specialization was choreography, it comes as no surprise that he spent much time on his revision of "Magpie Bridge" and "Weaving Brocade." In the traditional version of the play, these scenes are quite static, with the Immortal Maidens singing their songs while standing or sitting. In the performance of the revised play, these scenes emphasize dance as the Immortal Maidens imitate the actions of a fisherman, a woodcutter, a farmer, and a student, as well as a wedding procession in "Magpie Bridge," and the actions of spinning and weaving in "Weaving Brocade." When experiments with extended "water-sleeves" in the latter scene failed, the director opted for inclusion of a "Red Ribbon Dance." Qiao Zhiliang also discussed at great length how each gesture and gaze was intended to convey the inner emotions of the characters.[114] The degree of detail in his reminiscences, translated in full in this volume, strongly suggest that he relied on a "case book" that directors were instructed to prepare for each play in the early 1950s when the "Stanislawski method" enjoyed great prestige.[115]

The performance of *Married to a Heavenly Immortal* at the East China Theater Festival in the fall of 1954 was a resounding success. But critics find fault with even the most accomplished play, and *Married to a Heavenly Immortal* too came in for its fair share of criticism. In late November 1954 Lu Hongfei published an article in the *Anhui Daily* entitled "On the Revision of *Married to a Heavenly Immortal*,"[116] reacting in particular to comments by Yi Qun 以群 that had appeared in *Liberation Daily* (*Jiefang ribao* 解放日報). Both the venue of the publication and the status of Yi Qun required that these comments be taken seriously. Yi Qun (pen name of Ye Yiqun 葉以群, 1911–1966) had joined the Chinese Communist Party in 1932 upon his return from study in Japan and had long been active as an organizer and theorist in literary and cultural affairs. In 1954 one of his many functions was that of vice-director (and party secretary?) of the Shanghai Film Studio.[117] In his article Yi Qun commented on several plays that had been showcased at the East China Theater Festival. His comments on *Married to Heavenly Immortal* started out very positively:

> Through the love of Seventh Immortal Sister and [a member of] the laboring people Dong Yong the … play on the one hand exposes the dark "years and months in the heavenly palace" that "can be compared to a prisoner in jail," and sings the praises of joys and pleasures of a life of labor and love in "the mortal world"; on the other hand, it manifests a strong resistance to the rapacious and cruel landlord and eulogizes the laboring people's love of labor, love of freedom, and their spirit of mutual love. The effect of the performance of the full play was lively, as it was filled with the healthy and fresh atmosphere of popular theater. It was observable that

> the revisers had made a rather meticulous study of the original play and they had also considered other materials in order to enrich their play. The attitude of the revisers was one of high seriousness.[118]

But *Married to a Heavenly Immortal* also came in for criticism: Yi Qun noted a jarring stylistic discrepancy between those scenes of the play that were permeated with a fairy-tale atmosphere and those that aimed at a realist description of class struggle (though still using magical elements), and the resulting "insufficient concentration in the expression of the main thought." His blunt advice was to drastically simplify scenes such as "Starting Out on the Job" and "Completing the Job" and to completely do away with the character of Young Master Fu:

> The editing of *Married to a Heavenly Immortal* may already have achieved considerable achievements artistically, but the above-mentioned problem is equally present. The whole play is unified in style as far as the four scenes "Magpie Bridge," "Meeting on the Road," "Weaving Silk," and "The Separation" are concerned because they give expression to the hopes and needs of the laboring people under oppression by feudal forces using the method of fantasy and myth (fairy tale). But "Starting Out on the Job," "Embroidery" (already deleted in this performance), and "Completing the Job" give expression to the contradiction between landlords and laboring people with the simplest realist writing style; these two writing methods are obviously not unified in style. According to my information, the original intention in rewriting the play in this manner was "to highlight the irreconcilable contradiction between peasant slaves and slave owners and to show how Dong Yong as one of these peasant slaves frees himself of his cruel shackles by borrowing the powers of the Seventh Immortal Maiden after a determined struggle." This intention of course is good but we also have to acknowledge that it is not the case that all good intentions can be accommodated in one play, and if you attempt to forcibly accommodate them, you definitely will produce all kinds of defects. For instance, the story of Seventh Immortal Sister's love for Dong Yong is an imaginary fairy tale that praises freedom and opposes oppression; it is lively and moving. But if in the realist scenes you allow the laboring people in their struggle against the landlords to make use of the powers of an Immortal Maiden, then this not only lacks the power to convince, but also can produce the contrary effect. In order to ensure that *Married to a Heavenly Immortal* becomes even more refined and perfect,

> scenes such as "Starting Out on the Job" and "Completing the Job" have to be drastically pared down—a character such as Young Master Fu is completely superfluous.[119]

In his reaction Lu Hongfei meekly acknowledged this criticism as correct. When we compare the text of *Married to a Heavenly Immortal* in the version prepared for the participants at the East China Theater Festival and the text that was published in the following year (1955),[120] we can clearly observe the impact of Yi Qun's remarks: while the character of Young Master Fu is not eliminated (that would only happen in the movie adaptation), the space allocated to the direct confrontation between the indentured servant and his master is greatly limited. According to the 1954 version of the text, the play started on earth rather than in heaven, and the first scene is not "Magpie Bridge" but "Selling One's Body to Bury One's Father." In this scene Dong Yong enters lamenting his poverty following the death of his father and writes an empty contract for the sale of his body. The second curtain opens in the study of Young Master Fu, who cannot distinguish even the most common characters. When Dong Yong enters and offers himself for sale, Young Master Fu consults with his father who agrees to the profitable proposal, and the scene concludes with a short dialogue contrasting Dong Yong's filial piety to Young Master Fu's utter lack of moral feelings.

YOUNG MASTER FU. Dong Yong, here you have your silver and your linen.

DONG YONG. Many thanks, Young Master.

YOUNG MASTER FU. What are you going to do with this linen when you get home?

DONG YONG. I will make my father a burial shroud and a burial cap.

YOUNG MASTER FU. Your way of doing this is truly. … If it would be me, I would have it made into a pair of trousers for myself!

DONG YONG. As a son, I want to give expression to my filial piety.

YOUNG MASTER FU. And what are you going to do with this silver when you get home?

DONG YONG. I will buy a coffin.

YOUNG MASTER FU. Ha! Since ancient times it is said: "What's dead is dead, pull down what is dead!" If it were me, I would take it with me to the main street and buy myself some wine to drink!

DONG YONG. Isn't that an utter lack of natural goodness?

YOUNG MASTER FU. What do I care about an utter lack of natural goodness? Dong Yong, my father orders that you to report for work within three days—no delay is allowed!

(YOUNG MASTER FU *exits.*)

DONG YONG. How would I ever dare be late? (*Sings.*)
Now I've taken the linen and received the silver,
My body is tied with a rope of ten thousand yards.
From now on I'm not my own master anymore—
I seem to have jumped into a pit of raging fire!

(DONG YONG *exits.*)[121]

This scene very much resembles the corresponding sections in the traditional play. In the 1955 edition of the play, however, this scene has disappeared without a trace.

"Starting Out on the Job" is almost identical in the 1954 and 1955 versions of *Married to a Heavenly Immortal*, but we can observe major changes in "Completing the Job" in the 1955 edition. In the 1955 edition, as noted before, "Completing the Job" is preceded by a scene called "Eating Dates," which takes place during the last evening that Dong Yong and Seventh Sister spend at the house of the Fu family. Dong Yong arrives home bringing some dates and he learns from Seventh Sister that she is pregnant; after she reminds him that the next day will be the hundredth day of their stay with the Fu family, they look forward to their happy family life together after they will have returned to Dong Yong's own place. In the 1954 version of the play, however, a somewhat shorter version of this episode is combined with "Completing the Job." Furthermore, the scene opens with a short interlude played before the screen as Young Master Fu informs his father that the term of Dong Yong's servitude is coming to an end. Master Fu thereupon tells his son to order Dong Yong to cut trees on Dragon-Tiger Mountain. When his son objects that the mountain is infested with man-eating tigers, his father tells him that if Dong Yong is killed by a tiger Seventh Sister cannot but stay as the family's slave and continue to produce her marvelous silk. This little interlude is an echo of an earlier version of the story in which it is the young master who, on his own initiative, orders Dong Yong to cut trees on the bandit-infested Dragon-Tiger Mountain in the hopes that he will be killed, thus making it easier for him to get his hands on Seventh Sister after she becomes a widow.[122] In the 1954 version the interlude highlights the rapaciousness of the landlord who does not even shirk from murder in order to achieve his economic objectives. One may well feel that this interlude turns the characterization of the evil landlord into a caricature, and thus applaud its deletion in the 1955 version. But it also removes the dramatic irony as the audience watches the couple's happy anticipation of their imminent departure from the Fu Mansion. In the 1955 version the shortened "Completing the Job" opens with a brief dialogue between the landlord and his son, in which the young master informs his father that the couple intends to leave and the old landlord tells his son to order Dong Yong to go to the fields as he intends to renege on his promise to set them free after one hundred days. Interestingly, the 1955 version of this scene also hints at Young Master Fu's infatuation with Seventh Sister (perhaps compensating for the deleted scene "Embroidering") as it describes him as a peeping tom. But in both the 1954 and the 1955 versions of the play, the character of the landlord's daughter is completely written out of the script.[123]

One difference between the 1954 and the 1955 versions that cannot be directly tied to Yi Qun's comments is the already mentioned reintroduction of the long song by Dong Yong upon departing from home before "Meeting on the Road." In the version of "Meeting on the Road" printed by Wang Zhaoqian this is simply the opening song of this scene, but in the 1955 version of the play the song is expanded and becomes an independent scene entitled "Leaving the Hovel" (*Ciyao* 辭窯). While this is not specified in the text, the scene most likely was performed in front of the middle screen to allow for a change of scenery. The use of a modern stage with multiple screens is indicated in "Magpie Bridge." When near the end of the scene the seven sisters all exit and Seventh Sister returns by herself because she has fallen in love with Dong Yong and wants to descend to earth, the 1955 edition specifies that the middle screen has to be lowered as soon as the Immortal Maidens have cleared the stage, implying that the final aria by Seventh Sister and her dialogue with Eldest Sister are performed before the screen. In the version of the play that was printed in 1959, Dong Yong's long song upon setting out for the Fu Mansion is again incorporated into "Meeting on the Road" but it is now specified following Dong Yong's exit that the middle screen is to be opened to reveal Seventh Sister singing her aria of descending to the mortal world.

The Movie's Impact on the Play

The resounding success of *Married to a Heavenly Immortal* at the East China Theater Festival of 1954 also resulted in the decision to turn the play into a movie. The movie stuck to the basic outline of the play, from "Magpie Bridge" to “The Separation,” but had to shorten the text considerably. Unfortunately, the whereabouts of Sang Hu’s original screenplay are unknown (if it even still exists). We know that the director Shi Hui made major changes to the script during the filming. As the movie was envisioned as “a fairy-tale movie with song and dance,” it focused on the four scenes, “Magpie Bridge,” “Meeting on the Road,” “Weaving Brocade,” and “The Separation,” and drastically shortened “Starting Out on the Job” and “Completing the Job.” As it also replaced the role of Young Master Fu with that of an obsequious majordomo, it followed even more closely Yi Qun’s suggestions than any revisions of the revised play. But if Shi Hui removed the role of Young Master Fu, he stressed the exploitation of Dong Yong as his landlord has Dong Yong labor both day and night. The shots of poor Dong Yong pushing the mill also have the virtue of breaking up the long and monotonous action of “Weaving Brocade.” The long shots of the fisherman, woodcutter, farmer, and student at work that interrupt the song and dance of “Magpie Bridge” of course have the same function. But whereas Sang Hu envisioned a rather thoroughgoing revision of “Meeting on the Road” Shi Hui maintained the original design of that scene, giving full range to Wang Shaofang and Yan Fengying as comic actors. Basically the only change made to “The Separation” was that the disembodied backstage voice calling Seventh Sister back to heaven was replaced by a celestial warrior appearing in the clouds, which allowed the same actors to play this sentimental scene for all it was worth as the mood changed from happy joy to apprehension and finally despair.[124]

The huge popularity of the movie, released in February 1956, resulted in further rewritings of the script of the play as the Anhui Provincial Huangmei Opera Company tried to capitalize on the movie’s success by incorporating some of the features of the film into its stage performance.[125] In the spring of 1956 the task of making further revisions to the text of the play was entrusted to Jin Zhi. In his recollections Jin Zhi explains the choice of him and not of Lu Hongfei by referring to the fact that they both had been “scrutinized” (presumably as part of the 1955 campaign against Hu Feng) and that he had been cleared while Lu Hongfei’s case still was pending. Although Jin Zhi mentions that in the second half of the 1950s posters and programs often credited the text of the revised play to “Lu Hongfei, Sang Hu, and Jin Zhi,” he very much belittles his own contribution. He does, however, take credit for following the lead of Sang Hu to move the final duet by Dong Yong and Seventh Sister in “Meeting on the Road” to the very beginning of “The Separation” and to add two lines. In view of the extreme and enduring popularity of this song in China, one can understand the eagerness of the various revisers of the play to be associated with this song. Jin also claims that the performance version at that time still included "Selling the Body" as the first scene, and that it was his decision to begin the performed play, like the movie, with "Magpie Bridge."[126]

One of the reasons for Jin Zhi's assignment was the expectation that later in 1956 a second national theatrical festival would be convened in Beijing. This did not occur, but the Anhui Provincial Huangmei Opera Company took its *Married to a Heavenly Immortal* on the road and performed the play in places as far apart as Beijing and Guangzhou. The performance in Beijing resulted in a blistering condemnation of the revised version by Kang Sheng 康生,[127] an old Party stalwart and great lover of traditional theater who had just emerged from years of retirement. Even though Kang Sheng's letter was not openly published at the time, some newspaper articles voiced regret that certain attractive aspects of the traditional play had been omitted from the revised version. In Beijing, for instance, Wu Zuxiang questioned the characterization of Seventh Sister in the revised version,[128] while in Guangzhou Dong Meikan deplored the omission of several traditional acting techniques from "The Separation."[129] The majority of voices, however, were limited to expressing a preference for the revised version as performed in the fall of 1954 in Shanghai over the 1956 production of the play.[130] Writing in 1962 Jin Zhi called the 1956 script "a failed attempt at 'moviefication'"; he mentions as examples of the movie's impact the change in the characterization of Eldest Sister who had been turned from an "open and optimistic" person into a "somber and serious" character, the omission of some comic elements from "Meeting on the Road," and lyrics that did not fit the tunes.[131] The extent of the changes in the 1956 production is perhaps best suggested by the catalogue of changes that were undone, as provided in *The Process of the Rewriting of* Married to a Heavenly Immortal (*Tianxian pei de gaibian jingguo* 天仙配的改編經過), a publication of the Anhui Provincial Huangmei Opera Company:

> We restored "Selling the Body," "Leaving the Hovel," and "Starting Out on the Job" and the manipulation of the pack, the umbrella, and the white fan as they were found in the original play in order to highlight the traditional performance of Seventh Sister's character as well as her dialogue that is full of charm. In our treatment of the *dramatis personae* we turned the majordomo back into Young Master Fu; Eldest Sister once again united the whole play with the performance style of a *caidan*;[132] and the appearance of the heavenly warrior again became a back-stage voice.

> As for the performance, we restored the silk-weaving dances in which singing and acting are synchronized and in which the style of the whole play is unified. As for the music, we fittingly increased the role of the drum.[133]

One of the concrete points of criticism by Kang Sheng was the inclusion of the Red Ribbon Dance in "Weaving Brocade" and for a while that dance was not performed. Qiao Zhiliang in his recollections of directing the play also refers to the various changes that were made in imitation of the movie and that later were rejected.

In the spring of 1957 Lu Hongfei was brought in once again to revise the manuscript, and that script became the standard version from then on. Both Jin Zhi and Lu Hongfei alert us, however, to the fact that there existed a considerable difference between the text as published and the text as performed. Directors and actors would continue to make large and small changes. For instance, while in earlier versions Seventh Sister is summoned back to heaven in "The Separation" by a disembodied backstage voice, the text printed in 1979,[134] in an obvious borrowing from the movie, still has a heavenly warrior appear onstage, not only once but twice. However, the 1979 edition dropped some earlier changes that had been made to highlight the solidarity of the working class by omitting any references to Dong Yong's fellow workers.[135]

Conclusion

Performers and playwrights and directors and screenwriters, both east and west, have adapted stories in other genres to the stage and to the screen ever since the origin of theater and film, and they also have continuously reworked existing plays and movies in order to make optimal use of new stage and cinematic techniques and to capture new and larger audiences. Of course, they also have reworked existing plays and movies in order to impose their own interpretations of these old materials; other adaptations and rewritings have been produced to meet the demands of censors or to avoid the sensitivity of religious or political authorities. Many changes are made merely to follow the fashion of the times. Even without the founding of the People's Republic and without an explicit government policy of theater reform, Huangmei Opera would have continued to develop and as long as *Married to a Heavenly Immortal* remained on the repertoire, it would have been continuously adapted and revised. It is very unlikely, to say the least, that the traditional version would have continued to be performed in exactly the same way that it was performed in the 1930s and 1940s. But instead of one revised version of

Married to a Heavenly Immortal we probably would have been confronted by a number of versions, each of which would have been adapted to the needs of the contemporary theater in its own way.

But in such a case, many of those changes probably would have mirrored changes we encounter in the actual revised version of *Married to a Heavenly Immortal* as these were part and parcel of the ongoing modernization of traditional theater throughout the twentieth century. Even without any explicit policy of theater reform, those versions of *Married to a Heavenly Immortal* that were intended for performance on the modern urban stage would have been shortened considerably, would have enlarged the orchestra and diversified the musical repertoire, would have embellished the stage with more or less elaborate scenery, and would have enlivened the action with dances and special effects. Such versions most likely also would have stressed the mutual attachment between Dong Yong and Seventh Sister and might well have changed their status. Most likely, these versions also would have provided the play with a happy ending of some sort, which in view of modern notions of romantic love probably would have involved doing away with Master Fu's daughter as Dong Yong's wife. Many of the changes made by Ban Youshu and Lu Hongfei, Yan Fengying and Wang Shaofang, Li Liping and Qiao Zhiliang, Sang Hu and Shi Hui, and Party cadres who remain anonymous were quite acceptable not only to large audiences inside the PRC, but also to Chinese audiences outside the PRC, and they were eagerly copied in the Shaw Brothers' Hong Kong remake of the movie in the early 1960s. After all, irrespective of political persuasion, practically all Chinese were eager to modernize their culture, or at least they were eager to benefit from all the amenities of modern technology and fashion while enjoying those selected aspects of traditional culture that they wanted to continue to enjoy.

So if adaptation is not new and certainly is not something unique to China, the policy of theater reform certainly was new. Whereas the theater-reform policy continued earlier local and/or bottom-up initiatives to modernize the stage by building Western-style theaters, enhancing the status of actors, and producing plays with a modernizing message, the theater-reform policy was national and top-down. It relied on the power and the authority of the Communist Party, which in the 1950s enjoyed widespread support among a wide range of both the rural and urban population. Many of the involved scriptwriters may have had little or no prior experience in regional theater, but they were young and enthusiastic, and the new state-run companies (with their own Party committees), made up from selected, re-educated actors and actresses and provided with directors, were cooperative partners to stage their scripts in the best local theaters available. There is no reason to doubt the sincerity of these scriptwriters when they claim they were restoring *Married to a Heavenly Immortal* to its original meaning—precisely because the message of the "original" was fully in line with the Party message of class struggle and the struggle for free love.

We will never be able to fully reconstruct the spectacular impression *Married to a Heavenly Immortal* made when it was performed in Shanghai in the fall of 1954. By 1956 some commentators were already complaining that the performances by Yan Fengying and Wang Shaofang lacked some of the freshness of the 1954 performances. What we still have is the movie. Even though it shared the same star actors, the movie was never intended to be a shortened recording of the play, but rather a further adaptation of the story in a different medium. The movie was scripted and directed by China's greatest cinematic talents of the mid-twentieth century, fully utilizing its own brand of Huangmei Opera music and starring Yan Fengying and Wang Shaofang at the tops of their career. The movie may have been made on the cheap, but it brought intense pleasure and joy to millions, both inside and outside China, and it is still extremely enjoyable. But part of the movie's charm for contemporary audiences is precisely its quaint datedness: it comes to us not only from a different era of film technology but also from an era of Chinese history that is quickly fading from living memory. At the same time, any enjoyment of the movie is now colored by an awareness of the tragic fate that befell some of those who were involved in making it.

III. The Old Play

We have two sources for the pre-1949 Huangmei Opera version of *Married to a Heavenly Immortal*. The first is a printed version, available in two woodblock editions, from the Kunji shuju in Anqing and the Shunyitang 順義堂 in Gaoshafu respectively, and entitled *Dong Yong Sells his Body: Married to a Heavenly Immortal* (*Dong Yong maishen Tianxian pei* 董永賣身天仙配). On the basis of these two editions Du Yingtao prepared a collated edition in his *Dong Yong Chenxiang heji* of 1957.[1] This edition serves as the basis of the complete translation presented in the following pages. The second version of the pre-1949 Huangmei Opera version of *Married to a Heavenly Immortal* was dictated by the veteran actor Hu Yuting. This version is included in Wang Chang'an's *Zhongguo Huangmeixi* of 2009 in a selection of traditional plays entitled *Married to a Heavenly Immortal*.[2] It should be pointed out, however, that Hu Yuting's text as presented in Wang Chang'an's edited volume was collated against a copy of the printed version by the Kunji shuju. Wang Chang'an's edition serves as the basis of the partial translation presented in this chapter, which covers the section of the play that is not found in the printed version.

Hu Yuting's version makes it clear that the woodblock printings are only a very incomplete guide to the play as it was actually performed. Hu Yuting's performance edition provides far more detailed dialogues and contains a number of scenes and episodes that are not included in the printed version. I do not provide a complete translation of Hu Tingyu's performance version, limiting my translation to two major episodes that are lacking in the printed version (and therefore also could not have been collated against the printed version).[3] These two episodes respectively deal with the presentation of the silk to Old Master Fu, who thereupon decides to adopt Dong Yong and Seventh Sister as his son and daughter, and with the attempts by Young Master Fu to seduce Seventh Sister—attempts that fail and result in his groping of his own sister! The entrance of the Lord of Thunder and Mother of Lightning at the end of this second scene shows that in actual performance gods and ghosts of various kinds helped to fill out the stage. This episode is followed by a short scene in which Old Master Fu sees Dong Yong off at the end of the one hundred days. The episodes translated here did not make it into the revised edition of the play, but it should be obvious why they were so objectionable to the cultural bureaucrats of the early 1950s. The first episode shows Landlord Fu in a positive light, and the second episode mostly consists of bawdy clowning.

The prose dialogue in both versions of the traditional play may include couplets and four-line poems that are recited. In the woodblock printings, the arias are all made up of seven-syllable lines, but in Hu Yuting's performance text we also encounter arias that are wholly or partially made up of ten-syllable lines. Both versions specify how the arias should be sung.

§

Dong Yong Sells His Body: Married to a Heavenly Immortal

Part I. Dong Yong Sells His Body

Dong Yong (*performed by the young male* [xiaosheng],[4] *enters, and recites an introductory couplet*).

My dear mother unfortunately passed away early on,
Now my dear father is bedridden because of an illness.

Dong Yong (*speaks*).

Frost beats down on withered autumn leaves,
The spring plum is by heavy snow oppressed.
If one suffers a serious illness in a cold hovel,
To whom can one complain of one's poverty?

I am Dong Yong. Alas, my father has attracted a serious illness, but I lack the money to take care of him. So what should I do now? Perhaps I should go and borrow some silver from my uncle on my mother's side, so let me ask my father to come here so we can discuss the matter. Father, please come here.

Dong Yong's father (*performed by the old male* [laosheng], *enters and speaks*). OK. My son, what do you want to discuss with me?

Dong Yong (*speaks*). My father, how are you doing?

Dong Yong's father (*speaks*). My illness is extremely serious.

Dong Yong (*sings*).

Ever since you have been so ill,
I've lacked the money to take care of you.
I have asked you to come here and discuss the matter:
I'd like to go and borrow some money from my uncle.

Dong Yong's father (*sings*).

My son, the first word you utter is misspoken!
What an idea to go and borrow money from your uncle!
Your uncle will be willing enough to help us out,
But your aunt, I'm afraid, doesn't care for poor relatives.

Dong Yong (*sings*).

My father, the words you utter reflect your age!

Why do you say my aunt doesn't care for poor relatives?
Even if he fails to achieve fame and merit, the student still lives;
If I fail to borrow some silver, I will come back empty-handed.
I will support you, my father, while you go back inside—
I'm firmly determined to borrow some silver from my uncle.
Walking along, I have arrived at the house of my uncle,
And I politely greet my uncle, my dear mother's brother.

UNCLE (*performed by the clown* [chou], *enters and speaks*).
From the day of my birth fate has been set against me,
But I brought home a bride as beautiful as a flower.
Let me open the door to see who may be there—
Well, our visitor turns out to be Dong Yong!

DONG YONG (*speaks*). Dear uncle!

UNCLE (*speaks*). What brings you here?

DONG YONG (*speaks*). My father is bedridden because of some illness, and I would like to borrow some silver. Dear uncle, would that be possible?

UNCLE (*speaks*). You have come at the wrong moment, because it is your aunt who is now in charge.

DONG YONG (*speaks*). So let me speak to my aunt.

AUNT (*performed by the female clown* [choudan], *enters and speaks*).
Once again I hear my old man shouting,
I'll walk over and ask what's going on.

Stand to attention!

UNCLE (*speaks*). Your nephew Dong Yong is here.

AUNT (*speaks*). You stand over there. I can see that. Dong Yong, what brings you here?

DONG YONG (*speaks*). My father is bedridden because of some illness, and I would like to borrow some silver from you, my aunt.

AUNT (*speaks*). Too bad we are short of silver ourselves.

UNCLE (*speaks*). But we still have some money left from the pig we sold yesterday. Let's lend him some of that!

AUNT (*speaks*). The money in our house we need for our own livelihood. You are dismissed!

AUNT (*sings*).

If you are suffering starvation,
We're suffering starvation too:
How could we have a granary stacked with grain?
As soon as I see Dong Yong, I'm filled with vexation:
Why did he have to come to us to borrow fine silver?
I will get my cudgel and give him a beating,
Give him a sound beating and chase him out!

(*She acts out beating* DONG YONG, *and exits.*)

DONG YONG (*sings*).

How I hate my aunt deep down in my heart:
She gave me a beating and chased me away!
Suffering in silence, my eyes filled with tears, I enter this pavilion,
Once I've greeted my uncle, he welcomes me kindly.

UNCLE (*speaks*). You are crying—did your aunt lend you some money?

DONG YONG (*speaks*). She did not lend me any money, but gave me a beating and chased me away.

UNCLE (*speaks*). Here I have one skirt. Pawn it for money on the main street so you can take care of your father. Return the pawn slip to me. (UNCLE *exits.*)

DONG YONG (*sings*).

How grateful I am for my uncle's lofty sense of duty:
He managed to steal a skirt which I can pawn for silver.
Suffering in silence, my eyes filled with tears, I enter our hovel,
And stepping forward I make a deep bow to greet my father.

DONG YONG'S FATHER (*sings*).

My son Dong Yong left to borrow some silver and still hasn't returned—
But there I suddenly see my darling son once again stand at my side.
The first question I have for my darling son is this:
Did you borrow some rice and silver from your uncle?

DONG YONG (*sings*).

How I hate my aunt deep down in my heart:
She did not lend me any silver but gave me a beating!
How grateful I am for my uncle's lofty sense of duty:
He managed to steal a skirt which I pawned for money.

DONG YONG'S FATHER (*sings*).

Hearing the words of my son how I hate this aunt:
She didn't lend him any silver but gave him a beating!
In a single moment it makes me so mad I have to spit blood;
And I'm afraid that a man like me will not be able to survive.
My son, when I will have died, make sure to study the books:
Blue Heaven will not destroy a man who puts in his efforts.[5]
As I speak, I suddenly have to give up a mouthful of blood:
When Death arrives, all things are finished—my life is done!

DONG YONG'S FATHER (*acts out weeping*). Dong Yong, my son, alas! (*He acts out dying, and exits.*)

DONG YONG (*acts out weeping*). Daddy, my father, alas! My father, oh!

DONG YONG (*sings to the rapid beat*).

Now I see that my dear daddy has passed away, I know
I lack the money to provide him with a decent funeral.
As I lower my head, I come up with a plan in my heart:
I cannot but sell my body in order to bury my father.
I take out the Four Treasures of the Scholar's Study[6]
And write out an advertisement for selling my body,
And write out an advertisement for selling my body.
So I write: "I, Dong Yong, offer my body for sale,
Selling myself to any buyer to become his servant.
The price I am asking certainly is not too high:
Five bolts of white cloth[7] and five ounces of silver.
In selling myself I don't sell myself for all time:
When three years are finished, I will go back home."
I've quickly finished writing this sales advertisement,
But I don't know which family might buy a servant.
With lowered head, tears coursing down, I leave this hovel,
To ask you distinguished gentlemen for your advice.

DONG YONG (*speaks*). Please, you gentlemen, which family can buy a servant?

BACKSTAGE (*speaks*). The Fu Mansion on the other side of the street wants to buy a servant.

DONG YONG (*sings*).

Many thanks, you gentlemen, for giving me this direction—
They say that the Fu Mansion wants to buy a servant.
Walking on, I have arrived outside the gate of the Fu Mansion,
So let me ask for the Young Master.

DONG YONG (*speaks*). Young Master Fu!

THE YOUNG MASTER FU (*performed by the young clown* [xiao chou], *enters and speaks*).
All of a sudden I hear someone calling for me,
I go to the gate to find out what's the matter.
When I get to the gate and have a good look,
Well, Dong Yong has come to pay us a visit!

Dong Yong, what are you doing here?

DONG YONG (*speaks*). Is the Old Master perhaps at home?

THE YOUNG MASTER (*speaks*). He is inside.

DONG YONG (*speaks*). Could you ask him to come outside and see me?

THE YOUNG MASTER (*speaks*). Father, there's a visitor for you.

THE OLD MASTER (*speaks*).
All of a sudden I hear my son calling for me,
So I go to the gate to see what's going on.

What's the matter?

THE YOUNG MASTER (*speaks*). Dong Yong is here.

THE OLD MASTER (*speaks*). Tell him to come and see me.

THE YOUNG MASTER (*speaks*). Sir Dong, my father will see you.

DONG YONG (*speaks*). Mr. Fu, thank you for seeing me.

THE OLD MASTER (*speaks*). Dong Yong, please take a seat. What brings you here?

DONG YONG (*speaks*). My father has passed away and I do not have a coffin to encoffin him properly. So I want to sell my body and I hope you will be interested.

THE OLD MASTER (*speaks*). Did you bring a contract of servitude? Let me have a look.

DONG YONG (*speaks*). Mr. Fu, this is the contract of servitude, so please read it through.

THE OLD MASTER (*speaks*). So let me have a look: For five bolts of white cloth and five ounces of fine silver Dong Yong sells his body to be his buyer's servant for three years. That's phrased very well, but it does not yet mention my name.

DONG YONG (*speaks*). Allow me to borrow your Four Treasures of the Scholar's Study. So I will write: Dong Yong sells his body to Mr. Fu to be his servant for three years. Mr. Fu, please read it through.

THE OLD MASTER (*speaks*). So let me have a look. Guanbao,[8] place this contract of servitude in the strongbox. The silver we have here at hand, but we are short two bolts of white cloth.

THE YOUNG MASTER (*speaks*). There are still two bolts of white cloth left from the debts I collected yesterday.

THE OLD MASTER (*speaks*). Hand the white cloth and silver over to Dong Yong and ask him when he will start his job. (*He exits.*)

THE YOUNG MASTER (*speaks*). Hey, Sir Dong! Here you have your cloth and silver, so when will you start your job?

DONG YONG (*speaks*). On the seventh day I will come here and start my job.

THE YOUNG MASTER (*speaks*). Make sure to be here!

DONG YONG (*speaks*). How could I fail to be here? (THE YOUNG MASTER *exits.*)

DONG YONG (*sings*).

How grateful I am for Mr. Fu's lofty sense of duty:
Five bolts of white cloth, five ounces of fine silver!
With lowered head, tears coursing down, I enter our cold hovel,
And go into the backroom to encoffin my dear father.

(DONG YONG *exits.*)

* * *

SEVENTH SISTER (*enters and recites an introductory couplet*).

In the burner the incense is not yet finished,
As I leisurely walk away from Jasper Pond.[9]

SEVENTH SISTER (*speaks*).

In pair upon pair the magpies bump into the golden bell,
Through five-colored clouds they rise to the empyrean.
Buffalo Boy and Weaving Maiden, separated by the Heavenly River,
Are allowed a happy reunion at least once every year.[10]

I am Seventh Sister. Because I am feeling down here in the Palace of Dipper and Buffalo[11] I want to go to Magpie Bridge[12] to have some fun, and I've invited all my sisters.

(Eldest Sister, *performed by the female clown* [choudan], *and the other sisters, performed by females* [zhongdan], *enter.*)

Eldest Sister (*speaks*).

All of sudden receiving Seventh Sister's invitation,
We go over to her place to see what is going on.

Seventh Sister, what's the idea?

Seventh Sister (*speaks*). I would like to go and visit Magpie Bridge for fun. How about that idea?

Eldest Sister (*speaks*). We had the same idea, so let's go there, riding our clouds.

Eldest Sister (*sings*).

In the Palace of Dipper and Buffalo the clouds are surging;
The Way and its Method are lofty in front of Mt. Emei.
Old Gardener Zhang is a disciple of the Eight Immortals;
The failed student Ziya was the one to protect the Zhou.[13]
Riding on our clouds we soon arrive at Magpie Bridge
And watch the hustle and bustle of the mortal world.

(A fisherman *crosses the stage.*) Eldest Sister (*speaks*). Dear sisters, what kind of man is that man in the world below who is holding a fishing rod?

The other sisters (*speak*). That is a man angling for fish.

Eldest Sister (*speaks*). Let me characterize him in a few lines.[14]

The other sisters (*speak*). You have to characterize him well!

Eldest Sister (*speaks*). Sisters, please listen.

Eldest Sister (*sings*).

That man who is angling for fish doesn't need to worry!
With his angling rod in his hand he goes to the river bank.
Upon catching a bundle of fish, he sells it in the market;
Selling the fish he buys some rice, so making his living;
Selling the fish he buys some rice, so making his living.

(A woodcutter *crosses the stage.*) Second Sister (*speaks*). Dear sisters, what kind of man is that man in the world below who is carrying a carrying pole on his shoulder?

The other sisters (*speak*). That is a woodcutter.

SECOND SISTER (*speaks*). Let me characterize him.

THE OTHER SISTERS (*speak*). You have to characterize him well.

SECOND SISTER (*speaks*). Dear sisters, please listen.

SECOND SISTER (*sings*).

The man who is cutting firewood doesn't have to worry!
With his carrying pole in his hand he goes into the hills.
Having cut a load of firewood, he sells it in the market;
Selling the firewood he buys some rice, so making his living;
Selling the firewood he buys some rice, so making his living.

(A FARMER *crosses the stage.*) THIRD SISTER (*speaks*). Dear sisters, what kind of man is that man in the world below who passed by a moment ago?

THE OTHERS (*speak*). That is a farmer.

THIRD SISTER (*speaks*). Let me characterize him.

THE OTHERS (*speak*). You have to characterize him well.

THIRD SISTER (*speaks*). Dear sisters, please listen.

THIRD SISTER (*sings*).

The man who plows and sows doesn't have to worry!
Leading his plowing buffalo he goes to work his fields.
Then he waits for the end of the year to fill his granary;
Old and young in his family enjoy ease and prosperity;
Old and young in his family enjoy ease and prosperity.

(A STUDENT *crosses the stage.*) FOURTH SISTER (*speaks*). What kind of man passed by in the world below?

THE OTHERS (*speak*). That is a student of books.

FOURTH SISTER (*speaks*). Let me characterize him.

THE OTHERS (*speak*). You have to characterize him well.

FOURTH SISTER (*speaks*). Dear sisters, please listen.

FOURTH SISTER (*sings*).

The man who studies the books doesn't have to worry!
Carrying his books in his hands he enters the schoolroom.
When next year the Imperial Poster will be put up,[15]
The Imperial Brush will list him as Top-of-the-List;
The Imperial Brush will list him as Top-of-the-List![16]

(*A bride-fetching procession enters.*) SEVENTH SISTER (*speaks*). What kind of people are passing by with all their blaring and banging?

THE OTHERS (*speak*). That is a groom fetching his bride.

SEVENTH SISTER (*speaks*). Let me characterize him.

THE OTHERS (*speak*). You have to characterize him well.

SEVENTH SISTER (*speaks*). Dear sisters, please listen!

SEVENTH SISTER (*sings*).

The man who is fetching a bride doesn't have to worry!
Blaring and banging they take her to the wedding room.
Once groom and bride have exchanged one cup of wine,
They enjoy bliss throughout the night till the break of dawn;
They enjoy bliss throughout the night till the break of dawn.

ELDEST SISTER (*sings*).

Seventh Sister, you little slut, you have no shame at all!
Visiting Magpie Bridge you long for the mortal world.[17]
In case the Jade Emperor learns of your indiscretion,
We, your sisters, will all be punished as accomplices.
Inside the Third Gate of Heaven bell and drum resound:
Sisters, step forward to welcome our father, the king!

THE JADE EMPEROR (*enters and speaks*). Immortal Maidens, kneel down on seeing this edict.

THE SISTERS (*speak*). May Your Majesty live a myriad of years!

THE JADE EMPEROR (*speaks*). At present in Danyang District there lives a certain Dong Yong, who has sold his body in order to be able to bury his father, thus greatly pleasing the Jade Emperor. You, Seventh Sister, when visiting Magpie Bridge, conceived a longing for the mortal world. We order you to descend to the mortal world to be Dong Yong's wife for one hundred days. You will descend to the mortal world on the fifth day of the Fourth Month, and you will resume your position on the thirteenth day of the Seventh Month. This Imperial Edict allows no doubt. (THE JADE EMPEROR *exits.*)

THE SISTERS (*speak*). Your Majesty, please accept our gratitude.

ELDEST SISTER (*speaks*). This is the edict we have received: At present in Danyang District there lives a certain Dong Yong, who has sold his body in order to be able to bury his father, thus greatly pleasing the

Jade Emperor. You, Seventh Sister, when visiting Magpie Bridge, conceived a longing for the mortal world. We order Seventh Sister to descend to the mortal world to be united in wedlock with Dong Yong for one hundred days. You will descend to the mortal world on the fifth day of the Fourth Month, and you will resume your position on the thirteenth day of the Seventh Month. Seventh Sister, please accept my congratulations on your good luck!

Seventh Sister (*speaks*). Why do you call me "lucky"?

Eldest Sister (*speaks*). Because that is your name!

Seventh Sister (*speaks*). Now I have to descend to the mortal world, I am starting to become afraid, because I fear I may run into trouble down in the mortal world.

Eldest Sister (*speaks*). I will give you one stick of orchid incense.[18] If you run into trouble, just light this stick of orchid incense, and we, your sisters, will all descend to the mortal world to help you out!

Seventh Sister (*speaks*). Dear elder sisters, please allow me to express my gratitude by this bow.

Seventh Sister (*sings*).

Dear elder sisters, please allow me to express my gratitude
With a thousand bows, a myriad of bows, as is only fitting.
Dear elders sisters, please also be so kind as to take a letter,
To take a letter for me to Her Majesty, our mother the queen.
As I take my leave of my sisters I step on my fancy cloud;
At the end of one hundred days we'll go to heaven together.

(Seventh Sister *exits.*) Eldest Sister (*sings*).

We watch Seventh Sister riding off on her auspicious cloud;
We, her immortal sisters, all are filled with a happy feeling.
The six of us, elder and younger sisters, ride our fancy clouds;
At the end of one hundred days we'll all go to heaven together;
At the end of one hundred days we'll all go to heaven together.

(*They all exit.*)

Part II. Married to a Heavenly Immortal

Dong Yong (*enters and sings*).

Since ancient times few people reach the age of seventy;
Light and shade resemble an arrow, race on like a horse.
Never treat yellow gold as priceless pearls and treasures,
It won't buy you a replacement on the Yellow Springs road.[19]
With lowered head, tears coursing down, I arrive at our hovel,
And I bow in front of my father,[20] who's gone off to the shade.
Please do not blame your son for not wearing mourning—
It's impossible to dredge up the bright moon from a river.[21]
Now I've finished my bow, I gather my bedding and luggage,
Say goodbye to the ancestral tablets and set out for the Fus.

(Dong Yong *exits.*)

* * *

Seventh Sister (*enters and sings*).

In high heaven my father the king pronounced an edict,
Ordering me to descend to earth and marry Dong Yong.
Riding my cloud I went to the gate of the Third Heaven,
Where I saw my sisters with happy smiles on their faces.
Who would dare oppose the edict of our father and king?
What problem is there in my sisters all laughing at me?
Now I've arrived in Danyang, I do away with my cloud,
And I order the God of the Soil to serve as a go-between.

Seventh Sister (*speaks*). Local God of the Soil, where are you?

God of the Soil (*enters and speaks*).

God of the Soil, yes, God of the Soil,
Receiving offerings twice each year:
On the first day of the Second Month
And on the first day too of the Eighth.

Immortal Maiden, this lowly divinity greets you by bowing down to the ground. What orders do you have for me now you have called for me?

Seventh Sister (*speaks*). I will be united in wedlock with Dong Yong for one hundred days, and I order you to act as go-between and matchmaker.

GOD OF THE SOIL (*speaks*). Your wish is my command, but where should I hide myself?

SEVENTH SISTER (*speaks*). You can hide behind this Shady Scholartree.

GOD OF THE SOIL (*speaks*). How often will he call on me before I should answer?

SEVENTH SISTER (*speaks*). You should answer when he calls for the third time.

GOD OF THE SOIL (*speaks*). I will obey your instructions.

SEVENTH SISTER (*speaks*). I will give you your orders only once.

GOD OF THE SOIL (*speaks*). How would I dare speak too early?

(GOD OF THE SOIL *exits*.)

SEVENTH SISTER (*speaks*).

Because Dong Yong is devout in his filial piety,
He meets on the road with a heavenly immortal.
For one hundred days they'll be husband and wife,
And for all eternity his fame will be transmitted.

SEVENTH SISTER (*sings*).

I order the God of the Soil to hide behind the Shady Scholartree,
And I change myself into a mortal wench of sixteen summers.
This is still me, the youngest of those Seven Immortal Sisters,
But who'll be able to recognize me as Chang'e of the Moon?[22]
Riding my cloud, I take my seat here on the upper road,
And over there my brother Dong Yong is coming already.

DONG YONG (*enters and sings*).

An icy frost and freezing cold, and suffering starvation:
I'm surnamed Dong and my given name is Yong.
When my father passed away, I saw no other solution
But to sell my body to some buyer and become a laborer.
With my luggage on my shoulders I travel the main road,
But there by the side of the road is sitting a pretty wench of sixteen summers!
While traveling on the road I should not invite any trouble—
Banter between a boy and a girl often gives rise to scandal.
So I will not greet this pretty girl, but just sneak past her,
Imitating those devotees I'll recite the name of Maitreya![23]

SEVENTH SISTER (*sings*).

This good Mr. Dong is truly too well-behaved and serious:
As soon as he sees me, his face turns peach-blossom pink!
But even if you would weary out dragons and fly on phoenixes,
How could you escape from me to the west, flee to the east?
I'll walk over to the lower road—here I sit down as before,
And here I'll wait for that Mr. Dong, that nice gentleman.

DONG YONG (*sings*).

Confucius wept for his disciples Yan Hui and Zi Lu,[24]
Cao Cao wept because of Kongming and his storm;
Sun Quan wept for Zhou Yu, also known as Gongjin,
And Liu Bei wept for his second brother, Lord Guan.[25]
I, Dong Yong, am not sighing for me, Dong Yong;
As I walk on the road, I weep for my revered father.
I will not take the upper road, I'll go the lower road,
But on the lower road I once again run into that girl!

DONG YONG (*speaks*). Dear girl, you show no decency at all. A moment ago you blocked my way on the upper main road, and now you block my way once again on the lower main road. What kind of behavior is that?

SEVENTH SISTER (*speaks*). Oh, oh, oh! "The great road leads to heaven / And each walks on one side!" Do you want to tell me that I am not allowed to sit where you are allowed to walk?

DONG YONG (*speaks*). Please do me a favor here on the road.

SEVENTH SISTER (*speaks*). If so, sir, please go on ahead!

(*They speak together*). Let's each do the other a favor!

DONG YONG (*speaks*). Oh, oh, oh! Dear miss, why do you have to bump me down with your hip while I am walking by in a most proper way?

SEVENTH SISTER (*speaks*). Young man, don't you have some hidden motive? You walk on all flurried and flustered, and when you bump into me, you have the nerve to say that I bumped into you!

DONG YONG (*speaks*). Yes, you are right, I certainly have something on my mind. While walking I am all flurried and flustered, so perhaps it was me who bumped into you. Please let me walk by you once again.

SEVENTH SISTER (*speaks*). Sir, please go on ahead!

DONG YONG (*speaks*). Oh, oh, oh! This time it is absolutely clear. It obviously was you who bumped into me, but still you say that I bumped into you!

SEVENTH SISTER (*speaks*). That is not the way to start a conversation. Where do you live? And what is your name? If you tell me everything in all detail, I will let you pass.

DONG YONG (*speaks*). Dear miss!

DONG YONG (*sings*).

Chinese goldthread and Amur cork:[26] more bitter than bitter!
I am known as Dong Yong, I'm an orphan by fate.
When my father passed away, I didn't even have a coffin,
So I sold my body to some buyer and became his slave.
Dear miss, be so kind as to step aside for a moment,
So this poor man won't be too late in starting his labor.

SEVENTH SISTER (*sings*).

No need to ask at the gate about your hidden emotions;
If one observes your expression, they are easy to know.
You resemble a dragon that has not yet found its pool,
But the time will come it rises on mists and on clouds![27]
As long as you, young man, do not despise or reject me,
I'm happy to marry you so we may be husband and wife.

DONG YONG (*sings*).

Dear miss, the first word you speak is truly misspoken,
How can you talk about marrying me, becoming my wife?
My father has barely died and his corpse is not yet cold;
In the first month of mourning there can be no wedding!
Over my head I don't have a single tile to cover my body;
Under my feet I don't have one inch of land I call my own.
I also don't have the money to marry you as my wife,
And whom will you blame when later on you will suffer?
Here applies: "When a man is poor, he is beset by demons;
When the times are against you, you're by demons seduced."

SEVENTH SISTER (*speaks*). Dear sir, listening to you it would seem that I have offended you.

DONG YONG (*speaks*). If it isn't you who has offended me, it definitely isn't me who has offended you.

SEVENTH SISTER (*speaks*). How could I have offended you? But let me make a bow to you to make up for it. Sir, please accept my bow.

DONG YONG (*speaks*). And let me bow in return.

SEVENTH SISTER (*speaks*). Sir, you must have read the books of the ancient Sages.

DONG YONG (*speaks*). Indeed, as I used to be a student at the prefectural academy. I am now just temporarily down and out of my luck.

SEVENTH SISTER (*speaks*). As you are a student at the prefectural academy, you might be expected to know the correct forms.

DONG YONG (*speaks*). What do you mean?

SEVENTH SISTER (*speaks*). Shouldn't you first put down your luggage and your umbrella before you return my bow?

DONG YONG (*speaks*). In truth, "even a gentleman is criticized by his inferiors." Let me put down my luggage and my umbrella. Sister, please accept my bow. Hey, hey, hey! Sister, I am making a bow to you, so how come you run off with my luggage and umbrella?

SEVENTH SISTER (*speaks*). Your pack and your umbrella are mine.

DONG YONG (*speaks*). No, they are mine!

THE METAL STAR OF GREAT WHITE[28] (*enters and speaks*). Hey, hey, hey! You pervert, in broad daylight you are trying to rape a woman! What kind of crime is that?

DONG YONG (*speaks*). As if it is not enough that I have to deal with this one person bereft of reason, here comes another!

THE METAL STAR (*speaks*). And she turns out to be my little niece!

SEVENTH SISTER (*speaks*). So it's you, my uncle!

DONG YONG (*speaks*). Because they are niece and uncle, it will not be easy to be vindicated. Uncle, please let me explain. As I was walking on this road, she blocked my way. When she greeted me with a bow, I bowed to her in return, but she complained I had not yet put down my pack and umbrella. But when I put down my pack and umbrella and returned her bow, she snatched away my pack and umbrella. Uncle, please be so kind as to help me out.

THE METAL STAR (*speaks*). You are in the right. Let me talk some sense into her. Dear niece, this student says that he bowed in return and you ran off with his pack and umbrella. What kind of behavior is that?

SEVENTH SISTER (*speaks*). Dear uncle, please let me explain. Three days ago he passed in front of our door and promised me that we would travel together, of one heart and mind.[29] Now three days later he wants to dump me, so this pack and umbrella are mine.

THE METAL STAR (*speaks*). Sister, you are in the right. Student, my niece just told me that three days ago you and she were of one heart and mind, but now you want to dump her, so the pack and the umbrella are hers.

DONG YONG (*speaks*). Uncle, what does she have as proof of this marriage agreement? And what did she give me as evidence?

THE METAL STAR (*speaks*). Indeed! Little girl, what did this man give you as proof of this marriage agreement? And what did you give him as evidence?

SEVENTH SISTER (*speaks*). He gave me this pack and this umbrella as proof, and I gave him a white fan as evidence.

THE METAL STAR (*speaks*). And where is that fan now?

SEVENTH SISTER (*speaks*). At the back of his neck.

THE METAL STAR (*speaks*). Student, please come here.

DONG YONG (*speaks*). Uncle, what for?

THE METAL STAR (*speaks*). She says that you gave her this pack and this umbrella as proof, and that she gave you a white fan as evidence.

DONG YONG (*speaks*). I'm so poor I don't even have a black fan!

THE METAL STAR (*speaks*). I will have to pat you down.

DONG YONG (*speaks*). You still won't find it.

THE METAL STAR (*speaks*). Here, at the back of your neck!

DONG YONG (*speaks*). She must have planted that on me!

THE METAL STAR (*speaks*). She didn't plant it on anyone else, but of all persons she did plant it on you. Now let me ask you: Do you want an official mediation or would you like to settle privately?

DONG YONG (*speaks*). What would an official mediation look like?

THE METAL STAR (*speaks*). An official mediation means that we take you to the office of the authorities and you get a beating of forty strokes of the heavy cudgel.

DONG YONG (*speaks*). And if we settle privately?

THE METAL STAR (*speaks*). If you settle privately, the matter is settled if you marry my little niece as your lawfully wedded wife for one hundred years of bliss.

DONG YONG (*speaks*). We are here far from any village, so who will be the bride-giver and who will be the go-between?

THE METAL STAR (*speaks*). The student asks: Who will be the bride-giver and who will be the go-between?

SEVENTH SISTER (*speaks*). Uncle, you can be the bride-giver and the go-between.

DONG YONG (*speaks*). That is nonsense. How can one person fulfill two functions? The bride-giver cannot serve as go-between, and the go-between cannot serve as bride-giver.

THE METAL STAR (*speaks*). My little niece, the student says that a single person cannot fulfill these two functions.

SEVENTH SISTER (*speaks*). Uncle, then you will be the bride-giver, and the scholartree will be the go-between.

THE METAL STAR (*speaks*). Student, the scholartree will be the go-between and I will be the bride-giver.

DONG YONG (*speaks*). That scholartree is a dumb tree, so how can it be the go-between?

THE METAL STAR (*speaks*). If it answers when you call out to it, it can be the go-between.

DONG YONG (*speaks*). And if it doesn't answer?

THE METAL STAR (*speaks*). Then it cannot be the go-between.

DONG YONG (*speaks*). How often should I call out to it?

THE METAL STAR (*speaks*). Three times is the rule.

DONG YONG (*speaks*). Uncle, Sister, I'm out of here! People call me a fool, but you two are even more foolish than I am. The scholartree is a dumb tree that will not give an answer even if you call out three thousand times, let alone three times! Uncle, Sister, just listen! Shady Scholartree! If I am going to marry this girl as my lawfully wedded wife for one hundred years of bliss, you have to talk to me. Uncle, Sister, have you heard anything?

THE METAL STAR (*speaks*). I haven't heard a thing.

DONG YONG (*speaks*). Then I say goodbye.

THE METAL STAR (*speaks*). Three times is the rule. You have only called one time, so you should try it two more times.

DONG YONG (*speaks*). So let me call a second time.

THE METAL STAR (*speaks*). You definitely have to call.

DONG YONG (*speaks*). I definitely will call. Shady Scholartree! If I am to marry this girl as my lawfully wedded wife for one hundred years of bliss, you have to talk to me. Uncle, the tree doesn't say a word, so give me my luggage and my umbrella.

THE METAL STAR (*speaks*). You have only called two times, you still have one time.

DONG YONG (*speaks*). Do you really want me to call?

THE METAL STAR (*speaks*). I definitely want you to call!

DONG YONG (*speaks*). Let me call one final time. Shady Scholartree! If I am to marry this girl as my lawfully wedded wife for one hundred years of bliss, you will have to talk to me.

(THE GOD OF THE SOIL *enters and speaks.*)

The Shady Scholartree opens its mouth and speaks as follows:
Dong Yong, make sure to listen very carefully to my words!
Now you are to marry this girl as your lawfully wedded wife,
I, this scholartree, will be your matchmaker and go-between.

DONG YONG (*speaks*). How on earth is this possible?

DONG YONG (*sings*).

This is weirder than weird; this is truly weirder than weird!
Where did one ever see a dumb tree that learned to speak?
So I turn around and I greet this scholartree with a bow,

To express my thanks to a tree that serves as go-between.
Then I turn around and, Uncle, bow to show my respect.
Uncle, Sister, now make sure to listen carefully to my words.
Above my head I have not a single tile to shelter my body;
Under my feet I have no fertile fields to earn a livelihood.
In my freezing hovel I don't have even half a pint of rice,
So whom will she blame for her hunger and for her cold?

The Metal Star (*sings*).
Dong Yong, there is no need at all to cry such sad tears,
Make sure to listen very carefully to the words I'll say:
She will not blame you for having no tile over your head;
She is only too eager even if you have no fertile fields.
Once husband and wife have consummated the marriage,
I happily guarantee you one hundred days of wedded bliss.

Dong Yong (*speaks*). Uncle, come here! First you talk about one hundred years of marriage bliss, and now it has become one hundred days of wedded bliss! I don't want her!

The Metal Star (*speaks*). [I meant to say "sunny days" as in] "a bright sky and sunny day."[30] If you are not husband and wife during broad daylight, how could you still be husband and wife in the dark of night?

Dong Yong (*speaks*). Uncle, I have a comparison for you.

The Metal Star (*speaks*). What will you compare me to?

Dong Yong (*speaks*). To a knife made of tinplate.

The Metal Star (*speaks*). And for what reason?

Dong Yong (*speaks*). Because your mouth[31] turns so quickly.

The Metal Star (*speaks*). Don't talk nonsense. You take her with you to Fu Mansion, and I say goodbye.

Dong Yong (*speaks*). Let me see you off.

The Metal Star (*speaks*). There is no need to see me off. (The Metal Star *exits.*)

Seventh Sister (*speaks*). Sir, which way will we take to Fu Mansion?

Dong Yong (*speaks*). We'll take the upper road.

SEVENTH SISTER (*speaks*). Sir, you go first.

DONG YONG (*speaks*). Sister, you go first.

SEVENTH SISTER (*speaks*). The wife follows as the husband leads.

DONG YONG (*speaks*). If you're poor and destitute, the wife leads and the husband follows.

SEVENTH SISTER (*speaks*). Then there's luck and longevity.[32]

DONG YONG (*speaks*). Sister, you go first.

SEVENTH SISTER (*speaks*). I will walk on ahead, but you have to follow immediately behind me. (SEVENTH SISTER *exits.*)

DONG YONG (*speaks*). Uncle has set out on the upper road, and now Sister has set out on the upper road too, so this is my chance to sneak away along the lower road!

(THE METAL STAR *entering unexpectedly confronts him and speaks.*) You student, you really want to dump her! Where do you think you are going?

DONG YONG (*speaks*). Uncle, you were so kind as to be the bride-giver, but I forgot to ask you for your name.

THE METAL STAR (*speaks*). My name is Jin Risheng,[33] and I hail from Penglai.[34] Don't forget!

DONG YONG (*speaks*). Uncle, let me see you off! (THE METAL STAR *exits.*)

(SEVENTH SISTER *enters and speaks.*) Sir, what's keeping you?

DONG YONG (*speaks*). The upper road was blocked by a river, so I took the lower road.

SEVENTH SISTER (*speaks*). Sir, this time I will ask you to walk on ahead, and I, your wife, will follow you.

DONG YONG (*speaks*). Oh, oh, oh! But a moment ago you said: "When the wife leads and the husband follows, there is luck and there is longevity"!

SEVENTH SISTER (*speaks*). Sir, but this time you have to come. (SEVENTH SISTER *exits.*)

DONG YONG (*speaks*). Uncle has set out on the lower road, and the girl has also set out on the lower road, so this is my chance to sneak away to the upper road.

(The Metal Star *entering again unexpectedly confronts him and speaks.*) Oh, oh, oh! Where do you want to go this time?

Dong Yong (*speaks*). Uncle, are you some sprite?

The Metal Star (*speaks*). I am not some sprite.

Dong Yong (*speaks*). Are you some ghost?

The Metal Star (*speaks*). I am not some ghost either.

Dong Yong (*speaks*). How come you keep haunting me if you are not a sprite or a ghost? What's behind this?

The Metal Star (*speaks*). You cannot escape from me even if you fly up into the sky, and you cannot escape from me even if you sink into the earth. If you move one foot, I move a yard, and if you run one hundred steps, I catch up with you in one step. Be careful! I'm leaving you now. (The Metal Star *exits.*)

Dong Yong (*speaks*). Uncle has gone. This is really strange!

(Seventh Sister *enters and speaks.*) Sir, why do you stay behind once again?

Dong Yong (*speaks*). Darling!

Dong Yong (*sings*).

It is not the case that I, Dong Yong, want to dump you,
But there are so many aspects of the matter to consider.
When I get to Fu Mansion as an indentured laborer,
How can you, my darling, be able to stand such misery?

Seventh Sister (*sings*).

Even though I will be a slave when I get to their place,
I still will know how to wash clothes and starch gowns.
And when the three years of servitude will be finished,
We'll return to your home together, husband and wife.

Dong Yong (*sings*).

Darling, what you say shows your wisdom and insight,
As a result, it frees your husband's mind of its worries.
On the hills the songbirds loudly sing their love songs,
And the fishes in the water also frolic and jump about.[35]
Darling, while walking on the road let's take our time.

Seventh Sister (*sings*).

Unexpectedly we have already arrived at Fu Family Bay.

Dong Yong (*sings*).

Here we have now arrived in front of the gate of the Fus—
What do you want me to say when I will see old Mr. Fu?

(The Young Master *enters and speaks*.)

Not too poor and not too rich:
At twenty I'm running a pawnshop.
If people ask me for my name,
I'm Young Master Fu Guanbao!

Dong Yong, you're here to start on your job?

Dong Yong (*speaks*). Yes, indeed.

The Young Master (*speaks*). Father, Dong Yong has arrived to start on his job.

(The Old Master *speaks from backstage*.) Take him to the office and have him copy the accounts.

The Young Master (*speaks*). Follow me to the office.

Dong Yong (*speaks*). My luggage is still outside.

The Young Master (*speaks*). Then go and get it!

Dong Yong (*speaks*). Darling, please give me my pack.

Seventh Sister (*speaks*). Did you tell them that I also came along?

Dong Yong (*speaks*). No, not yet.

Seventh Sister (*speaks*). This second time you have to tell them you brought your wife.

Dong Yong (*speaks*). Yes, I will. Young Master, I fetched my luggage.

The Young Master (*speaks*). Then follow me so we can have something to eat.

Dong Yong (*speaks*). Young Master, I still left my umbrella outside the gate.

The Young Master (*speaks*). Then go and get it!

Dong Yong (*speaks*). Yes, I will. Darling, where is my umbrella?

Seventh Sister (*speaks*). Did you tell them this second time your wife came along?

Dong Yong (*speaks*). Oops, I didn't.

Seventh Sister (*speaks*). Then we will enter the mansion together. Young Master, here I am.

The Young Master (*speaks*). What's her relation to you?

Dong Yong (*speaks*). She is my wife.

The Young Master (*speaks*). Too bad! Dong Yong, you must have abducted her. Father, please come over here!

(The Old Master *enters and speaks.*)

All of a sudden I hear my son is calling for me,
So I'll have to go over and see what's the matter.

What's going on?

The Young Master (*speaks*). Dong Yong brought along a wife!

The Old Master (*sings*).

As soon as I see Dong Yong, I am filled with disgust!
You miserable creature, you're no better than a beast!
As soon as your father has died, barely been laid to rest,
You pick up a woman while on the road and seduce her!
No matter what happened, now tell me the full true story,
Because if you don't, my cudgel won't show any mercy.

Dong Yong (*sings*).

Dear Mr. Fu, there is no need for your towering rage—
Ask this "hairpins and skirt," and you'll know the facts.

The Old Master (*sings*).

Hearing these words, I will indeed inquire into the facts.
So I turn around and direct my questions to this woman.
From which prefecture do you hail? From which district?
What is your surname and given name? Tell me clearly!

Seventh Sister (*sings*).

Dear Mr. Fu, there is no need to ask for my full name:
From early on I've been the wedded wife of Dong Yong.
Wherever he goes, a wife is bound to follow her husband,
So I've come along to your mansion to pay off the debt.

The Old Master (*sings*).

As you've come along to pay off his debt by your labor,
Allow me ask you what kind of skills you may possess.

SEVENTH SISTER (*sings*).

I have no intention to brag, I don't want to exaggerate,
But in a single night I can weave ten bolts of fine satin.

THE OLD MASTER (*sings*).

This wife of Dong Yong is exaggerating and bragging:
How can one weave ten bolts of satin in a single night?
So without further ado I will instruct my son Guanbao
To provide them with tangled silk without a beginning.

THE OLD MASTER (*speaks*). Guanbao, come here. If Dong Yong's wife tomorrow in the fifth watch[36] at break of dawn has woven ten bolts of satin, things are fine.

THE YOUNG MASTER (*speaks*). And if she hasn't?

THE OLD MASTER (*speaks*). Then we throw them into jail. (THE OLD MASTER *exits.*)

THE YOUNG MASTER (*speaks*). Dong Yong, where are you? My father tells me that I have to lock the two of you in the weaving room, and tomorrow we want ten bolts of satin.

DONG YONG (*speaks*). And what if we cannot produce them?

THE YOUNG MASTER (*speaks*). Then we will beat your feet to a pulp!

DONG YONG (*sings*).

Hearing these words, my heart is filled with frustration—
Darling, please listen carefully to the cause of this mess.
Upon entering this mansion you had to brag and to boast;
If tomorrow at dawn we don't have the satin, we'll suffer!

SEVENTH SISTER (*sings*).

Dear husband, there is no need to be flurried and flustered!
These ten bolts of fine satin are only a minor matter indeed.
Don't worry at all, lay down to sleep in the weaving room:
In the fifth watch, at break of dawn, the satin will be there.

DONG YONG (*sings*).

At a loss what to do, I'm filled with anxiety—she only smiles.
My heart is feeling as if it were placed over a hot raging fire.
These ten bolts of fine satin are not some minor matter at all,
So how can we produce this fine satin by the fifth watch?
My eyes filled with sad tears, I go off to catch some sleep;

I'm like a pig or a goat about to be sacrificed to the gods and now waiting for dawn!

(DONG YONG *exits.*)

SEVENTH SISTER (*sings*).

When I set out on the road my immortal sisters informed me
That if I ran into problems, I should burn this orchid incense.
Holding this pure incense in my hands, I pray for assistance.

(THE OTHER IMMORTAL SISTERS *cross the stage and sing.*)

I'm afraid that we immortal sisters must descend to earth.

(THE OTHER IMMORTAL SISTERS *enter again and sing to the tune of the immortals.*)

The smoke of incense wafts upwards into heaven's court:
This must mean that Seventh Sister encounters a problem!
We, her sisters, riding together on our auspicious clouds,
Now descend as fast as we can to the Fu Family Mansion.

THE OTHER IMMORTAL SISTERS (*speak*). Seventh Sister, where are you?

SEVENTH SISTER (*speaks*).

All of a sudden I hear people talking,
So I will go over to see what's going on.

Welcome, my sisters!

ELDEST SISTER (*speaks*). For what reason did you call us down to earth?

SEVENTH SISTER (*speaks*). After I descended to the mortal world, I foolishly bragged that I could weave ten bolts of satin in a single night, so I have to bother you, my sisters, to help me out.

ELDEST SISTER (*speaks*). This is only a minor matter. Let me take care of it.

SEVENTH SISTER (*speaks*). Dear sister, thank you very much!

ELDEST SISTER (*speaks*). Dear sisters, what does one hear when weaving in the first watch of the night?[37]

THE OTHERS SISTERS (*speak*). In the first watch the mosquitoes are buzzing about.

ELDEST SISTER (*speaks*). So let me weave mosquitoes buzzing about.

ELDEST SISTER (*sings*).[38]

In the first fifth of the first watch one would like to sleep;

In the first fifth of the first watch one would like to sleep,
But in the first watch the mosquitoes are buzzing all through that watch.
Dear brother mosquito,
You are buzzing over there,
And I am listening over here,
And your buzzing fills my heart with pain.
It fills my heart with pain—
The more you buzz, the more the pain!
The mother asks her daughter: What's the noise?
Dear mother, please go to sleep—why those many questions?
Dear mother, please go to sleep—why those many questions?

ELDEST SISTER (*speaks*). Dear sisters, what does one hear in the second watch of the night?

THE OTHER SISTERS (*speak*). In the second watch it is the croaking frogs.

ELDEST SISTER (*speaks*). So let me weave croaking frogs.

ELDEST SISTER (*sings*).

In the second fifth of the second watch one would like to sleep;
In the second fifth of the second watch one would like to sleep,
But in the second watch the frogs keep on croaking all through the watch!
Dear brother frog,
You are croaking over there,
And I am listening over here,
And your croaking fills my heart with pain.
It fills my heart with pain—
The more you croak, the more the pain!
The mother asks her daughter: What's the noise?
Dear mother, please go to sleep—why those many questions?
Dear mother, please go to sleep—why those many questions?

ELDEST SISTER (*speaks*). What does one hear in the third watch of the night?

THE OTHER SISTERS (*speak*). In the third watch one hears the honking of a lonely goose.

ELDEST SISTER (*speaks*). So let me weave a honking lonely goose.

ELDEST SISTER (*sings*).

In the third fifth of the third watch one would like to sleep;
In the third fifth of the third watch one would like to sleep,

But in the third watch the lonely goose keeps on honking all through the watch!
Dear brother lonely goose,
You are honking over there,
And I am listening over here
And your honking fills my heart with pain!
It fills my heart with pain—
The more you honk, the more the pain!
The mother asks her daughter: What's the noise?
Dear mother, please go to sleep—why those many questions?
Dear mother, please go to sleep—why those many questions?

ELDEST SISTER (*speaks*). What does one hear in the fourth watch of the night?

THE OTHER SISTERS (*speak*). In the fourth watch one hears the barking of the spotted dog.

ELDEST SISTER (*speaks*). So let me weave a barking spotted dog.

ELDEST SISTER (*sings*).

In the fourth fifth of the fourth watch one would like to sleep;
In the fourth fifth of the fourth watch one would like to sleep,
But in the fourth watch the spotted dog keeps on barking all through the watch!
Dear brother spotted dog,
You are barking over there,
And I am listening over here,
And your barking fills my heart with pain!
It fills my heart with pain—
The more you bark, the more the pain!
The mother asks her daughter: What's the noise?
Dear mother, please go to sleep—why those many questions?
Dear mother, please go to sleep—why those many questions?

ELDEST SISTER (*speaks*). What does one hear in the fifth watch of the night?

THE OTHER SISTERS (*speak*). In the fifth watch one hears the call of the Golden Rooster.[39]

ELDEST SISTER (*speaks*). So let me weave the Golden Rooster announcing dawn.

ELDEST SISTER (*sings*).

In the fifth fifth of the fifth watch one would like to sleep;
In the fifth fifth of the fifth watch one would like to sleep,

But in the fifth watch the Golden Rooster keeps on crowing throughout the watch!
Dear brother Golden Rooster,
You are crowing over there,
And I am listening over here
And your crowing fills my heart with pain!
It fills my heart with pain—
The more you crow, the more the pain!
The mother asks her daughter: What's the noise?
Dear mother, go to sleep—why those many questions?
Dear mother, go to sleep—why those many questions?

(*They all exit.*)

Part III. Saying Goodbye to Dong Yong

Dong Yong (*enters and sings*).

Thanks to my wife's skill in weaving satins and silks
My three years of servitude became one hundred days.
The Fus treated us to a farewell dinner and now we leave,
It really was difficult to say goodbye, to take our leave.
In a single step I have arrived at this fork in the road:
Let me wait here for my wife so we can travel together.

Seventh Sister (*enters and sings*).

Lady Fu treated me to a farewell dinner and now we leave,
It really was difficult to say goodbye, to take our leave.
I never should have loved the red dust's embroidered brocade![40]
I never should have become the lover and mate of Dong Yong!
My husband Dong Yong is slowly walking on ahead—
How could he know that now I'm about to dump him?
Walking on, I've quickly arrived at the fork in the road:
Greeting my husband I put on a smile, hide my sorrow.

Dong Yong (*speaks*). My darling, what took you so long?

Seventh Sister (*speaks*). My feet are hurting,[41] so it's hard for me to walk.

Dong Yong (*speaks*). Then wait here for a while.

Seventh Sister (*speaks*). Where are you going?

Dong Yong (*speaks*). I'll hire a small sedan chair, so it can carry you, my wife, to our home.

Seventh Sister (*speaks*). My husband, wouldn't that be a waste of your money? It's only a short walk—I can manage.

Seventh Sister (*sings*).

Despite the pain I hurry on, despite the pain I hurry on:
Today we will be separated but he does not yet know.
Arriving at the Shady Scholartree I come up with a plan,
And I say: Dear husband, I have something to tell you!

Dong Yong (*speaks*). My wife, why do you stop for a second time?

Seventh Sister (*speaks*). Let me explain it to you. When you and I were married, it was all thanks to the scholartree that served as a matchmaker and go-between. Now we, husband and wife, today go back home, we definitely must express our thanks.

DONG YONG (*speaks*). We have already passed that scholartree.

SEVENTH SISTER (*speaks*). As human beings we cannot forget our roots, so let's go back.

DONG YONG (*speaks*). Here we have arrived below the Shady Scholartree. When earlier we, husband and wife, were married, it was all thanks to your assistance as matchmaker and go-between. Now we are going home, we express our thanks to you. My wife, you should also come here and express your thanks.

SEVENTH SISTER (*speaks*). I am pregnant, carrying your child, so I cannot lower my head and perform a bow.

DONG YONG (*speaks*). Dear scholartree, my wife is pregnant and cannot lower her head and perform a bow, so allow me to perform a bow on her behalf.

SEVENTH SISTER (*speaks*). Dear husband, the weather is stiflingly hot, so let's each get a stone and sit down for a while. (SEVENTH SISTER *sits down.*) Back at the Fu Mansion, who treated you well and who treated you fine?

DONG YONG (*speaks*). The Old Master treated me well and the Young Master treated me fine.

SEVENTH SISTER (*speaks*). In what manner?

DONG YONG (*speaks*). Before our departure they treated me to a farewell dinner with fine wine.

SEVENTH SISTER (*speaks*). So how many cups did you down?

DONG YONG (*speaks*). I didn't drink a single cup!

SEVENTH SISTER (*speaks*). That's a brazen lie, your face is all red!

DONG YONG (*speaks*). Let me have a look.

SEVENTH SISTER (*speaks*). Dear husband, we are here out in the fields, without a clear spring or a bright mirror, so how do you think you can see your own face?

DONG YONG (*speaks*). My dear wife, you are right. Back at the Fu Mansion, who treated you well and who treated you very well?

SEVENTH SISTER (*speaks*). Her Ladyship treated me well, and the young mistress treated me very well. Before our departure they treated me to a farewell dinner with fine wine, but I didn't drink a single cup.

DONG YONG (*speaks*). My dear wife, at other times you could down a hundred cups, so how come you didn't drink a single cup today?

SEVENTH SISTER (*speaks*). Let me explain. Today is the birthday of my father and mother, so I will abstain from alcohol for one hundred days.

DONG YONG (*speaks*). Hey, it's a good thing you mention it because I had forgotten. Wait here for a while.

SEVENTH SISTER (*speaks*). My husband, where are you going?

DONG YONG (*speaks*). Let me go to the market and buy some peaches of longevity and fruits of longevity with which to wish my father-in-law and mother-in-law many added years.

SEVENTH SISTER (*speaks*). My husband, isn't that a waste of your money? It is quite enough if we here perform a bow while facing the sky.

DONG YONG (*speaks*). Dear father-in-law and dear mother-in-law up above,[42] today on your birthday allow your son-in-law to perform a deep bow. May your good fortune be as extensive as the Eastern Ocean and may your longevity be as long lasting as the Southern Mountains, and may you both live to the age of one hundred and twenty!

SEVENTH SISTER (*speaks*). Dear heaven!

DONG YONG (*speaks*). Hey! I said "one hundred and twenty years." Should I still add some years?[43] Or do you want to tell me they don't want mine? Let me add some to you![44]

SEVENTH SISTER (*speaks*). Too bad that today I must say goodbye to him, but he doesn't yet have the faintest idea. I can only take out two hairpins and change them into a couple of mandarin ducks[45] in order to give him a hint.
May by the power of Heaven and Earth
A couple of mandarin ducks appear!

DONG YONG (*speaks*). What are those birds on that slope?

SEVENTH SISTER (*speaks*). That is a couple of mandarin ducks.

DONG YONG (*speaks*). Why is the female duck shedding tears with lowered head?

SEVENTH SISTER (*speaks*). It must mean that that female duck is an immortal bird and that she has to ascend to heaven, so she therefore sheds tears with lowered head. My husband, let me call out to her: Female duck, female duck, you are united in love with that male duck. Today you have to ascend to heaven, so why do you still not leave?

DONG YONG (*speaks*). Why doesn't that male duck ascend to heaven?

SEVENTH SISTER (*speaks*). The female duck is an immortal bird, and I am an immortal woman. That's why I can tell her to ascend to heaven. But you are a mortal man, and the male duck is a mortal bird, so it will not react when you call.

DONG YONG (*speaks*). Let me call too. Male duck, male duck, you are united in love with that female duck. Today that female duck ascends to heaven, so why do you still not go? Let me get a pebble and hit him so he will ascend to heaven!

SEVENTH SISTER (*speaks*). My dear husband, please let me explain. I am an immortal woman, so I can tell the female duck to ascend to heaven. But you are a mortal man, so how can you tell the male duck to ascend to heaven?

DONG YONG (*speaks*). That's a joke. If you are an immortal woman, then I must be an immortal male from highest heaven!

SEVENTH SISTER (*speaks*). How could I have woven ten bolts of silk in a single night if I hadn't been an immortal woman?

DONG YONG (*speaks*). My wife, why do you suddenly tell me such a different story today?

SEVENTH SISTER (*speaks*). My dear husband Dong Yong, I am Seventh Sister from heaven above. Because you practiced filial piety, my father the king dispatched me to the mortal world to become your wife, but only for one hundred days. Today that period has come to an end, and you and I will have to say goodbye.

(*Suppressing his weeping,* DONG YONG *sings.*)

Because we will have to say goodbye, say goodbye,
I am weeping and weeping, crushed by bitter tears.
My darling, now you are leaving, I cannot let you go,
I really cannot let you go, really cannot say goodbye!

DONG YONG (*speaks*). If you want to leave, I will go and find that old bride-giver!

SEVENTH SISTER (*speaks*). That was Metal Star Li of Great White.

DONG YONG (*speaks*). Shit!

DONG YONG (*sings*).

Li Changgeng, oh you Li Changgeng,[46]
I am weeping and weeping, as my tears gush down.
My darling, now you are leaving, I cannot let you go,
I really cannot let you go, really cannot say goodbye!

DONG YONG (*speaks*). Darling, let me count the days. Whichever way I count, it only comes to ninety-eight days.

SEVENTH SISTER (*speaks*). Add the day when we came and the day when we left.

DONG YONG (*sings*).

Add the day when we came, add the day when we left—
I am weeping and weeping, and tears keep on falling.
Let me get out the sword at my waist that cuts waists,
And cut that couple of mandarin ducks apart, in two.

DONG YONG (*speaks*). Let me go and find that Shady Scholartree!

SEVENTH SISTER (*speaks*). That is a dumb tree.

DONG YONG (*sings*).

That is a dumb tree, oh yes, now it is a dumb tree—
If you call, it doesn't react, so my tears freely flow.
My darling, with both my hands I grasp your hand,
Please take your husband along on the road to go.

SEVENTH SISTER (*sings*).

I, Seventh Sister, step forward in one single step.
My dear husband, please listen to my confession.
On the Southern Gate of Heaven a glare appears
As four serving officers proclaim the royal edict:
"If you don't return by noon, you'll be beheaded;
Heaven's regulations don't allow for an extension."
So I steel all my feelings and make a clean break,
Step on my auspicious cloud and fly up to heaven.
Yet unable to abandon Dong Yong, I look down:
My husband has collapsed by the side of the road!
He has lost consciousness by the side of the road—
I, Seventh Sister, am so upset it breaks my heart!
Lowering my head, I come up with a clever plan:

I'll have to write a letter and attach it to his waist!
But out on the road I have no paper, so what to do?
I'll tear a piece of my skirt and use that as paper.
Now I have a piece of my skirt, but still have no writing utensils—
So I'll have to bite my finger and use that as a brush.
Mustering my courage I bite in my middle finger—
The pain in my finger and heart is unsupportable!
And I write: "My dear husband Dong, be greeted!
My husband, please read the following with care.
My father the king, seeing your great filial piety,
Ordered me to be your wife for one hundred days.
One day of wedded bliss is one hundred days of love,
After one hundred days of bliss we are inseparable!
As husband and wife we love each other dearly,
And now I am pregnant, heavy with your child.
Whether it will be a boy or a girl, I don't know,
But once it is born, we'll know it without a doubt.
If I give birth to a boy, his name will be Zhongshu;[47]
If I give birth to a girl, she'll stay here in heaven.
This one white fan is a truly priceless treasure;
I give it to you so you may present it to the court.
At the capital His Majesty loves pearls and jewels;
The glory of office, high or low, depends on Him!
When you ride your horse across Magpie Bridge,
I will come and hand you your son at that bridge.
If you hope to be married for the rest of your life,
Take the daughter of the Fus as your second wife.
I wanted to write this in blood and let you know,
But the blood doesn't flow, my strength has gone!
The third quarter of the hour of noon has arrived:
Dear husband, I say goodbye and return to heaven!"

SEVENTH SISTER (*speaks*). My husband! (SEVENTH SISTER *weeps and exits.*)

DONG YONG (*sings*).

I lost my consciousness, I lost my consciousness,
All of a sudden I collapsed by the side of the road.
When I opened my eyes and looked for my wife,
I found a piece of her skirt by the side of the road.
That piece of skirt carried a letter written in blood,
And I carefully read each character and each line.
The letter said: "My dear husband Dong, be greeted!

My husband, please read the following with care.
My father the king, seeing your great filial piety,
Ordered me to be your wife for one hundred days.
One day of wedded bliss is one hundred days of love,
After one hundred days of bliss we are inseparable!
As husband and wife we love each other dearly,
And now I am pregnant, heavy with your child.
Whether it will be a boy or a girl, I don't know,
But once it is born, we'll know it without a doubt.
If I give birth to a boy, his name will be Zhongshu;
If I give birth to a girl, she'll stay here in heaven.
This one white fan is a truly priceless treasure;
I give it to you so you may present it to the court.
At the capital His Majesty loves pearls and jewels;
The glory of office, high or low, depends on Him!
When you ride your horse across Magpie Bridge,
I will come and hand you your son at that bridge.
If you hope to be married for the rest of your life,
Take the daughter of the Fus as your second wife.
I wanted to write this in blood and let you know,
But the blood doesn't flow, my strength has gone!
The third quarter of the hour of noon has arrived:
Dear husband, I say goodbye and return to heaven!"
Reading this letter, my heart feels as if poked by a knife,
And I weep and I weep, and I cry and cry loudly.
The gate of the house is not far, I arrive at the Fus,
So let me ask the Old Master to finance my trip.

THE OLD MASTER (*enters and speaks*). My son,[48] you are back! But where is your wife?

DONG YONG (*speaks*). She abandoned me halfway.

THE OLD MASTER (*speaks*). She is an immortal, so how can she remain the wife of a mortal man? My son, this year is the year of the metropolitan examinations, so why don't you go to the capital to seek fame while we wait here for you. My son, here you have your luggage.

DONG YONG (*speaks*). Then I will set out on the road immediately.

THE OLD MASTER (*speaks*). Now you leave it is the Third Month of spring.

DONG YONG (*speaks*). When I return, gold will cover the ground.

Goodbye! (DONG YONG *exits.*)

THE OLD MASTER (*speaks*).

My son has left and gone to the capital,
Now I'll wait for his letter coming back.

(THE OLD MASTER *exits.*)

* * *

(EUNUCH *and* RETINUE *enter.*) EUNUCH (*speaks*).

In heaven the mansions of the immortals,
On earth the houses of the prime ministers—
But if you want true wealth and nobility,
Nothing compares with the imperial palace!

Because the Empress Dowager has to keep to her bed because of an illness, I have received the emperor's order to summon the rarest treasures of the whole world. Boys!

MEMBERS OF RETINUE (*speak*). Yes sir!

EUNUCH (*speaks*). We have all arrived at the Pavilion for Presenting Treasure. Here we have a poster that we will post outside. Report immediately to me if anyone takes this poster away.[49]

(DONG YONG *enters and speaks.*)

Having left the land of my home far behind me,
I arrive at the Pavilion for Presenting Treasure.

Let me take this poster away.

EUNUCH (*speaks*). Tell the man who took away the poster to come inside and report.

DONG YONG (*speaks*). Sir, I am the man who took away the poster.

EUNUCH (*speaks*). You who present treasure, where do you live? What is your surname and given name? What treasure do you present? Please tell me in all detail!

DONG YONG (*speaks*). I hail from Danyang District and my name is Dong Yong. I present ten bolts of patterned satin and one precious fan. Sir, please have a look.

EUNUCH (*speaks*). Worthless trifles! But let me show them to the emperor.

(DONG YONG *exits.*) EUNUCH (*speaks*). Let me set out on the road and go to the court.

Arriving in front of the golden steps
I submit a report to His Majesty.

A myriad years to Your Majesty!

(*Backstage speaks.*) All put down your report!

EUNUCH (*speaks*). Many thanks to Your Majesty! (*All exit.*)

* * *

(DONG YONG *enters and speaks.*)
The eunuch left to submit his report to the emperor,
Now I arrive at the Pavilion for Appointing Officials.

(EUNUCH *and* RETINUE *enter.*) EUNUCH (*speaks*). An imperial edict has been conferred. Kneel down and listen to its recitation. His Majesty states: "When the Empress Dowager saw the treasures, she fully recovered from her illness. Seeing this, We were pleased and We hereby award you the title of Top-of-the-List for Presenting Treasure. Danyang District will become Xiaogan District,[50] and Descending Magpie Bridge will become United Karma Bridge. Above the bridge the Temple of the Immortal Maiden will be erected, and the image of the Immortal Maiden will be carved of sandalwood. We gift you three sticks of Guangnan incense, so you may burn incense in the morning and change the water in the evening." Now the imperial edict has been recited, face the imperial palace and express your gratitude.

DONG YONG (*speaks*). Many thanks to His Majesty!

EUNUCH (*speaks*). I will return to the palace to report on my mission.

DONG YONG (*speaks*). Allow me to see you off. (EUNUCH *and* RETINUE *exit.*)

DONG YONG (*speaks*).
At the Gate of Yu I thrice drowned in the waves;[51]
The thunder once resounds now under a blue sky.

Bring my horse! (DONG YONG *exits.*)

* * *

(MAIDENS *lead* SEVENTH SISTER *onstage, and she sings.*)
An imperial edict allows me to descend to the world of dust;
For one hundred days I was married to my husband Dong Yong.
In the Palace of Dipper and Buffalo I gave birth to a boy,

And I now am bringing the baby to Dong Yong as his heir.
The maidens lead the way as I enter the immortal's temple,
And from afar I see Dong Yong arriving to burn incense.

(Servants *lead* Dong Yong *onstage, and he sings.*)

I this official arrive at the Temple of the Immortal Maiden.
By whom was this temple erected? It truly is spectacular!
On this side hang the Three Stars[52] that provide their light;
On that side hang the Four Great Officers of high heaven.
I cannot find a Buddha image as I search under the canopies;
This statue of a divinity looks exactly the same as my wife!
I rush forward and embrace my own darling …

Seventh Sister (*sings*).

But I push my husband away, who falls down on the bridge!
My husband, I see, now wears on his head a gauze cap;
My husband, I see, is now wrapped in a crimson gown.[53]
Maidens, now hand the baby boy to my husband, his father;
This is the last time we will be allowed to see each other.

(The maidens *precede* Seventh Sister *as she leaves the stage.*)

Dong Yong (*sings*).

I had lost consciousness, yes, I had lost consciousness,
And all of sudden I, Dong Yong, fell down on the bridge.
When I opened my eyes, lifted my eyes, and had a look,
I saw that my darling had delivered this baby boy to me.
Servants, clear the road, so I can go to my benefactor[54]
And inform him of all that has happened and also why.

(The servants *precede* Dong Yong *as he leaves the stage.*)

* * *

(The Old Master *enters and speaks.*)

My eyes watch for the banners of victory,
My ears listen for news that is favorable.

(Servants *lead* Dong Yong *onstage.*) The servants (*speak*). Sir, the Top-of-the-List returns home.

The Old Master (*speaks*). Strike up music and ask him inside! My son, you went to the capital, and I was indeed waiting for this moment of glory. But there is one matter, which I would like to discuss with you.

Dong Yong (*speaks*). Dear benefactor, what may that be? Please speak freely and frankly.

The Old Master (*speaks*). I have a daughter who is not yet married. I would like to promise her to you, and I hope you will not reject this offer.

Dong Yong (*speaks*). I have not yet repaid your earlier favors, so how can I dare accept this one?

The Old Master (*speaks*). My daughter, where are you? There is this baby boy that Seventh Sister handed to Dong Yong at Descending Magpie Bridge. Take him with you and raise him. I have promised you for the rest of your life to the Top-of-the-List as his wedded wife. After you will have bowed to the ancestors in the front hall, we'll have a banquet in the back hall and everyone will have a great time! (*They all exit.*)

§

Scenes from *Married to a Heavenly Immortal*

(based on the version dictated by Hu Yuting, collated with the printed edition by the Kunji shuju in Anqing)

The fragment translated here starts following the song on the fifth watch of the night during the night-long weaving scene. In the performance version, the elder sisters have told Seventh Sister to spend the night with her new husband. While Eldest Sister has been weaving, singing her songs to the Five Watches Tune, the other sisters have been using their time embroidering shoes.

THE OTHER SISTERS (*speak*). I've finished my pair of shoes. I've finished my pair. Eldest Sister is dead tired. Let's pick a straw and put it up her nose!

ELDEST SISTER (*speaks*). Ohatchee! We'll have a storm!

THE OTHER SISTERS (*speak*). We'll have some rain!

ELDEST SISTER (*speaks*). I'm done weaving this silk. Let me cut it from the loom and count how many bolts there are.

THE OTHER SISTERS (*speak*). Five, six, seven, eight, …

ELDEST SISTER (*speaks*). Hey, you are all shortchanging me. I will not count them out loud, I will just pout my lips, and then I will know the number in my heart.

THE OTHER SISTERS (*speak*). Eldest Sister, how many bolts do you have?

ELDEST SISTER (*speaks*). Ten bolts and some more. Let me get a ruler and measure.

THE OTHER SISTERS (*speak*). Here is a ruler.

ELDEST SISTER (*speaks*). One, two, three. …That means an additional three feet and six inches, which we will give to brother-in-law Dong so he can make himself a green hat.

THE OTHER SISTERS (*speak*). In the mortal world a green hat is a source of shame.[55]

ELDEST SISTER (*speaks*). In that case, we will give it to our little nephew so he can have it later made into a silk coat. Where did Seventh Sister go?

SEVENTH SISTER (*enters and speaks*). Dear sisters!

THE OTHER SISTERS (*speak*). We have finished the flowered shoes with phoenix-heads!

ELDEST SISTER (*speaks*). I have woven ten bolts of silk. There is an additional three feet and six inches, which we leave here so you can later make a silk coat for our little nephew.

SEVENTH SISTER (*speaks*). Many thanks for your hard work all through the night!

ELDEST SISTER (*speaks*). It is only normal that we as sisters should come and help you out. Younger sisters, please go ahead back to the palace.

THE OTHER SISTERS (*speak*). Eldest Sister, please come with us.

ELDEST SISTER (*speaks*). I will come in a moment, I have something to discuss with Seventh Sister.

THE OTHER SISTERS (*speak*). Eldest Sister, don't conceive a longing for the mortal world! (*They exit.*)

ELDEST SISTER (*speaks*). Would I long for the mortal world?

SEVENTH SISTER (*speaks*). Let me see you sisters off!

ELDEST SISTER (*speaks*). There is no need to see us off. Let me ask you: Who has treated you well and who has treated you very well since you descended to the mortal world and entered the Fu Mansion?

SEVENTH SISTER (*speaks*). Mrs. Fu treats me well and Miss Fu treats me very well.

ELDEST SISTER (*speaks*). And what about Young Master Fu?

SEVENTH SISTER (*speaks*). He is always trying to flirt with me.

ELDEST SISTER (*speaks*). Damn, that scoundrel has the guts to flirt with an Immortal Maiden. Younger sister, this time it is you who has descended to the mortal world. If it had been me who had descended to the mortal world, I would have invoked the Five Thunders[56] and had him struck to pieces.

SEVENTH SISTER (*speaks*). How can you do that to the son of a good family?

ELDEST SISTER (*speaks*). Well, if he is the son of a good family, you invoke the Five Thunders to scare him, and you don't let them hurt his life. I cannot stay here any longer with you. When your one hundred days are up and you return to the palace, make sure to bring some fine present from the mortal world with you for your elder sister.

SEVENTH SISTER (*speaks*). What would you like?

ELDEST SISTER (*speaks*). Let me whisper it in your ears. (*Acts out blowing, and exits.*)

(SEVENTH SISTER *[sings as] level verse.*)

I see that my sisters are walking back toward the palace,
But I, Seventh Sister, now am filled with joy in my heart.
With a happy smile on my face here in the weaving room
I call for Dong Yong: Husband and wife now are ready.

(DONG YONG *enters.*)

(DONG YONG *[sings as] level verse.*)

All night in the weaving room I never closed my eyes,
Dazed and dizzy during the five watches of the night.
I step forward and I ask my darling: Did you indeed
Finish weaving those ten bolts of silk as you promised?

(SEVENTH SISTER *[sings as] level verse.*)

This last night
I spent with you
Sleeping in the weaving room,
So how can I now
Out of the blue
Suddenly have ten bolts of silk?[57]

(DONG YONG *[sings as] level verse.*)

When I hear this one word, I'm overcome by a daze:
I'm a hot man who is thrown into a basin of icy water.
Who told you to start bragging upon entering the mansion
That you could weave ten bolts of silk in one single night?
What can we do if we do not have those ten bolts of silk?
I fear you and I will not be able to suffer the punishment!

(SEVENTH SISTER *[sings as] level verse.*)

This one word of mine
Scared my husband so much

He is overcome by a dizzying daze,
So I will have
To hand him the silk
So he can clearly see it for himself.
My husband, wake up and have a good look:
Indeed I have woven these ten bolts of silk.
Here I hand these ten bolts of silk to you,
So take courage
And see the Old Master
And hand him this silk!

(Dong Yong *[sings as] level verse.*)
I look at this silk and see that all the colors are fresh,
Darling, you indeed possess both talent and skill.
When you weave a dragon, it shows all its claws;
When you weave phoenixes, the birds are frolicking.
If the people of this world will not believe me,
They only have to glance at the Golden Rooster.
Darling, my wife,
You worked so hard,
While I slept in the weaving room.

Seventh Sister (*sings*).
Your wife's skills are nothing out of the ordinary.

Dong Yong (*speaks*). Darling, you're the best!

Seventh Sister (*speaks*). Not at all! (*Exits.*)

(Dong Yong *[sings as] level verse.*)
My darling has gone to sleep in the weaving room,
I, Dong Yong, can finally lay all my worries aside.
With a swagger I'll walk into the mansion's hall,
And say, "Sir, please allow me to present the silk!"

Dong Yong (*speaks*). Sir!

(Young Master Fu *enters.*)

Young Master Fu (*speaks*). Dong Yong, you must be asking for him in order to present the silk.

Dong Yong (*speaks*). I am here to see the Old Master!

Young Master Fu (*speaks*). Slowly! Slowly! Did your wife weave ten bolts of silk?

Dong Yong (*speaks*). Indeed, she did. Please ask the Old Master to come here so I can hand him the silk in person.

Young Master Fu (*speaks*). Father, may I see you!

(Old Master Fu *enters.*)

Old Master Fu (*speaks*). Guanbao, what's going on?

Young Master Fu (*speaks*). Dong Yong wants to hand you the silk.

Old Master Fu (*speaks*). Tell him to come and see me.

Young Master Fu (*speaks*). Fine. Dong Yong, my father tells you to come over and hand him the silk.

Dong Yong (*speaks*). Sir!

Old Master Fu (*speaks*). Don't stand on formalities. Did she indeed weave those ten bolts?

Dong Yong (*speaks*). Indeed, she did. Sir, please have a look.

(Old Master Fu *[sings as] level verse.*)

As soon as I see this brocade with all its bright colors—
Dong Yong's wife indeed has a special talent and skill!
When she weaves a dragon, the dragon shows its claws,
And when she weaves phoenixes, they frolic in the sky.
Now if the people of this world would not believe me,
They need only to cast a glance at the Golden Rooster.

(*speaks*). This silk has really been woven in an excellent manner. Guanbao, tell your sister to come here. Here are ten bolts of silk. Hand them to her so she can count them.

Young Master Fu (*speaks*). Fine. Sister, are you coming or not?

(Miss Fu *enters.*)

Miss Fu (*speaks*). I'm coming, I'm coming! What's going on?

Young Master Fu (*speaks*). Just look in what an excellent manner the wife of Dong Yong wove these ten bolts of silk! When she weaves a dragon, it really resembles a dragon.

Miss Fu (*speaks*). When I weave a dragon, it also resembles a dragon!

Young Master Fu (*speaks*). When you weave a dragon, it looks like a snake on a mud wall. Look how her phoenixes really resemble phoenixes.

Miss Fu (*speaks*). So when I weave a phoenix, it doesn't resemble a phoenix?

Young Master Fu (*speaks*). When you weave a phoenix, it looks like a rain-soaked rooster. Here are ten bolts of silk. Father tells you to count them and store them in a box.

Miss Fu (*speaks*). I'll do so. This is really superior weaving! My brother cannot count, so I will hide one bolt. Brother, there are only nine bolts.

Young Master Fu (*speaks*). When father counted them a moment ago, there clearly were ten bolts, so how can there only be nine? Let me count them once again: One, two, three, four, five, six, seven, eight, nine. Indeed, we are one bolt short. Let me count them in reverse order: Ten, nine, eight, seven, six, five, four, three, two. Hey, now we are two bolts short.

Miss Fu (*speaks*). How come we are two bolts short?

Young Master Fu (*speaks*). If we are missing the tenth bolt and the first bolt, we must be missing two bolts!

Miss Fu (*speaks*). No. If we have the first, then we don't have the tenth, and if we have the tenth, then we don't have the first, so we are only missing one bolt.

Young Master Fu (*speaks*). Hola! You must have hidden one bolt from me. Walk in a circle for me.

Miss Fu (*speaks*). I'll walk in a circle if you want.

Young Master Fu (*speaks*). Walk in a really large circle.

Miss Fu (*speaks*). I'll walk in a really large circle if you want!

Young Master Fu (*speaks*). Great! That is great! This is amazing! If you can squeeze a bolt of silk between your thighs at you mother's place, you will squeeze your husband between your thighs once you go to your mother-in-law's place! Take it into the backroom and store it in a box.

Miss Fu. I will. (*Exits.*)

(Old Master Fu *enters.*)

Old Master Fu (*speaks*). Dong Yong!

Dong Yong (*speaks*). Yes sir.

OLD MASTER FU (*speaks*). Your wife has made herself very useful here by weaving this silk. So I would like you and Guanbao to become sworn brothers, and I would like your wife and my daughter to become sworn sisters. Will you agree?

DONG YONG (*speaks*). This …

OLD MASTER FU (*speaks*). How can you have any objections? I guess it must be because I have not yet burned the contract by which you sold your body. Guanbao, open the strongbox and get out that contract. I will burn it here in the presence of Dong Yong!

YOUNG MASTER FU (*speaks*). Yes, yes! The contract has been burned to ashes.

DONG YONG (*speaks*). Sir, please allow me to express my gratitude with a bow. Here I bow to my adoptive father. Darling, are you coming or not?

(SEVENTH SISTER *and* MISS FU *enter.*)

SEVENTH SISTER (*speaks*). Husband, here I am.

MISS FU (*speaks*). Father, here I am.

DONG YONG (*speaks*). Darling, you and Miss Fu will become sworn sisters. Please bow to your adoptive father.

SEVENTH SISTER (*speaks*). My husband, I will do as you say.

OLD MASTER FU (*speaks*). Daughter, come forward and recognize Dong Yong's wife as your sworn sister.

SEVENTH SISTER (*speaks*). Sir, please allow me to express my gratitude with a bow. Here I bow to my adoptive father.

MISS FU (*speaks*). I bow to my father.

OLD MASTER FU (*speaks*). Don't stand on formality. Daughter, please take your sister with you to the embroidery room and do some embroidery.

MISS FU (*speaks*). Father, I will do as you say. Elder sister, come with me.

SEVENTH SISTER (*speaks*). Younger sister, please lead the way. (*She exits following* MISS FU.)

YOUNG MASTER FU (*speaks*). I'll go there too!

OLD MASTER FU (*speaks*). None of that! You will take your elder brother along and go to the Hall of the Sage[58] to study your books.

YOUNG MASTER FU (*speaks*). Fine. Elder Brother, come with me. (*Exits.*)

DONG YONG (*recites*).

Filling the court, the nobles clad in red and purple

(*Exits.*)

OLD MASTER FU (*recites*).

Are all people who started out as poor students.
Now I have adopted the son of a different family,
I will treat him as if I had fathered him myself.

(*Exits.*)

* * *

(DONG YONG *and* YOUNG MASTER FU *enter together.*)

(DONG YONG *[sings as] level verse.*)

"On this gorgeous day I search for flowers on the banks of the Si;
This unlimited brilliant scenery has been renewed all of a sudden.
Without any effort I now know the features of the easterly winds:
A myriad of purples and thousands of reds together are spring."[59]
My younger brother leads the way toward the Hall of the Sage.

(YOUNG MASTER FU *[sings as] level verse.*)

But my belly hurts so much I cannot take any more steps.

(*Speaks*). Aiya, aiya! My belly hurts so much I cannot study.

DONG YONG (*speaks*). Brother, how can your belly hurt so much that you cannot study? Fine, I will go on ahead all by myself, and you go back home to recover from this illness. (*Exits.*)

YOUNG MASTER FU (*speaks*). Great, that worked well. I feigned to have a stomach ache, and I induced Dong Yong to go and study all by himself. His wife is embroidering flowers tonight in the upstairs room, so I will have to grab this opportunity to go upstairs tonight and try to seduce his wife. Let me go back. (*Exits.*)

* * *

(SEVENTH SISTER *and* MISS FU *enter together, followed at some distance by* GUANBAO.)

(SEVENTH SISTER *[sings as] level verse.*)

The stars in the sky are shining clearly, oh so clearly;
The orange osmanthus tree is blooming, oh so fragrantly.
It may happen that people don't respect the gods above,
But in the underworld King Yama[60] cannot be deceived.
Above the highest mountain there is heaven:
A man who commits evil cannot last for a long time.
My younger sister takes me to the embroidery room:
I pull the thread,
    She pushes the needle,
        As we artfully embroider mandarin ducks.

(SEVENTH SISTER *sits down to the east, and* MISS FU *sits down to the west.* YOUNG MASTER FU *stealthily enters from the west, but when he sees that* SEVENTH SISTER *is seated on the opposite side, he unobtrusively exits and reenters unobtrusively from the east.*)

(SEVENTH SISTER *[sings as] level verse.*)

I hear the drum tower
    Beat out the roll
        For the first watch of the night,
While we sisters
    In the embroidery room
        Artfully embroider flowery patterns.
Let me make flowery shoes with bright phoenix heads
For my husband so he can present them to the emperor.
On the drum tower
    They beat out the first watch,
        And there is no end to my sighs,
When suddenly I am assailed by a vulgar smell!

SEVENTH SISTER (*speaks*). Sister, the vulgar air here is truly oppressive, let's change places!

MISS FU (*speaks*). Fine, the two of us will change places. (YOUNG MASTER FU *acts out embracing* MISS FU.) Hey, father ordered you to study your books in the Hall of the Sage, so why did you run back here?

YOUNG MASTER FU (*speaks*). I came here for some fun. A moment ago I saw you sitting over at the other side, so why did you run to this side? I'm afraid there must be some buttock-biting beast over there!

MISS FU (*speaks*). If you still refuse to go downstairs, I will inform daddy in a moment, and he will give you a beating.

Young Master Fu (*speaks*). Well, that's fine. (*Acts out gazing at the western side and exits to reenter at the western side.*)

(Miss Fu *[sings as] level verse.*)

I hear the drum tower
Beat out the roll
Of the second watch of the night;
When I observe
My elder sister,
She has superior arts and skills.
When she embroiders a dragon, the dragon shows its claws;
When she embroiders phoenixes, the couple is frolicking.
On the drum tower
They beat out the second watch,
And there is no end to my sighs,
So I listen to the drum to know the watch of the night.

Seventh Sister (*speaks*). Sister, the vulgar air here is too oppressive, let's switch seats again.

Miss Fu (*speaks*). Fine, I will switch seats with you. (Young Master Fu *steps forward and acts out embracing* Miss Fu.) How come you still haven't gone downstairs?

Young Master Fu (*speaks*). Shit! A moment ago I clearly saw Dong Yong's wife sitting on this side, so how come she is once again sitting over there? All I end up doing is groping my own younger sister. That's really dumb. (*Exits.*)

(Seventh Sister *[sings as] level verse.*)

I hear the drum tower
Beat out the roll
For the second watch of the night;
When I think of that
Young Master Fu,
My heart is filled with resentment.
Younger sister,
You've worked so hard,
So go and sleep in the room behind,
But I will have to
Invoke the Five Thunders
To scare and frighten that fellow!

SEVENTH SISTER (*speaks*). Now wait. This Guanbao is always trying to flirt with me, so let me invoke the Five Thunders to scare him off. (*Recites.*)
May by the power of Heaven and Earth
The Thunder God descend to the mortal world.

(*The* LORD OF THUNDER[61] *and* MOTHER OF LIGHTNING *enter.*)

LORD OF THUNDER (*speaks*). Immortal Maiden, here I am!

SEVENTH SISTER (*speaks*). Forget about formalities. Let's get to business.

LORD OF THUNDER (*speaks*). Many thanks, Immortal Maiden. For what kind of mission have you called us down to this world?

SEVENTH SISTER (*speaks*). The only reason why I ordered you to descend to this mortal world is that this Guanbao is always trying to flirt with me, so I order you to go ahead and frighten him. But as he is the son of a good family, you are not allowed to hurt his life.

LORD OF THUNDER (*speaks*). We will execute your orders! (*Exits with* MOTHER OF LIGHTNING.)

(YOUNG MASTER FU *enters.*)

YOUNG MASTER FU (*speaks*). Hey, clouds are covering the skies! Listen to the thunder! The thunder is getting closer and closer! Did any one of you do something bad? If you did something evil, you have to confess. Make sure not to implicate me!

(*The* LORD OF THUNDER *and the* MOTHER OF LIGHTNING *enter. They strike* YOUNG MASTER FU *who kneels down.*)

SEVENTH SISTER (*speaks*). You gods may leave.

LORD OF THUNDER (*speaks*). Yes, we will. (*Exits with the* MOTHER OF LIGHTNING.)

SEVENTH SISTER (*speaks*). Guanbao, dear Guanbao, why are kneeling there on the floor?

YOUNG MASTER FU (*speaks*). This is great! My father feeds you and you still have to ask these two chicken hawks to swoop down on my head!

SEVENTH SISTER (*speaks*). Chicken hawks? Those were the Lord of Thunder and the Mother of Lightning descending to the mortal world!

YOUNG MASTER FU (*speaks*). Alas!

SEVENTH SISTER (*speaks*). Guanbao, will you still try to grope your elder sister the next time?

YOUNG MASTER FU (*speaks*). What about groping?

SEVENTH SISTER (*speaks*). If you are not willing to say it, you will not be able to get up!

YOUNG MASTER FU (*speaks*). I will get up anyway. Damn, I've grown roots!

SEVENTH SISTER (*speaks*). As soon as you say that you will not try to grope me next time, you can get up.

YOUNG MASTER FU (*speaks*). I will not try to grope you.

SEVENTH SISTER (*speaks*). Well, then get up! Guanbao, let me tell you: If you ever grope me again, I will invoke the Five Thunders who will strike you dead. (*Exits.*)

YOUNG MASTER FU (*speaks*). Dong Yong has at home "a big soft-shell turtle of thirty pounds—one big evil tortoise"! She can even invoke the gods of thunder! Let me tell all of you: Next time you see a fine woman who belongs to someone else, don't try to touch her. If you will try to touch her, the gods of thunder will swoop down on your head and will tell you to confess or they will strike you. (*Exits.*)

* * *

(OLD MASTER FU *enters.*)

(OLD MASTER FU *[sings as] level verse.*)

Today is the thirteenth day of the Seventh Month,[62]
So King Yama opens the gate to release all ghosts.
Dong Yong went to the grave tumulus of his father,
And I could not but
    Order Dong Yong
        To present there some wine and rice.
Upon his return
    I called for him,
        And I said to him: "Dear Dong Yong,
My dear son,
    Please come to the hall,
        I have something to discuss with you."

(DONG YONG *enters.*)

(DONG YONG *[sings as] level verse.*)

What a wonderful father
Master Fu has been:
His favors are far from shallow;
He has treated me
As a son of the family:
I study the books of the Sages.
In front of the hall
I greet my father
And present myself with a bow,
And I ask my father:
"What do you want
To discuss with your adoptive son?"

(OLD MASTER FU *[sings as] level verse.*)

My son Dong Yong,
Don't stand on ceremony,
And just stand there on one side;
Your adoptive father
Has something to say,
Please listen and take it to heart.
You and your wife sold your bodies and came to my place,
And from slave and servant you became my own children.
Today it is the Seventh Month, it is the Middle Prime,
So each and every family burns money made of paper.[63]
Your own father
In his grave tumulus
Has his wine and also his rice;
Your adoptive father
Has provided fine wine
For you, my son, as a parting feast.
Today you and your wife will go back to your home,
I hope you'll live in harmony with your smart wife.

(DONG YONG *[sings as] level verse.*)

My adoptive father,
You treat your son
With favors that are not shallow:
In the painted hall
You provide fine wine

To your son for this parting feast.
Your son will not drink
This cup of wine
But offer it up to Heaven and Earth,
Praying they may protect
My adoptive old father,
So he may live to one hundred years!
When I turn around
And see my adoptive father
I greet him with a bow of gratitude:
Your son still has
To ask you, dear father,
To provide him with traveling money.

(Old Master Fu *[sings as] level verse.*)

My son, you wait here in front of the hall for a while,
Your father will give you silver for you to go home.
Today the two of you, husband and wife, will go home,
But make sure to come and visit us once in a while.
Now it is up to you of course to come and visit or not,
But it would honor the one hundred days your father took care of you.

(Dong Yong *[sings as] level verse.*)

I have greatly benefited
From the way my father
Has taken such good care of me;
You have given me
This fine wine at my departure;
You've given me traveling money.
If your son today upon returning home,
Would forget you, adoptive father, he'd be deceiving Heaven.
Saying goodbye to my adoptive father, I go outside,
Hoping my adoptive father will tell my wife to come back with me.

(*Exits.*)

Old Master Fu (*sings*).

I see my
Son Dong Yong
Walk farther and farther away.
This fills me,
His adoptive father,

With sorrow and worries galore.
Now I cannot see
My son anymore,
I will go inside.

(*[Sings to] the tune of the immortals.*)

And in the rear chambers
I will tell my adoptive daughter
To go back together with him.

(*Exits.*)

IV. The Revised Play

The text of the revised version of *Married to a Heavenly Immortal* is available in a large number of printings. These many printings rarely present an identical text because the revised edition continued to be further revised and adapted. The earliest printing dates from 1954 and was prepared as an internal publication in connection with the 1954 East China Theater Festival.[1] It presumably provides us with the text of the play as it was performed on that occasion. The first public printing of the play appears to be the edition put out by the Shanghai wenhua chubanshe in Shanghai in 1955, which is translated here.[2] Whereas the 1954 version starts with the scene of Dong Yong selling himself as an indentured servant to the Fu family, the 1955 edition starts in heaven. The 1955 edition inserts a short scene following the opening scene in which Dong Yong is setting out for the Fus after he has buried his father. The 1955 edition separates the scene "The End of the Term" into two separate scenes by greatly developing the first section of the scene as "Eating Dates." There are also a host of minor changes throughout the play.

Later editions continue to make larger and smaller changes to the text. The text included in the Anhui volumes of the *Zhongguo difang xiqu jicheng* of 1959[3] once again specifies how each of the arias should be sung, information that is not provided in the 1954 and 1955 editions. Formally, it has one less scene than the 1955 edition because it incorporates the short scene with Dong Yong leaving his home into "Meeting on the Road." The text that was printed in 1979 in the *Anhui xiqu xuanji* (and reprinted in Li Jianye and Dong Jinyan's *Dong Yong yu xiaowenhua* of 2003)[4] clearly shows the impact of the movie. For instance, in "Weaving the Silk" Dong Yong is not only sent to sleep by Seventh Sister, but also he is ordered by his master to push the mill throughout the night. "Eating Dates" has disappeared as an independent scene and is once again much simplified and incorporated into "The End of the Term." This is because the revelation of Seventh Sister's pregnancy is now postponed to the final scene of "The Separation," when a warrior in golden armor appears onstage to transmit the Jade Emperor's edict ordering that his disobedient daughter return to heaven immediately.

Married to a Heavenly Immortal

A Huangmei Opera

Orally transmitted by Hu Yuting

Adapted by Hong Fei

Shanghai: Shanghai wenhua chubanshe, 1955

Preface

The original play was very beautiful, but it also contained chaff and dregs, the most important of which are the following two points: 1.) The play used "filial piety" as its main theme, and it used the method of "predetermined fate" to determine the meeting and separation of Dong Yong and Seventh Sister; 2.) The play nullified the struggle between Dong Yong (a serf) and the slave-holding Fu family, and thus did away with class struggle. The revised edition retains Seventh Sister's descent to earth, but it excises the scene of Dong Yong moving Heaven and Earth by his filial piety; it preserves the marriage of one hundred days, but it excises the use of "predetermined fate"; it retains Seventh Sister's pregnancy, but it excises the scenes of Dong Yong traveling to the capital and presenting treasure, and of the Immortal Maiden bringing the baby; and following Dong Yong and Seventh Sister's wedding below the Shady Scholartree, when the ten bolts of cloud brocade have been completed and on the eve of completion of the term of servitude, it adds descriptions of the details of Dong Yong and Seventh Sister's daily life . Through their mutual concern and care, it gives expression to the deep love for life of the laboring masses of ancient times and their beautiful hopes for the future.

This play was first revised in 1953 by Hong Fei,[5] of the Creative Group of the Bureau for the Management of Cultural Heritage in Anhui province, who based his revision on the orally transmitted version by the old Huangmei Opera artist Hu Yuting and also consulted *The Shady Scholartree* in Sichuan Opera and Jinhua Opera (*Wuju*). When it was later performed by the Anhui Provincial Huangmei Opera Company, the opinions of experienced artists like Wang Shaofang, Yan Fengying, and Zhang Yunfeng 張雲鳳 and of directors Li Liping and Qiao Zhiliang were incorporated. Later, it was revised more than ten times by Hong Fei. During this process of revision Hong Fei received concrete direction and assistance from the responsible cadres of the Anhui Provincial Party Committee of the Chinese Communist Party and from the Bureau for the Management of Cultural Heritage.

When it was performed at the 1954 East China Theater Festival, it received first prize for its script. Following the performance at this meeting, it was once again revised, taking into account the opinions of all sides.

Dramatis Personae

Dong Yong

Seventh Sister

God of the Soil

Eldest Sister

Second Sister

Third Sister

Fourth Sister

Fifth Sister

Sixth Sister

Fu Guanbao

Old Master Fu

Scene 1. Visiting Magpie Bridge

(Seventh Immortal Sister *enters.*)

Seventh Sister (*sings*).

Incense smoke wafts upwards while colored clouds surge:
Seventh Sister sits morosely by the side of Jasper Pond.
Mortal men may say that the divine immortals live well,
But who knows the innermost secrets of these immortals?

Sitting all the while in the Palace of Dipper and Buffalo I feel very much depressed. Today my father the king is treating the divine immortals of the four seas to a grand banquet, so I must use this opportunity to invite my immortal sisters to have some fun outside of the palace. Sisters, please come!

(The immortal sisters *arrive as if floating through the air.*)

Eldest Sister (*recites*). Sitting all day long in Dipper and Buffalo,

The other sisters (*recite*). We are overcome by an endless depression.

Seventh Sister, why did you invite us to come here?

Seventh Sister. I am feeling down and depressed, so I wanted to have some fun outside of the palace with my sisters.

Second Sister. The regulations of our father the king are very strict. It can't be done!

Seventh Sister. Second Sister, don't be afraid. Today our father the king is treating the immortals of the four seas to a grand banquet, so we are free to do what we want.

The other sisters. Eldest Sister, what do you think?

Eldest Sister. Our father the king is treating the divine immortals of the four seas to a grand banquet, so we are free to do what we want. It should be quite possible to go out and have some fun.

The other sisters (*excitedly*). Eldest Sister, where shall we go?

Eldest Sister. Let me see. ... Let's go to the Imperial Pond!

Third Sister. What's the fun in going there?

ELDEST SISTER. There you have immortal fishes, immortal cranes, immortal geese, immortal ducks. …

THE OTHER SISTERS. Boring! Boring!

THIRD SISTER. Seventh Sister, where do you want to go?

SEVENTH SISTER. I want to go to the Heavenly River!

SECOND SISTER (*hesitatingly, flinching*). To the Heavenly River?

THIRD SISTER. You, you have no courage at all! (*Addressing* SEVENTH SISTER.) Seventh Sister, what's the fun in going to the Heavenly River?

SEVENTH SISTER. On both banks of the Heavenly River you have immortal flowers and immortal plants. And if you stand on Magpie Bridge you can view the scenery of heaven and earth all together!

THE OTHER SISTERS. Great! Let's go to the Heavenly River!

(*They all take off, but* ELDEST SISTER *doesn't make a move.*)

THIRD SISTER. Eldest Sister, let's go to the Heavenly River!

ELDEST SISTER (*angrily*). You all go! I will look after the house. (*She prepares to go inside.*)

FOURTH SISTER and SIXTH SISTER. Eldest Sister, please!

ELDEST SISTER. I should not go out and play together with you little kids.

SEVENTH SISTER. Eldest Sister, the proverb says: "Time does not exist in the palaces of heaven; age does not apply to the divine immortals." In my eyes, Eldest Sister, you are even younger than we are!

ELDEST SISTER (*turning anger into a smile*). You, you always have a ready answer! That's why I love you so much!

THE OTHER SISTERS. Eldest Sister, let's all go together to Magpie Bridge!

ELDEST SISTER. Fine!

THE OTHER SISTERS. Eldest Sister, you lead the way!

ELDEST SISTER. Follow me!

THE OTHER SISTERS. Most happily!

(THE IMMORTAL SISTERS *rise and dance as if floating through the air.*)

THE IMMORTAL SISTERS (*sing*).

As if borne on the wind we arrive at the Heavenly River,
The Heavenly River like a floating belt of white waves.
From Magpie Bridge we seven sisters, elder and younger,
Watch fresh flowers bloom in the world of mortal men.

THIRD SISTER. Eldest Sister, Seventh Sister's proposal really was better! Look at all those pretty sights in the mortal world!

ELDEST SISTER. Indeed, it really is great fun!

(THE IMMORTAL MAIDENS *look in all directions, with happy smiles on their faces.*)

SEVENTH SISTER (*hopping like a sparrow*). Sisters, look!

THE OTHER SISTERS. Look at what?

SEVENTH SISTER. Look at that old man. On his head he is wearing a large bamboo hat and he is covered by a straw cape. Holding his punting pole he is standing at the prow of his boat. …

ELDEST SISTER. That is a fisherman.

THE OTHER SISTERS. A fisherman!

ELDEST SISTER. Sisters, let me characterize him in a few lines.

THE OTHER SISTERS. You have to characterize him really well.

ELDEST SISTER. Listen!

(THE IMMORTAL MAIDENS *dance, imitating the actions of the fisherman.*)

ELDEST SISTER (*sings*).

The fisherman lives in the middle of rivers and lakes;
On both banks the reeds resemble a surrounding wall.
Punting his boat from the shore he throws out his net—
One net full of fishes and shrimp is one net of food!

THE OTHER SISTERS. You have characterized him well!

SEVENTH SISTER. Eldest Sister, look at that young man on top of that high hill. On his shoulder he carries a carrying pole and in his hand he holds an axe. …

ELDEST SISTER. That is a woodcutter.

SEVENTH SISTER. How can that young man cutting wood in the deepest mountains not be afraid of wolves and tigers?

ELDEST SISTER. He has his axe with him.

SECOND SISTER. Let me characterize that woodcutter in a few lines.

THIRD SISTER (*mockingly*). "The regulations of our father the king are very strict. It can't be done!"

SECOND SISTER. You sharp-tongued hussy!

SEVENTH SISTER. Allow Second Sister to characterize him in a few lines!

THE OTHER SISTERS. You have to characterize him very well.

SECOND SISTER. Listen!

(THE IMMORTAL MAIDENS *dance imitating the actions of the woodcutter.*)

SECOND SISTER (*sings*).

In his hand he holds an axe with which to open mountains;
Carrying a carrying pole on his shoulder, he climbs a hill.
He is not afraid of jackal and wolf or of tiger and leopard—
From the firewood he sells he buys rice, thus making a living.

THE OTHER SISTERS. You characterized him well.

THIRD SISTER. Seventh Sister, please look. …

SEVENTH SISTER. On the fields of the farms people are coming and going, plowing and sowing and transplanting the seedlings. …

ELDEST SISTER. Those farmers really have a busy life!

THE OTHER SISTERS. Really too busy!

SEVENTH SISTER. The farmers are fully occupied throughout all four seasons of the year. They really have a bitter life!

THIRD SISTER. Let me characterize them in a few lines.

SECOND SISTER (*taking revenge*). But you'll have to do away with your sharp tongue!

SEVENTH SISTER. Third Sister, you have to characterize them really well!

THIRD SISTER. Listen! (*She sings.*)

The people who work the fields have no moment for leisure;
Their faces face the yellow earth, their backs face the sky.
Their only wish is to reap a good harvest of the five grains,
So they'll have no worries about food, no worries about clothing.

THE OTHER SISTERS. You have characterized them well.

SEVENTH SISTER. Sisters, look at that student seated in the Hall of Loving the Sage!

FOURTH SISTER. Where?

SEVENTH SISTER. Over there!

ELDEST SISTER. How come it had to be you who spotted him?

FOURTH SISTER. Sisters, let me characterize him in a few lines.

THE OTHER SISTERS. You have to characterize him very well!

FOURTH SISTER. Listen! (*She sings.*)
Seated by the cold window the student studies the books,
At midnight by the light of the lamp, till the sky brightens.
For ten years by the window he perseveres in his studies,
Hoping that his name will be listed on the golden plaque![6]

SEVENTH SISTER. Here they come!

ELDEST SISTER. Here they come who?

SEVENTH SISTER. Look at them blowing the pipes and beating the gongs, the sound of the drums resounding to heaven. …

ELDEST SISTER. That is a wedding procession taking the bride to the house of the groom.

SEVENTH SISTER (*deep in thought*). A wedding procession!

SECOND SISTER (*not daring to look directly*). A wedding procession?

THIRD SISTER. Second Sister, just look! This wedding procession is so much fun!

SECOND SISTER (*reluctantly*). Oh. …

SEVENTH SISTER. Sisters, let me characterize it in a few lines!

SECOND SISTER (*filled with fear*). This …

THIRD SISTER (*supporting* SEVENTH SISTER). Go ahead, characterize it!

SEVENTH SISTER. Eldest Sister?

ELDEST SISTER. Characterize it in a few lines.

SEVENTH SISTER. Dear sisters, please listen! (*She sings.*)

The world of men is quite different from the heavenly world:
Over there men and women get married, becoming a couple!
The love between husband and wife is beyond description,
Resembling a pair of mandarin ducks on the reservoir pond.

(The other sisters *are surprised.*)

Third Sister (*smiling sympathetically*). You dead hussy, you truly have no shame!

Second Sister (*addressing* Seventh Sister). You, you are too reckless and wanton!

Eldest Sister. Enough! Enough! As long as nobody snitches, nothing has happened.

Second Sister (*filled with concern*). Sisters, shouldn't we go back?

Seventh Sister (*looking at the mortal world as if her eye has been caught by something, and answering lackadaisically*). Oh …

Third Sister. It's still early!

Eldest Sister. Hey, look at him!

The other sisters. At whom?

Eldest Sister. At that peasant boy!

(Seventh Sister *looks intently at the mortal world; she remains silent but her face reveals her sympathy.*)

Seventh Sister. He has heavy eyebrows and big eyes and a good and honest face, but why is he weeping and crying, crying and weeping?

Eldest Sister. That guy? He lives in Danyang and his name is Dong Yong. Together with his father he made a living tilling the fields. But because the family was destitute, when his father died he did not have a coffin for a proper funeral and he had no other way but to sell himself as a slave. That's why he is overcome with sorrow, and cries and weeps, weeps and cries!

The other sisters. Such filial piety is truly rare!

Seventh Sister (*filled with sympathy*). He is so lonely and forlorn, without anyone to rely on. He is really pitiable!

Third Sister. I would say you are falling in …

(*A bell resounds.*)

SECOND SISTER. Eldest Sister, let's hurry back!

THE OTHER SISTERS. Eldest Sister, please!

ELDEST SISTER. Please!

(THE IMMORTAL SISTERS *exit.*) (*The middle screen comes down, and* SEVENTH SISTER *enters by herself.*)

SEVENTH SISTER (*sings*).

Returning to the palace following a visit to Magpie Bridge,
I, Seventh Sister, suddenly feel ill at ease, deeply disturbed.
Don't mention the five-colored bright clouds and their dazzling luster—
How can they compare to flowers blooming in pairs in the world below?
Don't mention the immortals happily united at the banquet of peaches—
How can it compare to husband and wife in the world below, shoulder to shoulder enjoying their simple fare?
Don't mention to me the pure bliss the divine immortals enjoy—
They live a life like that of criminals who are locked up in jail.
When I turn back and once again look at the mortal world,
I see green hills and blue rivers that are tightly intertwined;
A bamboo fence, a straw-thatched cottage, a bustling crowd,
And then that dilapidated hovel leaning against some hill.
That Dong Yong is gathering his belongings in that cold hovel;
As he faces his pack and his umbrella, his tears continue to fall.
He there is overcome with sorrow, I here am filled with depression;
He there is shedding tears, while my heart is filled with emotion.
I, Seventh Sister, would like to descend to earth—

(*The bell resounds.*)

But once again I hear the resounding bell and drums!
My father the king is seated in Lingxiao Hall and
The divine immortals of the four seas wait at his sides.
While on his left side a blue dragon encircles a pillar,
A white tiger with wide-open maw sits on his right side.
I am not at all afraid of that blue dragon or that white tiger,
But what I indeed fear are the strict regulations of Lingxiao Hall …
But if I do not descend to the mortal world now today,
Until what year will I have to wait, alone and forlorn?

(*Determined.*)

I will go to the mortal world—off to the mortal world;
I've made up my mind: I will go to the mortal world!
Deceiving my father the king and also my elder sisters,
I will oh so quietly descend to the mortal world below.

(Eldest Sister *enters.*)

Eldest Sister. Seventh Sister, you are staying behind!

Seventh Sister (*flustered*). Eldest Sister!

Eldest Sister. Where are you going, all by yourself?

Seventh Sister (*seeking an excuse*). Oh … I dropped something a moment ago at Magpie Bridge!

Eldest Sister. If you dropped something at Magpie Bridge, you should be going to Magpie Bridge to find it, so why are going to the Southern Gate of Heaven? The Southern Gate of Heaven is the road to the mortal world!

Seventh Sister. This …

Eldest Sister. Don't be afraid. Silly kid, I am fully aware of your innermost secret!

Seventh Sister. Eldest Sister!

Eldest Sister (*with concern and urgency*). This is not some funny game. We definitely cannot allow our father the king to know about it!

Seventh Sister. What, our father the king?

Eldest Sister. I've been told that our father the king, now that he has treated the divine immortals of the four seas to a banquet, will go to the Queen Mother of the Western Heaven.

Seventh Sister (*elated*). So our father the king will go to the Western Heaven!

Eldest Sister. When you descend to the mortal world this time, some hills will be high and some low, and some people will be good and some bad, so you have to be very careful indeed.

Seventh Sister. This …

Eldest Sister. This white fan is given to you by Third Sister.

SEVENTH SISTER. Does she also know?

ELDEST SISTER. If you want other people not to know, you'd better not do it at all.

SEVENTH SISTER. Please convey my thanks to her!

ELDEST SISTER. I am giving you a stick of Disaster Incense. When you meet with disaster, burn this stick of incense, and we your six elder sisters will come down to earth to help you out.

SEVENTH SISTER. Eldest Sister, many thanks! (*She finds it hard to let go of* ELDEST SISTER.)

ELDEST SISTER. Take care of yourself on the road!

SEVENTH SISTER (*sings*).

Many thanks, my eldest sister, for all your kindness
In giving me this white fan and this Disaster Incense.

(ELDEST SISTER *exits.*)

Riding on my auspicious cloud I run as fast as is possible,
I am determined to find Dong Yong in the world below.
I want to be united with him in a right and proper marriage;
May the love of husband and wife last for one hundred years.

(*Exits.*)

Scene 2. Leaving the Hovel

(Dong Yong *enters.*)

Dong Yong (*sings*).

My father has now been buried on an abandoned hillside;
I, Dong Yong, weep so much that my tears will never dry.
Because we are so poor as if washed clean by water,
I sold my body in order to bury my father—how sad!
In the village ahead lives a certain magnate, old Mr. Fu;
He is extremely wealthy, his gold is piled up like mountains.
He gave me two bolts of white linen, five ounces of silver,
But wanted me to become his laborer for a full three years.
He told me to mourn at the grave for three full days
And then to start on the job and not to procrastinate!
So I got together my luggage and picked up my umbrella;
This bare and empty hovel is now a most distressing sight!
When in days now past I would open the door and go out,
My father saw me off, accompanying me part of the way.
With hundreds and thousands of words he instructed me,
Afraid that I might suffer from hunger, and afraid I might suffer from cold.
Today as I open the door and go out, no one shows any concern;
To whom can I tell the bitter suffering in my innards?
Let me get a piece of rock, block the door of this hovel!
Oh, this inexpressible bitter sorrow, this unresponsive heaven!
Alas, year upon year we encountered famine and drought,
Filling our stomachs with the bark of trees, the roots of grass.
And now today I depart to become an indentured laborer—
I am afraid that my torment and suffering will only increase.
This truly is a case of a pig's gall attached to the huanglian tree;[7]
Bitter suffering on top of suffering, a heart pierced by arrows!
Wiping the tears from my eyes I set out on the road ahead—
There is no other way out for me but to go to Fu Family Bay.

(Dong Yong *exits.*)

Scene 3. Meeting on the Road

(Seventh Sister *enters.*)

Seventh Sister (*sings*).

A myriad rays of morning glow, auspicious clouds without number:
Descending to earth below, I, Seventh Sister, run as fast as a shuttle.
At the Southern Gate of Heaven I take off my immortal garments,
And in an instant change myself into a beauty of the human realm.
Arriving in Danyang District I step down on the ground,
And all I see by the side of the road is this one scholartree.
Its dark branches and green leaves grow most luxuriantly;
On its branches there are also birds that build their nests.
And in these nests the birds are staying in couples, in pairs,
Enjoying greater happiness than even the divine immortals.

Dong Yong (*backstage*). Such bitter suffering!

Seventh Sister (*sings*).

Suddenly I hear the voice of a man complaining bitterly:
This must be Dong Yong, who is approaching this spot.
I will be standing here on the main road, waiting for him,
And see what he chooses to do once he has noticed me.

(Dong Yong *enters.*)

Dong Yong (*sings*).

Carrying my umbrella, with my luggage on my back—
Tear after tear coursing down, soak the pit of my breast.
Hastily, hurriedly I hasten on in a hurry on the road—

(*He notices* Seventh Sister, *is taken aback,* [*then sings*].)

From where appeared such a heavenly beauty[8] here on the road?
She has her eyes fixed on me and is watching me;
What is the reason she is flashing me such smiles?
My heart is in such turmoil it can easily catch on fire,
So I don't have the stomach to look at this beauty.
My father also has warned me on many occasions
That banter of boys and girls will result in scandal.
I will not travel the upper road, but will sneak off to the lower road,
So I will not stir up stormy waves on level ground.

(Dong Yong *exits.*)

SEVENTH SISTER (*sings*).

Just look how discreet and prudent that Dong Yong is!
As soon as he sees me, his face is suffused with red!
If he and I were to be married as husband and wife
Our love and affection would be without any limit.
But alas, it is impossible to propose to him in person;
I'll have to ask the scholartree to be our go-between.

Local God of the Soil, where are you?

(GOD OF THE SOIL *enters*).

GOD OF THE SOIL (*recites*).

God of the Soil, yes, God of the Soil,
Receiving offerings twice each year:
On the second day of the Second Month
And on the first day too of the Eighth.

Immortal Maiden, my greetings!

SEVENTH SISTER. Take your ease.

GOD OF THE SOIL. Immortal Maiden, why have you called for me on coming to this place?

SEVENTH SISTER. Because Dong Yong has left his cold hovel and is on his way to the Fus to start his job, I want to help him out. Wouldn't that be a good idea?

GOD OF THE SOIL. Dong Yong is a good and honest person. Immortal Maiden, if you are ready to help him out, I will be happy to make my small contribution.

SEVENTH SISTER (*happily*). Are you willing to help me out?

GOD OF THE SOIL. Yes, I want to be of assistance.

SEVENTH SISTER. If so, I will ask you to do something for me.

GOD OF THE SOIL. Please let me know what to do.

SEVENTH SISTER. I want to be married to him as husband and wife, so I want you to serve as the matchmaker and go-between.

GOD OF THE SOIL. This is … wonderful, definitely wonderful, but I'm afraid that if the Jade Emperor comes to know about it, I will be blamed!

SEVENTH SISTER. The saying goes: "The one who is responsible takes the blame." How could I be willing to involve you in my misfortune?

GOD OF THE SOIL. I am happy to serve as the go-between, but how should I go about it?

SEVENTH SISTER. I'll whisper it in your ear. (*She whispers to the* GOD OF THE SOIL.)

GOD OF THE SOIL. Congratulations, Immortal Maiden, I will do exactly what you told me to do.

(GOD OF THE SOIL *exits.*)

SEVENTH SISTER (*sings*).

I, Seventh Sister, have firmly made up my mind,
I've told the God of the Soil to serve as go-between.
The jade cage has been broken, the phoenix flies off:
I am at liberty to go to the west or go to the east.
When an immortal walks, she seems carried by the wind:
On the lower road I'll greet Dong Yong most politely.

(DONG YONG *enters.*)

DONG YONG (*sings*).

While living in poverty I unfortunately lost my father;
This boat that has sprung a leak runs into a head wind!
Suppressing my sadness, eyes filled with tears, I walk the lower road.

(DONG YONG *notices* SEVENTH SISTER.)

And on this lower road I run again into that upper road girl!

Sister, it's you who is in the wrong!

SEVENTH SISTER. And why is it me who is in the wrong?

DONG YONG. When a moment ago I was walking on the upper main road, you blocked my way, and now I walk on the lower main road, and you again block my way. That's why I say that it is you who is in the wrong.

SEVENTH SISTER (*deliberately*). Bah! (*Friendly.*) Brother, since ancient times they say: "The main road leads to heaven, and each walks on his own side." You are not going to tell me that I am not allowed to stand where you are allowed to walk?

DONG YONG (*speaking to himself*). She makes sense. Indeed, I cannot claim that she is not allowed to stand where I am allowed to walk. (*Addressing* SEVENTH SISTER.) Sister, please do me a favor and let me pass by.

SEVENTH SISTER. Now that sounds reasonable. So, please.

(*They both start walking, but* SEVENTH SISTER *deliberately bumps into* DONG YONG.)

DONG YONG. Sister, why do you bump into me?

SEVENTH SISTER. You carry a pack on your back and hold an umbrella in your hand. You are preoccupied, flustered and flurried, and bump into me, but have the gall to blame me!

DONG YONG (*speaking to himself*). Indeed, I am preoccupied, flustered and flurried, and I may well have bumped into her. (*Addressing* SEVENTH SISTER.) Please allow me to pass once again.

(*They both start moving, but when* SEVENTH SISTER *again wants to bump into* DONG YONG, *the latter observes her intention.*)

DONG YONG. This time it was clearly you who wanted to bump into me!

SEVENTH SISTER. I don't care whether you bumped into me or I bumped into you, but let me ask you this: Do you want to pass?

DONG YONG. Of course I want to pass!

SEVENTH SISTER. Come to think of it, it must be because of a karmic bond that you and I have run into each other here on the road. Where do you live? And what is your surname and your given name? If you tell me, I will let you go on your trip.

DONG YONG. Sister! (*sings.*)

I live in Danyang and have lost my father and mother;
I am known as DongYong, I am an orphan by fate.
Because I didn't have a coffin when my father died,
I sold myself to the Fu family: I now am their slave.
Please, Sister, be so kind as to step aside for a while,
Enable this destitute person not to be late for his job!

SEVENTH SISTER (*sings*).

As I hear you narrate your most innermost feelings,
I, Seventh Sister, also am overcome by emotion.

You are like a rice seedling that lacks rainwater,
But a day will come when you will flower and bear fruit.
You're like a goose that is separated from the flock,
Battered by the rain and blown about by the wind.
Dear brother, my hope is you won't reject me,
Because I would like with you …

DONG YONG. What would you like?

SEVENTH SISTER (*sings*).
To soar on shared wings!

DONG YONG (*sings*).
Hearing her words, my heart is filled with joy:
She would like with me to soar on shared wings!
Roosting together, soaring together, utterly free—

(*Realizing his difficult situation.*)
But alas, I have met with disaster, like a chicken in a cooking pot!
I am now a slave, I am not my own master:
How can I dare hope to be united with her as husband and wife?

(*Thinking again of his extremely difficult situation, he does not know how to react.*)

(*Inserted speech.*) Sister!
Why did you speak these words just a moment ago
Of wanting to soar on shared wings with Dong Yong?
You are like a fresh flower blooming in early spring,
And I resemble a tender willow ravaged by frost!
I hope you will allow me to pursue my journey—
Look, the red sun in the sky is moving to the west!

SEVENTH SISTER. Oh, oh, oh! I am delaying your journey, so please allow me to offer my apologies by making a bow.

DONG YONG. Allow me to bow in return!

SEVENTH SISTER. Brother, you carry a pack on your back and hold an umbrella in your hand. Not just one bow, but even ten bows or one hundred bows in this way could not count as a proper bow.

DONG YONG. You are right. With a pack on my back and an umbrella in my hand, not just one bow, but even ten bows or one hundred bows wouldn't count. (*Addressing* SEVENTH SISTER.) Fine. Let me put down my pack and my umbrella, and then perform a bow. Sister, please accept my bow.

SEVENTH SISTER (*recites.*)

Whether it is the proper manner of a bow or not,
I grab your pack and your umbrella and take off!

(*While* DONG YONG *is performing his bow,* SEVENTH SISTER *sticks a white fan in the back of his neck, and also takes away his pack and his umbrella.*)

DONG YONG (*speaking to himself*). Let me get my luggage and my umbrella and pursue my journey. Hey, how come my pack and umbrella have disappeared? (*Addressing* SEVENTH SISTER.) Hey, Sister, why did you make off with my pack and my umbrella?

SEVENTH SISTER. This pack and this umbrella are mine!

DONG YONG. These are clearly mine!

SEVENTH SISTER. These are mine! Mine!

(GOD OF THE SOIL *enters.*)

GOD OF THE SOIL. Haha! Haha! One boy and one girl, out in the fields, pulling and grabbing—what does it look like?

DONG YONG. As if it were not enough that I have to deal with this one person bereft of reason, here comes another!

GOD OF THE SOIL. Who says that I am bereft of reason?

DONG YONG. Uncle, if you can reason with her that would be great. Let me tell you the story.

GOD OF THE SOIL. Go ahead!

DONG YONG. When a moment ago I was traveling on the upper main road, this girl blocked my way, and when I took the lower main road, she once again blocked my way. We exchanged some words, and then she made a bow as an apology and I returned her bow. But she said that my bow did not count because I did not put down my pack and my umbrella, but when I put down my pack and my umbrella and made my bow, she took off with my pack and my umbrella. Now tell me, who here is in the right?

GOD OF THE SOIL. If you tell it like this, you are in the right.

DONG YONG. Uncle, and how much am I in the right?

God of the Soil. As much as a sesame seed.

Dong Yong. Big or small, in the end I am in the right.

God of the Soil. Sister, (Seventh Sister *and* God of the Soil *exchange a smile of understanding*) that fellow says that a moment ago when he followed the upper road you blocked his way, and that you again blocked his way when he took the lower road. When the two of you had some words, you made a bow to him to offer your apologies, and he in turn made his bow. But you said that it could not count as a bow since he had not yet put down his pack and his umbrella, and when he put down his pack and his umbrella, you took off with his pack and his umbrella. Doesn't this mean that you are in the wrong?

Seventh Sister. Uncle, you cannot listen to only one side of the story. I also have my side to tell.

God of the Soil. Go ahead.

Seventh Sister. This fellow is called Dong Yong. Three days ago he passed in front of our door and he promised me that we would travel together. But today here on this bright and sunny road he wants to dump me! Now tell me who is in the right?

God of the Soil. He wants to dump you?

Seventh Sister. Yes, he does!

God of the Soil. If that's the case, you are in the right!

Seventh Sister. How much am I in the right?

God of the Soil. As much as a mung bean.

Seventh Sister. Big or small, in the end I am in the right!

God of the Soil. Fellow, it turns out that you are in the wrong.

Dong Yong. How can you conclude that I am in the wrong?

God of the Soil. That girl there says that three days ago you passed in front of her door and promised her that you would go together, but here today on this bright and sunny day you wanted to dump her. That's why I say you are in the wrong.

Dong Yong. If we promised each other to go together, what did I give to her as proof and what did she give to me as evidence?

GOD OF THE SOIL. Indeed. Girlie, if you promised each other to go together, what did he give you as proof and what did you give him as evidence?

SEVENTH SISTER. There's proof and there's evidence.

GOD OF THE SOIL. What proof and what evidence?

SEVENTH SISTER. He gave me his pack and his umbrella as proof. (*She points to the pack and the umbrella.*) And I gave him a white fan as evidence.

GOD OF THE SOIL (*addressing* DONG YONG). There's proof and there's evidence.

DONG YONG. What proof and what evidence?

GOD OF SOIL. You gave her the pack and the umbrella as proof, and she gave you a white fan as evidence.

DONG YONG. And where is that white fan?

GOD OF THE SOIL (*addressing* SEVENTH SISTER). And where is that white fan?

SEVENTH SISTER. Behind his neck.

GOD OF THE SOIL. Behind your neck.

DONG YONG (*feels, and finding the fan is flabbergasted.*) Hey, that's weird! (*Looks at* SEVENTH SISTER, *looks at* GOD OF THE SOIL, *at a loss what to do.*)

GOD OF THE SOIL. Do you want an official mediation? Or do you want a private settlement?

DONG YONG. What would an official mediation mean?

GOD OF THE SOIL. Since ancient times it is said: "An official mediation leads to a painful situation." We will take you to the offices of the authorities, and you will be punished with forty strokes by the heavy cudgel.

DONG YONG. And a private settlement?

GOD OF THE SOIL. Now a private settlement. … (*Looks back at* SEVENTH SISTER, *who is visibly overcome by shame.*) The matter is settled as soon as you marry this girl as your lawfully wedded wife for one hundred years of bliss.

DONG YONG (*looking at* SEVENTH SISTER *and speaking to himself*). Well, this girl looks quite beautiful, she is straightforward and has a ready answer, so it definitely would be great if we could become husband and wife. … But alas, first of all, my parents have passed away and I've been reduced to poverty, and second, I've sold my self as a slave and I am not my own master. … (*Addressing* God of the Soil, *finding an excuse.*) Uncle, that would indeed be wonderful, but … there is no bride-giver and no go-between.

God of the Soil. I can serve as bride-giver and go-between!

Dong Yong. Uncle, one head cannot wear two hats: the bride-giver cannot serve as the go-between, and the go-between cannot serve as the bride-giver.

God of the Soil (*addressing* Seventh Sister). That fellow says that one head cannot wear two hats; that the bride-giver cannot serve as the go-between and that the go-between cannot serve as the bride-giver.

Seventh Sister. Why on earth? So the bride-giver cannot serve as the go-between. … Uncle, you are advanced in years, can you give me away?

God of the Soil. I can give you away.

Seventh Sister (*lifts her head and looks.*) Let's ask this scholartree to be the go-between!

God of the Soil. What? This scholartree, the go-between?

Seventh Sister. You go and tell that fellow to go over and call out to the tree three times, and if the tree opens its mouth and starts talking, then we will become husband and wife for one hundred years. But if the tree does not answer, he can follow his road to the end of the world and I will cross my single-log bridge.

God of the Soil (*addressing* Dong Yong). Is it fine with you if I am the bride-giver?

Dong Yong. That is fine with me.

God of the Soil (*lifts his head and looks.*) How about asking this scholartree to be the go-between?

Dong Yong. That scholartree is a dumb tree!

God of the Soil. You go up to the tree and call out to the tree three times. If the tree opens its mouth and starts to speak, you and the girl will be husband and wife for one hundred years. If the tree does not respond, you travel your road to the end of the world, and she will cross her single-log bridge.

DONG YONG. That tree cannot speak even if I call thirty times or three hundred times, let alone three times!

GOD OF THE SOIL. You just try.

DONG YONG. Old scholartree! This girl and I hope to be married for one hundred years of bliss, so please open your mouth and speak if you are willing to be the matchmaker and go-between! (*There is no reaction.*) Uncle, do you hear anything?

GOD OF THE SOIL. I don't hear a thing! (*Addressing* SEVENTH SISTER.) Give the pack to him! (*Addressing* DONG YONG.) Try a second time!

DONG YONG. Old scholartree! This girl and I hope to be married for one hundred years of bliss, so please open your mouth and speak if you are willing to be the matchmaker and go-between! (*There is no reaction.*) Uncle, do you hear anything?

GOD OF THE SOIL. I don't hear a thing! (*Addressing* SEVENTH SISTER.) Give him his umbrella.

SEVENTH SISTER. I've given him his pack and his umbrella. If he now runs off, I will get even with you!

GOD OF THE SOIL. She has given you your umbrella. You have tried two times, so that still leaves one try, so call out to the tree!

DONG YONG. Old scholartree! This girl and I hope to be married for one hundred years of bliss, so please open your mouth and speak if you are willing to be the matchmaker and go-between!

(SEVENTH SISTER *works her magic on the scholartree by waving her fan.*)

(*Backstage sings.*)

The scholartree opens its mouth and starts speaking,
Addressing Dong Yong, it says: Now listen carefully!
You and this girl will be united in wedlock together,
Because this scholartree will serve as the go-between!

DONG YONG (*sings.*)

This is truly something unprecedented, miraculous!
Since when do dumb trees have the gift of speech?
I turn around and honor you, Uncle, with a deep bow,
But there is something that I have to inform you of.
Above my head I don't have a single tile to shelter my body;
Under my feet I don't have one inch of land to call my own.

In my cold hovel I did not have even half a pint of rice,
So I sold myself as a slave to suffer my owner's abuse.
If this girl is going to be married to me, I am afraid
That she'll blame me when she suffers hunger and cold!

(SEVENTH SISTER *gives a hint to* GOD OF THE SOIL.)

GOD OF THE SOIL (*sings*).

Dong Yong, don't be filled with doubt and anxiety!
Unless I explain the situation, you won't understand:
You may not have a single tile, but she won't reject you;
You may not have one inch of land, but she's only too eager!
All she wants is to live in harmony as husband and wife—
What does she care about suffering hunger, suffering cold?
Come, come, come! Greet each other, filled with harmony,
To be wedded below the scholartree as husband and wife.

(DONG YONG, *objecting, does not move forward.*)

GOD OF THE SOIL. Now come!

DONG YONG. Uncle! (*sings.*)

It's not that I, Dong Yong, don't want to move forward,
But there still is a major problem that I have to tell you.
I have become an indentured servant of the Fu family,
I have sold my body to be their slave for a full three years.
The sales contract says I am unmarried, have no dependents—
How can we now arrive there together as husband and wife?
If those people in the Fu family will treat you badly,
How will I be able to support that, be able to be at ease?

(GOD OF THE SOIL *looks back at* SEVENTH SISTER. SEVENTH SISTER *walks over to* DONG YONG.)

SEVENTH SISTER (*sings*).

Dong Yong, please stop shedding this stream of tears,
Because in my heart I've clearly made up my mind.
While you will be the long-term laborer at that place,
I will wash the clothes and starch the shirts over there.
Since we are united in wedlock as husband and wife,
I have no fear of any temporary misery and vexation!

DONG YONG (*sings*).

Hearing these words, I am secretly filled with joy:
It is hard to find someone with such a good heart!

(*Inserted speech.*) Sister,

> Today you and I are wedded as husband and wife,
> I only fear I will make you suffer misery and pain.

GOD OF THE SOIL. Fine! There is no need for all that talk! Come, bow to each other as husband and wife! (DONG YONG *and* SEVENTH SISTER *bow to each other.*) So now you are married as husband and wife, the happiest event in the world! But out on the road I have no present I can give you—please don't blame me for that.

SEVENTH SISTER. Uncle, don't be so formal.

GOD OF THE SOIL. Dong Yong, you and this girl go to the Fu Mansion to start on your job, and I now have to say goodbye.

DONG YONG. I will see you off.

GOD OF THE SOIL. There is no need to see me off.

DONG YONG. Well, goodbye then!

GOD OF THE SOIL. Bye! (*Exits.*)

SEVENTH SISTER. Which road do we have to take to the Fu Mansion?

DONG YONG. Let's take the upper road.

SEVENTH SISTER. Please, go ahead!

DONG YONG. We'll walk together as husband and wife!

DONG YONG (*sings*).

> A moment ago I was a single person, alone and forlorn,
> But out of the blue I've found a fine match on the road.
> Hand in hand with my darling we travel the highway,

SEVENTH SISTER (*sings*).

> Husband and wife, together we walk to Fu Family Bay.

DONG YONG (*sings*).

> Alas, it's too bad that I will have to be a long-time worker,

SEVENTH SISTER (*sings*).

> But when the three years are finished, we will go home.

DONG YONG (*sings*).

> I am afraid that the Fu family will treat you abusively,

Seventh Sister (*sings*).

But our love and affection will turn bitter into sweet.

(Dong Yong *and* Seventh Sister *sing*.)

Husband and wife can be compared to mandarin ducks:
Sharing bitter and sweet, standing shoulder to shoulder!

(*Exit together*.)

Scene 4. Starting Out on the Job

(FU GUANBAO *enters.*)

FU GUANBAO (*sings*).

As long as there's no wind, I do not fear the cold;
Loaded with money, I don't worry about poverty.
I'm now just waiting for the arrival of Dong Yong,
Who is bound to come to our place to report for his job.

(DONG YONG *and* SEVENTH SISTER *enter together.*)

DONG YONG. Here we are at the Fu Mansion. Darling, you wait outside for a moment while I go in.

SEVENTH SISTER. Dong Yong, once inside the mansion, you must tell them that you brought your wife with you!

DONG YONG (*enters the gate and greets* FU GUANBAO). Young Master, I have arrived to report for my job.

FU GUANBAO. Ha! So you have arrived. Go and fetch water!

DONG YONG. Outside the gate I ….

FU GUANBAO. You still have some stuff outside the gate?

DONG YONG. I left my luggage and my umbrella outside.

FU GUANBAO. Hurry and get it!

DONG YONG (*going out through the gate*). Darling, get me my luggage and umbrella.

SEVENTH SISTER. Dong Yong, once inside the mansion did you tell them that I had come too?

DONG YONG. Oh no, not yet.

SEVENTH SISTER. Don't forget now that you enter the mansion for a second time. (*She hands his luggage to* DONG YONG.)

DONG YONG (*entering the mansion*). Young Master!

FU GUANBAO. Hurry up and take care of the firewood!

DONG YONG. Outside the gate I still have …

Fu Guanbao. What is it this time?

Dong Yong. Eh … I also left my umbrella outside the gate.

Fu Guanbao. You are really a pain in the ass. Hurry up and get it.

Dong Yong. Darling, get me my umbrella.

Seventh Sister. You must have told them that your wife has come too now that you have entered the mansion for a second time, didn't you?

Dong Yong. Oh no, not yet!

Seventh Sister. So why didn't you tell them?

Dong Yong. The sales contract clearly states that I am a single person, a bachelor, so how can I today arrive with a wife?

Seventh Sister. Just tell them I'm a wife you picked up by the side of the street.

Dong Yong. That would be wrong. You are a human being, so how could I just pick you up?

Seventh Sister. That's only to fool the Young Master!

Dong Yong. This …

Seventh Sister. Dong Yong, you are too honest. Let me go inside by myself!

(Seventh Sister *goes inside, and when* Fu Guanbao *sees her, he is stupefied.*)

Fu Guanbao. Dong Yong, (*pointing at* Seventh Sister) who is this person?

Dong Yong. That … That is my wife!

Fu Guanbao. How can it be that she is your wife! Fine, the sales contract clearly states that you are unmarried and have no dependents, so where does this wife come from today? (*Facing backstage.*) Father!

(Old Master Fu *enters.*)

Old Master Fu. Guanbao, what's the matter?

Fu Guanbao. Dong Yong has abducted a charming young girl.

Old Master Fu. How can that be possible? (*addressing* Dong Yong.) Dong Yong, what's the background of this girl?

Dong Yong (*at a loss for words*). Sir, she …

Old Master Fu. Back then I thought that you were selling your body in order to bury your father and that you were fully sincere, that's why I gave you two bolts of white linen and five ounces of silver. Who could have known that you would be a scoundrel who abducts women from respectable families by making false promises!

DONG YONG. Sir …

OLD MASTER FU (*addressing* FU GUANBAO). Guanbao, repossess Dong Yong's silver and linen and chase these two people away!

(YOUNG MASTER FU *looks at* SEVENTH SISTER, *and then has his own secret designs.*) Father, have you lost your mind? Three years of labor for only two bolts of white linen and five ounces of silver—where are we going to find such a cheap deal?

OLD MASTER FU. Mm… Dong Yong, take this girl back to her home and return to report for duty.

(*On the side* FU GUANBAO *is wringing his hands in desperation.*)

SEVENTH SISTER. Sir, you must know the old proverb: "When the husband has a load of a thousand pounds, his wife will carry five hundred pounds." How can I run away and soar off while Dong Yong works here at your place as a laborer?

OLD MASTER FU (*not knowing how to answer her and turning to* DONG YONG). Dong Yong, now tell me what is the background of this girl?

DONG YONG. We met each other out on the road, and she became my lawfully wedded wife!

OLD MASTER FU. Even under these circumstances you still persist in your story! How can this be possible? (*sings.*)
How I hate deep down in my heart this little Dong Yong!
With tricky words and false statements he tries to fool us.
The great affair of one's lifetime[9] depends on the command of one's parents,
So how could you secretly take a wife while out on the road?
It is obvious that your conscience lacks proper norms:
The abduction of a woman is not a minor misdemeanor!
Holding my rod, I will administer you a beating …

(OLD MASTER FU *tries to give* DONG YONG *a beating, but* SEVENTH SISTER *waves her fan.* DONG YONG *turns around and* OLD MASTER FU *is overcome by a dizzy spell, hitting* GUANBAO *every time he tries to beat* DONG YONG.)

Fu Guanbao (*sings*).

But time and again you hit the body of your own son!

Old Master Fu.

But time and again I hit the body of my son Guanbao!
This must mean that this woman is a devilish monster!
Damned Dong Yong, where did you raise the courage
To bring here this devilish monster, murdering whom?

(Dong Yong *is totally befuddled, so* Seventh Sister *hastily covers up for him.*)

Seventh Sister (*sings*).

I am not some devil, and I am not some monster either,
I am just a "skirt and hairpins" from the mortal world.

Old Master Fu (*sings*).

If you're just a "skirt and hairpins" from this mortal world,
What is the reason why you have come to our mansion?

Seventh Sister (*sings*).

My husband has come to your place to work in the fields,
But I can weave brocade and embroider floral patterns.

Old Master Fu. Can you weave brocade?

Seventh Sister. Yes, I can weave brocade.

Old Master Fu. And can you also embroider flowers?

Seventh Sister. Yes, I can also embroider flowers.

Old Master Fu. OK. Dong Yong, the background of this woman is unclear, so we really should chase her out, but for the time being we'll allow her to stay here in our house because of her skills in embroidering flowers and weaving brocade.

Dong Yong. Sir, many thanks!

Fu Guanbao (*speaking to himself*). This is great!

Old Master Fu (*addressing* Seventh Sister). I want you to weave ten bolts of cloud-patterned brocade in a single night!

Dong Yong. Sir, how can that be possible?

Old Master Fu. You don't expect me to feed her for free, do you?

DONG YONG. Darling, this is my fault!

SEVENTH SISTER. Sir, if I weave ten bolts of cloud-patterned brocade in a single night, what will you do?

DONG YONG. Darling!

OLD MASTER FU. In that case. … If you can weave ten bolts of cloud-patterned brocade in a single night, I … will reduce his three years of labor to one hundred days.

DONG YONG. And if she doesn't complete the ten bolts?

OLD MASTER FU. Then another three years will be added to your three years!

SEVENTH SISTER. Sir, are you speaking in earnest?

OLD MASTER FU. I do not speak my words in jest!

SEVENTH SISTER. In that case, let's draw up a contract.

DONG YONG. Darling, this is really impossible!

OLD MASTER FU. Fine, let's draw up a contract.

SEVENTH SISTER. Fine, let's draw up a contract!

FU GUANBAO. Father, this is not a case of selling land or selling fields, this is not a case of selling a wife or children, and it is also not a case of selling one's body to become a slave, so what kind of contract will you draw up with her?

OLD MASTER FU (*whispering to* FU GUANBAO). If she cannot weave ten bolts of cloud-patterned brocade in a single night, then after three years of labor we get a bonus of another three years! (*Writes out the contract and hands it to* SEVENTH SISTER.) Here, take this!

SEVENTH SISTER. Dong Yong, carefully store this contract away. (DONG YONG, *filled with foreboding, takes it from her.* SEVENTH SISTER *comforts him.*) With this contract we will be able to return home very quickly!

OLD MASTER FU. Guanbao, take Dong Yong and his wife to the weaving room.

(DONG YONG *and* SEVENTH SISTER *exit.*)

OLD MASTER FU. Guanbao!

FU GUANBAO. What?

OLD MASTER FU. Give her a pile of tangled thread without a beginning, so she will be unable to finish those ten bolts of cloud-patterned brocade even in ten years!

FU GUANBAO (*speaks*). Yes, I will. (*Exits.*)

OLD MASTER FU (*pleased with himself*). Dong Yong, my dear Dong Yong, don't hold a grudge against me when tomorrow morning at the break of dawn you cannot produce those ten bolts of cloud-patterned brocade and you have to work for me as a slave for another three years! (*Exits.*)

Scene 5. Weaving Brocade

(Dong Yong *and* Seventh Sister *enter together.*)

Seventh Sister (*sings*).

No wonder Dong Yong is filled with anxiety in his heart—
He doesn't know I'm an Immortal Maiden from highest heaven!
Having come to the weaving room, he quickly sits down;
His brow knit in a frown, his face betrays his worries.

Dong Yong, why do you have to be so anxious?

Dong Yong. Look at this tangled thread without a beginning! How can you weave ten bolts of cloud-patterned brocade in one single night?

Seventh Sister. It's still too early to say whether or not I can weave ten bolts, but such a worried and bitter expression is of no use at all!

Dong Yong. Darling, now that you have brought about this disaster that reaches to heaven, not only will my suffering be doubled, but you too will be punished because of me!

Seventh Sister. Dong Yong, don't be so upset!

Dong Yong. Darling, you don't realize how cruel this Old Master is!

Seventh Sister. How cruel is he?

Dong Yong. When the Young Master a moment ago handed me this yellow silk, he also told me this: If we don't come up with those ten bolts of cloud-patterned brocade tomorrow morning at the break of dawn, they will not only fine me another three years of labor, but they will also tie us up, husband and wife, in the corner of the western corridor and give us a sound beating!

Seventh Sister. That's only to scare a sincere person like you!

Dong Yong. Do you think they don't dare give us a beating? Darling, you should try to escape this very night. It would be better if I all by myself get the beating and suffer punishment.

Seventh Sister. Dong Yong, it is I who spoke those words; it is I who called down this disaster. Could I leave you behind by yourself to suffer while I make my escape?

DONG YONG. Darling! (*sings.*)

I beg you not to be concerned about me, Dong Yong—
Sneak away and escape and flee to some faraway place!
Even if you were to have ten pairs of hands, you couldn't
Finish weaving the ten bolts of cloud-patterned brocade!

SEVENTH SISTER (*sings*).

There is no need to be worried, no need to be upset!
When weaving brocade your wife has superior skills.
Ten bolts of cloud-patterned brocade are a minor matter,
Your wife can provide one hundred, one thousand bolts!

Dong Yong, you go to sleep in the back, and let me weave these ten bolts of cloud-patterned brocade.

DONG YONG. How can I sleep when I'm filled with anxiety?

SEVENTH SISTER. Well … (*She takes out her white fan.*) Great, this will do it … (*Addressing* DONG YONG.) If you stay here, I would have to entertain you with my conversation and that would interfere with my weaving. I will come and keep you company as soon as I have finished weaving these ten bolts of cloud-patterned brocade. Take with you your luggage, your umbrella, and this white fan. Make sure to put the white fan under your cushion so it won't get lost.

DONG YONG. Fine. (*Exits.*)

SEVENTH SISTER (*sings*).

So Dong Yong as soon as possible may go home
We tomorrow must hand over ten bolts of brocade.
When I descended to the world, Eldest Sister said
I should burn this Disaster Incense in times of disaster.
Now this Disaster Incense is an immortal treasure;
Its blue smoke will rise up straight to highest heaven.
I very much hope my sisters will notice it quickly,
And hurry down to the mortal world here below!

(SEVENTH SISTER *lights the incense.* THE OTHER IMMORTAL SISTERS *enter.*)

ELDEST SISTER (*sings*).

The rising blue incense smoke reaches high heaven.

THE OTHER IMMORTAL SISTERS (*sing*).

Why is the incense smoke whirling in this manner?

ELDEST SISTER (*sings*).
It must mean Seventh Sister is in trouble right now!

THE OTHER IMMORTAL SISTERS (*sing*).
So the six of us have to go down to the world below!
Riding on our auspicious clouds, carried by the wind,
We arrive in the blink of an eye at Fu Family Bay.

SEVENTH SISTER. Welcome sisters.

THE OTHER IMMORTAL SISTERS. Seventh Sister, you have truly transformed yourself into a pretty girl of the mortal world!

SEVENTH SISTER. Does our father the king know that you have descended to the mortal world?

THIRD SISTER. How would she (*pointing at* SECOND SISTER) have dared to come along with us if it weren't the case that our father the king has left for a banquet in the Western Heaven!

SECOND SISTER. You shouldn't say all these things!

SEVENTH SISTER. This ...

THIRD SISTER (*curiously looking inside and seeing* DONG YONG). Sister, look over there! There's a guy sleeping there!

ELDEST SISTER. So he is that Dong Yong who sold his body to bury his father!

THE OTHER SISTERS (*addressing* SEVENTH SISTER). You are so reckless and daring!

THIRD SISTER. Wake him up, so we can greet him!

SEVENTH SISTER. Third Sister, when I saw how worried and upset he was, I placed my white fan by his side so he could get a good night's sleep.

ELDEST SISTER. Why is he so worried and upset?

SEVENTH SISTER. Because Old Master Fu wants me to weave ten bolts of cloud-patterned brocade in a single night.

THE OTHER IMMORTAL SISTERS. That Old Master is truly terrible!

ELDEST SISTER. That's only a minor matter. Not only ten bolts—even one hundred bolts or one thousand bolts I can finish with one or two throws of the shuttle!

SEVENTH SISTER. Sisters, if you all help me out, it is only a minor matter. But if I were here all by myself it would be quite a problem.

ELDEST SISTER. Seventh Sister, do you have silk thread?

SEVENTH SISTER. Here it is.

ELDEST SISTER. Aiya! These people have no conscience at all! They have messed up this yellow silk, so how can you use it to weave brocade?

THE OTHER IMMORTAL SISTERS. Eldest Sister, why don't we ask for heavenly silk?

ELDEST SISTER (*recites*).
May heavenly silk descend to the mortal realm
To weave in the world of men cloud-patterned brocade.

THE OTHER IMMORTAL SISTERS. Let's all gather up the silk!

THIRD SISTER. Seventh Sister, you and your husband have just married, so you should not allow these happy times to slip by. We, your sisters, will take care of this weaving business for you!

FOURTH SISTER, FIFTH SISTER, SIXTH SISTER. Go and keep your husband company!

SEVENTH SISTER. Sisters, I want to learn from you!

FOURTH SISTER, FIFTH SISTER, SIXTH SISTER. We don't want you here! We don't want you here!

SEVENTH SISTER. Since ancient times it is said: "Husband and wife are married for one hundred years." There are still many days to follow!

ELDEST SISTER. Enough! There's no need for any further discussion. The time of a single night is easily passed, so let's quickly start to straighten and comb the thread.

(THE IMMORTAL MAIDENS *start working by straightening and combing the thread. The watch is sounded.*)

ELDEST SISTER. Which watch was that?

THE OTHER IMMORTAL SISTERS. The drum sounded the first watch.

ELDEST SISTER. So let's start weaving!

THE OTHER IMMORTAL SISTERS. Let's start weaving! (*sing.*)
The first fifth of the first watch: the moon is round;

In the first watch the cuckoo cries throughout that watch.
That pitiable little cuckoo
Cries till its heart is hurting,
Cries till its mouth is dry,
Cries till heaven sheds tears,
Cries till earth too sheds tears!
Every night it cries and cries—
But in the end for what reason?

ELDEST SISTER (*sings*).
Little sisters, let me ask you, why does it cry?

THE OTHER IMMORTAL SISTERS (*sing*).
Eldest Sister, weave your brocade—why these many questions?
In the first watch the cuckoo cries all through the first watch!

ELDEST SISTER. Ah, it is the cuckoo that cries. So I will weave a "cuckoo crying on its branch."

(*The drum sounds the second watch.*)

ELDEST SISTER. Which watch was that?

THE OTHER IMMORTAL SISTERS. The drum sounded the second watch!

ELDEST SISTER. So let me go on weaving!

THE OTHER IMMORTAL SISTERS (*sing*).
In the second watch the moon hangs at heaven's edge;
In the second watch the magpie cries throughout the second watch.
Listen to that little magpie:
When it cries out over there,
Its cry makes all people happy.
When the happy magpie cries on its branch
Good things are bound to happen at any moment!
When magpies construct a bridge,
Immortals are allowed to cross the Silver River![10]

(*They smile at* SEVENTH SISTER.)

ELDEST SISTER (*sings*).
Little sisters, let me ask you, what bird is crying?

THE OTHER IMMORTAL SISTERS (*sing*).
Eldest Sister, go on weaving—why these many questions?
In the second watch the magpie cries throughout the second watch.

ELDEST SISTER. How come we still hear the happy magpie even though the drum has sounded the second watch?

THIRD SISTER. This is Seventh Sister's happy day, so the happy magpie keeps on crying throughout the night!

ELDEST SISTER. So let me weave "heavenly immortals crossing Magpie Bridge."

THE OTHER IMMORTAL SISTERS. Let's go on weaving!

(*The drum sounds the third watch.*)

ELDEST SISTER.Which watch was sounded?

THE OTHER IMMORTAL SISTERS. The drum sounded the third watch.

ELDEST SISTER. So let me go on weaving!

THE OTHER IMMORTAL SISTERS (*sing*).

In the third watch the moon shines on my window;
In the third watch turtledoves coo throughout the third watch.
One pair of little turtledoves
Are cooing to each other
As if sharing their secrets.
During the day they soar on paired wings;
At night they sleep with necks intertwined.
Roosting together and flying together
They surpass the divine immortals!

ELDEST SISTER (*sings*).

Little sisters, let me ask you, what bird is calling?

THE OTHER IMMORTAL SISTERS (*sing*).

Eldest Sister, keep on weaving—why these many questions?
In the third watch turtledoves are cooing throughout the third watch!

ELDEST SISTER. So the turtledoves are cooing. I will weave "turtledoves soaring on paired wings."

THE OTHER IMMORTAL SISTERS. Go on weaving!

(*The drum sounds the fourth watch.*)

ELDEST SISTER. Which watch was sounded?

THE OTHER IMMORTAL SISTERS. The drum sounded the fourth watch.

ELDEST SISTER. So let me go on weaving!

THE OTHER IMMORTAL SISTERS (*sing*).

In the fourth watch the moon is inclining toward the west;
In the fourth watch a migrating goose calls throughout the fourth watch.
It is one little migrating goose,
Flying this way and that way,
It is oh so lonely and forlorn.
For whom is it delivering a letter
Now that it lands on this sandy bank?[11]
Go and find yourself a companion—
There is no need to sleep all alone!

ELDEST SISTER (*sings*).

Little sisters, let me ask you, which bird is calling?

THE OTHER IMMORTAL SISTERS (*sing*).

Eldest Sister, go on weaving—why these many questions?
In the fourth watch a migrating goose calls throughout the fourth watch!

ELDEST SISTER. So a goose is calling. I will weave a "migrating goose delivering a letter."

THE OTHER IMMORTAL SISTERS. You go on weaving!

(*The drum sounds the fifth watch.*)

ELDEST SISTER. Which watch was sounded?

THE OTHER IMMORTAL SISTERS. The drum sounded the fifth watch.

SEVENTH SISTER. The drum sounded the fifth watch, and the ten bolts of cloud-patterned brocade are still not finished, so what do we do now?

ELDEST SISTER. Don't get flustered, don't be flurried. I will make some extra effort!

THE OTHER IMMORTAL SISTERS (*sing*).

In the fifth watch the moon sinks behind the hills;
In the fifth watch the Golden Rooster brightens the sky with its call.
When we hear that little Golden Rooster
Loudly raising its cry over there
It causes people to feel ill at ease.
The Golden Rooster in its cage announces dawn,
And it stirs the heart-strings of those separating.

Once we say goodbye to each other,
When will we ever be able to meet again?

Eldest Sister (*sings*).
Little sisters, let me ask you, which bird is calling?

The other immortal sisters (*sing*).
Eldest Sister, keep on weaving—why these many questions?
In the fifth watch the Golden Rooster brightens the sky with its call!

Eldest Sister. Aiya, I'm exhausted! Let me cut the brocade from the loom and count how many bolts I have. (*She counts.*) One, two, three ...

The other immortal sisters. seven, eight, nine ...

Eldest Sister. Stop it! Stop it! You are going to shortchange me. I only need to pout my lips and then I know the number in my heart. (*She counts the brocade.*)

The other immortal sisters. Eldest Sister, how many bolts?

Eldest Sister. Ten bolts, and three feet and six inches.

Third Sister. She can make a nice jacket for her husband to wear from those leftovers!

Eldest Sister. In my opinion, we should allow Seventh Sister to keep these. When later she will have given birth to a little baby boy, she can make from it a silk gown for him to wear.

(Seventh Sister *shows by her expression that she feels embarrassed.*)

The other immortal sisters. Eldest Sister, you really think of everything!

Seventh Sister. Thank you, sisters, for helping me out. My gratitude knows no bounds.

Third Sister. It is enough if you and your husband, united in love, do not forget our bleak and desolate life in the Palace of Dipper and Buffalo!

Seventh Sister. Here in this mortal world I think of you every hour and every minute!

Third Sister. How can you still remember us now that you have such a perfect husband!

Second Sister. Seventh Sister, you definitely should not linger here in the red dust. You better accompany us back to heaven.

SEVENTH SISTER. This …

THIRD SISTER. Seventh Sister, don't worry. Now our father the king has gone to the Western Heaven for a banquet. He will stay there for a few months before he returns. And even when our father the king has returned, we will be able to find some means to keep him in the dark.

SECOND SISTER. That will depend on your ability!

ELDEST SISTER. The sky has turned bright, so mortals and immortals can no longer mingle. We have to hurry back to heaven.

SEVENTH SISTER. Let me see you off my dear sisters!

THE OTHER IMMORTAL SISTERS. No need to see us off. (*They sing.*)
Because Seventh Sister was confronted with disaster,
We arrived in the mortal world on our colored clouds.
In one night we wove ten bolts of cloud-patterned brocade:
A fine divine miracle, renowned throughout eternity.

(THE OTHER IMMORTAL SISTERS *exit.*)

SEVENTH SISTER (*sings*).
My immortal sisters have returned to heaven above;
I am busily folding and checking these bolts of silk.
We have woven ten bolts of cloud-patterned brocade—
Now a smile covers my face and joy fills my heart.

Dong Yong!

(DONG YONG *enters.*)

DONG YONG (*sings*).
I had a really good sleep! Oh, I really slept quite well,
I slept all through the night till the fifth watch arrived.

(*As if suddenly awakening from a dream.*)
I step forward and ask my darling: Did you finish
Weaving those ten bolts of cloud-patterned brocade?

SEVENTH SISTER (*deliberately hiding the brocade behind her back*). Aiya, I am not yet done.

DONG YONG. I knew that you were unable to weave that much!

SEVENTH SISTER (*imitating the voice of* OLD MASTER FU). That will be an additional three years on top of your three years!

DONG YONG. In a situation like this you are still cracking jokes! Darling, it still would be best if you tried to escape!

SEVENTH SISTER. And you?

DONG YONG. I? I can only stay here, suffer the beating and accept the punishment.

SEVENTH SISTER. Dong Yong, look what I have here! (*She shows the cloud-patterned brocade.*)

DONG YONG (*overcome by joy*). Where does this come from?

SEVENTH SISTER. Your wife produced this in a single night!

DONG YONG. Darling! (*sings.*)

I see this cloud-patterned brocade with its fresh colors:
My darling, you indeed have a special talent and skill!
When you weave a dragon, the dragon shows its claws,
And when you weave phoenixes, they frolic in the sky.
If in a single night you finished weaving ten bolts.
It must be because you are the Weaving Maiden Star!

SEVENTH SISTER (*sings*).

Your wife, I assure you, is not the Weaving Maiden Star;
A famous teacher taught me her skills, which were superb!
I now hand these ten bolts of cloud-patterned brocade to you,
So you may deliver them to Mr. Fu and ransom your body.

DONG YONG (*very pleased*). Darling, I will take this cloud-patterned brocade to the Old Master. You have been busy all night, you should get some sleep.

SEVENTH SISTER. Deliver these ten bolts now! (*She exits.*)

DONG YONG (*deeply moved and filled with hope.*) In this way we can return home after one hundred days! (*Exits.*)

Scene 6. Eating Dates

(Seventh Sister *enters.*)

Seventh Sister (*sings*).

Under the high sky of the Seventh Month the air is clear and crisp;
When the evening wind blows in your face, it is pleasantly cool.
Summer has gone and fall has arrived, the time has passed quickly.
Since arriving at the Fu Mansion, we've been busy night and day.
Until late at night I keep working on the young lady's wedding gown,
And before the sky turns bright I must go to the river and wash clothes.
But Dong Yong's sufferings are even much more bitter than mine,
In wind and in rain he has to go to the fields and slave there all day!
When I can find a moment of rest from my labors I repair his torn clothes.

(Dong Yong *enters unobtrusively.*)

So my darling Dong Yong will not have to suffer the biting cold!

Dong Yong. Darling!

Seventh Sister. Dong Yong, are you back?

Dong Yong. I'm back.

Seventh Sister. How come you are back so late?

Dong Yong. The very moment I returned from the fields the Old Master ordered me to pound the rice. Each and every day you have to wait for me till this time, it really makes me feel …

Seventh Sister. "Filled with concern and ill at ease!"

(Dong Yong *smiles.*)

Seventh Sister. You sit down. Let me get a bowl of hot water so you can wash your hands and feet.

Dong Yong. Darling, I already washed my hands and feet in the kitchen.

Seventh Sister. Don't try to fool me, you are covered in dust all over!

(Seventh Sister *wants to leave and get water, but* Dong Yong *pulls her back.*)

Dong Yong. Darling, I have here some dates for you.

SEVENTH SISTER. Where did you get those?

DONG YONG. A farmhand in the other village, a good friend of mine, gave them to me.

SEVENTH SISTER. Then you eat them!

DONG YONG. I saved them for you. Darling, I recall a lucky phrase.

SEVENTH SISTER. Which lucky phrase?

DONG YONG. The proverb says it well: "Eat a date, eat one more date, and give birth to a boy at an early date!"[12]

SEVENTH SISTER. You Dong Yong! (*She whispers in his ear, telling him that she is pregnant.*)

DONG YONG. Darling, if you are in blessed circumstances, I have to express my gratitude to Heaven and Earth!

SEVENTH SISTER. Dong Yong, what day is it today?

DONG YONG. The twelfth of the Seventh Month.

SEVENTH SISTER. And tomorrow?

DONG YONG. Why do you have to ask me! That's the thirteenth of the Seventh Month!

SEVENTH SISTER. You and I reported for work on the fifth of the Fourth Month, and tomorrow will be the thirteenth of the Seventh Month, so you will have served out your one hundred days of servitude.

DONG YONG. I have also counted the days, but I have only arrived at ninety-eight days!

SEVENTH SISTER. How about the day of arrival and the day of departure?

DONG YONG. Darling, you think of everything!

SEVENTH SISTER. Just say goodbye to the Old Master in the fifth watch, at the break of dawn, and we can go back home!

DONG YONG. Darling, first of all you are in blessed circumstances, and second, the one hundred days of servitude are finished. This really may be called "Bringing home a daughter-in-law and marrying off a daughter!"

SEVENTH SISTER. What does that mean?

DONG YONG. Good fortune arrives in pairs!

SEVENTH SISTER. Dong Yong, you seem to be as happy as a three-year-old who is celebrating the New Year in a flowered jacket and a flowered cap!

DONG YONG. You are quite right! Darling! (*sings.*)
When I imagine tomorrow that we will go back home,
I am so happy that flowers bloom in this heart of mine.
As husband and wife, a couple, we'll enter the cottage
And hasten to whitewash the walls of our dwelling.
The bed we will place against the eastern side, and
The kitchen stand we will place against the western side.
From today I will fetch the water and you'll cook the rice,
I will plant the fields and then you will bring me tea.
I will raise cotton flowers and you will weave linen,
I will grow sticky rice and you will make rice cakes.
I will go up the hills to cut firewood, catch fish in the river;
You at home will raise chicken, raise geese, and raise ducks!
As long as husband and wife work hard and live simply,
We will have plenty to eat and also plenty to wear.
And when next year the hundred flowers start to grow,
Darling, you're bound to give birth to a little baby child.
If you will give birth to a boy, a stripling fellow,
He will follow me to the fields to plow and rake;
If you give birth to a baby girl, she'll stay with you
Here at home, weaving brocade, embroidering flowers.
Darling, you and I see the light at the end of the night:
As soon as the sun has come out, we will go back home!

SEVENTH SISTER. Dong Yong, by the looks of it, you are going mad with joy! It is late at night, so please get some sleep.

DONG YONG (*unable to suppress his elation*). Darling, you get some sleep first. I will collect our luggage. As soon as the eastern sky turns bright, I will wake you up so we can return home together!

SEVENTH SISTER. Let's pack our luggage together. (*Takes out a well-made piece of clothing.*) Dong Yong, this is a set of clothes that I just repaired. Put on these clothes so you won't feel the chilly wind. When you go home wearing a nice set of clothes, the neighbors will say that you look like a man who has a wife!

DONG YONG. Darling, when you and I go back home as husband and wife, that is the happiest event in the world, so you too should wash your face, comb your hair, and change your clothes.

SEVENTH SISTER. That's something for tomorrow morning.

(*A rooster crows.*)

DONG YONG. The rooster has crowed, so what's this talk about "tomorrow morning"?

SEVENTH SISTER. Then I'd better wash my face and comb my hair. (*Exits.*)

DONG YONG (*sings*).

We hear the Golden Rooster loudly announcing dawn;
The east turns white, and then the sky becomes bright.
I bundle my luggage together as tight as tight can be,
And when I pick up this umbrella, I remember the past:
When I left that cold hovel, it was me all by myself,
But today I have my darling, we'll be traveling together.
My darling will walk in front, and I will follow behind;
Husband and wife will enter the cottage as a couple, a pair!
If only my father and mother were both still alive,
How happy they would be on seeing us, me and my wife!

(SEVENTH SISTER *enters.*)

SEVENTH SISTER. Dong Yong!

DONG YONG. Are you ready? (*He stares intently at* SEVENTH SISTER.)

SEVENTH SISTER. I am ready. Why do you keep looking at me?

DONG YONG. When I look at you … (*Sings.*)

The clothes you are wearing perfectly suit your figure;
The red flowers on your gown seem to be blooming on a tree!
Your face, it seems to me, resembles the moon in the sky;
Your eyes, so it seems, resemble the stars next to the moon!
Darling, when you move your feet while walking outside,
You resemble a colored cloud that is floating in the sky;
Darling, when you open your mouth and I hear your voice,
It resembles a silver bell that is sounding in an empty valley.
Darling, you truly have a perfect figure from birth—
Now when I look at you this morning, I love you even more.

SEVENTH SISTER. Dong Yong, you are praising me way too much!

DONG YONG. Darling! (*Sings.*)

I will never be able to describe in full your perfections:
I'm grateful to you for the devotion you have shown me.
You have sewed clothes for me, you have repaired them;
You have suffered on my behalf, worried on my behalf.
If you had not woven ten bolts of brocade in a single night,
How would I have been able to escape from this fiery pit?

Look, the red morning clouds have appeared in the east.
(*Enthusiastically he pulls* SEVENTH SISTER *with him and starts walking.*)

Now you and I are set to leave this mansion of the Fus.

Darling, let's go to the hall and say goodbye to the Old Master.

SEVENTH SISTER. What about your pack and your umbrella?

DONG YONG. I'm so excited that I almost forgot my luggage and my umbrella!

SEVENTH SISTER. You! And what about my white fan?

DONG YONG. That's on the bed. I will go and get it for you. (*Exits.*)

SEVENTH SISTER (*speaking to herself*). Today is the first time since our wedding that I have seen Dong Yong as excited as this!

(*Drums resound, as if an emperor rides out.* [SEVENTH SISTER] *sings.*)

I hear drums resounding in the high heavens up above,
And involuntarily I'm suddenly startled in my heart.
Could it be that my father the king has returned to his palace from the Western Heaven?
Could it be that my father the king is touring and inspecting the expanse of heaven?
If by any chance on arrival at the Dipper and Buffalo Palace
He finds out that I descended to earth, he will explode in rage.
This is called: a blazing fire that is doused by a tub of snow—
Freezing water showers my skull and even chills my heart!

(*Inserted speech.*) Well, it doesn't matter!

Third Sister promised me that she would find some way
To keep my father in the dark so he would be deceived.
Third Sister is a woman who knows many cunning tricks,
She combines courage with care, she has many skills.
And then there also is my Eldest Sister who is very kind,
She surely will be able to take care of this matter for me!

(DONG YONG *enters unobtrusively.*)

DONG YONG. Darling, what are you thinking about?

SEVENTH SISTER. Oh! I was thinking about going back home together!

DONG YONG. Here is your fan. (*He hands her the fan.* SEVENTH SISTER *takes it from him.*)

SEVENTH SISTER. So let's say goodbye to Old Master Fu and go home.

DONG YONG. Please.

(DONG YONG *and* SEVENTH SISTER *exit.*)

Scene 7. Completing the Job

(OLD MASTER FU *enters.*)

OLD MASTER FU (*sings*).

Even though men say wealth and status are fated by karma,
One still must be very careful when keeping one's accounts.
For only five ounces of silver and two bolts of white linen
I managed to buy this young Dong Yong as a bonded slave.
On top of that his wife turned out to have excellent skills:
In a single night she managed to weave ten bolts of brocade.
Now the autumn winds are blowing and the rice is ripening:
Each and every kernel of grain resembles yellow gold!
The rooster has crowed three times, the sky turns bright,
So I will order Dong Yong to go to the fields immediately.

Guanbao!

FU GUANBAO. Father, there is something I wanted to tell you!

OLD MASTER FU. Why are you making such a fuss?

FU GUANBAO. Last evening Dong Yong and his wife kept on chattering and talking, and they were so excited that they never went to sleep all night.

OLD MASTER FU. How do you know?

FU GUANBAO. Eh… Eh… I was listening outside their door.

OLD MASTER FU. And what were they talking about?

FU GUANBAO. They said they wanted to go back home. Is the term of his servitude perhaps almost finished?

OLD MASTER FU. How do you know that they think they have served out their servitude?

FU GUANBAO. Was is not you who said that if she could weave ten bolts of brocade in a single night, the three years of servitude would be shortened to one hundred days?

OLD MASTER FU. Don't talk such nonsense. Tell Dong Yong to go to the fields.

(DONG YONG *and* SEVENTH SISTER *enter.*)

Dong Yong (*recites*).

The cock has crowed three times:

Seventh Sister (*recites*).

We say goodbye and go back home!

Fu Guanbao. Dong Yong, you arrive at the right moment. My father orders that you go to the fields.

Dong Yong. I won't go.

Fu Guanbao. You won't go? If you have the guts to do so, go and tell my father! Father, I told Dong Yong to go to the fields, but he said he won't go.

Old Master Fu. How is that possible? (*Addressing* Dong Yong.) Why won't you go?

Dong Yong. Sir, my term of servitude is finished.

Old Master Fu. You have only worked off a few months of your three years of servitude, so how can you say that your term is completed?

Seventh Sister. Three years of servitude?

Old Master Fu. Guanbao, get me Dong Yong's sales contract!

(Young Master Fu *exits, reenters immediately*.)

Young Master Fu. Father, here is the sales contract concerning Dong Yong.

Old Master Fu. Dong Yong, just look! This contract clearly states "Selling my body I do not sell it for all eternity; when three years are finished I will return home."

Seventh Sister. Isn't there yet another contract?

Old Master Fu. What contract?

Seventh Sister. You're not going to tell me you forgot how I produced ten bolts of cloud-patterned brocade in a single night? (*Takes the contract from* Dong Yong*'s hands*.)

Sir, just look! This contract clearly states: "If ten bolts of brocade are produced in a single night, the three years of servitude become one hundred days."

Old Master Fu. But even if we set the term at one hundred days, then today still cannot count as the end of the term!

DONG YONG. Today is the end of the term!

OLD MASTER FU. Please, count the days!

DONG YONG. I started work on the fifth of the Fourth Month, and today is the thirteenth of the Seventh Month …

OLD MASTER FU. Indeed, from the fifth of the Fourth Month to the thirteenth of the Seventh makes only ninety-eight days of labor.

FU GUANBAO. So there are still two days left? (*Addressing* DONG YONG.) So you think you can go back home?

SEVENTH SISTER. Sir, how can you say it is only ninety-eight days? What about the day of arrival and the day of departure?

OLD MASTER FU. Why should I count the day of arrival and the day of departure?

SEVENTH SISTER. "Each day on the emperor's calendar is a day of work for the people." How can you not count them?

OLD MASTER FU (*in a fix, and coming up with a different strategy*). Fine, if you say we have to count those days, we will count them.

DONG YONG and SEVENTH SISTER. Old Master, goodbye!

OLD MASTER FU. Not so fast!

DONG YONG. Now what?

OLD MASTER FU. Were you planning on taking that girl with you back home and enjoying your bliss? That seems to me a stupid thought and a silly idea.

DONG YONG. What is so silly and stupid about it?

OLD MASTER FU. The background of this woman is unclear, so I will have to report you to the authorities. Not only will I make sure that husband and wife are separated, but also that you will be locked up in jail for a long, long time!

DONG YONG. Darling! (SEVENTH SISTER *whispers in his ears.*)

DONG YONG. Old Master, don't repeat that I abducted my darling. But in the case that I have abducted her, your crime would be much bigger than mine!

OLD MASTER FU. How so?

DONG YONG. Where did we live since our marriage?

OLD MASTER FU. You lived at my place.

DONG YONG. And for whom did she weave her cloud-patterned brocade?

OLD MASTER FU. She wove the cloud-patterned brocade for me.

DONG YONG. So ever since we were married we lived at your place and she wove her cloud-patterned brocade for you. Why didn't you report us to the magistrate right away? Why didn't you report us to the authorities right away?

OLD MASTER FU. This …

DONG YONG. Sir, I've told you right from the start that we were married in a legal manner with a go-between and witnesses. If you report us to the authorities, the go-between will testify and the witnesses will show up. You will be condemned for making a false accusation, and if they don't fine you one thousand, they will fine you at least eight hundred!

OLD MASTER FU. Well … (*Coming up with yet another scheme.*) Dong Yong, I always have had your best interests at heart.

DONG YONG. Yes, I know.

OLD MASTER FU. Dong Yong! (*Sings.*)

If you stay here at my place, you'll enjoy your ease;
Why do you have to be in such a hurry to go home?
At home you have no father and you have no mother,
You also do not have even the smallest plot of land.
If you go home to that cold hovel, you'll suffer misery,
The thought of which makes me feel uncomfortable!

DONG YONG (*sings*).

Dear Sir, I sincerely appreciate your good intentions,
But I still prefer to go back home and suffer my misery.
The cottage may be a mess, but it keeps out wind and rain,
And we'll suffer hunger and starvation most happily!

OLD MASTER FU. Dong Yong, don't be so stubborn! From now on I will treat the two of you like my own children. Here, Guanbao will become your sworn brother!

Fu Guanbao (*addressing* Dong Yong). You will be my sworn brother! (*Addressing* Seventh Sister.) You will be my adoptive elder sister!

Dong Yong and Seventh Sister (*together*). Long arms in short sleeves do not reach up to high branches!

Old Master Fu. Don't talk about long arms in short sleeves not reaching up to high branches! Let me tear to shreds this sales contract! (Old Master Fu *tears the contract to shreds.* Dong Yong *hastily collects the pieces.*)

Seventh Sister. Let's go back home!

Dong Yong. Goodbye! (*He and* Seventh Sister *exit together.*)

Old Master Fu. At the busiest time of the year they just leave!

Old Master Fu and Fu Guanbao. This is truly too detestable! (*They exit together.*)

Scene 8. Separating at the Scholartree

(DONG YONG *and* SEVENTH SISTER *enter together.*)

DONG YONG (*sings*).
The sun rises on the eastern hills, then travels toward the west:

SEVENTH SISTER (*sings*).
Husband and wife have survived the full one hundred days.

DONG YONG (*sings*).
Today we return as a couple, a pair, to my cold old cottage,

SEVENTH SISTER (*sings*).
Like birds escaped from the cage going home to the forest.

DONG YONG (*sings*).
Sweet follows now that bitter is gone, and it is all thanks to you:
In a single night you produced ten bolts of cloud-patterned brocade.

SEVENTH SISTER (*sings*).
I for you and you for me: we're a couple, husband and wife,
There's no need whatsoever to mention such a minor matter.

DONG YONG. Darling, look! (*Sings.*)
All over the place the chrysanthemums show friendly smiles;
Even the high hills are so happy that they lower their heads.
The people passing by on the road talk softly to each other,
Praising you and me as a wonderful pair, husband and wife!

(*Drums resound.* SEVENTH SISTER'*s mood turns somber.*)

SEVENTH SISTER. Dong Yong, that farmhand in the other village was your best friend and treated us, husband and wife, with the greatest affection. Now that your term of servitude is finished today, you should go ahead and tell him goodbye.

DONG YONG. Darling, you are right. Let me go ahead.

SEVENTH SISTER. Make sure you will be waiting for me there.

DONG YONG. Darling, make sure to be there quickly. (*Exits.*)

SEVENTH SISTER (*sings*).
Today as we were going home my heart was filled with joy,

But now I hear the bells and drums that repeatedly urge me on.
I am so afraid that my father the king has found out about me,
And that he insists that I leave Dong Yong and abandon him.
My only wish is to go back home, to live in peace and harmony,
The love and affection of husband and wife is a joy without end!

(*The drums resound again. Speech from backstage.*) Seventh Sister, listen! Visiting the Palace of Dipper and Buffalo the Jade Emperor has learned that you on your own authority have descended to the mortal world here below, so his dragon-heart is greatly enraged and he orders you to return to the courts of heaven by the third quarter of the hour of noon! If you do not obey, he will dispatch heavenly soldiers and heavenly officers who will cut Dong Yong's body into ten thousand pieces!

Seventh Sister (*sings*).

From heaven's palace my father the king sends down an order,
And like a thunderclap out of the blue he sends down disaster.
Go ahead and arrest me, your seventh daughter—I'm not afraid,
But it is totally impossible to wound and harm my Dong Yong.
Ever since I met with Dong Yong in the shade of the scholartree,
The affection of husband and wife has been as deep as the ocean.
If we had one cup of cool water, the two of us drank it together;
If we had one bowl of bland rice, the two of us shared it together.
Alas, while at the Fu Mansion we suffered many tribulations,
And we hardly had any opportunity to express our mutual love.
We had hoped that today, now that the term of servitude was finished,
Husband and wife would go home, never to be parted day or night!
I truly hoped that he would till the fields while I would weave brocade,
"The husband will plow, his wife will weave": joy without limit!
I truly hoped that in the spring of next year, in the Third Month,
Dong Yong would be holding our baby in his arms by the door.
I never expected my father the king to be so devoid of feeling
That he would ruin this beautiful dream, not allow it to happen!
If by any chance I would have to abandon Dong Yong midway,
How could he make a living all alone back in his cold cottage?
Alas, Dong Yong has no father and he also has no mother—
Except for me, Seventh Sister, he has no relative in this world.
Who will repair his shoes and socks for him if they have holes?
Who will mend his clothes for him when they're tattered and torn?
Who will boil water for him and make his tea when he is thirsty?

Who will steam rice and vegetables for him when he is hungry?
Who will comb his hair for him, who will wash his face when rising early at dawn?
Who will make sure late at night to warm his blanket for him?
To whom can he tell the injustices he suffers, the wrongs he receives?
Who will inquire how he is doing when the weather is cold or hot?
Above his head he doesn't have a single tile, under his feet not an inch of land!
His destitution is so extreme, he will have to sell his body again!
When he will have fallen into that trap, he cannot save himself.
Who then will weave cloud-patterned brocade to pay his debts?
Considering all possibilities, I find it impossible to say goodbye;
I find it truly impossible to abandon the love of husband and wife.

(*Inserted speech.*) Dong Yong!

It's not the case that your wife has a heart that is unfeeling,
That I dump you halfway to ascend to the heavenly realm.
My father the king is the one to blame for his cruel rules,
So cruel that I must fear you too will suffer disaster!
I'll happily go to the execution grounds to be hacked to pieces
But I can't allow that you will suffer such trepidation and fright!
A love and affection without bounds, an unlimited hatred;
A separation while alive and in death: overcome by emotion.
I hastily hurry along the main road, looking for Dong Yong;
As soon as I see him, I will tell him my innermost feelings!

(*She exits.* Dong Yong *enters.*)

Dong Yong (*sings*).
The dragon returns to the ocean, a bird to the woods:
Today, husband and wife will go back to their home.
All of a sudden I have arrived below the scholartree,
Where I'll wait for my wife so we may walk together.

(Seventh Sister *enters.*)

Seventh Sister (*sings*).
Dong Yong over there is running as quick as he can,
While, I, Seventh Sister, am following awash in tears.
His face is wreathed in a smile, his heart filled with joy—
How could he know the boundless sorrow in my heart?
We truly hoped to be husband and wife for all eternity,
Who could have known that today we would be torn apart?

Here out in the fields I carry a grudge against my father:
Why can't we, husband and wife, be united till old age?

DONG YONG. Darling, there you are!

SEVENTH SISTER (*sings*).
I find it hard to express the bitter sorrow in my heart,
So, seeing Dong Yong, for the moment I wipe my tears away.

DONG YONG. Darling, how come you are walking so slowly?

SEVENTH SISTER. Dong Yong, it is difficult for me to walk fast because I am heavy with child.

DONG YONG. Darling, let me leave you here alone for a while.

SEVENTH SISTER. My husband, where do you want to go?

DONG YONG. Just have a look, here out in the fields there is no tea shed and no wine house. You are pregnant, so let me go to the main market street ahead and hire a sedan chair to carry you back home.

SEVENTH SISTER. Wouldn't that be a waste of your money, my husband?

DONG YONG. So what would you suggest?

SEVENTH SISTER. As long as you support me for a stretch, it should be fine.

DONG YONG. So let me support you. (*Sings.*)
Let me help you to your feet and support you as you walk.

SEVENTH SISTER (*sings*).
The heart of mine, Seventh Sister, is filled with bleak sadness.

DONG YONG (*sings*).
We, husband and wife, are like birds soaring on paired wings.

SEVENTH SISTER (*sings*).
But now a freak storm is about to rise up and to rip us apart.
Like a sparrow hopping about in a basket filled with chaff,
I am one moment filled with joy, the next filled with sadness.
And when I turn around and see the shady old scholartree,
My heart is filled with even more sadness and desolation.
I remember how when I first descended to the mortal world
We clung to each other as dark branches and green leaves.
But today that unfeeling autumn wind has started to blow,
Breaking apart these intertwined branches with all its might.

(*Stops, filled with pain.*)

DONG YONG. Darling, why don't you walk any farther?

SEVENTH SISTER. Dong Yong, what was this spot where we were a moment ago?

DONG YONG. We were below the Shady Scholartree.

SEVENTH SISTER. Husband, when you and I were married on that day, it was all thanks to the scholartree that served as go-between. So we should express our thanks to him with a bow now that we today come to this spot.

DONG YONG. Darling, if you hadn't mentioned it, I would have forgotten. Dear scholartree, when earlier we, husband and wife, were married, it was thanks to your good services as go-between, so please allow me, Dong Yong, to now express my gratitude with a bow today as we pass below you. Darling, I have performed my bow.

SEVENTH SISTER. Husband, I am pregnant, so I cannot lower my head, kneel down, and bow, so why not also make some bows on my behalf?

DONG YONG. Darling, you are pregnant, so let me perform some bows on your behalf. (*Bows again.*) Darling, I have made my bows on your behalf, so let's walk on.

SEVENTH SISTER. Husband, it is still early. Let's each get a stone and sit down for a while.

DONG YONG. Here I have a stone for you to sit on. Darling, just look at these two stones: one is higher and one is lower, resembling a chair.

SEVENTH SISTER. I don't think they resemble a chair.

DONG YONG. So what do they resemble?

SEVENTH SISTER. They resemble stairs.

DONG YONG. How so?

SEVENTH SISTER. Just look at these two stones! One is higher and the other is lower, so they are just like a ladder for your wife to ascend to heaven.

DONG YONG. That's a very apt comparison! Now today when we go back home, it is just like climbing from hell to heaven!

SEVENTH SISTER. Dong Yong, you …

DONG YONG. What?

SEVENTH SISTER. Dong Yong, I have here a bundle of thread. You keep it with you.

DONG YONG. Where does it come from?

SEVENTH SISTER. My female friend in the other village gave it to me.

DONG YONG (*sings*).
I now carry this bundle of yellow thread in my hands—
But darling, why on earth do you give this bundle to me?

SEVENTH SISTER (*sings*).
If at some later date your clothes and socks are tattered and torn,
You can repair them yourself and sew them yourself.

(*The two of them sit down on the stones.*)

DONG YONG. It would indeed be a good thing if I were able to repair my own clothes when you are busy. (SEVENTH SISTER *sadly sheds tears.*) Darling, you …

SEVENTH SISTER. Why are you staring at me?

DONG YONG. Did they treat you badly at the Fu Mansion?

SEVENTH SISTER. Why do you say so?

DONG YONG. Because I see traces of tears on your cheeks.

SEVENTH SISTER. These … These are tears caused by the wind.

DONG YONG. Darling, you are fooling me. The proverb goes: "Tears caused by the wind fall drop by drop; tears from a broken heart gush down the cheeks." (*He wipes away* SEVENTH SISTER*'s tears.*) Darling, from now on we will never again have to suffer any maltreatment by the Fus!

SEVENTH SISTER. Dong Yong! (*She wishes to say something, but stays silent.*)

DONG YONG. Well, let's go back home! Look how high the red sun has risen in the sky!

SEVENTH SISTER (*surprised*). Aiya, the sun is at its highest point! Enough, let's go home!

DONG YONG. Hey, darling! You are going in the wrong direction, that's the way to the Fu Mansion. We have to go this way to my place.

SEVENTH SISTER. You have your home, I have my home.

DONG YONG. Now what? Do you want to live separately even as husband and wife?

SEVENTH SISTER. It is absolutely not so that I want to live separately, but I do want to go back to my natal home.

DONG YONG. Aiya, how could I have been so muddle-headed? Ever since we were married as husband and wife, I tilled the fields during the day and you wove your brocade during the night. I forgot all about my father-in-law and my mother-in-law. Darling, let's go and visit your natal home together today!

SEVENTH SISTER. You cannot go to my mother's place.

DONG YONG. Why can't I go there?

SEVENTH SISTER. Well, today is the birthday celebration for my father and mother, so how can you and I go there empty-handed?

DONG YONG. So what's your idea?

SEVENTH SISTER. It should be enough if you bowed facing the sky.

DONG YONG. So let me make my bow facing the sky. Dear father-in-law and dear mother-in-law, today on the occasion of the celebration of your birthday I offer you my congratulations and I wish you happiness like eastern happiness[13] and the long longevity of one hundred years.

SEVENTH SISTER. Oh heaven!

DONG YONG. The proverb says: "Those who live to seventy years have since ancient times been rare." But when I say "one hundred years" you still want me to add more.[14] So let me extend their longevity to one thousand years, to a myriad of years! Haha!

SEVENTH SISTER (*speaking in an aside*). Dong Yong is plain dumb! Let me use my white fan to enlighten him. (*Addressing* DONG YONG.) Dong Yong, have a look at this white fan.

DONG YONG. I've seen it many times before. (*Accepting the fan.*) It definitely is a fine white fan.

SEVENTH SISTER. The front side is fine, but the backside is even better!

DONG YONG. Let me have a look then. (*Recites.*)

The fan is truly white like snow;
Its picture shows a rounded moon.

And on the moon you see Chang'e,
Quite different from mortal women.[15]

SEVENTH SISTER. Husband, can you read those lines of verse?

DONG YONG. I can read those, yes.

SEVENTH SISTER. Do you also understand them?

DONG YONG. No, I don't understand them.

SEVENTH SISTER (*in an aside*). If he doesn't understand the meaning, then it is all of no use. Let me take these golden hairpins and draw a couple of mandarin ducks to give him another hint. (*Recites.*)
The hundred kinds of birds all fly through the empty sky:
May a couple of mandarin ducks descend to the mortal dust.

(*Addressing* DONG YONG.) Husband, look, what are those?

DONG YONG. Over there on that sandy bank? They seem to be a couple of mandarin ducks.

SEVENTH SISTER. Yes, it is a couple of mandarin ducks.

DONG YONG. One female duck and one male duck?

SEVENTH SISTER. Of course, one female duck and one male duck! The one on the side of your wife is the female duck, and the one on my husband's side is the drake.

DONG YONG. Darling, why is this female duck shedding tears with a lowered head?

SEVENTH SISTER. Dong Yong, this female duck and this male duck are a loving couple of husband and wife, but today the female duck is about to leave the male mandarin duck behind and ascend to heaven. That is why she is shedding tears with a lowered head.

DONG YONG. I can't believe that.

SEVENTH SISTER. Let me call out to her. Female duck, female duck, today you will ascend to heaven, so why don't you spread your wings and soar on high? (*The sound of a bird flying off.*)

DONG YONG. Let me also tell that male duck to ascend to heaven. Male duck, male duck, you and that female duck are a loving couple of husband and wife. Today the female duck is ascending to heaven, so why don't you follow her in her ascent to heaven? Fly off! Get of the ground! (*Upset.*) Let me chase him up to heaven with a pebble. Darling, why can't I make him move?

Seventh Sister. My husband, the female mandarin duck is an immortal bird, and I, your wife, am an immortal woman, and that is why I can chase her back to heaven. That male mandarin duck is a mortal bird, and you, my husband, are a mortal man, so how would you be able to tell him to ascend to heaven?

Dong Yong. If you are an immortal woman, then I am an immortal man!

Seventh Sister. I am truly an immortal woman.

Dong Yong. You truly are an immortal woman?

Seventh Sister. How could I have woven ten bolts of cloud-patterned brocade if I weren't an immortal woman?

Dong Yong. What?

Seventh Sister. My husband, you haven't forgotten that, have you?

Dong Yong. But why do you look so sorrowful today if you are an immortal woman?

Seventh Sister. Husband, your wife is the seventh daughter of the Jade Emperor. Without authorization I descended to the mortal world to marry you, hoping that we could be a loving couple of husband and wife for all eternity. Unfortunately, my father has now found out about this and he commands me to ascend to heaven by the third quarter of the hour of noon!

Dong Yong. Darling!

Seventh Sister. Dong Yong!

Dong Yong (*sings*).

Jade Emperor, Oh, Jade Emperor, what is your intention?
Why have you made up your mind to rob me of my wife?

(*Inserted speech.*) Darling,

The two of us were married in the shade of this scholartree,
Will we also have to part in the shade of this scholartree?

Seventh Sister (*sings*).

We, this loving couple of husband and wife, have to part—

Even a heart made of iron or stone is wounded by sadness.
Your wife's intention was to stay with you, accompany you,
But alas, an imperial command cannot be altered or changed.

DONG YONG (*sings*).

It is nonsense to say an imperial order cannot be altered—
Let me ask the bride-giver to explain the matter in detail.

SEVENTH SISTER. Who do you think the man who gave me away may have been?

DONG YONG. This …

SEVENTH SISTER (*sings*).

He was a transformation of the God of the Soil of this place!

DONG YONG (*sings*).

When I realize that the bride-giver was the God of the Soil,
I am in such a fix that I have no idea what I now should do.
Other witnesses can be located, found, and brought back,
But where would I have to go to find the God of the Soil?

(*Inserted speech.*) Darling!

I take this bundle of thread and I hand it over to you again.
Even if I have all this thread, what benefit will it be to me?
Even if I were to have a thousand yards, ten thousand yards
Of thread, I still would be unable to tie down my dear wife!

Darling, when we were married back then, this scholartree was the go-between, so let me go over and find him!

SEVENTH SISTER. You won't be able to find him.

DONG YONG. Scholartree, when we, husband and wife, were married, you kindly opened your mouth and spoke out. So why don't you keep my darling here now as today she wants to ascend to heaven? Scholartree, open your mouth and speak out! Open your mouth and speak out!

SEVENTH SISTER. There is no use in yelling to that tree!

DONG YONG. Darling, earlier it responded when I called a third time. So let me call out to it once again! Scholartree, open your mouth and speak up!

SEVENTH SISTER. It's a dumb tree, you know.

DONG YONG. A dumb tree … (*Sings.*)

You dumb tree, yes, you dumb tree!
I, Dong Yong, weep and cry hot tears.
On the day of our wedding you were the go-between,
So why don't you try to keep my darling here today?

SEVENTH SISTER (*sings*).

Husband and wife, united in love, impossible to part—
But very soon the red sun will reach its highest point!
The third quarter of the hour of noon is about to arrive.

DONG YONG (*sings*).

I grasp your hand, my darling, unwilling to let you go.

SEVENTH SISTER (*sings*).

It's not the case that I, your wife, am eager to leave;
But I am truly in a fix both to the left and to the right.

DONG YONG (*sings*).

You, my wife, are star-crossed, and I am star-crossed;

SEVENTH SISTER (*sings*).

Husband and wife, we are both equally star-crossed.

DONG YONG (*sings*).

The husband star-crossed like a dragon outside his pool;

SEVENTH SISTER (*sings*).

The wife star-crossed like a tiger far from his mountain!

DONG YONG. Jade Emperor, Jade Emperor, why do you cruelly and deliberately want to separate us, this loving couple of husband and wife?

(*The drum resounds.*)

SEVENTH SISTER. Don't hurt my Dong Yong! I'm coming! (*She is about to leave.*)

DONG YONG (*seeing that* SEVENTH SISTER *wants to leave, tries to catch up with her but fails, and then he collapses and faints on the ground*). Darling! Darling!

(SEVENTH SISTER *rushes over to* DONG YONG.)

SEVENTH SISTER (*sings*).

Once I see that he, Dong Yong, has fainted and collapsed,
I, Seventh Sister, weep so much my tears resemble waves.

I lower my cloud, and then quickly kneel down beside him.
And from the skirt I am wearing I take one piece of fabric.
I want to write him a letter to leave him a full explanation,
But here I don't have paper and ink, I don't have a brush.
So I cannot but bite my middle finger till blood flows out,
My ten fingers as well as my heart are overcome by pain!

(*She writes a letter in blood.*)

I urge my dear husband not to be worried and anxious,
I leave this letter written in blood for my man to see.
One night as husband and wife is one hundred days of love—
So how can I ignore one hundred days as husband and wife?
At present, I, your wife, am pregnant, heavy with your child,
But I do not yet know whether the baby will be a boy or a girl.
If I give birth to a boy, I'll give him the name of Dong Xiao;
If I give birth to a girl, I'll give her the name of Green Peach.
Next year in the balmy spring, when flowers are blooming,
Here under the scholartree I'll hand the baby over to you …

(*The drum resounds.*)

(*Backstage speech.*) This is third quarter of the hour of noon. Seventh Sister, quickly return to heaven!

Seventh Sister (*sings*).

One thousand words, a myriad phrases are not enough—
Alas, an imperial edict cannot be extended or ignored!

Dong Yong! (*She exits.*)

Dong Yong. Darling! (*He sings.*)

A moment ago I fainted and collapsed here on the field;
Suddenly I see a piece of skirt, a letter written in blood.
It states: One night as husband and wife is one hundred days of love—
So how can I ignore one hundred days as husband and wife?
At present, I, your wife, am pregnant, heavy with your child,
But I do not yet know whether the baby will be a boy or a girl.
If I give birth to a boy, I'll give him the name of Dong Xiao;
If I give birth to a girl, I'll give her the name of Green Peach.
Next year in the balmy spring, when flowers are blooming,
Here under the scholartree I will hand the baby over to you …
Reading this letter written in blood my heart feels pierced,
Up into heaven, down into earth, I will follow my darling!

SEVENTH SISTER (*from backstage, as if from the clouds*). Dong Yong!

DONG YONG. Darling, please wait, I am coming! (*Exits.*)

(*The end.*)

V. Reflections and Criticisms

The Rewriting

The early discussions of the revision of *Married to a Heavenly Immortal* were focused on the ideological aspects of the process and the revision was hailed as a restoration of the original nature of the legend. A tale of exceptional filial piety rewarded by divine intervention became a story of heroic search for free love and staunch defiance of the traditional secular and celestial authorities. In the process Dong Yong's rich benefactor became a rapacious landlord (and his lecherous son was reduced to a stupid oaf).

The revision was an ongoing process as the editors tried to keep pace with the evolving political situation outside of the theater. The revision involved not only the scriptwriters and actors but also the local Party bosses who used *Married to a Heavenly Immortal* to showcase their achievements in theater reform to the national authorities in Shanghai and beyond. The many changes in music, performance, costume, and scenery were hardly mentioned as these were considered improvements without a clear ideological content.

Ban Youshu

The Revised Huangmei Opera *Married to a Heavenly Immortal*[1]

November 25, 1953

The old Huangmei Opera *Married to a Heavenly Immortal* has been formally performed in Anqing following revision by the Creative Group of the Provincial Bureau of Culture. This is a happy event in our work on the reform of Huangmei Opera and, more widely, in the work of reform of regional opera in Anhui province. It makes us realize that among the old plays of Huangmei Opera there are many pieces that are rich in popular character (*renminxing* 人民性).[2] But these pieces were de-natured by the reactionary ruling classes and lost their original brilliance. Now they only need to be cleaned up to be able to once again display a dazzling and blinding light.

Following the revision and performance of *Married to a Heavenly Immortal*, the results have been positive. First of all, [the editors] have removed the feudal poison that was inserted by the ruling classes in the past. For many years the old *Married to a Heavenly Immortal* only propagated the feudal teachings of filial piety on behalf of the landlord class. It told the story of how one Dong Yong[3] sold himself to bury his father (one of the *Twenty-four Exemplars of Filial Piety*) and "by his filial piety moved Heaven and Earth." Therefore, the Jade Emperor ordered the Seventh Immortal Sister to descend to the mortal world to marry him, providing him with all kinds of advantages. In this way, the story indoctrinated the common people with the idea that they should all practice filial piety. "To rule all-under-heaven with filial piety" was one of the magic treasures by which the feudal emperors controlled the masses. In *Married to a Heavenly Immortal* as performed following the revision there are no longer any items that propagate reactionary feudal morality. This new *Married to a Heavenly Immortal* clearly embodies the efforts and struggles of young men and women in feudal society to free themselves from the shackles imposed on them in their pursuit of happy lives of love and ideals. Of course, because of the limitations of the historical conditions, their resistance is limited and what they aspire to can only be based on the small family economy made up of individual households where the husband plows and the wife weaves. Without a doubt this represents the aspirations of the millions of oppressed peasants at that time. Therefore, such a theme is healthy.

Next we can observe that the editor and director made considerable effort with respect to the arrangement of the scenes. In the new revised play the first scene "Burying the Father" (which includes Dong Yong going to his uncle to borrow money) has been dropped, the scene "Longing for the Mortal World" has been added, and the performance ends with "The Separation." In this way [the editors] daringly remove scenes, such as Dong Yong becoming Top-of-the-List and Dong Yong recognizing millionaire Fu as his benefactor and marrying his daughter, which from an objective standpoint dampen the class contradictions. This procedure corresponds to the principal spirit of removing the dross and saving the essence. The newly-added scene "Longing for the Mortal World" represents the convoluted process of Seventh Sister's internal turmoil and the contradictions in the heavenly palace before descending to the mortal world, rendering the anti-feudal theme much richer and clearer. That is why we experience an even greater *renminxing*.

Third, in the scene "Visiting Magpie Bridge" the character of the vilified Eldest Sister is changed (originally her character was played by a *caidan* 彩旦),[4] and the appearance onstage of the fisherman, woodcutter, farmer, student, and the wedding procession is deleted. Now the seven Immortal Maidens are singing of them in turn, while they accompany the songs with a dance. In fact, the scene "Visiting Magpie Bridge" has become a beautiful ancient-costume group dance. The dance has been created based on the original Huangmei Opera and by absorbing the performance methods of dances from elsewhere. In this way, although we cannot yet say that [Huangmei Opera] has fully matured, it basically has not yet lost its original character and has achieved a unity of content and form.

Of course, this is not the same as saying that the newly performed *Married to a Heavenly Immortal* is without defects. There are still some places where it feels rough. The dance in the scene "Weaving Silk" is nothing more than a mechanical representation of the manual production process of weaving silk. This is inconsistent with the spirit of Chairman Mao's precious guideline that art in comparison to life "is more focused and more typical." Also the ending of the play requires more study. This is where it is most difficult to satisfy the audience, but it is also the greatest shortcoming of the original play. Of course, it will not do to end with Dong Yong becoming Top-of-the-List, even though this too represents the aspirations of the laboring masses at that time. Should the play end instead with "Delivering the Son"? If this is treated well, it is not impossible, but the problem is that once Dong Yong and Seventh Sister have been separated, the climax has already passed and there is nothing else that can still be presented. Even more importantly, it would not provide the audience with any greater stimulus and inspiration.

In addition, the play still suffers from abstract generalization (for instance, in its treatment of millionaire Fu and Young Master Fu) and formalism (for instance, in "The Separation" a god in golden armor appears as soon as the heavenly drum resounds).[5] In the scene "Longing for the Mortal World" the complex moods of a young girl hoping for a life of love are not yet sufficiently grasped.

The above are some of my personal impressions upon watching *Married to a Heavenly Immortal*. In order to allow this extremely popular fairy-tale play[6] on its present basis to be continuously improved and to establish a good example for those who later will revise old plays I offer these insights for consideration and as reference for further study by comrades working on drama. I hope that in the near future they will be able to revise this play even more perfectly and to perform it even more splendidly. At the same time, I hope that more excellent plays that have been revised will come out in quick succession so that by "overturning the old and bringing out the new, and allowing one hundred flowers to bloom together" they will serve the needs of the enterprise of the great construction of our fatherland!

Hong Fei

On the Revision of *Married to a Heavenly Immortal*[7]

December 10, 1954

Editor's note: *Married to a Heavenly Immortal* is a play that is extraordinarily popular with the masses of the people in this province. At the great East China Theater Festival which recently took place this play obtained first prize for its script, and prizes for beautiful performance, direction, and musical performance. Comrade Hong Fei was the person "who held the brush" during the rewriting of this play. This article, relatively completely introducing the process of revising this play, may serve as reference for theater workers analyzing the ideological content of our heritage of regional drama.

I

The laboring people of the past have created many beautiful fairy tales[8] on the basis of their own imagination. Over a long period these were created by numerous people, and as a result they were continuously enriched and developed. In this way, *Married to a Heavenly Immortal* has grown from a simple legend into a play that is rich in episodes. The story of Dong Yong meeting an immortal is first found in *Investigations of the Supernatural* (*Soushen ji*) by Gan Bao (early fourth century) of the Jin dynasty (265–416), and the story is set in the Han dynasty (206 BCE–220 CE).[9] There are social reasons why this historical period produced such a story with a peasant as its protagonist. The Han dynasty still retained remnants of the slave system. "For those who sold themselves and their dependents as slaves there were pens on the street, and they were put in these pens just like animals. The common price for a slave was 15,000 coins" (*A Brief General History of China*, ch. 2).[10] Peasants who were forced to sell themselves into servitude suffered merciless oppression and exploitation. But they were thirsting for freedom and they all cherished an idea of a beautiful life. Of course, they also hoped to have a beautiful and smart wife who would share their life for better or worse and who would help and assist them, and [they hoped] to escape their cruel shackles and live an independent life in which "the husband would plow while the wife would spin." The story of Dong Yong meeting an immortal reflects precisely the ideals of the millions of oppressed peasants during those days.

The "Transformation Text on Dong Yong" of the Tang dynasty (a document discovered at Dunhuang),[11] and the "Tale of Dong Yong Meeting with an Immortal," one of the "plain tales" of the Song dynasty (found in *Reclining on a Cushion Next to a Rainy Window*)[12] not only turned [the legend] from a story narrated in prose into a *chantefable* text in prose and song, but also contributed to the gradual completion of the characteristics of the two protagonists in the story—Dong Yong and Seventh Sister. Unfortunately, these texts also included many fatalistic and absurd elements. Later, when drama arose during the Yuan and Ming dynasties, the story of Dong Yong meeting an immortal was adapted in dramatic form. The *Comprehensive Catalogue with Content Abstracts of the Sea of Songs* (*Quhai zongmu tiyao*) includes a content summary of *Weaving Brocade*,[13] and *Autumn Night Moon* (*Qiuye yue* 秋夜月) contains a complete script of the scene "The Immortal Maiden Takes her Leave at the Scholartree."[14] At present, nearly all genres of regional theater in China include plays on Dong Yong and Seventh Sister. Huangmei Opera's *Married to a Heavenly Immortal* and Sichuan Opera's (*Chuanju* 川劇) *The Shady Scholartree* (*Huaiyin ji* 槐陰記), Jinhua Opera's (*Wuju* 婺劇) *The Shady Scholartree* (*Huaiyin shu* 槐陰樹), *Seventh Sister Descends to Earth* (*Qijie xiafan* 七姐下凡) in the repertoire of Tea-Picking Opera (*Caichaxi* 採茶戲) from Jiangxi, and *Married to Seventh Star* (*Qixingpei* 七星配) in the repertoire of Daoqi Opera (*Daoqixi* 倒七戲) from Anhui all treat the same story, but each play has its own characteristics.

The episodes of *Married to a Heavenly Immortal* (this also applies to *Weaving Brocade*) correspond to the first half of the "Tale of Dong Yong Meeting an Immortal." The story goes that upon the death of his father Dong Yong is unable to provide him with a funeral and thus sells himself to the Fu family as a slave. The Jade Emperor is moved by his filial intention and orders that Seventh Sister descend to earth to team up with him as husband and wife for one hundred days. After the marriage, the Immortal Maiden weaves ten bolts of silk in a single night, thus lessening the burden on Dong Yong. When the one hundred days are over, Seventh Sister ascends to heaven. Upon her departure she offers Dong Yong a silk skirt and a white fan and tells him to go to the capital to present these treasures. Dong Yong later obtains the title of Top-of-the-List for Presenting Treasure. As he rides home, the Immortal Maiden is ordered to deliver to him his son, and when she meets with Dong Yong, she also instructs him to take young Miss Fu as his second wife. The complete story of Dong Yong meeting an immortal is healthy and beautiful, but it also includes some dross.

II

The healthy, beautiful aspects of this play are found in its ideology that reflects the past struggles of the laboring people on behalf of their beautiful ideals. The protagonists in the play, the laborer Dong Yong and Seventh Sister, characters who conform to the ideals of workers, are relatively lovable as far as the description of their characters is concerned. Dong Yong is sincere and good and is concerned about others in tight situations. When Seventh Sister wants to follow him as his wife, he honestly and straightforwardly declares: "Above my head I have not a single tile to cover my body/ Under my feet I have not one inch of land to make a living./ It's very kind of you, young lady, to follow me,/ But regret will come too late once you suffer hunger and cold." At the same time, he also contemplates the following: "If you, young lady, accompany me,/ I am afraid that Mrs. Fu will deliberately find fault with you./ And if Mrs. Fu were to abuse you,/ How will I be able to bear that? How will you be at ease?"[15] Such a character is precisely the uniquely good character of the laboring people. Seventh Sister is a rebel from the palace and daringly pursues a life of true happiness among men. When she descends from heaven and sees Dong Yong as he is leaving his hovel, she brazenly sets out to catch up with him: "Today, I reckon is the day that he is starting on his job/ So I will go with him and we'll become a couple." But when Dong Yong, concerned about her and hesitant, is faced with the issue of marriage, he cannot make up his mind. She immediately declares: "If the Fu Mansion treats us poorly,/ I will shoulder one-half of that heavy load." After she and Dong Yong marry, she uses her intelligence and her labor (weaving ten bolts of silk in a single night) to shorten the long term of his bitter servitude. But the very day that husband and wife leave the Fu family unexpectedly is also the end of her one hundred days and the Jade Emperor orders her to ascend to heaven. At this moment, her feelings of resistance are extremely strong. Just have a look: "Here on the road I am filled with anger toward my father,/ I'm angry because his royal edict lacks all reason!/ As he ordered me to descend to the world below/ He should not call me back after one hundred days." We enjoy these two characters because they manifest the superior quality of our nation.

But the negative, backward parts of this play are also very serious. That is because it uses all kinds of ingenious machinations to cover up and distort the fighting spirit of laborers struggling for their ideals and leads people to comply with "Heaven's fate," to accept their poverty, and to see everything as determined by karma. Why does Seventh Sister descend to earth? Even though the original play indicates that "Seventh Sister when visiting Magpie

Bridge conceives a longing for the mortal world," the true reason for her arrival in the mortal world is "My husband's filial piety moved Heaven and Earth,/ So the Master of Fate informed the Jade Emperor./ When my father the king saw his exceptional filial piety,/ He ordered me to descend to the world to become his wife." "Filial piety" is the dominant thread throughout the original play. All Dong Yong's and Seventh Sister's experiences are determined by the fact that Dong Yong's filial piety moves Heaven and Earth and that the Jade Emperor orders Seventh Sister to descend to earth to become his wife for one hundred days. We do not oppose the correct feelings between father and son and we do not oppose the fact that Dong Yong displays filial piety toward his good father, but we do oppose "filial piety as the foundation of all moral behavior," and we do oppose that a person's fate is determined by filial piety. We know that the poverty of laborers in the past, to the extent that like Dong Yong they had to sell themselves into servitude, was not because of the machinations of Heaven's fate but because of the cruel exploitation by the rulers. The contradiction between the exploiters and the exploited allowed for no compromise, but in the original play this confrontational contradiction was nullified. For instance, Dong Yong first becomes a sworn brother with the son of Master Fu, and he later marries Master Fu's daughter. At the same time, a negative worldview is forcibly imposed on an oppressed laborer. When Dong Yong goes to the Fu family to begin his job, he even has the following thoughts: "Light and shadow resemble an arrow carried along by the wind,/ As they lightly float by they leave not a trace./ In one thousand years fields change hands eight hundred times;/ After thirty years "east of the river" has become "west of the river."/ What is the point of amassing great amounts of money?/ As soon as Impermanence arrives, all things are empty./ The sun sinks in the western hills to return to the east again,/ So I urge people to practice filial piety and not to practice evil./ The Hegemon King practiced evil and died at Raven River,/ But Han Xin also lost his life in Weiyang Palace. . . ."[16]

Once we became aware of the cream and the dross in the original play, we wanted to preserve the positive parts that are advantageous to the people, and we also wanted to mercilessly remove the negative parts that are harmful to the people. Therefore, when revising the play, we kept the scene of Dong Yong being forced to sell himself but we removed "the filial piety that moved Heaven and Earth"; we kept Seventh Sister's longing for the mortal world at Magpie Bridge, but we removed the order by the Jade Emperor; we kept the marriage of one hundred days, but we removed the fatalistic arrangement;[17] we kept Seventh Sister's pregnancy, but we removed the scenes of Dong Yong presenting the treasure and of Seventh Sister bringing him his son. Because we kept some parts and removed other parts we had to make a number of changes and additions based on the needs and possibilities because only in this way could we ensure that the play would be a perfect work of art. For instance, "Visiting Magpie Bridge" in the original play only consisted of the Immortal Maidens standing on benches and waiting for the fisherman, the woodcutter, the farmer, and the student to cross the stage and singing a song for each of them; after their songs, the Jade Emperor issues his edict ordering Seventh Sister to descend to earth. Now we changed it as follows: Seventh Sister feels depressed and invites her six elder sisters to come along with her to Magpie Bridge to observe the scenery of the mortal world, thus highlighting the Immortal Maiden's displeasure with her boring life and her yearning for the human realm; moreover, with Seventh Sister as the main character, as they watch the life of labor of the fisherman, the woodcutter, the farmer, and the student, they give expression to their sympathy and concern, and from this is produced Seventh Sister's extreme sympathy and concern for Dong Yong. As far as form is concerned, we removed the fisherman, the woodcutter, the farmer, and the student from the stage, and through the songs and dances of the Immortal Maidens imitating the laborers of the human realm we achieved our aim of theatrical simplicity and liveliness. As far as Dong Yong's relation to the Fu family is concerned, we based ourselves on the original episodes, but we also consulted the records in the *Provincial Gazetteer for Hubei* concerning Dong Yong's meeting with an immortal (this contains the factual record of how the rich man abused Dong Yong),[18] and we wrote "Starting Out on the Job" and "Completing the Job" in order to reflect the confrontational contradiction between the peasant slaves and the slave owners. The reason for this change is that we wanted to present the laborer Dong Yong as the main character onstage, to show him sympathy and support, and to give more prominence to the positive part of the original play, that is, the struggle of the laborers of the past for their beautiful ideals. Because of this, we also came up with some scenes that describe Dong Yong and Seventh Sister's married life. After they become husband and wife in the shade of the scholartree, on the eve of weaving ten bolts of silk and upon completion of the job, through their life as husband and wife we reflect their mutual attachment, closeness, and hopes for a beautiful future. Precisely because their mutual attachment and closeness are so encompassing, precisely because their life ideals are so beautiful, an even stronger explanation is provided for the oppression they suffer at the hands of the rulers in heaven and on earth, and the destruction of their ideals becomes incomparably cruel. This is the new face that we have attempted to give to *Married to a Heavenly Immortal.*

III

The rewriting of *Married to a Heavenly Immortal* took two years, and changes were made more than ten times. From October of last year it has been staged by the Anhui Provincial Huangmei Opera Company and it has been repeatedly performed in Anqing and Hefei and also for comforting the People's Liberation Army. Recently, it participated in the performances at the first East China Theater Festival. Because of this performance we received evaluations by specialists and friends in the theater world. Everyone recognized that the main theme of this play shows a strong popular character (*renminxing*), that it reflects the strong love and great hopes of the laboring people for freedom and happy lives, and that it reflects the daring and persistent struggle of the people against the forces of evil. Moreover, [they felt,] the story is very beautiful and refined and can give expression to the theme in a focused manner; even though the characters are simple, the story is not at all monotonous. The impression that Dong Yong and Seventh Sister leave behind is very fresh. They also recognized that this is because we continued the realist methods of expression in our theatrical heritage. That these strong points were pointed out by our comrades is to a large extent because they were meant as encouragement as actually the play's artistic creation has not yet achieved that level. If you say that this play has some accomplishments, you have to give credit to the precious heritage that has been bequeathed to us by our ancestors, you have to give credit to the theater-reform policy of the Party, and you have to give credit to the concrete and patient leadership of the Party. Despite their busy work schedule, the responsible cadres of the Party committee in our province have come to us to discuss the problems in the revision of *Married to a Heavenly Immortal*, and they have presented suggestions for improvement with respect to the theme, the characters, and even the tiniest of details. Their assistance and encouragement have been very important to us. Moreover, the leadership of the Bureau of Culture of Anhui province and comrades in the world of literature and art have time and again considered the many problems in the revision of this play. This has made us deeply realize that, just like any enterprise, the production of a work of art can only achieve success by relying on the leadership of the Party and by obtaining the assistance of the masses. At the same time, the revision of *Married to a Heavenly Immortal* was also a collective creation. The revisers were continuing the creative work of their predecessors and summarizing everyone's wisdom.

How did we go about the concrete work [of revision]? First of all, we collected all kinds of records about *Married to a Heavenly Immortal* and scripts of plays on the same topic in other theatrical genres. The collection of the records assisted us in understanding the social background of the origin of the story, and it also allowed us to find evidence for our changes in the process of developing and enriching [the play]. The collection of the scripts of plays on the same topic in other theatrical genres allowed us to borrow the strong points of others to complement the weak spots of our own. For instance, "Magpie Bridge" in Sichuan Opera and "Separating at the Scholartree" in Jinhua Opera are more complete than the original script of *Married to a Heavenly Immortal*, so this allowed us to borrow some things. Once we had these rich materials at hand, we still had to collaborate very closely with the directors and experienced artists. Based on their individual stage experiences, they provided us with suggestions on many aspects, from the construction of the story and the shaping of the protagonists to the wording of the arias and the dialogues (in this respect the Huangmei Opera directors Li Liping and Qiao Zhiliang and the experienced artists Wang Shaofang and Yan Fengying came up with many ideas). The final arbiter of the art of theater is the broad audience, and every time this play was performed we received many suggestions from enthusiastic members of the audience. These suggestions came from all sides, so it was unavoidable that at times they would also contradict each other. This demanded that the revisers consider these suggestions from all sides and carry out multiple experiments so that after repeated study they could come up with their own ideas. For instance, members of the audience held two views regarding the ending of *Married to a Heavenly Immortal*: Some people were of the opinion that this play completed the task of its theme and was artistically complete in ending with "The Separation," but others were not satisfied with "The Separation" as the ending and suggested keeping the scene "Delivering the Son." When our first revised script was performed onstage, we simply ended with "The Separation." Later we experimented with "Delivering the Son." The first time we changed it in such a way that, with the assistance of Eldest Sister Seventh Sister breaches the rules of the Jade Emperor and bravely takes her son to the world below. Later we changed it in such a way that in the shade of the scholartree Dong Yong, while waiting for Seventh Sister, in a dream meets with Seventh Sister who brings him his son. Eventually we feared that this treatment would lessen the positive import of this tragedy, and, at the same time we also had great difficulty in making the concrete action of Seventh Sister descending to earth convincing and rational. That is why in the end we decided to conclude with "The Separation."

Even though quite some labor was expended on this play and even though it has been well received, it still contains many deficiencies. As pointed out by Comrade [Yi]qun in the *Liberation Daily* of November 5, the most important of these is that the play as a whole is insufficiently unified with respect to style and is insufficiently focused in its expression of its theme. Therefore the play as a whole leaves disparate feelings. According to Comrade [Yi]qun, "the whole play is unified in style in the four scenes 'Visiting Magpie Bridge,' 'Meeting on the Road,' 'Weaving Silk,' and 'The Separation' because these give expression to the aspirations and needs of the laboring people under the oppression of feudal forces through the methods of fantasy and borrowing from fairy tales. But 'Starting Out on the Job,' 'Embroidery' (already deleted), and 'Completing the Job' all give expression to the contradiction between landlords and the laboring people using the simplest realist method, and these two ways of writing are obviously not unified in style." The reason why we initially put so much emphasis on the writing of "Starting Out on the Job" and "Completing the Job" is that we wanted to highlight the irreconcilable contradiction between peasant slave and slave owner and, in this way, to elucidate how one peasant slave, Dong Yong, by utilizing the power of an Immortal Maiden and through an obstinate struggle is able to free himself from his cruel shackles. At first, we believed that this endeavor was justified, but we did not realize that "not all good endeavors can be accommodated in a single play and forcibly accommodating these definitely would produce all kinds of defects." This criticism provided us with some new inspirations and we came up with the following: Originally we had planned on greatly expanding "Starting Out on the Job" and "Completing the Job," but how should we now pare them down? How should we write up Master Fu and his son as truthful characters? Moreover, our comrades also offered us some suggestions for deepening the characterization of our protagonists and purification of the language, which are all very precious. In sum, artistically the play is not yet perfect and it is in need of further work. So we hope that everyone will continue to offer their criticism. Only through continuous criticism and assistance can we ensure that the ideological nature and the artistic nature [of the play] will be raised to a higher level.

November 20, 1954

The Performance

In 1956, when the Anhui Provincial Huangmei Opera Company visited Beijing, interviews with Yan Fengying and Wang Shaofang appeared in the Beijing press. The articles discussed the differences between the traditional and the revised *Married to a Heavenly Immortal*, and how Yan and Wang had changed their own performances of the leading characters accordingly. Both Yan Fengying and Wang Shaofang also stressed the huge gulf in the lives of performers before and after the establishment of the People's Republic.

In their detailed analyses of the characters that they performed and in their insistence on their personal identification with their characters they reflect the wide-ranging influence of the Stanislavsky system in China in the 1950s.[19] We find the same influence in Qiao Zhiliang's reminiscences of directing *Married to a Heavenly Immortal.* Even though these memories were recalled during the 1990s, they appear to rely heavily on the extensive "directorial plan" of forty years earlier. Li Liping's 1981 essay provides us with a survey of the different stages in the production of the 1953 and 1954 plays. The articles by Li Liping and Qiao Zhiliang clearly illustrate the division of labor between the two directors. Li Liping taught the individual actors to analyze the characters they played and to identify with these characters. Qiao Zhiliang focused on the interaction of the actors on stage; as a choreographer he was also responsible for the dances. The articles also bring out how freely the directors borrowed from other theatrical genres in their staging of the revised version of *Married to a Heavenly Immortal.*

Yan Fengying

How I Perform Seventh Sister[20]

1956

Married to a Heavenly Immortal is an item in the traditional repertoire of Huangmei Opera. I have sung Huangmei Opera since my earliest youth. In the beginning I only entered onstage to scamper about as a little maid, but in those days I also saw performers of an earlier generation perform *Married to a Heavenly Immortal*. Later I myself also performed in this play. But to tell the truth, what did I understand in those days? When my teacher told me to sing in a certain manner, I sang in a certain manner. I sang opera only to make a living; I felt neither love nor hatred toward the character of Seventh Sister. Whether I watched other people perform this opera or whether I myself performed this play, I did not feel any special interest toward it.

I preferred to perform some plays that had a strong emotional flavor and that had plenty of arias, such as *The Small "Leaving the Inn"* (*Xiao cidian* 小辭店),[21] *Meeting in the Western Room* (*Xilou hui* 西樓會),[22] and *Meeting at Indigo Bridge* (*Lanqiao hui* 藍橋會).[23] In the region of Anqing and Tongcheng (the area where Huangmei Opera grew up), when watching Huangmei Opera the audiences (primarily peasants), just like the Beijing audiences watching Peking Opera, mostly came to listen to the singing. Many experienced performers had their own special characteristics when singing the tunes, and the audiences were absorbed by these special styles.

In the old *Married to a Heavenly Immortal* the role of Dong Yong is somewhat more important. You can say that it was primarily Dong Yong's play. Its central idea was quite different from that today. First, it glorified the story of Dong Yong selling his body to bury his father in the *Twenty-four Exemplars of Filial Piety*—Dong Yong sells his body and buries his father, his filial piety moves the Jade Emperor, and the Jade Emperor gives Seventh Sister to him as a wife for one hundred days. Following the "Separating at the Scholartree," Dong Yong marries the daughter of Old Master Fu and obtains the rank of "Top-of-the-List for Presenting Treasure." On his way home, Seventh Sister descends to the mortal world and hands him his son. Dong Yong receives "Multiple Blessings All at Once" as his filial piety is properly rewarded.

The old *Married to a Heavenly Immortal* also contains the two scenes

"Meeting on the Road" and "The Separation." In these two scenes Seventh Sister plays a considerable role. But Seventh Sister in these two scenes was usually performed by two different performers. In "Meeting on the Road" she was often performed by the "leading lady" and in "The Separation" as a rule she was performed by the "second *dan*" (the second-placed *huadan* 花旦).[24] I have performed both these scenes, but in those days I usually only performed one of them. So it is difficult to say that I had a complete impression of Seventh Sister.

When putting on a play in the past the older generation would explain the story and the dialogues. Occasionally we would memorize the dialogues as we were applying our stage make-up. It would also happen that when performing plays consisting of multiple installments there would be no dialogue. Having heard the story and its major incidents we would immediately ascend the stage and "freely bandy about" with our dialogues that we improvised on the spot. Huangmei Opera performers called this "opening the sluices."

These phenomena nowadays would most likely be considered "a lack of responsibility toward the audience." But in those days we had to perform two plays or even three plays in one day, and each play had to be different. Apart from some experienced performers of an earlier generation who had received some education, the ordinary performers—especially someone like me who at that time was very young and had never attended school—could not come up with any other trick.

The only other way was to "steal a play." When you saw that some actor played a part very well or sang some role very well, you would stand in the wings and secretly and carefully memorize everything. In this way on occasion you could memorize a complete plot.

Eventually I slowly developed a habit. When I came across a play, I would make sure to find out which story it told, what kind of person I was performing, and what she did once onstage. When I entered the stage, I thus would know what to do and what to say.

On top of that, I also put quite some effort into the singing. Should I sing loudly or should I sing softly? Should I sing rapidly or should I sing slowly in order to give expression to the thoughts and feelings of the given role (if the lyrics were more plentiful, I could fully display my talents).

When performing the old *Married to a Heavenly Immortal* I was very much at a loss. There is not much singing in "Meeting on the Road," but that was not the major problem. What exactly was this Seventh Sister doing in descending to earth? It goes without saying that in those days I had no capacity for analysis to speak of, and I had even less understanding of a "historical perspective." All I knew was that Seventh Sister descended to earth because she had been told to do so by her father and that after one hundred days she had to return to heaven. In this way, of course I could not say that she had a true "love" for Dong Yong. If I think back on it today, the whole purpose of this scene would appear to be to come up with some method to secretly insert the fan in the back of Dong Yong's neck and to secretly run off with his pack and his umbrella so that Dong Yong would take me along. Of course, the reason why I had these incorrect impressions had everything to do with my level of understanding of that role at the time.

I also could not get a clear idea of the status of Seventh Sister after she descends to earth. In the [old] play Dong Yong was a student, and Seventh Sister's costume and make-up were not very different from that of an ordinary *huadan*, so you could not tell whether she was the dainty daughter of a noble family or a village girl. She was wearing a skirt and a vest, and in her right hand she held a fan and in her left hand she held a handkerchief. When she was standing, she loved to put her left hand on her hip. Such an image, of course, did not correspond to that of a peasant woman.

There was no scenery. A stage hand followed Seventh Sister and placed a chair at the entrance or exit gate to the stage, and this chair represented the two rocks where one entered or left the main road. Seventh Sister "sat down" on these two "rocks" and blocked Dong Yong's way.

Dong Yong was purely costumed as a "filial son."[25] He wore a wig of long, unbound hair (*shuaifa* 甩髮), capped by a white mourning kerchief. In this scene he showed a face that was mostly weeping and mourning, and only at the very end would he smile a bit.

In the traditional repertoire of Huangmei Opera there were very few large dance numbers—we mostly relied on singing.

In this scene, Seventh Sister does not do much singing, but it was not clear to me what this character was doing onstage. But in order to make a living, I went ahead and sang, but in my heart I was not happy.

In 1954, because we were to participate in the East China Theater Festival, the leadership once again ordered me to play Seventh Sister. This time we performed the revised play. Initially I still was not happy, but later, in the process of rehearsing this play, I slowly changed my earlier opinion.

According to what the comrades who had done the revision told me, they did some research and found that Dong Yong had really existed and also that he had truly sold his body to bury his father. And there truly was a very capable girl who accompanied him and who helped him by weaving more cloth than any ordinary person could have done (but not ten bolts of brocade) in a single night. They told me that Dong Yong had been a peasant and that the reason that he later became a student was due to the revisions [of the play] by the feudal class. So we restored Dong Yong to his original role. When we performed in Beijing there were also comrades who argued that we should reverse that change.

Because Seventh Sister could weave silk, she definitely must have loved "labor." When she descended to the mortal world, she must have become a village girl.

In addition, an even greater change was that Seventh Sister's descent to the mortal world was changed from a passive action into an action undertaken on her own initiative. Unable to withstand the chilly years and months at the celestial palace and yearning for a fulfilled life in the human realm she secretly descends to the mortal world.

These changes created quite a number of new problems for me. I wanted to perform her as a village girl and I also wanted to perform this village girl as truly and sincerely in love with Dong Yong.

When I was little and still living at home, I would herd buffalo and I had many "village girl" friends. You could also say that I was a "village girl." If you mention village life, I am immediately reminded of how when I was little I would mischievously get into fights on the hillside with the other girls herding buffaloes. I am relatively familiar with their lives. On the stage I have performed various different village girls, for instance Tao Jinhua 陶金花 in *Collecting Pig Fodder* (*Da zhucao*) and Yang Siya 楊四伢 in *Shazigang* 砂子崗.[26] But even though I was told that this Seventh Sister was a village girl, she was still wearing an ancient costume with long sleeves and a plaited skirt, and she still made some bodily movements from classical theater. This caused me all sorts of difficulties.

Seventh Sister is a divine immortal, so it is reasonable to analyze her from the perspective of a divine immortal. I had never met a divine immortal and I had no way of meeting one, but I could deal with her according to the feelings and circumstances of "human beings."

When performing Tao Jinhua in *Collecting Pig Fodder* I primarily went for a spontaneous and vivacious young girl from a farming village. When I performed Yang Siya in *Shazigang* I primarily went for a suffering wife who is beaten and abused. But when performing Seventh Sister in *Married to a Heavenly Immortal* I considered that she had the courage to flee from heaven to earth and that she also had the courage to take the initiative and propose marriage to a man she had never met. In addition, she could come up with some clever schemes to move Dong Yong and to counter the evil Old Master Fu. … Thus, she clearly must have been both a courageous and intelligent and a passionate and capable young woman.

Analysis and understanding were not the most difficult part. I feared I would not be able to play her like this on the stage. From the moment we started rehearsing, we ran into the following problem: the director disliked my performance for being too "cultured" (*wen* 文). For opera performances there are a set of traditional artistic conventions. On the one hand, I wanted to play her in a verisimilar way, but, on the other hand, I wanted to perform her in a beautiful way. These were the two main tasks that confronted me.

Why did I fail to perform her in verisimilar way and in a rustic manner? It took me quite a while to find out. When a village girl and a dainty daughter of a noble family are confronted with the same problem, the way in which their emotions are expressed and the way in which they confront other people are not the same. For instance, in "Meeting on the Road" Seventh Sister sings: "I would like to be united in wedlock." Initially I performed this in the usual way of a high-born young lady. While indicating with my two index fingers to Dong Yong the idea of "united as a pair," I bashfully lowered my head. This style of performance was applicable not only here; I have also used it in other plays, but when used in the case of Seventh Sister, it was too "cultured." I still remember how when I was little, some grownups would curse their daughters for "not having any shame." In fact, these girls were some very capable friends of mine, but they did not abide by the regulations of the old folks and they selected partners in accordance with their own wishes. I imagined that Seventh Sister also must have been such a "character." I would grasp the opportunity and daringly express my true feelings to Dong Yong because otherwise he would run off (I didn't really remember that I still had "miraculous powers"). I would immediately tell him that I wanted to marry him. This was not Lin Daiyu 林黛玉 meeting Jia Baoyu 賈寶玉 in the dark of the night, amidst the flowers by the light of the moon.[27] This was "in the bright light of day," on the road to nowhere, when a village girl who had failed to find refuge with relatives ran into Dong Yong who had sold his body to bury his father. If he would not take me in, I would have "no place to go." Filled with these emotions, I sang, filled with urgency and in a clear voice, as my eyes were fixed on him: "I would like with you. …" But how could I truly be like those girls who were cursed by their parents for "not having any shame"? So when it came to singing "to be united in wedlock," I bashfully lowered my head.

In this part of the play I still performed Seventh Sister as a divine immortal masquerading as a village girl. It is "a play within a play." I am a divine immortal, but I am also a village girl. I wanted to bring both these two different statuses across in my performance in order to perform this play in a verisimilar manner. Furthermore, I was truly in love with Dong Yong!

For the rest of the play, apart from those few scenes in which Seventh Sister appears as a divine immortal, I appear as the good wife of Dong Yong. I love him from the bottom of my heart.

As for Seventh Sister's love of Dong Yong, the work of analysis was very simple. But if you transport it to the stage and want me to love comrade Wang Shaofang (who played Dong Yong) exactly as if he were my lover, then that was somewhat more difficult. We are just regular comrades, and in the end we are not true lovers, so as soon as we started rehearsing, it was truly contrived and awkward.

When we discussed this, we wanted to develop these "marital feelings" offstage. There was a time that we joked together and ate our food together, with the result that we became exceptionally close to each other. When performing onstage we also reacted perfectly to each other, so in performance you really could not distinguish whether I loved Dong Yong or I loved Wang Shaofang.

In "Meeting on the Road" I enter onstage first, and while Wang Shaofang has not yet entered onstage, in my mind I see his image as he had already put on his make-up, and I truly feel that he is lovable in every aspect. Because I am filled with this love, I naturally become somewhat mischievous. Once when we were performing onstage, I suddenly realized that a girl will always show off in front of her lover as somewhat younger and loving to be cute, so I stressed this a bit in my performance. Later we kept this in the play and we also developed it fully in other places.

In the first half of "The Separation" my thoughts are extraordinarily beautiful. I have such a good husband, and on top of that I am also pregnant. As I am imagining my future happy life, scenes of this life start to come alive in my brain, as if being shown in a movie: my husband Dong Yong plowing the fields, me weaving cloth at home, and our son playing in front of the loom. I also imagined how I would have a baby for the first time and what the baby would look like once it was born. ... In this way, my emotions were easily aroused.

This "love" not only helped me to perform the scenes filled with happy emotions, it also helped me to perform the tragedy of a cruel separation in "The Separation."

I am truly in love with Dong Yong and have these wonderful illusions, but then suddenly Dong Yong and I have to part. What to do? I do not want to leave him and ascend to heaven! But if I do not ascend to heaven, Dong Yong's life will be in imminent danger. I do not think all that much about my own future, and in all that I do I try to find a solution for Dong Yong. I am only concerned about him! How can I tell him this without being too sudden, with the result that he may become too heart-broken? How can I make him realize my enduring love for him? When I have barely ascended to heaven and storm and thunder make Dong Yong collapse, of course I am concerned! Just like Eldest Sister, I don't care at all whether I will be "locked up in heaven's jail" after I have returned. I want to comfort Dong Yong and tell him that he has to find the courage to continue living because next year when the flowers bloom in balmy spring, I will come and bring him his son.

All my actions emerge from a heart that truly loves him. This heart is firmly tied to his body. If I leave him, you truly will have to cut loose this heart with a knife. How can I go on living without Dong Yong! Whenever I came to this point in the performance, I would be unable to suppress the sadness in my heart and I would start weeping. I would continue to weep until I had taken off my costume and make-up. I would tell myself: "This is only a play!" but that would be of no use because I was so afraid that some disaster might strike him. I was so afraid that he might leave me!

This love made me actively pursue Dong Yong, cleverly oppose Old Master Fu, meticulously care for my husband and protect him no matter what. … In short, it was all because I loved Dong Yong.

My close cooperation with comrade Wang Shaofang imbued this "love" with a strong feeling of truth.

Huangmei Opera primarily relies on singing. Plays such as *Husband and Wife Watching the Lanterns* (*Fuqi guan deng* 夫妻觀燈),[28] in which song and dance are equally important, only appeared after Liberation when Huangmei Opera had absorbed some elements of Peking Opera. Huangmei Opera later also included some dances. In general, you would hold a fan in one hand and a handkerchief in the other, and once you started dancing it would appear somewhat like modern "flower-drum lanterns." Earlier I most often performed my plays dressed in skirt and jacket, but what I was wearing this time resembled an ancient costume, as in Shaoxing Opera (*Yueju*), and then I had to do some dances, so this was yet another problem. The rehearsals in preparation for participation in the East China Theater Festival took place in June and July, exactly the hottest time of the year. When we were rehearsing, I took part in the rehearsals, and when we were not rehearsing, I practiced my movements in a long skirt. Only after I had practiced them for two months in this manner did they improve somewhat. In the beginning, when I noticed that my movements were "cultured," I wanted them to be somewhat more "rustic," but then they turned out not to be beautiful. During that time, I was reminded of some innovations in movements by Mr. Xun Huisheng 荀慧生 when performing *Reddy* (*Hongniang* 紅娘),[29] and I also was reminded of some other examples. After we arrived at the East China Theater Festival, my teacher Bai Yunsheng 白雲生[30] gave me some instructions to improve my movements. This all provided me with great assistance and inspiration. Of course, my actual performance did not live up to their demands.

Married to a Heavenly Immortal has been turned into a movie that has already been released. I am sure that from the silver screen the comrades will discover even more of my deficiencies. I sincerely hope that everyone will help me.

November 14, 1956, in Ji'nan

Wang Shaofang

How I Perform Dong Yong[31]

1956

I

From my earliest youth I traveled with my parents from place to place performing opera, so I myself was not a peasant, but I very much liked to interact with peasants. When we were traveling from this place to that place and stopping for a meal or staying at an inn, I quickly befriended them. Even today I still remember very clearly those little companions with whom, when I did not have to perform, I emptied sparrow nests and dug up wild greens, and those destitute friends who often gave me, only "a player,"[32] some fresh vegetables that they had picked in their own gardens.

I remember their faces, and I also remember their attitudes.

At times, they might seem to be very weak and docile. If the landlord wanted them to give up the grain that was barely enough to feed themselves in order to pay their rent, they might kneel on the ground and implore him most piteously. But if one really wanted to rob them of their subsistence, they would risk their lives and they would not pay any attention to "the law of the land" or "profit and harm."

I had an addiction (I still have it to this very day): I like to stand by and "watch the commotion." At times when I see two elderly women cursing each other, I am unable to leave until I have heard the end of the fight. At times I also liked to watch my little companions. They were different from "city people." For instance, those students from the city who have studied books may feel "somewhat uncomfortable" when encountering someone, but they still will show some "civility," and even when they are red in the face, they still will affect a "serious" and "reserved" manner. My little companions were not like that. If they felt unhappy, they felt unhappy, and their faces would turn red, their necks would bulge, they would not know where to place their hands other than to grasp at everything, and they would very directly tell you: "I am so pissed off!" Or they would put on some airs, saying, "No, no, it doesn't matter at all!"

II

I have played the roles of several young men, such as Student Zhang 張生,[33]

Liang Shanbo 梁山伯,[34] Xu Xian 許仙,[35] Wei Kuiyuan 韋奎元 (the *xiaosheng* in the Huangmei Opera [*Meeting at*] *Indigo Bridge*),[36] and Wu Sanbao 吳三寶 (the *xiaosheng* in the Huangmei Opera *Roaming in Spring* [*Youchun* 遊春]).[37] These men were all students who had studied in the city or tradespeople.

I had also earlier played the role of Dong Yong, but in those days he was still a student, so he too was a man who "studied books."

When *Married to a Heavenly Immortal* was revised, the original shape of this legend about the laboring masses was restored in terms of plot and theme. Because of this, Dong Yong regained his original character. According to the comrades who did the revision, they consulted the local gazetteer of Xiaogan District in Hubei and found that it contained the story of "Dong Yong Selling his Body." But this Dong Yong was not a student but rather a peasant.[38]

So Dong Yong was a peasant, and this presented me with a major problem.

III

When I was young, my father and my teacher often told me this story:

> Student, lady, villain, servant,or clown—
> Whether you're a lion, a tiger, or a dog:
> If you play a dragon, act like a dragon;
> If you play a tiger, then act like a tiger!

Even though they did not know any theory, their demands on me were extremely strict. For instance, even though their characters belonged equally to the repertoire of the *xiaosheng*, Student Zhang and Liang Shanbo each had their own requirements. If Liang Shanbo was not played well, he could easily become "silly,"[39] and if Student Zhang was not played well, he could easily become "rakish."[40] Their manners of speech each had their own measure, and their movements onstage each had their own style. From these aspects one could distinguish who was romantic and who was sincere.

How could I perform this Dong Yong? And even more, how could I perform this Dong Yong who was a peasant?

IV

I racked my brains and I reconsidered once again the characters that I had played and the characters that I had seen other people play. There were some methods that were of some assistance. But the most important memories were those of my boyhood years, as I remembered those little companions from the countryside.

I also remembered my teacher. My teacher's strict training of bodily movements made me form a "set view" with respect to artistic creation, whereby I had to pay attention to hands, eyes, body, method, and stride, and my bodily movements had to be clean, crisp, and beautiful. There was a time when some comrades—especially comrades who worked in spoken drama—expressed severe criticism of my acting and said that my method was a kind of formalism. At the time, I did not accept that criticism seriously, because on the one hand I had my set view, and on the other hand I was not capable of anything else on the stage.

I considered the set [of conventional movements] my teacher had taught me as a precious treasure, but I did not consider them to be sufficient. I wanted them to be even more beautiful and richer because otherwise they would not be suitable.

A problem arose in performing Dong Yong. Peasants have made an appearance on the opera stage, but in *Hunting the Tiger* (*Liehu ji* 獵虎記) they are *wusheng* 武生, and a *wusheng* has a *wusheng*'s postures and movements. However, Dong Yong could not be categorized as a *wusheng*.[41]

The stride of the *xiaosheng* role-type reflects the way students walk, so that was even less suitable. And I was also not eager to resemble spoken drama. So I thought: "Let me be creative! Let me make some changes to the 'Four-Direction Step' (*sifangbu*) of the *xiaosheng*." For a normal square stride one needs thick-soled shoes, but Dong Yong would not have had that training, so no thick-soled shoes. The square stride is oh so leisurely and oh so cultured, so I would make it somewhat quicker and more robust.

Once I had changed the stride, I also had to change the speech. It might still be stylized speech, but when students say a sentence, they love to "evaluate" its "taste" in a very overdone manner, so I would make it cleaner.

V

Not only were other people not used to going about this in this way, I too felt uncomfortable. I imagined that if my teacher were present, this style definitely would not pass muster because it was lacking in the old plays. But now that I had encountered this new problem, I had to be somewhat more daring. The image of my little companions of my boyhood years provided me with courage. I could not perform Dong Yong as a weakly student, and I also could not perform him as a martial hero. So I had to perform him like my peasant friends whom I had liked so much. At my present level, I could only act in this way.

Not only in my stride onstage and in my speech, but also in a number of detailed movements did I imitate my peasant friends as much as possible. When Dong Yong meets Seventh Sister, isn't he very bashful? So I imagined my peasant friends' posture, red in the face with thick necks, not knowing where to put their hands and feet. When Heaven forces Seventh Sister to ascend to heaven, I imagined how the landlords forced my peasant friends to pay rent: like them I implored piteously and then furiously rose up in rebellion.

In short, as much as possible I wanted to play Dong Yong as a peasant.

VI

From the beginning I felt an emptiness on the stage. I would walk in this way, I would speak in that way, and even the smallest movements I designed to perfection. But still, an emptiness. I had analyzed my character, Dong Yong's social background, his duty, his. … The director had also provided me with explanations in accordance with the new methods. But still there was this emptiness.

I truly needed to once again honestly taste the thoughts and emotions of my peasant friends and truly experience them in my own body.

For instance, why does Dong Yong in "Meeting on the Road" not agree to Seventh Sister's marriage proposal? Doesn't he love her? Or is there some other reason? The script prescribes that "he is afraid to involve Seventh Sister in his suffering." This shows that he not only loves her but also is very concerned about her. I thought of my destitute friends. They might have been destitute, but they had a simple and pure yearning for a happy life. A single husband and a single wife, they would lead their bitter lives of "crying together covered by rags," but they would truly love each other. And when they really had nothing to eat, they would go begging on the streets together and they would share together whatever food they obtained, whether hot or cold. Such a pure love that is based on an honest heart is of course much more valuable than a love that is based on money. That is why I thought that Dong Yong must have been able to love her, especially when she says that she is willing to share with him those days of hardship—then he loves her even more.

The script does not give much expression to this aspect of Dong Yong. There is little about love and a lot about sneaking away. I felt that Dong Yong was not very sensitive. Later, when the movie was made, with the help of the director I added this one line of dialogue: "This girl is not bad looking at all and she is filled with sincerity toward me, so if she were to become my wife. . . ." Only in this way are Dong Yong's true feelings expressed ever so slightly.

In this respect, the first half of "Separating at the Scholartree" was greatly developed. For instance, Dong Yong's yearning for a future life in which "I will plow the fields and you will weave cloth," and his joy when he discovers that Seventh Sister is pregnant—I felt that these emotions were in accordance with human feelings.

In this way I very quickly ascertained: I am a good and honest peasant. In the scene "Meeting on the Road" I am filled with sadness about my father's death. When we go to Fu Family Bay, I discover that Seventh Sister can withstand hardship and, moreover, even though I have no place to which to turn, she loves me sincerely. I very quickly develop sympathy for her and always feel concerned about her, fearing that I will involve her in my suffering. At the same time, I develop a love for her and am only too happy to marry her.

In scenes such as "Starting Out on the Job" and "Completing the Job," as soon as I see her, in one way or another I want to be more cheerful and happier. In the latter half of "The Separation" I want to protect her with all my might, and in one way or another I want to make her stay with me.

In this way I gradually found what I needed on the stage: I love her, I protect her, I am close to her. … With every performance, these feelings in my heart increased. Slowly I lost that awkward feeling of "emptiness."

Then I also had the strength to perfect my movements.

In this way, through repeated polishing and more practical experience, I gave shape to the Dong Yong who nowadays lives on the stage.

I do not dare to affirm that this Dong Yong is verisimilar. Because I am still performing this role and still polishing this role, I cannot predict the future changes.

Li Liping
Production of the Stage Version of *Married to a Heavenly Immortal*[42]
1981

Before participating in the first East China Theater Festival of 1954 *Married to a Heavenly Immortal* underwent roughly one year of rehearsals, during which time there were three relatively big changes (the shooting of the movie was a later event). As one of the people responsible, I will recount some memories about those rehearsals.

The first time that *Married to a Heavenly Immortal*, a play from the traditional repertoire of Huangmei Opera that had been revised by comrade Lu Hongfei, was staged was in the fall of 1953 in Anqing. I always called these performances tryouts because I was a director who had just been transferred from a spoken drama company and definitely was a new recruit as far as Huangmei Opera was concerned. Directing *Married to a Heavenly immortal* occurred at the beginning of my study of traditional opera.

The work of this tryout progressed relatively smoothly. The first reason was that the leadership which was very concerned had dispatched comrade Qiao Zhiliang, who was well-versed in the performance techniques of Peking Opera, to take on the task of choreographer. The second reason was that we had assistance and guidance from famous experienced actors, such as Ding Yongquan 丁永泉 (Ding Laoliu 丁老六) and others. The actors rehearsed during the day, and at night they took part in the performances of the two drama companies, Victory and The Masses. This was very convenient for our study and practice.

During this first staging, the roles of Seventh Sister and Dong Yong were performed respectively by comrade Chen Yuehuan 陳月環 and comrade Zha Ruihe 查瑞和 (at that time some of the province's Huangmei Opera performers had left for Korea to entertain the troops, and comrade Yan Fengying was on leave because she was pregnant). The six other sisters, Landlord Fu, and the other roles were performed by comrades such as Zhang Liangjun 張良俊 and Zhang Man 張曼. Pan Hanmin 潘漢民 was the composer. Just like me, he was a new recruit at the time. Later he would always modestly claim that his only work was writing down the score, but he really did make a major contribution. For instance, he recognized the languorous and melodious character of the "underworld tune," a melody that was exclusively used by ghosts and he broke all taboos by using it in this fairy-tale play. He went to a lot of trouble to employ it in "Magpie Bridge." Some people were of the opinion that the immortals in Huangmei Opera had their own "tune of the immortals," the buddhas had their Buddhist melodies, and the underworld tune was sung by ghosts, so the Immortal Maidens definitely could not use it. But practice resulted in insight, and in "Magpie Bridge" it was used in the happy and lively "bride-fetching dance" where it truly had a special effect.

When we talk about performance, we first have to talk about the revised version. For the first time, comrade Lu Hongfei completely revised this *Married to a Heavenly Immortal* that propagated feudal morality and changed it into an anti-feudal *Married to a Heavenly Immortal.* In the work of repertoire reform in the early 1950s it can be said that he marched in front. The original play tells of how Dong Yong sells his body to bury his father and how his filial piety moves Highest Heaven. The Jade Emperor thereupon sends his youngest daughter down to earth to become Dong Yong's wife for one hundred days. The revised version tells of how Seventh Sister falls in love with the honest and sincere Dong Yong and the beautiful human world and, in disregard of the strict rules of the heavenly palace, stealthily descends to the mortal world and teams up with Dong Yong. Following their separation at the scholartree once the bond for one hundred days had come to an end, the original play still includes "Seventh Sister Delivers the Boy" and "Dong Yong Becomes Top-of-the-List." Dong Yong also marries the daughter of Landlord Fu. This explains how, because of his filial piety, Dong Yong gains riches and glory for both husband and wife. Originally, this was a glorification of, and a song of praise for, feudal rule. The revised version ends with the separation near the scholartree. It describes how there is no end to Seventh Sister's miseries after her mortal longings have been stirred. It is an act of resistance, it is an accusation! In the original, the climax of the entire play is the "grand reunion of husband and wife in riches and glory." In the revised version we wanted to put Seventh Sister and Dong Yong's "Separating at the Scholartree" in that tricky position.[43] But now the theme of the play had changed and the melodrama had become a tragedy, so we necessarily had to change the manner of performance. Thus we devoted great effort to the staging of "Magpie Bridge," "Meeting on the Road," and "Weaving Silk" so we could provide good preparation for the climax in "The Separation." If the forced separation of Seventh Sister and Dong Yong made people cry as much as possible we would have achieved our theme of resistance and attack on feudal persecution. As far as the work of staging is concerned, first of all I have to mention how comrade Qiao Zhiliang successfully designed the dances for "Magpie Bridge" and "Weaving Silk." This provided the entire play with graceful and dazzling colors, and it was a major reason why *Married to a Heavenly Immortal* could be so loved by the audiences. When we participated in the 1954 East China Theater Festival we often performed the two scenes, "Magpie Bridge" and "Weaving Silk," for our beloved Premier Zhou [Enlai] and the accompanying leaders of the fraternal parties participating in the national celebration of the fifth anniversary of the founding of the People's Republic and we were praised by the Premier and the international guests.

The traditional performance of "Magpie Bridge" and "Weaving Silk" was relatively simple. In "Weaving Silk" originally it was only Eldest Sister who placed a board over a chair onstage and treated it as her loom. In "Magpie Bridge" the Seven Immortal Sisters stood closely together on a Magpie Bridge that was made by placing two tables next to each other, and the actors who performed the fisherman, the woodcutter, the farmer, and the student crossed the stage in front of the tables. While they were standing on these tables the Immortal Maidens sang the "Four Characterizations." Using this method it was obviously impossible to give expression to the play's required atmosphere of "a myriad purples and a thousand reds show off their brilliant colors/ men and women busy themselves amidst the sounds of laughter and banter," and of course it was also not possible to express the longing of Seventh Sister for the human realm. During the tryouts we decided to instead use dances that could imitate situations in the human realm; we allowed the Immortal Maidens who had always led lives of "each morning, each evening, some fleeting clouds" to suddenly sweep aside the mist and to see the human realm with its myriads of purples and thousands of reds and to start to dance as they are overcome with joy. The heavenly realm and the human world are contrasted and not only are the seven Immortal Maidens spellbound, but the audience is also moved. This has a powerful supporting and stimulating function with regard to Seventh Sister's rebellion against His Majesty the Jade Emperor and her stealth descent to the mortal world. The manner in which "Weaving Silk" is performed became much more active, lively, and filled with vitality by adding the silk-weaving dance performed by the seven Immortal Maidens.

After only a month or so, the play was put together. The first tryout took place in The Masses Theater in Anqing, where we performed it a total of nine times, and almost every evening we played to a full house. At that time, the Anqing audience was still accustomed to seeing a different play every day, so it was quite an accomplishment that a newly revised play, without any famous actors taking part in the performance, could have such drawing power. The performance had a large impact, but there were many different reactions. In general, this tryout met with the approval of the majority of the audience in the hometown of Huangmei Opera, and the audience was positive about the revision. As for the negative reactions, the audience felt that ending the performance with "The Separation" was way too sad with all that weeping and sobbing. It was hoped that we could retain the scene of "Seventh Sister Delivering the Baby [to Dong Yong]" to provide the audience with some traditional satisfaction. One day, when the play was over, the audience did not disperse and instead insisted that we also perform "Delivering the Baby." To be honest, at that time my level was limited and having become a prisoner-of-war of the well-intentioned audience, I too wanted to allow Seventh Sister another opportunity to meet with Dong Yong by delivering the baby to him. But how should she deliver the baby? After quite some deliberation, the only solution seemed to be to have Seventh Sister deliver the baby to Dong Yong in a dream. After several rehearsals, but before we had put it onstage, I came to oppose this idea. But I learned a valuable lesson from this: if you insist on adding a "brilliant tail" to tragic materials like *Married to a Heavenly Immortal*, you definitely are "adding legs to a snake" and you will destroy the positive meaning of the play's theme.

The second production occurred in the spring of 1954; these rehearsals took place after a number of the members of the Anhui Provincial Huangmei Opera Company had returned to Hefei and had performed before the Provincial Party Committee and the Provincial Bureau of Culture. In this production Seventh Sister was performed by comrade Yan Fengying. In her creation [of the role] she was serious and strict, and daring to investigate and to review. At the beginning of the rehearsals we analyzed together the character of Seventh Sister. She is not only, as commonly acknowledged, lively and brave and daring to resist, but she is also, because she is the youngest daughter of His Majesty the Jade Emperor, willful and naughty—at times she can even be flirtatious. Once this tune was established, she had no problem singing her part. With her delicate acting that had long been molded in her heart and her superior singing that excelled in expressing the emotions of her character, she did away with the established way of performing Seventh Sister as a kind and good young lady of the upper classes to create a lively and naughty peasant girl. But at the same time she also did not lose the nature of an Immortal Maiden. In "Meeting on the Road" there is an episode in which Seventh Sister wants to bump into Dong Yong but she fails to do so because he is aware of her intention. The original way of performing this was that Seventh Sister, having failed to bump into Dong Yong, turns around and covers her face with her water-sleeve to express her shame, but then she pulls aside a corner of her water-sleeve to take a peek at Dong Yong.[44] Comrade Yan Fengying changed this stolen glance from behind the water-sleeve that covered her face into the following: she retreats with small rapid steps (*suibu* 碎步), covers her face with both hands, and ever so lightly shakes her shoulders to give expression to her regret and shame. Then she looks at Dong Yong through her fingers to see his reaction. When an angry Dong Yong asks her, "Is it you who is bumping into me, or is it me who is bumping into you?" comrade Yan Fengying adds a long extended "Ah!" before she answers. In a very lifelike manner she portrays the naughty and flirtatious silliness of a girl in front of a person she respects (love by its nature always contains respect).

In the old play performance of "The Separation" Seventh Sister has to wear a wig (*shuaifa* 甩髮)[45] and a long skirt, and use water-sleeves;[46] when weeping at the separation she has to repeatedly "fall forward" (sit down).[47] If one did not have some training in martial arts it was not possible to play this scene to the end. When coming to this scene in the performance of the old play [the actress playing] Seventh Sister would be replaced by a martial *dan* (*daoma dan* 刀馬旦) or by an actress who had basic martial training, and when coming to "Delivering the Baby" Seventh Sister would again be played by the original actress. In the past when Yan Fengying played in *Married to a Heavenly Immortal* she too was replaced by someone else in "The Separation." But as the revised version moved the climax to this scene, it was not possible to replace her with a different actress. In order to maintain the performance characteristics of this play, we also had to preserve some traditional movements. This created some trouble for comrade Yan Fengying. After the first rehearsal I went to her house to visit her, with the idea of asking an experienced performer to provide her with individual coaching. But as soon as I entered the door I was dumbstruck because she was wearing the long skirt and the wig and she was practicing the movement of "falling forward" in front of a mirror. I saw that she was covered in sweat from head to toe and that her face was all dirty. Should I tell her to take some rest or should I talk about something else? At that moment, I really was in a quandary. That comrade Yan Fengying could become such a fine actress who is remembered by the audience at large is certainly not only because, as is commonly considered, she had such sparkling eyes and such a good singing voice. Most importantly, it was due to her spirit of diligent study and hard training, and her daring to experiment.

In the summer of the same year *Married to a Heavenly Immortal* was selected by the Provincial Party Committee and the Provincial Bureau of Culture to participate in the first East China Theater Festival. They also decided to strengthen our team so we could enhance the level of our work. This was the third production. This time Wang Shaofang, Pan Jingli, Wang Shaomei 王少梅, Zhang Yunfeng, Ding Zichen 丁紫臣, Wu Laibao 吳來寶, and many others took part and respectively played the parts of Dong Yong, Eldest Sister, Second Sister, Landlord Fu, and others. Comrades Wang Wenzhi 王文治 and Wang Shaochi 王紹墀 joined us as composers, and the stage design was entrusted to comrade Wang Shiying 王士英. It can be said that at that time all talent in Hefei had been assembled in one room. Even though the weather was stifling hot, the rehearsals continued in strict order. For "Meeting on the Road" there was a revised version by comrade Ban Youshu (he and Lu Hongfei had made their own changes) which had been performed by Wang Shaofang and Pan Jingli in the leading roles for close to one hundred times in Nanjing and Shanghai and on the Korean front. Therefore, one might say that Wang Shaofang was already an experienced Dong Yong before he participated in this production of *Married to a Heavenly Immortal.* During the rehearsals, comrades Wang Shaofang, Pan Jingli, and Zhang Yunfeng immediately grasped their roles and they also made creative contributions. This time, the time needed for rehearsals was most limited, but the achievements were most spectacular, and each scene saw conspicuous improvements. This applied especially to "The Separation" in which comrade Wang Shaofang, using his sincere and noble singing voice and his graceful and fluent dance movements, gave full expression to Dong Yong's emotions, from his happiness and joy upon returning home after completing the job to his rage and pain when his lover is abducted.

In "The Separation" the key to propel the play to its climax was how to handle Seventh Sister's inescapable return to heaven. In the original play Seventh Sister arrives obeying orders and she leaves obeying orders, so both her arrival and departure are easily handled. But in the revised version Seventh Sister stealthily descends to the mortal world because she loves the human realm, and she is forced to separate from Dong Yong according to the strict rules of heaven. Because of this "inescapable return to heaven" we carried out some experiments during our rehearsals. Only at the last moment did we decide on the formula that later was performed onstage: we had the warrior dressed in gold appear once when Dong Yong goes to a nearby village to fetch some water and we had him exit after transmitting the imperial edict; when Dong Yong is holding on to Seventh Sister and refusing to release her, we used a thunderous backstage voice (in the movie the warrior appears in the clouds), loudly shouting, "If Seventh Sister still does not return to heaven, Dong Yong will be smashed to pieces!" So first he shows his shape, and later his voice is heard. With his shape and his voice the impression is strengthened, and Seventh Sister's inescapable return to heaven makes some sense.

The fall of 1954 was a golden autumn. Our socialist fatherland achieved great successes on every front. Participating in the East China Theater Festival, *Married to a Heavenly Immortal* brought glory to Huangmei Opera. Under the leadership of the Party Anhui theater-reform work achieved stellar results.

Qiao Zhiliang

Memories of Directing *Married to a Heavenly Immortal*[48]

1996

Source: 1995 *Huangmeixi* Performance Art Conference, Collection of Selected Essays

Compiler's Note: Mr. Qiao Zhiliang long ago switched careers from his well-known position in Peking Opera to become a director of the Provincial Huangmei Opera Company, collaborating with Yan Fengying, Wang Shaofang, and other performance artists. The many stage performances that he directed include *Married to an Immortal.* He was not only witness to a period of growing excellence in Huangmei Opera, but he was also a participant who made important contributions to Huangmei Opera. Due to his advanced years, it is difficult for Mr. Qiao to take up the pen to record the creative processes and rich artistic experiences during those years. Therefore, Yao Yuwen and Zhang Chuancai, students in the class of '92 of the Department of Chinese in Anhui University organized the content of Mr. Qiao's oral history into this essay. We believe it will be meaningful for research both on the history and the artistic experience of Huangmei Opera.

Dictated by Qiao Zhiliang

Recorded and Compiled by Zhang Chuancai and Yao Yuwen

Married to a Heavenly Immortal was the first major drama performed by the Anhui Provincial Huangmei Opera Company after its formation. The play was originally titled *The Hundred Days Match* (*Bairi yuan* 百日緣), one of the *Twenty-four Exemplars of Filial Piety*. Dong Yong sells himself into servitude to pay for his father's funeral. His filial spirit moves Heaven and Earth, so the Jade Emperor orders his seventh daughter to descend to the mortal realm to marry Dong Yong for one hundred days. After the prescribed period, Seventh Sister must return to heaven. Comrade Lu Hongfei set about making changes on the basis of this old script. He took out the superstitious elements, removed the phrase "the hundred days match," and made significant changes to the theme, plot, and structure. Thus, a univocal song of praise for filial piety was developed into a tragedy of romantic youth filled with rich connotations and endowed with a stronger and more elevated realist meaning beyond that of a colorful fairy tale.[49]

Due to the changes to the script, the staging of the earlier *The Hundred Days Match* could only serve as a reference. As director, I was faced with the concrete off-stage work of analyzing and studying the play's central thought. The personalities of the characters and the related design of the stage aesthetics, music, tunes, and action all had to go through a period of fine-tuning. It can be said that, to a great extent, *Married to a Heavenly Immortal* threw off the shackles of the old theater, while at the same time it enriched and developed Huangmei Opera's techniques for artistic expression.

1. The Seven Heavenly Sisters Share the Stage, Singing and Dancing

In the opening scene, "Magpie Bridge," we first faced the problem of establishing the scene.

When the curtain rises, the first thing to emerge in front of the audience should be a lonely and cheerless Heavenly Palace. In order to create this kind of atmosphere, we made black clouds swirl inside the Heavenly Palace and placed a faintly visible pavilion in the distant background. The colors were exaggerated, but this kind of scene created a feeling of emptiness. Since there were props but not people onstage at this point, the relationship between the environment and the characters was a bit unclear. So, the second time we set it up, we placed the seven sisters centerstage in the middle of the misty clouds to accentuate a sense of the levels onstage. At the same time, the desolation of the environment became a foil to the lonely emotional landscape of the Seven Immortal Sisters in the Heavenly Palace. With mind becoming matter and matter becoming mind, the characters and the environment achieved a momentary harmony. Afterwards, the seven sisters lifted up the clouds and mist, and from "the ground" rose a beam of light, which dispersed the oppressive atmosphere. When the Seven Immortal Sisters looked upon the bustling, lively human world—betraying their feelings of delight in it—the great contrast between the heavens and the mortal realm was completed.

Next came the choreography for the Seven Immortal Sisters. With the Seven Immortal Sisters [all] onstage at once, it was a big scene. If there were no choreography, the stage would have seemed drab and flat. However, if the choreography were not beautiful, it would be easy to make people feel dazed and confused. In comparison, drabness and flatness is the other extreme. So we used the "arranging flowers" formation only after Eldest Sister had assented to the pleas of her sisters and said, "After you." Following the lead of Eldest Sister, they all raised their cloud brooms[50] and, taking cloud steps, meandered toward Magpie Bridge just as if they were "fluttering in the breeze." "Arranging flowers" is a single-file formation—it has a unified aesthetic, but we also produced an effect with each individual's pose by having the actors circumambulate the stage several times. This pairing of a single-file formation with standardized dancing, while avoiding the disorder of a full stage, expressed the elegance of the Seven Heavenly Sisters walking in the clouds.

When the Seven Immortal Sisters reached Magpie Bridge and lifted up the misty clouds, the single-file formation broke up. Each sister looked about from her own spot and then they took turns switching places. [Here we] adopted the "Dispersing the Army" device and used it to try to reveal each character's bearing, thereby strengthening the impression given by their first poses. It was not dispersal for dispersal's sake, but rather [a matter of] seeing differences among the characters in the midst of dispersion. This also occurred in the midst of the big group scene of the Seven Heavenly Sisters, and [followed] the primary principle of finding difference in similarity.

2. The Four Characterizations—Originating in Life, Surpassing Life

In the original *Hundred Days Match*, "the fisherman, the woodcutter, the farmer, and the scholar" enter and exit individually. The Seven Heavenly Sisters, standing on two tables and two chairs without dancing, separately sing their characterizations. This setup made the stage atmosphere appear to be dull. Moreover, if one had put real "fishermen, woodcutters, farmers, and scholars" downstage doing their real work, this would have been excessive and would have given the stage a cramped feeling. The "Four Characterizations" is a scene that primarily expresses the mentality and interests of the Seven Immortal Sisters, so to have "fishermen, woodcutters, farmers, and scholars" rush on and off the stage is clearly too bland. Thus, in our performance we resolved to cut them—we had no "fishermen, woodcutters, farmers, and scholars," but rather we had the actresses use pointing, bearing, gestures, and so forth to act out the "fishermen, woodcutters, farmers, and scholars." Fully taking advantage of the suppositional[51] nature of traditional opera, we used the seven sisters' eye movements to represent the "fishermen, woodcutters, farmers, and scholars," thus using spirit to convey feelings. When objects are *seen*, limitlessness and limitation are one.

The removal of the "fishermen, woodcutters, farmers, and scholars" from the stage made it possible to add song and dance as the Seven Immortal Sisters remain onstage, looking at things and mimicking them. This also brought difficulties—"looking" and "singing" were not difficult, but mimicking and dancing were blank slates.

How were we to represent the "fishermen, woodcutters, farmers, and scholars"? Speaking specifically in the language of dance, how were we to choreograph them? Huangmei Opera has always been known for its strong flavor of life, because it stresses in particular the imitation of life. But imitation should not be a complete copy, like a photograph, but rather it should be an artistic reworking of the movements of life on the basis of life's natural state. When a perfectly ordinary gesture in life is shifted onto the stage, it often seems to be nondescript; this is due to the difference in the environment. In accordance with the necessities of stage performance, the movements of life must be made dancelike, and ordinary conventional gestures must be combined with specific common knowledge. This allows natural beauty to become artistic beauty. If you want people to understand [this], you must grasp the aesthetics of stage performance; thus the choreography in the "Four Characterizations" was rooted in the principle of "seeing something and mimicking it," and it originated in life and surpassed life.

First, to praise the fisherman, how were we to imitate him? Making use of suppositional gestures, we took full advantage of the Seven Heavenly Sisters' cloud brooms to use them as props. The earliest design concept had the Seven Heavenly Sisters all pretending to be fishermen, with their cloud brooms as paddles. However, the total stage effect of paddling with cloud brooms did not look good, especially given that the movements appeared to be too unrefined for a group of young maidens. "Sculling" motions were much prettier, so we switched to using the cloud brooms as oars. For footsteps, the Seven Heavenly Sisters used cloud steps and moved their bodies up and down, imitating a boat bobbing on the waves. After these basic conventions for movement were established, the music started, and when the Seven Heavenly Sisters moved, they were dancing. Suddenly, the entire stage became more alive. It was just as if the waves were shimmering, dotted with fishing boats.

Since we couldn't have fishing boats just drifting helter-skelter onstage, we arranged them in a specific group formation. This way, we were able to intensify the visual effect and stress the expression of the lively energy on the lake. [At the line] "Fishermen live in the middle of rivers and lakes," the formation retreated from downstage to centerstage and formed two crisscrossed lines; at "On both banks the reeds resemble a surrounding wall," in a diagonal double-column formation they raised their cloud brooms over their arms, mimicking rippling reeds; at "Punting his boat from the shore he throws out his net," they used their cloud brooms as punting poles, and then swung their cloud brooms twirling above their heads, as their skirts also swirled around. After this pushing, swinging, and circling of the cloud brooms, plus the fluttering of water-sleeves and skirts, then came the first squat. It was as if the fishing nets were cast into the water. In the following beat, the cloud brooms also functioned as nets, with each actress grasping her broom with both hands. At "One net full of fishes and shrimp is one net of food!" the formation broke apart.

The design of any imitative gesture can only be a formal imitation, but a formal imitation is [actually] secondary. The goal of imitative gesture is to find a spiritual resemblance in the space between looking alike and looking different. In the staging of the "Four Characterizations," the principle of "seeing something and mimicking it" ran throughout our goal of spiritual resemblance through formal imitation. Concretely, this involved integrating the unique characteristics of stage performance and emphasizing the selection of movements from real life, the selection of conventions, and the synthetic utilization of props.

Our multi-purpose use of cloud brooms was not limited to the first song of praise for the fisherman. In the third song of praise for the farmer, we also made full use of the imitative potential of the cloud broom. When representing harvesters cutting rice and wheat, the cloud broom acted as a sickle; when representing threshing the wheat, it became a flail. Using a single implement as many things truly grasps an essential element of suppositionality.

The selection of movements from real life manifests the pursuit of artistic beauty. In addition to deciding between "paddling" and "sculling," the choreography representing the lyric "Their faces face the yellow earth, their backs face the sky" also followed aesthetic principles. Rather than the gesture of planting rice seedlings, we thought of the gesture of threshing wheat with a flail. We took into consideration beauty and ugliness, as well as the most efficacious use of the strength of the cloud brooms.

In terms of selecting conventions, we tried to preserve the unique characteristics of Huangmei Opera. For the part representing the fishermen, we could have copied conventions from other opera genres, especially Peking Opera. However, during the rehearsals we did not arbitrarily apply conventions from Peking Opera. Instead, we combined the plots and rhythms of the sung tunes to create a new design for playing fishermen. This made the gestures even more "plum-flavored"[52] and made them belong to Huangmei Opera. In the scene of the wedding procession after the "Four Characterizations," the dance formation absorbed the "cicada shell" formation from the flower-drum lantern performances, not Peking Opera's "two dragons rising from the water." Thus we avoided indiscriminate imitation of copying conventions and gave this lively play even more feeling and flavor of real life.

3. Movement and Stillness with Appeal, Rising to the Peak with Restraint

Making choreography more perfect may be a matter of formal factors but it must serve the plot and content that you wish to represent.

The "Four Characterizations" is an organic whole, but since each of its sections differs in content, they are distinct from one another. The formal factors thus become indices by which each [section] differentiates itself from the others. We fully took this into consideration during the rehearsals.

In terms of melodic expression, the first characterization, that is, of the fisherman, used a sweet and gentle tune to represent his carefree and contented life on the water. In the second song praising the woodcutter, we altered that sweetness and gentleness by pushing the tempo and intensifying the sense of motion. For the third song about the farmer, in order to stress the busy toil of a farmer's life, the melody was as hurried as his bustling through the four seasons. Our emphasis on "quiet" and "calm" in the fourth song in praise of the scholar naturally was related to a scholar's life.

At the same time, the "Four Characterizations" as a whole also adhered to an internal structural logic. Up to the fourth song of characterization, all three songs included both song and dance, but we did not add choreography to the fourth song. On the one hand, we wanted to draw a connection to the calmness of the scholar's life, but we also wanted to contrast this with the other three songs. In terms of the overall structure, movement and stillness were brought together, varying in an appealing way and giving the audience a chance to take a breather.

In terms of connecting the "Four Characterizations" with the following scene of the wedding procession, the song characterizing the scholar actually functioned as a buffer, just like a tune repeating in a middle range and then suddenly moving into a higher octave. The scene of the wedding procession is the height of liveliness, with an atmosphere of gaiety washing over the stage and into the hearts of the audience. Up to this point, everything employs the technique of spreading-the-word and generally foreshadowing the later [scene] in which the Seventh Sister will see the sad and touching Dong Yong. Thus, in striving for liveliness and jubilation in this scene, the higher the highs rise and the firmer the downward pressures press, the stronger the opposition between sadness and happiness becomes. Simultaneously, this bit also foreshadows the stirring of Seventh Sister's sympathy and her determination to descend to the mortal realm to aid Dong Yong. Because of this, everything can be expressed clearly through feelings and principles.

4. Myriad Amorous Feelings, Exhausted in a Backward Glance

The painstaking first scene, "Magpie Bridge"—just as in a cinematographic technique—initially featured a long shot in order to leave the audience with an impression of the Seven Immortal Sisters as a group. But within this group we also explored variety to display the subtle differences in character among the sisters, and this intention was concretely manifested in the opening scene and in the "Four Characterizations." As a result, the camera zoomed in little by little, adding a close-up on top of the foundation of that group image—a close-up of Seventh Sister. That is why our design was to have the Immortal Sisters hear the sound of the bell and return to the palace, with the exception of Seventh Sister who remains alone onstage. An especially meaningful movement was Seventh Sister's backward glance after her six sisters have returned to the palace and she too is about to leave. You could say that the rather long preceding narrative sequence was all an introduction to this backward glance. We used this moment to make explicit Seventh Sister's difference from her sisters.

The staging of this moment stressed "tranquility" and in this tranquility [we] magnified Seventh Sister's sympathetic nature. Furthermore, this tranquility was different from the calm and quiet fourth song of characterization, which took into consideration the structure of the plot as a whole. Instead, feeling arrived at [the stage of] natural tranquility and its limitless "taste" was here expressed through silence. This psychological space was required by both the actors and the audience. From Seventh Sister's expression, the audience could imagine the desolate suffering that Dong Yong has borne in the mortal realm, but this was not something that a single lyric expressing sympathy or a line of dialogue could have transmitted. For this kind of transmission, you can only rely on movement of the gaze and changes in the facial expression. Thus, this backward glance was the "gaze" of the whole Magpie Bridge scene, and if it was not performed well, it would have been as if the preceding scene existed in name only.

At the same time that "tranquility" is an expression of the scene's atmosphere, it is also a powerful unfolding of Seventh Sister's internal conflicts—on the surface she is as calm as still water, but beneath this veneer runs a rushing current. For one, it symbolizes the panic of the heart caused by the tolling of the bell [that proclaims] Heaven's rules, but it is also her pity for Dong Yong caused by his miserable suffering. Seventh Sister's [competing] desires to rebel and to obey raise havoc in her sympathetic heart—this is a fate-determining moment of truth, an intertwining of weakness and courage. In the midst of tranquility, the scene leads to new heights. For both the actors and the audiences, trying to communicate all kinds of words through wordless expression is a useful test. This so-called "reading a book without a word or phrase" is a key requirement not only for aesthetic beauty, but also for creative beauty.

Seventh Sister's scene further establishes the basic tone of the entire play. Because Seventh Sister lingers, Eldest Sister cannot but return and observe her younger sister's state of mind. Being the older sister, she first voices concern for her sister's best interests and then follows this up with her gift of "disaster incense."[53] Here we again used a bit of close-up, presenting Eldest Sister's motherly concern for Seventh Sister. At the same time, what Eldest Sister says makes the audience break out into a cold sweat on behalf of Seventh Sister. Not knowing if this portends disaster or felicity, suspense is suddenly born.

Seventh Sister resolutely descends to the mortal realm, and Eldest Sister gazes after her for a long moment. Seventh Sister is filled with anticipation of good fortune, but what she does not know is that a tragedy has just begun.

5. *Roadside Meeting—Pursuit and Flight with a Thousand Twists and Turns*

One special characteristic of this scene is its emphasis on the spoken lines. In contrast to the primacy of singing in the previous scene, the characters' personalities are revealed and their images are fleshed out in this dialogue. Spoken lines [must] conform to an important principle of the opera world: for every thousand pounds of words, [only] four ounces of song. Therefore, in this scene, singing retired to a subordinate position, while speaking became the primary element. One specific requirement is "when reciting, one must recite as if singing." In line with this thinking, we rigorously controlled the dialogues of the actors in performance, and we wanted this seemingly dull "recitation" to reveal the characters' every minutely different mood, thereby capturing the audience. "Recitation" may be just one of the "Four Skills," but no matter how much natural talent an actor may have, he or she cannot do without the skill of "recitation."[54] Otherwise, he or she will be without a firm foundation. If the spoken lines are not handled well in the "Meeting on the Road" scene, then the entire scene will be 70 percent worthless.

However, the lines still are only an external form. If you want to infuse that form with life, you must closely integrate hand gestures, gaze, body movement, steps, and so forth, and fully excavate the subtext of the lines. Only then can you make the lines have a lasting impression after they have been spoken and leave the audience with an imaginative space of limitless beauty.

Relative to other performances, this scene had even fewer established practices. Thus, in performing it, the actors were given more creative space to integrate it into the surrounding circumstances and to create a free and lively atmosphere.

When Seventh Sister wanted the God of the Soil to help her out, she made a hand gesture [and says]: "Hey … come here!" rather than the familiar "Come lend me your ear … (ha, ha, ha.…)" The free handling of this small detail was in consideration of the surrounding circumstances. Now the God of the Soil may be truly hard of hearing or just pretending to be confused, but Seventh Sister was too embarrassed to repeat herself, so she used hand gestures to suggest her intentions to the God of the Soil. These gestures were not only for the God of the Soil to see, but they also were an explanation to the audience to solve the riddle of what had been whispered between Seventh Sister and the God of the Soil. On an even deeper level, we also considered the shy heart of Seventh Sister as a young girl experiencing passion for the first time. Using gestures to make clear her thoughts showed that on the one hand Seventh Sister had the courage to love, but on the other hand she also had the timidity characteristic of young girls in love—even when she has fallen in love completely, she is still too bashful to speak. Thus, in addition to Seventh Sister's immortal nature, we also carved out her personality, making people feel as though she is one of us. However, the most indicative of Seventh Sister's shy heart was certainly the language in the hand gestures that she used when talking to Dong Yong.

The scene begins just after Dong Yong has explained his life experiences, and [in it] Seventh Sister comforts him by singing the verse: "I would wish with you … what is it? ... to be united in wedlock!" If we had not come up with certain hand gestures right here, but had wanted to communicate Seventh Sister's hesitancy to speak, we would have had to rely solely upon the actor's singing skill to express tactfulness at the end of the phrase. However, this would have given people only the faintest inkling [of her feelings]. After we added the hand gestures and lyrical ornamentation and pauses [to her singing], the [desired] effect was strengthened. The pause after "with you" drove Dong Yong to interject "What is it?" Since Seventh Sister was still hesitating as to whether or not to speak at this point, Dong Yong's "What is it?" seemed to give her courage. When she could no longer *not* speak, then out came "to be united. …" There was no accompaniment here, so Seventh Sister's *a cappella* solo reverberated on the stage. This made it necessary for the sung lyric to have ornamentation, and the ornamentation revealed Seventh Sister's inner vacillation between speaking and keeping silent. Combined with this were Seventh Sister's hand gestures. Her two hands pulled apart for a moment, representing her and Dong Yong. Following her singing of "in wedlock," her two hands came together side by side, then abruptly pulled apart again. This made one feel as if Seventh Sister's heart were beating frantically. Following this, flustered and shy, she hastily moved away [from Dong Yong]. At first, this set of hand gestures was not a side-by-side gesture, but a piling-up gesture, with the upper and lower hand changing positions. However, this seemed vulgar and unfitting for Seventh Sister's simple nature, so after reconsidering it, we decided to change to the current side-by-side gesture. This kind of hand gesture unified the image of Seventh Sister. Thus, the gestural language of this motion and the lyrics became fully fused, and without using a single *word* we painted a striking picture of the ever-changing heart of a girl in love that underpins Seventh Sister's simple lyrics.

The basic tone of "Meeting on the Road" was light brightness constructed on top of a free spirit. The entrance of the God of the Soil established this tone, and it was [also] expressed through the relationship among the characters. Through the comparison between Seventh Sister and the God of the Soil, the comparison between Seventh Sister and Dong Yong, and the triangle formed by the three of them, we made this light, sprightly tone pervade throughout [the scene]. Although the story of Dong Yong's life experiences is rather sad, the overall tone did not change. Fundamentally, this basic tone relied upon the "pursuing" and "fleeing" of Seventh Sister and Dong Yong because the relationships among all three characters depended upon this "pursuit" and "flight" to move to completion.

Dong Yong did not follow the steps or poses of the Peking Opera *sheng* character for his [actual] entrance because his sad and touching story had already been explained when Seventh Sister watched him from Magpie Bridge.[55] According to the structure of the play, Dong Yong should bear the weight of this earlier scene in his entrance: the pain of burying his father lowered his head and he did not use the Four-directions Step.[56] From the point of view of real life, he also should not walk with a measured gait or with small quick steps, but rather with natural steps. However, his steps still must follow the rhythm of his singing so that their movement and pauses are elegant, and he should physicalize the sorrowful emotions of his heart through these steps. After Dong Yong entered, the earlier and later light and sprightly tune is replaced by sadness. Relative to the great tragedy of the overarching plot, [Dong Yong's] sadness is not the end-point of the play's action, but rather it is a kind of turning point and artifice. Fundamentally, it is just a very small buffer against sprightliness and lightness so that the following scene is constructed atop Dong Yong's sorrow: as Seventh Sister "deliberately creates problems,"

Dong Yong does not notice her kindnesses. Hence, this kind of disharmony creates a series of comedic elements, which come out in the "pursuit" and "flight" of Seventh Sister and Dong Yong.

Seventh Sister has already made up her mind to marry Dong Yong, and it is she who creates the "Meeting on the Road" opportunity, so of course she wants to take full advantage of her chance to express her amorous feelings to Dong Yong. All that she can do is "pursue," and in her "pursuit" we come to see another aspect of her personality—her mischievous spirit. However, Dong Yong single-mindedly wants to arrive at Fu Mansion before sunset and does not have the presence of mind to understand Seventh Sister's kind intentions. So he stubbornly "flees," and in his "flight" we come to see his honesty and simplicity.

This scene of pursuit and flight is emphasized most of all in the "gazes." When Seventh Sister *sees* Dong Yong pass by, her first step is to block the road. Dong Yong is walking with his head hanging and, to his surprise, he finds his way blocked, so he suddenly raises his head. Here, he should hurriedly glance up, but because there is a young lady standing in the road, he cannot look her over like just anyone and he simply retreats in a hurry. And Seventh Sister's eyes should be filled with tenderness—finally, she is gazing upon the object of her affection! So Seventh Sister bravely stares at Dong Yong, but unfortunately Dong Yong in his confusion has no way of perceiving Seventh Sister's tender affections. Dong Yong has no idea why a country lass would be standing in the road blocking his way, but he wants to find out, so he covers himself with his umbrella and secretly takes a peek. The design of these two "gazes" requires that the actors use the expressions in their eyes with restraint. Only in this way can the "gazes" be physicalized and also show the differences between Seventh Sister's and Dong Yong's personalities and mentalities. Dong Yong wants to move forward but cannot, so he has to "take the road less traveled." But Seventh Sister also blocks the smaller path! Here we used two and a half circumambulations, and since Dong Yong could not move forward, he completed another half-circle and then turned around to go down the first road. But he still could not pass. This series of movements was completed without any dialogue (Dong Yong's few sung lines are all an internal monologue), and communicating the lines' subtext required eye expression and physical bearing. This was in order to fill the silence with endless meaning. Since Dong Yong *cannot* leave, only then does he come face-to-face with Seventh Sister for the first time. Structurally speaking, this series of actions of "pursuit" and "flight" is a method of postponement. Originally, there was just a simple motion, but it was painstakingly exaggerated to express the implications through "pursuit" and "flight," all of which can only be sensed but cannot be explained by words.

Next came a segment of dialogue between Seventh Sister and Dong Yong. Following the action of "pursuit" and "flight," [this dialogue] turned into another point of the personality-revealing plot. Dong Yong asks Seventh Sister why she is blocking the road—naturally she has a reason, but how can Seventh Sister explain herself to Dong Yong? Yet she cannot *not* explain. So, after first hesitating with an "Um"—showing that she understands she is in the wrong and is embarrassed about it, but even so cannot let him go—she says: "Just how is it that *I* am blocking *your* path? You ... you ... I'm not blaming you, and now you're blaming me?" This is just simple sophistry. Then she continues: "When you explain yourself clearly, *then* I'll let you pass"—just like the overbearing behavior of a spoiled little girl. This segment of dialogue seeks to form a juxtaposition between the two: Seventh Sister's "clear awareness and willful offense" versus Dong Yong's "ignorance and helplessness." In Dong Yong's ignorance and helplessness is revealed his simple and honest nature, and even if Seventh Sister's offenses are mischievous and sophistic, her overbearing behavior reveals her deep love for Dong Yong. Since this "clear awareness and willful offense" is founded on Dong Yong's pain at his father's funeral, if it did not carry the deepest of affections, then our image of Seventh Sister would remain shallow and superficial. Furthermore, the feelings of sympathy that we began to establish during the previous scene would be diluted, or even be destroyed, by this superficial comedic bit. Precisely because of this, the basic tone of the play shifts when Dong Yong begins to narrate his life experiences. Seventh Sister reins in her mischievous spirit and gives her full attention to Dong Yong as he pours out his heart. Thus when the actors are trying to grasp this comparatively ridiculous scene, they definitely cannot deviate from Seventh Sister's true intentions; if they do deviate, then we lose the foundation for the following scene in which Seventh Sister listens to Dong Yong pouring out his heart and then comforts him. It will be impossible to harmonize the innocent banter and later the outpouring of true feeling. In that case, the scene will not succeed in its goals. So the actress playing Seventh Sister absolutely must have a layer of loving affection behind her "clear awareness and willful offense." The difficulties that Seventh Sister intentionally creates are all in the name of love, and everything that happens in "Meeting on the Road" should revolve around "expressing love and accepting love."

All of this is united within "pursuit" and "flight," which should not stop with the physical actions, but should deepen into the unfolding of Seventh

Sister's and Dong Yong's inner hearts. In this sense, the tension between "pursuit" and "flight" is actually the tension between "expressing love" and "accepting love."

After Seventh Sister has bashfully expressed her love, Dong Yong still insistently flees from her. At this point, it is not that Dong Yong is unmoved by Seventh Sister's confession. In dire straits, he mainly needs a virtuous and considerate wife to give him courage and confidence. He also yearns for a fortunate life. His flight is founded upon plain and simple reasoning: with nothing to his name, he cannot bear to make Seventh Sister suffer with him. Such a simply motivated "flight" makes Seventh Sister think that she has made the right choice and it adds a layer of respect to her affection for him. So, seeing the contradiction between "pursuit" and "flight" from the contradiction between "expressing and accepting love," without a doubt we will gain yet another level of meaning. In addition, while "pursuit" and "flight" are as yet unresolved, there is another chance for the God of the Soil to take the stage.

After the God of the Soil appears, a new "character triangle" is created onstage. The God of the Soil becomes a bond between Dong Yong and Seventh Sister, motivates development of the plot, and facilitates resolution of the "pursuit-flight" tension. So the demands of the performance of the God of the Soil in this scene are relatively high. If the God of the Soil cannot handle his scene, then the harmony of the "character triangle" will be destroyed and the situation onstage will become unbalanced. The God of the Soil cannot but become a connector between the two of them and cannot but help to resolve the contradictions—otherwise, he will become a superfluous character. In the end, the necessities of the restricted space of the stage may be simple: the existence of each character has its own rationale (as do the set design and the props). The logic of the existence of the God of the Soil lies in being a "bond" and if he were divested of his reason for existence—severing this "bond"—the relationship between Dong Yong and Seventh Sister would not be able to progress and could only remain deadlocked at this point.

The scene with these three characters onstage at the same time still privileged dialogue [over song]. After Seventh Sister has spoken, she is both shy and happy; after Dong Yong listens to her and is surprised but happy, he thinks of his own miserable circumstances. Reason tells him to be content with his current situation and return to a calm state. When the God of the Soil enters, he feigns ignorance, but he actually has been keeping track [of everything] in his head. These three states of mind must be subtly appreciated, and only if they are grasped precisely can the scene be performed satisfactorily. This required fitting gestures that help to communicate the true inner meaning of the dialogue. Particularly worth noting was our use of the umbrella and the pack, which can be called "drawing on local resources" and naturally became interesting. At the same time, the design of the details in this scene was still based on the opposition between "pursuit" and "flight." The God of the Soil has had enough of this conflict, [but] Seventh Sister continues to "pursue." Her hesitancy has decreased markedly after her confession, so she becomes the primary agent. She controls the whole situation; however, while on the one hand she feels certain of her success, on the other hand she worries about her approach. Thus, after Dong Yong twice calls out to the Shady Scholartree, Seventh Sister might be a bit uneasy (mostly out of fear that Dong Yong will run away), but she still returns the umbrella and pack to Dong Yong. Dong Yong then single-mindedly "flees." But in fact he has been "pursued" into a corner. A simple and honest person, he also has a few frank ideas, so he brings up the "matchmaker" to put Seventh Sister on the spot. In the end, he cannot foil Seventh Sister—he cannot run away and he gets caught in his own promise when the Shady Scholartree suddenly opens its mouth to speak!

"Pursuit" and "flight" were united in the happy, expansive sound of drumming, and the "opposition" between Seventh Sister and Dong Yong was finally harmonized. The contradictory opposition between "pursuit" and "flight" actually manifested the good natures of Seventh Sister and Dong Yong, and due to this, the final peace between the two of them seemed to "occur reasonably and naturally." In the plot design of this series, all of the details, characterizations, and so forth have a close relationship with "pursuit" and "flight"—our "Roadside Meeting" scene succeeded precisely in this contradiction. Furthermore, given the final resolution of the twists and turns of "pursuit" and "flight," this [entire] progression amply showed that Seventh Sister and Dong Yong are a match made in heaven. Yet this perfect match will eventually be torn apart by life. Thus the process of "pursuit" and "flight" stays with the audience, and when the perfect marriage is destroyed, the audience has an even deeper appreciation of its tragic implications.

6. Reporting for Work—Cutting the Superfluous and Preserving the Core; Overt Plans and Counter-Plans

This scene is first of all about rearranging the relationships among the characters, [so] we eliminated any details that drifted away from the plot, such as Guanbao ogling Seventh Sister, who is "like bodhisattva Guanyin[57] descending to the mortal realm," and Landlord Fu rebuking Guanbao after he says "'grate' peace in the world," and so forth[58] The original play contained these minor episodes for no reason other than to show the ugliness of the villains, but if one uses ugliness to reveal ugliness and on top of that adds details that do not have much connection to the plot, then it is often all too easy to dilute the point of the scene. Villains (in supporting roles) should be subordinate to the positive roles (the leading roles)—you don't want the negative roles to shine by themselves and you don't want them to be too "flowery." Rather, their ugliness should come out in comparison to beauty or, in other words, ugliness brings beauty into relief by its contrast with beauty. Thus, Guanbao saying "'grate' peace in the world" is enough to reveal his ugliness, and Landlord Fu's step pattern (slow and leisurely), gestures and expressions (hunchbacked, extended neck, narrowed eyes), and speech (feeble and faint) bring to life his despicable ugliness. So, in our performance Landlord Fu did not point out the mistake in saying "'grate' peace in the world" and did not berate his son with foul language. He simply directly sent Guanbao to see whether or not Dong Yong had arrived. From this dialogue on its own Landlord Fu's image is quite clear: what he cares about is not "'grate' peace in the world"—he only cares about money.

Based on the above simplifications, we created an immediate segue into the main theme—Seventh Sister and Dong Yong's conflict with Landlord Fu—and we quickened the pace of the plot. This strategy of simplification is also evident in the scene "Completing the Work." When confronted with the husband and wife having finished their work and wanting to return home, Landlord Fu becomes angry and has his servants beat up Dong Yong. In the original play, this scene played out painstakingly, with Landlord Fu punching right and left while Dong Yong ducked back and forth. So in our performance we simplified this as much as possible as far as Landlord Fu was concerned, and Dong Yong and his wife took advantage of the opportunity to leave for home. This cut was made in nearly one fell swoop, with the reasoning that we should more quickly enter the "Husband and Wife Return Home as a Pair, as a Couple" scene rather than waste our time on minor episodes. When it is time to simplify, then simplify, when you need to complicate, then complicate; in order to be concise, you cannot have a single superfluous word, and in order to be complex, you cannot be short one single word. This principle is reflected in our handling of "Starting Out on the Job" and "Completing the Job," and it is a principle that runs through the entire play.

The "cruel plans" of Landlord Fu leave Dong Yong at a loss about what to do, but for Seventh Sister it is an entirely different matter. She has broken all of the rules of Heaven for the sake of her personal happiness, yet will she surrender to Landlord Fu's machinations? Here, Seventh Sister carries out a counter-plan that takes aim at Landlord Fu's plans, thus developing the resolute aspect of her personality one step further. Contravening the rules of Heaven was only an indirect expression [of this trait], whereas this incident involving her "counter-plan" is a direct expression of, and highlights, Seventh Sister's fearless spirit when fighting for her happiness. Only in this way can a logical comparison with her series of rebellious actions be created.

Because of the above-mentioned simplifications "The Plan" and "The Counter-Plan," which initially were not long, were effectively strengthened and the layers of Seventh Sister's personality were expanded one step further. At the same time, in the contrast between beauty and ugliness, ugliness is vilified and beauty is elevated. Thus, the use of the principle of simplification in this case not only did not weaken our portrayal of beauty and ugliness, but in fact it made it stronger and deeper.

7. Weaving Silk—Borrowing, Inheriting, Developing, Re-creating

At the time, weaving silk was a comparatively thorny scene—the primary difficulty being in "how to weave."

In the original *Hundred Days Match,* there simply was no dancing and only the Five Watches of the Night were highlighted. The main action was Eldest Sister sitting on a stool weaving, with both hands mimicking the smooth motions of a shuttle to the accompaniment of the "Five Watches Tune." The entire tableau was rigid, which appeared ridiculous and at odds with the atmosphere at the time. When we started to design this scene, we thought about changing it. Our point of departure was to take the "Five Watches Tune" as our foundation and to rework the scene from there. Following this, the movement and language were also changed—we wanted to make the weaving gestures more dancelike and to transform the scene from Eldest Sister weaving alone into the group of sisters weaving together. But this was just the overall structure, and actually implementing the specific operations of this structure was not easy.

Real weaving cannot appear onstage, thus real movements were not possible and the weaving gestures could only attempt to imitate. Similarly, for the heavenly threads we could only use lighting to symbolically mimic the threads descending into the mortal realm. The loom and threads were both imaginary, thus the weaving gesture also had to be imaginary. At "Sisters, let's get to work!" the actresses all moved to the rhythm of the music, imitating the gestures of spinning silk and weaving. Eldest Sister sang the "Five Watches Tune" while she wove, and all of the sisters sang along with her. All of their related movements were choreographed to correspond to the "Five Watches Tune," thereby melding song and dance into one form.

If the process of weaving was entirely mimed, then how could we deal with the ten bolts of brocade after they were finished? There had to be some sort of explanation about the ten bolts of woven fabric—at the very least we had to work in concert with the props that would later be placed on the table before the landlord. At the same time, in order to fully express the mood of the sisters at this moment, naturally we could not do without dance. Accordingly, we decided to employ a half-abstract, half-concrete method to choreograph the scene. At first, we looked to the actresses' water-sleeves. Using water-sleeves to represent brocade cloth seemed a natural choice, and we extended the length of the water-sleeves to 1.5 meters. However, the actresses' skill in this respect was comparatively weak; water-sleeves are not easy to work with in the first place, and with the increase from 1 meter to 1.5 meters, it became quite difficult for them to dance, let alone to communicate through the language of dance. To force them to dance like this and make mistakes was worse than not dancing. Following this, we thought of using red silk ribbons. Ribbon dancing is used in works in other drama genres, such as Peking Opera's *Hemp Maiden Drinks to Longevity* (*Magu shangshou* 麻姑上壽)[59] and *Tray of Silk Grotto* (*Pansi dong* 盤絲洞).[60] Using red silk ribbons made the gestures more accurate, and they were less difficult to dance with than the water-sleeves. So we had a Red Ribbon Dance within the weaving scene.[61] The silk strips symbolized real cloth, and also became an essential prop for the choreographed movements. When everyone shook out the brocade, they tossed it back and forth with an utterly lively feeling. Later, the Red Ribbon Dance faced criticism,[62] and for a brief period the silk dance detail was omitted. However, the vitality of the dance has already been proven over time. Through the crisscrossing and breaking apart of the red ribbons, the Red Ribbon Dance divided the stage into small segments. This both strengthened the sense of space and established and enriched the scene. As props, the red ribbons highlighted the beauty of the dance, completely saturating [the stage with] the cheerful mood of the immortal sisters after they complete weaving the brocade and anticipating the happy prospects for Seventh Sister and her husband.

The problems of borrowing and inheriting in this scene together stress a single point. We profitably explored borrowing the Red Ribbon Dance, along with inheriting and reworking the "Five Watches Tune." Between the premiere and the revival of *Married to an Immortal,* this play was also made into a movie that had a broad influence.[63] We therefore absorbed some parts of the film when we performed the revival. In this absorption, we insisted upon the principle of "using what you can, and not using what you cannot," and what we used had to be endowed with vitality. Given the difference between filming a movie and performing onstage, drawing upon expressive hand gestures was still useful to the stage performance. As for the advantages of those cinematic hand gestures that we could not absorb, they could serve as a comparison reflecting the disadvantages of the opera stage, which must do its best to transform its disadvantages into advantages. For example, when Seventh Sister sings, "I originally lived in the village of Penglai" in the film, there is a close-up on the screen of Seventh Sister's facial expression. Its purpose is to stress the look in her eyes when she tells a lie. The cinematic close-up cannot come to the stage, but the expressions in her eyes in the film and onstage are one and the same. So when we performed, we further strengthened our emphasis on the actress's eye movements at this time. Some things were comparatively easy to move onto the stage, such as the image of Landlord Fu, which in the revival was basically designed to follow the image in the movie. But there were several things in the film that we could not move onto the stage even if we tried, such as the "heavenly shuttle," which used a special effect to show the difference between the heavenly shuttle and the mortal weaving shuttle, or the superimposed projection of different related frames during the singing of the "Five Watches Tune" in the film. However, the stage drama of *Married to an Immortal* also has its own advantages, namely the unlimited freedom of imaginary space created through suppositionality. In this, the film version of *Married to an Immortal* could not compare. Thus, in drawing on the film we by no means wanted to completely omit the characteristics and advantages of the stage play, but rather we wanted to endlessly enrich and develop them.

Next is the attitude toward the "Five Watches Tune." The "Five Watches Tune" is specific to Huangmei Opera.[64] At the time, we wanted to change it, but we could not find anything suitable to replace it with. So we retained it, while making some changes to the music to make it more aesthetically pleasing. When dealing with traditional things, the key is to determine how to use them and to use them to exactly the right extent. Only then will one have a true inheritance, since this kind of tradition already possesses a renewed vigor. Take the use of the "Netherworld Melody" in the "Four Characterizations"—if we merely look at it from the concept of the "Netherworld Melody," then it is truly "carelessly used"; however, the use of this tune in the "Four Characterizations" and the traditional use of the "Underworld tune" are already on two [different] levels. Who can now say that using the "Netherworld Melody" to sing "The fisherman lives on rivers and lakes..." is not beautiful?

The "Five Watches Tune" is related to the emotional landscape of that moment. Even though after looking at the details, some people might point out that this segment of the "Five Watches Tune" strays from the plot, if we look at it holistically, the use of the "Five Watches Tune" makes the beauty of the dance and the beauty of the music reflect one another. The rhythm is bright and graceful, further stressing the atmosphere of happiness. This is closely related to Dong Yong and Seventh Sister's yearning for good fortune because their wishes will be realized along with the weaving. At the same time, holistically this scene is also a great postponement. It is a moment of postponement of happiness just before the arrival of tragedy, and overall it has a cushioning function.

At the same time that it settled the use of technique, the "Weaving" scene also had a deeper layer of significance—the transformation of the atmosphere in different segments of the scene. This transformation was based on the emotional transformation of the characters. From the moment when the six elder sisters and Seventh Sister look at one another, grieved about parting, to the attitude of delight when Dong Yong and his wife face a night's worth of brocade, the atmosphere must always be grasped accurately. Only by accurately unearthing the emotional shifts of the characters can one fully realize the change in the atmosphere onstage. This was all completed as if under natural conditions, allowing the audience to be unaware of savoring one hundred different "tastes" and to gain artistic appreciation.

8. Completing the Job—A Prologue to Great Sorrow: Foreshadowing and the Force of Piling Up

Overall, the scene "Completing the Job" is one of a young husband and wife placing their hopes on the pipe dream of freedom. This is the first time in the whole play that the affection between the young husband and wife is shown. Although it is very short, it simplifies their relationship and places the emphasis on their love, thereby intensifying their love.

From "Meeting on the Road" to just before "Completing the Job," their love grows more solid and more earnest by the day. With respect to the plots of the scenes before and after, this postpones the anticipation of happiness and prosperity and delays the arrival of the final tragic climax. Such a postponement does not dilute the tragic implications; rather, it more clearly augments the power and depth of the tragedy.

Looking at the entire play, from "Magpie Bridge" to "Completing the Job" to "Husband and Wife Return Home as a Pair," all of these scenes are actually a kind of postponement—the delay of the impending tragedy through happiness. Although there is a bit of mournfulness therein, as I have discussed above, compared with the final sorrow all other moments are part of a process of postponement that serves the greater tragedy. It is like giving you an exquisite flower vase and pointing out its splendors, letting you carefully savor each of them, but then forcefully pushing it over and shattering it. The process of postponement is thus a process of subtle savoring, and this process is the "force of piling up." The more, the higher—just like water continuously rising. One can imagine the force of impact and the rousing power when the dike breaks. So "piling up" becomes a turning point and latent feature in the preceding five scenes.

When the sisters were on Magpie Bridge praising the pleasures of the human realm with interest and admiration, it was a beautiful scene. The sisters naturally could not have imagined or wished that one day their sister would be punished by the rules of Heaven and would suffer the pain of being separated from her husband. "Meeting on the Road" did its utmost to emphasize that their match is ideal, so who could imagine or want the loving spouses to be unexpectedly wrenched apart by life? "Going to Work" and "Counter-Plan" gave the audience a sense of anticipation; the "Weaving" scene spared no effort to play up their boundless happiness; and "Completing the Job" showed prosperity waiting just around the corner. The audience could imagine their happy feelings in their hut, sitting under the oil lamps while awaiting daybreak. The "piling up" of this series of events filled up the stores of "force." It was everyone's hope that this couple, who had faced so many complications and adversities, might enter the palace of good fortune. This wish was also the result of all that which was "piling up." If not for the "stored force" of this "piling," then shattering the flower vase would be completely irrelevant. Even if there were a little bit of pity for them, it would be dry and meaningless—one certainly would not speak of sorrow that pierces to the quick.

The setting up of a pattern of suspense and foreshadowing was also part of the process of postponement. It was not the same as "piling up"—the two were different approaches with the same function. When facing elements of tragedy within happiness, people will feel anxiety. For example, the part when Eldest Sister and Seventh Sister make strong statements and when fear creeps in after the God of the Soil realizes that Seventh Sister intends to marry Dong Yong, and so forth—these scenes all are related to "piling up." If it were simply "a pile," then when "the pile breaks" in the end, it would be difficult to avoid giving the audience a feeling of abruptness. The audience would not be able to accept it, just as with the question: "How can what is clearly a horse suddenly transform into a donkey?" Instead, hiding the correct amount of tragic elements creates tension for the audience. In the end, the springs are wound too tightly and then they snap. Emotionally, this is a natural shift, a natural release. When we reconsider it in retrospect, we suddenly realize that all that has happened has had a logical relationship. That is to say, it is not that the vase has shattered without reason, even if it seems unexpected. If a tragedy can reach this point, then it has succeeded. Using the eyes of today to look back at our earlier performance, we can say that as a tragedy *Married to an Immortal* has ample ground to claim success.

9. Parting—Who Broke this Exquisite Vase?

The curtain rises, forcefully revealing the happy, excited mood of husband and wife as they are on their way back to their humble dwelling after having finished their work. Both the set design and the attitudes of the characters reflect the theme of this scene. The road to good fortune lies under their feet, and emotion rises in their hearts and materializes as "the smiling face of the clear streams and green mountains." It is as though the green mountains and clear streams are also infected with the joyful mood of the protagonists. In addition, the music and lighting serve the mood of the protagonists as well. In the duet in this scene between the two protagonists, we made full use of the language of physical movement to express their inner stirrings to the greatest [possible] extent. The operatic frame, dance gestures, and postures of spoken drama were all blended in the scene, intertwining the protagonists' words and hearts. Our scene attempted to make this known through the fusion of the "piling up" of the five prior scenes as the change of events was silently brewing.

The bad news brought by the Heavenly General deals a deathblow to the loving couple. If they cannot be together happily, what meaning can they find in this world? As a result, the "Parting" scene shifts to a sorrowful tune, and the entire play shifts from comedy to tragedy. Our use of the stage, lighting, and sound effects for the Heavenly General's entrance gave the audience a feeling of vanishing into darkness. The change in the exterior environment symbolized a change in the characters' fate, and at the same time emphasized the abyss that is Seventh Sister's inner suffering. One aria even more directly expressed Seventh Sister's inner suffering. With both eyes, she faced front toward the audience as if she were gazing at the image of Dong Yong, whom she loves with her whole heart. Beneath this, she is even more hurt inside. So we added a "Crying Tune" style of singing on top of the "Immortals' Tune" in this aria and the actress used a quivering voice to convey her choking back sobs. At this point, Seventh Sister did not use any relatively large gestures, since if her gestures were large this would impede the expression of her interior shifts. Only "stillness" could stress the mournful tone painted by the aria, and in that stillness lay all of the sufferings that had pierced her heart. So we thought of using a static posture while she was singing in order to draw the audience's gaze to her. In that way, when Seventh Sister sang, she could use her voice even better to communicate her emotions, infecting the audience and playing upon their heartstrings. She thereby transmitted her great suffering to every corner [of the room]. In terms of concrete singing techniques, the word "mend" in the line "when your clothes are worn, who shall mend them?" absorbed the *pingtan* singing method.[65] This singing style most precisely expressed Seventh Sister's feelings of suffering.

Although, on the one hand, Seventh Sister is touched to the quick, on the other she cannot fall apart in front of Dong Yong. Facing Dong Yong, she still holds herself together, thus creating another strong contrast between a difficult-to-articulate suffering (Seventh Sister) and an ignorant bliss (Dong Yong simply does not know what has happened since he left). Within this contrast, as before Dong Yong is awash in the "smiling face" of the "clear streams and green mountains," whereas Seventh Sister forces herself to put on a happy face. Regardless, it is difficult for her to hide her heavy heart. This contrast of great sadness and great happiness strengthens the tragic implications, giving the audience an indescribable heartache. The tragic and the comic are woven together, laced up side by side.

When Dong Yong realizes that Seventh Sister is crying, Seventh Sister runs away with tears glistening and holds him off by insisting that it is a speck of dust or the wind. Dong Yong does not believe her and says, "With a broken heart, tears gush down one's face, but facing the wind, tears fall drop by drop"—at this moment, the innocent turns shrewd. Seventh Sister has already given several hints to Dong Yong and she cannot bear to suddenly hurt him, but she also cannot *not* speak. Dong Yong is immersed in happiness, and in general cannot fully understand. In addition to the surface meaning of this exchange of hinting, there is another level of hidden meaning; in order to convey *this* meaning, the actors have to use their facial and eye expressions in exactly the right way. Furthermore, at this moment Dong Yong should still look as though he is completely unaware; the actor's acting must achieve this goal or the effect of the contrast will not be intensified. And after Dong Yong sees her tears, Seventh Sister must speak. For Seventh Sister's revelation of her identity, we did not follow the traditional technique that used drums, instead we did not use any background sound effects. This was meant to emphasize the shock of Seventh Sister's declaration. Dong Yong is greatly surprised—he had never suspected that his beloved wife was a daughter of the Jade Emperor, nor had he imagined that they would suddenly be separated in life as if parted by death, so he sings the line: "From heaven descends a heartless sword. …" Before he sings, he backs away in shock; singing at a distance from Seventh Sister represents his difficulty of accepting [this news]. This scene begins with the Peking Opera "High Splashing" tune, and then transitions into a Huangmei tune. Huangmei Opera does not have a method for singing without a fixed beat, so we handled this in such a way so as to reflect the sudden shift in Dong Yong's mood. Following this, Dong Yong is pleading with the Shady Scholartree—the object is the same as before, but it is no longer that old matchmaker who spoke to them. The bustling scene of Seventh Sister, the God of the Soil, and Dong Yong on that day flashes before his eyes—how could that have become today's bleakness and desolation? This scene uses the narrative of Dong Yong's sorrowful silence to strengthen the juxtaposition of now and then and to increase its tragic implications.

The final sounding of the Heavenly Drum is the prelude to the arrival of the greatest sorrow of the entire play. Although Seventh Sister cannot bear to be parted from Dong Yong, his life depends upon her departure. She cannot cast away Dong Yong, yet she also cannot watch him go to his death. Here, her subjective life is under such intense pressure that it appears too trivial to be worth mentioning, [like] a beautiful vase crushed under a great weight, with no power to resist—this is the great sorrow [of the play]. This scene used relatively large physical movements, and together they made manifest the final struggle between the two [protagonists]. With one large turn, Seventh Sister embraced Dong Yong and right at this moment, thunder and wind sounded onstage and with the large movements they brought to light the evil of the moment. Tragedy transforms into a kind of strength, and the support of this strength enables their final struggle. [Yet,] movements with great scope require a limit—going too far is as bad as not going far enough—and excessive movement often dilutes the point of this scene. In the original play, Dong Yong and Seventh Sister tumbled around the stage, but in our performance we simplified this: in the midst of the struggle, Dong Yong fainted in anger and grief.

When Seventh Sister sees Dong Yong swoon, she runs to him, crying. The original opera used kneeling steps,[66] but if the actor's skills are not up to the task, this appears ugly and it is worse than not doing it at all. In our performance we used staggering steps to walk over, as if she were stumbling to break away and descend from the clouds in order to return to Dong Yong's side. If one looks at it from the plot, there is no need for kneeling steps, whereas the use of staggering steps connected more concretely to the storyline. And, as a result, the following sung line "Dong Yong faints in desolation" flowed smoothly. In this series of actions, the tragic implications deepened even further. In the end, Seventh Sister's eye expressions are incredibly important—these should not be impatient or without hope, but rather full of bitterness and facing the clear sky: I am unafraid of your Heavenly Rules, one after another rendering us apart. Our hearts in heaven and in the mortal realm are one! With this, her eyes unite with the spirit and meaning of this last line and provide a speck of brightness to this great, heavy grief.

The Filming

One cannot say that the Shanghai Film Studio considered making *Married to a Heavenly Immortal* a priority project. Only a limited budget was made available and the task of directing the movie was entrusted (against his will) to the experienced but sidelined director Shi Hui. Sang Hu provided a script that envisioned drastic changes but many of these changes were abandoned as the project progressed. The huge success of the movie was totally unexpected.

As many operatic movies were made in the 1950s, opinions varied. Some directors were in favor of a purely documentary approach, whereas others favored a free adaptation that would make use of the possibilities of cinema. A conference to debate the pros and cons of both approaches was organized in 1956.[67] It is clear that Sang Hu and Shi Hui were among those who wanted to make full use of available cinematic techniques to create attractive feature films. More conferences on the topic followed in 1959 and 1963.

Sang Hu
Married to a Heavenly Immortal on the Silver Screen[68]
1956

In our country the story of Dong Yong and Seventh Sister is widely known amongst the people. In recent years genres of traditional opera such as Hubei Opera (*Chuju*), Jinhua Opera, Shaoxing Opera (*Yueju*), and Cantonese Opera all included this item in their repertoire. When a competitive performance of traditional operas from all over the country took place in Beijing in the fall of 1952, the representative company from the central-southern region performed the Hubei Opera *Marriage of a Hundred Days* (*Bairi yuan* 百日緣). This was the first time that I watched a stage performance of the story of Dong Yong. What was performed was "Separating at the Shady Scholartree." The strong tragic nature of the story and the consummate performance skills of the actors greatly moved the audience. When I returned to Shanghai after the conclusion of the Beijing event, I also saw *Married to a Heavenly Immortal* as performed by the Anhui Provincial Huangmei Opera Company that had visited Shanghai to participate in the Performance and Study Meeting held there. What was performed was the scene "Meeting on the Road."[69] This scene gave conspicuous expression to Seventh Sister's daring and ardent pursuit of love and Dong Yong's good and honest character. Content, construction, and performance were all filled with the vitality of spring, and the simple but beautiful music of Huangmei Opera added an even greater limitless luster to the performance as a whole.

Needless to say, the legend of Dong Yong selling his body to bury his father and moving heaven by his filial piety contains many elements of feudal superstition, but to judge from the effect of these operas in different localities, the audiences were most attracted by Dong Yong and Seventh Sister's miraculous marriage and their later cruel separation. That is why in each and every genre of opera the two scenes "Meeting on the Road" and "Separating at the Scholartree" most absorbed the people. In the perception of the audience, Seventh Sister in "Meeting on the Road" is not a lofty and unapproachable divine immortal but a poeticized daring and enthusiastic girl. She is filled with yearning and trust toward life, and her manner of head over heel enthusiastically pursuing love reflects the passion and hope of young women who for so long in the old society suffered the shackles of feudalism. In "Separating at the Shady Scholartree" the audience was one-sidedly sympathetic with Dong Yong and Seventh Sister, and it hated the Jade Emperor who forced Seventh Sister to ascend to heaven. When this play was performed according to the old script, Dong Yong's filial piety moved the Jade Emperor, who therefore ordered his own daughter to descend to the mortal world and marry Dong Yong and then to return to heaven after one hundred days. When the audience watched the scene of the parting at the Shady Scholartree, it would be filled with sadness because of the arbitrary separation of this loving couple, and it would strongly condemn the Jade Emperor for his cruel lack of feeling. This is due to the strong popular character (*renminxing*) that is present in the story of Dong Yong and Seventh Sister.

Guided and inspired by Chairman Mao's "Let One Hundred Flowers Bloom, Discard the Old and Bring Forth the New," since Liberation all genres of traditional opera have made conspicuous progress both in terms of the revision of traditional plays and in the creation of new plays that reflect modern life. In the case of *Married to a Heavenly Immortal*, in recent years comrades in the Anhui Provincial Huangmei Opera Company, directed by the Bureau of Culture of the province, undertook repeated revisions and improvements of this play. Therefore, the quality of its performances was continuously improved. At the 1954 East China Theater Festival in Shanghai *Married to a Heavenly Immortal* won a prize for its script, for its direction, for its excellent performance, and also for its music. The actors (Yan Fengying in the role of Seventh Sister; Wang Shaofang in the role of Dong Yong) each obtained a prize for their acting. When the Shanghai Film Studio decided to make this beautiful fairy tale into a movie and assigned me the task of revising the script, I therefore felt very fortunate and happy.

Because the stage version of *Married to a Heavenly Immortal* already had achieved such extraordinary success, it provided a very good basis for the work of revision. In order to make the central message even more distinct and focused, we made Dong Yong and Seventh Sister's resistance against Heaven the primary theme, and we made their resistance against their exploitation and oppression by Master Fu the secondary theme. Next, in the scene "Meeting on the Road" we appropriately adjusted the relations between the characters. This means that Dong Yong was not treated as a completely passive character and we emphasized his friendliness toward Seventh Sister—he refuses to promptly agree to her marriage proposal only because he does not want to involve her in his suffering. With respect to the scene "Separating at the Shady Scholartree," we not only portrayed the incomparably deep love between Dong Yong and Seventh Sister and exposed their cruel oppression by Heaven, but also, and more importantly, we delineated the unswerving and inflexible determination of the loving couple. Even though the story has a tragic ending, in the end Dong Yong and Seventh Sister never submit to the Jade Emperor. "I do not fear the heavenly regulations that tear us apart while alive,/ In heaven and on earth our hearts will always be one." This is their oath of love, and this is also their furious accusation.

Married to a Heavenly Immortal is a fairy tale,[70] and therefore a movie offers far more possibilities to use all kinds of means for enrichment. From the very beginning, we decided to shoot the movie in the manner of a fairy-tale feature film with song and dance and not as a documentary of theatrical arts. In this respect, the director[71] came up with daring and unique artistic solutions, and the performers put in back-breaking work. Moreover, in terms of camera movement, scenery, and special effects the director was appropriately creative. Therefore, I am of the opinion that this movie has a relatively perfect form. It fully preserves the strengths of our national theatrical arts, but it also employs the special features of cinematic art.

When it comes to the question of how to bring theater and film together even better, we have had successful experiences and we have also learned from our failures, as the concrete circumstances of each opera genre are different and as at present this project remains at the stage of a tentative experiment. But under these circumstances each and every little success is a reason for joy. In my capacity as the scriptwriter but also in my capacity as a member of the audience I want to congratulate the director, the performers, and the other comrades involved in this project for the creative labor they have put into this, and I happily share in the success and joy that they have achieved.

Shi Hui

Notes about Directing *Married to a Heavenly Immortal*[72]

1956

Recently the problem of how to shoot stage operas as movies has attracted the attention of quite a few people. Does it become very difficult to give full play to the characteristics of film if one stays too loyal to the arts of the theater? Or do we necessarily inflict damage on the arts of the theater if we go too far in "moviefication"? Is it best to shoot an opera without making any changes at all? Or is it right to go for "moviefication" without caring for the rest? Everyone has his own approach, and opinions are not very unified. What I know in this respect is very limited and I cannot come up with any big theory, but let me provide some simple experiences and suggestions based on my work in directing *Married to a Heavenly Immortal.*

My Earliest Creative Ideas

I first have to acknowledge that I am an outsider when it comes to our national traditional theatrical arts. I am only an enthusiastic member of the audience, filled with a strong and passionate love. Wherever we go to shoot on location with our production team, I seize the opportunity to watch the traditional opera of that locality, and I always greatly enjoy these performances. This applies even more to Peking Opera, which I have been listening to from my earliest youth—I am really addicted to it. I am a true opera fanatic! I also studied it for a while and learned to sing a few lines. I have performed onstage too, and have performed quite a range of characters, trying out every role-type. I have even sung in military plays, but I did not fight anyone and no one fought me. But according to what friends who watched my performances have told me, my performances belonged to the "self-indulgent style."

Love does not equal understanding. Love does not mean getting it right when it becomes your turn to be responsible, and people who criticize others for messing up will not necessarily do things in a proper style when they are in charge.

Before I undertook the task of directing *Married to a Heavenly Immortal,* I had never watched Huangmei Opera. What I saw first of all was the adapted literary script (in its first draft). That draft had thrown off the shackles of the set conventions of traditional theater and had given full expression to the nature and capacity of film; the fairy-tale[73] features were very much emphasized. Because the scriptwriter had also worked as a director, his script was very rich in "camera feeling." At the same time, it aroused in me some preliminary ideas about how to handle this future film.

I conceived of the idea of a new kind of cinematic style: a fairy-tale movie. The contents and incidents in the first draft of the literary script of *Married to a Heavenly Immortal* allowed for this possibility. It also inspired a creative impulse in me—in order to shoot it completely in conformity with cinematic demands, I wanted to compose a new score for which the original Huangmei Opera would only provide the materials. I wanted to create an original fairy-tale film using full-fledged cinematic techniques.

"An Immortal Maiden descends to earth and marries a peasant who has sold himself as a slave"—this was such a daring and intelligent image! In my mind all kinds of pictures emerged: heavenly palaces floating in emptiness, Immortal Maidens riding clouds, scenes of the human world, a scholar-tree opening its mouth, a God of the Soil serving as go-between, Immortal Maidens weaving silk, celestial soldiers and celestial officers from the Southern Gate of Heaven. ...[74] This really fascinated me. Because we had done away with the set forms of the stage, the original music was not suitable, so the music for the whole play had to be created anew, and the dance movements could be assigned to an extremely secondary position. Truly, this was a movie—a fairy-tale movie, preferably in full color! If I were to shoot it without any changes, sticking to the set forms,[75] the music and the dances of the stage performance, where would the creativity of us film workers be found? I was determined to undertake a daring experiment!

After Watching the Stage Performance

Not much later, the Anhui Provincial Huangmei Opera Company came to Shanghai, and the first work they performed was *Married to a Heavenly Immortal*. When I walked into the theater, I was carrying with me my original ideas about shooting this movie, and I had no intention at all of paying attention to the music, dance, and characteristics of Huangmei Opera. I only wanted to absorb some materials that corresponded to my original conceptions.

Strangely, however, the first thing to attract me was the music of Huangmei Opera—that thick earthy breathing was really moving! What I mean here is not some "novelty," because I know that things that are only novel do not last for long. What I liked was its clear national characteristics and heavy local coloring—its simplicity, its beauty, and its appeal.

This cast my original ideas very far away. In the theater I stubbornly clung to some of them, but the enthusiastic reaction of the audience made me waver again and again. In the end, I realized that I had to abandon my original ideas, that I had to dispassionately watch the play as a member of the audience, and that once I had seen the play I had to dispassionately reconsider how to go forward.

The more I saw the opera, the more I liked it; the more I listened, the more I became entranced. The melodies were relatively easy to remember, and during the second performance I could already follow along and sing the first line of a couplet or continue the second line. "Easy to remember" is, I am afraid, a characteristic of the music of our traditional opera. Even though "easy to remember" has some connection with "monotonous," it is not the same as "monotonous." Every genre of traditional opera has its own basic melody, and it is often the case that we only have to hum a melody to immediately determine whether it is Peking Opera, Sichuan Opera, Shaoxing Opera, or Cantonese Opera. When you have watched a performance of any kind of opera, there will be a basic melody that will haunt you after you leave the theater, even if you cannot sing the words. This is the most important characteristic of our local theater; it is a characteristic that is quite different from Western Opera, where every work has its own music. I decided that my future film should not have an original score with new melodies and new tunes, but rather it would have Huangmei Opera music!

As one scene after another was performed on the stage, step by step I entered more deeply into the world of the play. I was deeply absorbed by the beautiful folk legend, and the scene of "Separating at the Scholar Tree" even made me shed tears of sympathy. I had deeply fallen in love with this genre of local opera. Yet I could not watch the play completely like other members of the audience. What I wanted from the performance was to understand the problems of *Married to a Heavenly Immortal* in terms of genre, script, music, and dance. I did not miss this good opportunity and went to most of the shows, watching them from different seats and angles, from below stage and from backstage. This allowed me to become even better acquainted with these problems and it definitely stimulated my creative imagination.

I would very much like to stress the benefits I derived from watching over twenty performances. This transformed many of my ideas and fixed my basic direction and method to approach the film.

In the theater I paid special attention to the reaction of the audience: at what places was it happy and which parts aroused its emotions? I derived great benefit from sitting among the audience and listening to its many comments.

This allowed me to come up with quite a few suggestions for the scriptwriter about how to revise the script.

For instance, in the Magpie Bridge scene the Immortal Maidens have sneaked out to watch the mortal world, and there is a long section of song and dance describing the fisherman, woodcutter, farmer, and student. The audience was deeply absorbed by this part of the play and it showed its pleasure. This was the same at each performance, but in the first draft of the movie script this section of the play was removed. In my opinion, the reason the audience loved this segment was first of all because of the beauty of its form, and second because it embodied the strong love of the people for everyone who relies on his own labor for his livelihood. Because these two aspects were intertwined, the audience was very satisfied. Therefore, after an exchange of opinions with the author,[76] we eventually restored this scene.

Also, in the scene "Meeting on the Road" there is an episode in which Seventh Sister blocks Dong Yong's way onto the main road; when Dong Yong sneaks off to a side road, she once again blocks his way there; and when Dong Yong again goes back to the main road, she also goes to the main road and blocks his way, leaving Dong Yong extremely unhappy. Following a conversation, she allows him to pass by her, but then she bumps into him and says that he has bumped into her; when Dong Yong proceeds a second time, he manages to dodge her, with the result that Seventh Sister attempts to bump into him again but, to her great annoyance, she fails. The screenwriter and I originally held the same view about this episode: We felt that Seventh Sister blocking the road in this way and that way, and even bumping into Dong Yong, made little sense and came across as far-fetched. In the first draft of the movie script this episode was omitted, and we chose to have Seventh Sister appeal to Dong Yong's sympathy because she was "all alone in the world," which would then develop into mutual love. But why did the audience love the original performance so much? Seventh Sister is a young girl, so it would seem to be highly implausible to have her on purpose bump into a man she does not know. But why did the audience not experience it like this and why did it feel that Seventh Sister was extremely likable? The actors performed it in such a convincing way. I was puzzled by this problem for a long time.

In the end, I found an answer. First of all, this treatment was in accordance with the personality of the characters. Seventh Sister is neither the White Snake nor Zhu Yingtai.[77] Apart from her fearlessness, intelligence, and diligence, she is also characterized by her naughtiness. "Diligent and naughty" is her particular characteristic. Dong Yong cannot marry an elegant and sophisticated wife who is so weak that she is blown over by the wind and loves to eat but is too lazy to work. He has to share his life with a woman who does not fear poverty and suffering and who is willing to work. Only this would conform to the people's imagination. The stage performance of the three blockings and two bumpings greatly strengthens the characterization of Seventh Sister. At the same time, it develops the characterization of Dong Yong as loyal and honest, good and innocent. All of the later developments are causally connected to this episode, which helps to create the distinctive atmosphere of *Married to a Heavenly Immortal.* Using cinematic means, we could give full expression to the fairy-tale atmosphere that was hinted at in this episode. The author agreed with my suggestion, and we restored this episode.

In sum, I reaped many benefits from watching many performances, but there is no need to go into further detail here.

A Crucial Roundtable Conference

A roundtable conference was attended by all creative personnel, including the scriptwriter who attended at our invitation. At this conference, apart from conducting a detailed analysis, study, and discussion of the script, we also worked out a solution to the crucial problem of how to turn *Married to a Heavenly Immortal* into a movie.

Opinions initially were extremely divided. Some people argued that the best approach was to shoot the movie using a well-established documentary approach, because for many performance conventions we could not create a set of corresponding cinematic techniques within the very short period of time allotted for our task. Basically, it was argued that we shoot the movie exactly the way the play was performed onstage because that would result in a documentary record. At the same time, there were people who raised the following counter-question: When Seventh Sister flies down from heaven, it is obvious that that could best be filmed using cinematic techniques; so why would you want her to run in a circle onstage[78] in front of the camera? If she runs in a circle onstage, then that is easily understood by a theater audience, but in a movie it is quite different. A movie audience is not a theater audience. A theater audience will not demand that Seventh Sister fly up and down on the stage, but a movie audience will definitely be dissatisfied if Seventh Sister runs in a circle in front of the camera.

Starting our discussion from this point, with respect to the question of whether a movie audience comes to watch a movie or comes to watch a staged play, our general opinion was that such an audience comes to watch a movie. Of course, you can say that this only applies to a feature film. If the movie is a documentary of a staged performance of an opera, the audience will come to watch the opera. This resembles the scenery, design, and editing of a news feature—the audience comes for the facts. What we first had to determine was whether the movie *Married to a Heavenly Immortal* would be a documentary of a staged performance (a so-called documentary film) or whether we would shoot a creative movie (a feature film).

Determining the task of the filming had a clear advantage. At the very beginning, the leadership[79] had assigned us the task of making a documentary, and only later was this changed into making a feature film. This decision gave us a great inspiration: we could approach our creative work from a cinematic angle. But the leadership had attached one condition: We had to preserve the characteristics of Huangmei Opera. This gave rise to various contradictions because between an opera and a movie there are countless irresolvable contradictions. Even though the content of a script may allow for the adoption of some cinematic features, an operatic performance brings with it a whole set of problems that cannot be resolved within a short time, problems that have to wait for experimentation and discussion.

Was the task of this movie to provide a documentary recording of the performance methods of Huangmei Opera? It was not. Was it to document each movement and each set form of a particular performer to serve as teaching materials for later generations? It was not. Moreover, the current performance conventions of Huangmei Opera are very different from the codified and rigid conventions of Peking Opera and *Kunqu* Opera. Huangmei Opera has great flexibility and in going its own way it is not subject to the limitations of set conventions. Theatrical conventions [in other operatic genres], such as *qiyi* 氣椅,[80] "the stiff corpse,"[81] circling the stage, the horsewhip,[82] city towers,[83] *jiaotou* 叫頭,[84] *kutou* 哭頭,[85] *sijitou* 四季頭,[86] and fixed poses are all optional. These conventions do not constitute a codified, conventional performance method, where "everything goes wrong as soon as one link goes awry." The conventions of Huangmei Opera have formed a system of their own through a lively and organic process—the performances of comrade Yan Fengying especially highlighted this point. This implied that as far as *Married to a Heavenly Immortal* and cinematic form were concerned, the contradictions between the two were somewhat less than in the case of other genres of traditional opera, and therefore there was no reason at all to have the Immortal Maiden run in a circle onstage in front of the camera when she descends to earth. It would be quite acceptable to use special effects to have her "fly down to the human realm." At the same time, there was no need to preserve "miming an action" when the Immortal Maidens are weaving silk and it would be acceptable to use cinematic techniques to display their ingenuity and wisdom.

At the conference everyone tended toward this view, and the comrades of the Huangmei Opera Company were also very supportive. Even though this might still create quite a few contradictions during the actual filming, it was something we were eager to try out and experiment with. Eventually, we decided that Huangmei Opera would serve as the basis, that we would to the greatest extent possible use the nature and possibilities of film, and that we would make a fairy-tale feature film with song and dance.

First, we had to destroy the frame of the stage, jump out of this thing that shackled cinematic creativity, do away with everything that belonged only to the form of a performance onstage, change this beautiful lyrical fairy tale into something even more moving, provide it with a strong emotive power, and use the special qualities of film to convey through images everything the stage could not express.[87] This work was not simple; it was filled with contradictions, our capacities were limited, and objectively there were limits to what we could do. But no matter whether we would succeed or fail, we wanted to experiment and daringly create a new modality of turning an opera into a movie.

That we decided to work in this way should not lead to the conclusion that this is the only way to turn an opera into a movie. Our approach was determined on the basis of a specific genre, of a specific work, of a particular performance form, and of the available performers. *Pushing the Mill Together* (*Shuang tuimo* 雙推磨, a Wuxi Opera) is a pure documentary movie[88] and equally very good, but that is because the performance characteristics of this play consist in people miming an action. On a completely empty stage, the movements of the performers make the audience feel that they are busy pushing the mill and hauling water; that is why it was right to shoot this movie as a documentary. When some theatrical arts or the performances of some famous actors are intended as historical materials, as materials for study, or as teaching aids, we can achieve that task not only by a faithful registration but also by the added means of slow motion, diagrams, and explanatory captions on the side. *Married to a Heavenly Immortal* has a complete story, and when performed onstage it is not extremely conventional. Its contents and incidents are so rich in fairy-tale atmosphere and the music of Huangmei Opera is so rich in vitality and emotive power that we decided to treat it in the form of a "fairy-tale musical."

It is my opinion that adapting an opera to a movie provides an extremely broad array of performance options depending on the different circumstances, and this is bound to generate all kinds of different movies. The crucial issue is to base oneself on the particular situation.

Starting from the notion of a "fairy-tale musical," we concluded that the less dialogue the better, and it would be even better if the dialogues would rhyme. In this way, the dialogues would be rich in musicality and also be suited for dance. We did away with the drumbeat of the stage music, the most important reason being that the drumbeat had a very strong stage feeling and that retaining it would naturally remind the viewers of the stage. The drumbeat is the control center of operatic music and it serves as a conductor: it guides the cooperation between the orchestra and the performers onstage. But in a movie there is no need to see the orchestra, and therefore the method of conducting can be changed. During the singing of the arias, the rhythm of a drumbeat of one stress and three light beats may have two functions: One function is that it objectively tells the performers, "you have reached the middle beat, you have reached the stress," while the other is that it determines the speed of the tempo. The first is a kind of habit. When we asked our comrades, the performers, whether they could sing without the drum, they said they could do it, but they said that they relied entirely on the drum to determine the tempo. Apart from this, there was still the other function of creating atmosphere. In this case, the drum is used as one of the percussion instruments and this had to be preserved because then the drum is treated as part of the orchestra.

This decision was very daring, but it was very beneficial to the shape of our movie. We surmised that we would not lose the characteristics of Huangmei Opera on account of this, because we retained the drum's role as a musical instrument and we only did away with its role as an objective conductor that was devoid of any melody.

Some Experiences Gained from the Shooting

Often things that make sense in theory do not make sense in practice. The decisions that Huangmei Opera would serve as the basis, that we would to the greatest extent possible use the nature and possibilities of film, and that we would make a fairy-tale musical did not provide an easy road at all. As soon as we started to give expression to our vision with the movie camera, problems arose. The main difficulty lay in how to actually shoot the film.

I have watched *Romeo and Juliet*, starring Ulanova,[89] quite a number of times, and this movie has greatly inspired me. I will never forget the shot in which Juliet runs down endless stairs as she rushes to the priest to ask him for the drug. This is a technique that combines ballet and cinema, and at the same time it is an artful way to jump out of the confines of the stage. I also cannot forget how the camera movement is artfully combined with the dance. This provided me with an answer: if a director is not thoroughly acquainted with the complete music and dance of a work, he will be unable to proceed with his creative work. Therefore, thorough knowledge of the music and detailed awareness of the dance are an important weapon for the director who is directing this kind of movie, and the shots necessarily have to be produced on this basis.

I once met a friend from the Peking Opera world and he told me some of the circumstances surrounding the shooting of *Creating Havoc in the Heavenly Palace* (*Nao tiangong* 鬧天宫).[90] His original entry onstage [as Sun Wukong] took place while monkey soldiers, holding their banners, were entering to a rapid beat of the drum. He was hidden behind a big banner, covering his face with his gown. He released his gown only after the big banners had arranged themselves to his left and right, and then he briefly assumed a frozen posture. Thereafter he flipped his long sleeves, displaying his intense satisfaction and making the image projected as the Great Sage[91] extremely impressive. But before the audience had a chance to observe him very carefully, he immediately displayed his monkey nature, pulling his ears and rubbing his cheeks like a true naughty monkey. Afterward, he pulled in his long sleeves, raised his gown with his feet, and returned to his seat. This was his design for the performance of Sun Wukong's entry onstage. It made me think about how one could capture such a design on film. The usual manner of starting with a long shot followed by a medium shot, then by a medium close-up or a close-up, and finally by a full view of his returning to his seat would not adequately give expression to the actor's performance. But if the camera could follow the Great Sage through all his actions—when the banners parted and he covered his face with his gown, when full of satisfaction he flipped his long sleeves, pulled at his ears and rubbed his cheeks, grabbed his sleeves and lifted his gown—that would probably be somewhat better. The expressive movement that the actor had created through long-term observation of human characteristics should be the most important starting point.

On the basis of these two inspirations, the more than twenty performances that I saw of *Married to a Heavenly Immortal* became the most important consideration for generating the shots.

For the movie, the stage performance of over three hours had to be shortened to ninety minutes, so we had to change the original script. Eight lines became four, four lines became two; two arias became a single aria. We did away with all nonessential lyrics, and we added some film music to convey a sense of the surrounding atmosphere. The length of the instrumental transitions had to be adapted to the needs of the movie, so we had to change the original tunes. All this could not be separated for even a minute from the performances and dances of the actors. We knew that Huangmei Opera before Liberation had no stringed-instrument accompaniment—it did not even have the two-string fiddle! It only had percussion; the accompaniment of stringed instruments is a post-Liberation feature. Even the commonly used instrumental transition is a new invention. Due to unrelenting efforts in recent years by performers and composers, the music of Huangmei Opera has seen continual development. It may have its own characteristics, but it has not yet been solidified. Comrade Yan Fengying can sing many folk songs, and many of the tunes for a female voice have been created by her. ...[92] Comrade Wang Shaofang was originally a Peking Opera performer, and therefore he has borrowed some things from there. Huangmei Opera originated in Huangmei District in Hubei province, and only later did it spread to Anhui. Therefore, it is also intimately related to the Handiao and Huidiao tune systems. But the Xipi, Erhuang, and Qinqiang tune systems each have their own relationship with Huangmei Opera,[93] and therefore we can say that the digestive system of Huangmei Opera is extremely strong. It shows considerable elasticity in the various tempos, such as "level words," "tunes of the immortals," "colorful tunes," "fired-up styles," "two-beats," and "eight-beats," which are all manifestations of the basic tune. These can exist independently, but they can also be intermingled. This is a big difference from Peking Opera and *Kunqu* Opera, and this makes it relatively lively. This was a great asset for the movie. In dealing with the music we never departed from the needs of the movie camera. Everything was subservient to the needs of the camera, and the camera was subservient to the depiction of the characters and to the original and relatively fundamental performance design of the actors. This was our fundamental guideline in the creative work of shooting *Married to a Heavenly Immortal*.

In conclusion, I have to repeat once again that I am an outsider when it comes to traditional opera. I am only an amateur without any deep knowledge—I barely have any experience. I have mostly considered the problem from a cinematic standpoint, and in this way I have daringly experimented with this new genre. Unavoidably, my work has many defects and even failures. The contradictions between scenery and dance and the lack of stylistic unity in the movie as a whole testify to that. But the question is whether or not the direction of this experiment can be pursued so that these problems can be resolved one by one.

Touring the Country

When in the wake of the huge popularity of the movie the Anhui Provincial Huangmei Opera Company performed *Married to a Heavenly Immortal* in Beijing in September and October of 1956, it met with fierce criticism from an unexpected party. The high-ranking Politburo member Kang Sheng 康生 (1898–1975), who after many years of illness had reemerged in the spotlight earlier that year, manifested himself as vociferous supporter of traditional opera in its unrevised form.

Although Kang's opinions never became official policy, his high position required that his pronouncements be taken seriously. At a symposium on Huangmei Opera held in Beijing, many pundits expressed criticism of the 1956 performance.[94] However, whereas Kang Sheng called for an all-out return to the pre-1949 version of the play, they focused on details or criticized attempts by the stage version to incorporate elements of the movie. These criticisms did have some impact at the time, as the text of the play was once again revised and certain elements borrowed from the movie were abandoned, at least for the time being.

Kang Sheng[95]

Letter after Watching *Married to a Heavenly Immortal*[96]

September 27, 1956

The song melodies in this play are very beautiful and contain elements of Huidiao and Gaoqiang. But the play *Married to a Heavenly Immortal* is an example of dialogues to which songs have been added (*hua jia chang* 話加唱), and it is very difficult for people to watch it to the end.

Furthermore, the costumes, scenery, performance, and music in this play all imitate Shaoxing Opera (*Yueju*) and the traditional performance techniques have been completely abandoned. If this play represents the direction of work in drama in Anhui province, then this direction is very dangerous and it is necessary "to rein in the horse at the brink of the cliff and look back at the right shore"!

The history of theater in Anhui goes back a long way and as far as song melodies and performance techniques are concerned, it has preserved some quite excellent traditions. That is why I was filled with high hopes when I went to watch this performance "to report to the Capital." But as soon as I entered the theater, and even before I had taken my seat, my enthusiasm was already greatly dampened when I noticed the Shaoxing Opera modus operandi of covering up your poor skills with scenery and costumes. But because of the beauty of the song melodies (there are some parts of the melodies that also seem to have some kinship with Gaoqiang from Hubei. I do not know why), I felt that I should take my seat and listen. When the performance had advanced to the Immortal Maidens weaving silk, Dong Yong brought out a plate that was covered with red silk. When I saw that plate, it scared me greatly: I would have to watch another Red Ribbon Dance! Who could have known that that would indeed be the case because the girls soon started to dance in confusion?

In this way the excellent theater of Anhui and its artistic traditions said goodbye to me, and so I could not but immediately leave the theater and return home, filled with deep apprehension.

There are many theater companies that to this very day have not yet seen the light. They believe that when they come to Beijing "to report to the Capital" they have to do away with the original traditional performance techniques of each regional genre and their unadulterated excellent operas, and on the Beijing stage have to present revised bastard mongrels. This is clearly a major mistake. I hope that this time the Anhui Provincial Huangmei Opera Company can change this mistaken way of thinking and can perform some authentic Huangmei Opera using excellent traditional plays that have not been revised at all, using traditional performance techniques as well as song melodies and dialogues, and using traditional accompanying music, so the Beijing audiences can observe the excellent true face of Huangmei Opera.

Kang Sheng
Evening, September 27, 1956,
upon my return home after watching *Married to a Heavenly Immortal*

A Symposium on Huangmei Opera[97]

October 17, 1956

From September 22 to October 17 the Anhui Provincial Huangmei Opera Company visited Beijing and performed *Married to an Immortal*. … On October 17 a symposium on Huangmei Opera was jointly organized by the Bureau for the Arts of the Department of Culture, the Bureau of Culture of the City of Beijing, and the League of Chinese Playwrights. The discussion was chaired by Bureau Chief Tian Han. He introduced the development of Huangmei Opera as well as the excellent performers of this genre, for instance, comrade Wang Shaofang and comrade Yan Fengying, who are known and loved by audiences inside and outside of the country because of the movie *Married to a Heavenly Immortal*. He next invited Mr. Xun Huisheng to first say a few words; among those who later contributed to the discussion were comrades Zhang Aiding 張艾丁, Bai Yunsheng, Wei Xikui 魏喜奎, Lu Yangchun 陸陽春, Zhang Yao 張垚, Zhang Dinghe 張定和, and Dai Zaimin 戴再民.

Everyone at the symposium uniformly praised the performance of the Huangmei Opera Company. But they also expressed some opinions about the revisions of the script of *Married to a Heavenly Immortal*. They concluded that the procedure of changing the script of a play on the basis of the movie script needed more study because of the obvious differences between the expressive methods of cinematic art and the artistic arrangements on the operatic stage. To judge from the present performance, in many places the play had lost the characteristics of the traditional performance of Huangmei Opera, and some very fine things had been abandoned. For instance, "Selling One's Body to Bury One's Father" in the original play was a fine scene that greatly moved people, and it was very regrettable that it now had been removed. Eldest Sister in "Visiting Magpie Bridge" and "Weaving Silk" had been performed by a *caidan*, which was in accordance with the situation and very entertaining, but now she had lost her individual character. There were also some defects in the music, as some melodies had become songs and had lost their salient features. As far as the scenery was concerned, it one-sidedly pursued realism and in many places hampered the stage performance. In the design of the costumes one missed the unique features in this genre of opera. Some people pointed out that the current performance of *Married to a Heavenly Immortal* was not as good as the one performed at the East China Theater Festival, and this was mainly the result of the director blindly imitating the movie script and because of the movie's handling [of the plot].

Wu Zuxiang[98]

Watching *Married to a Heavenly Immortal*[99]

October 3–4, 1956

The Anhui Provincial Huangmei Opera Company has come to Beijing to perform. Its first performance took place in the Chang'an Theater on the evening of September 22. It performed *Married to a Heavenly Immortal* which has created quite a stir nationally and internationally since it has been made into a movie. When the movie was shown, I did not find an opportunity to watch it, which I very much regretted. But this time I was greatly indebted to the moving enthusiasm of a friend who intentionally came all the way from the city, wiping the sweat from his brow, to the suburbs to bring me two tickets, and so I took my daughter along to see once again the theater of my home village, which I had not seen for thirty or forty years.

"Huangmei Tunes" is the kind of opera I have watched since my earliest youth, and in my memory it has an unlimited poetic flavor and holds an unparalleled attraction. In the area of my home village almost every youth knew those brilliant operatic stories by heart and they all were able to sing that tune that enchanted people and could move their hearts and souls. Especially among those young laborers who did not have their own farms and worked long term for others, such as farmhands, craftsmen, shop clerks, peddlers, wheelbarrow pushers, and porters, there often emerged performers whose talent and art were outstanding and who were fancied by large audiences. Whenever the harvest was completed or in the First Month of the New Year, they would come together in groups of seven or eight people, find an out-of-the-way spot, and erect a small stage. From this family they would borrow some clothes, and from that family they would bring some gongs and drums, and throughout the night they would perform many moving plays.

I said that they would find an out-of-the-way place to erect their stage. This was necessary, because this kind of opera at that time was called "obscene opera," or "small opera." The local gentry said that it damaged morals and corrupted customs, and the stubborn family heads of the better-off families prohibited their children from watching it. But these condemnations and prohibitions were all in vain and only increased its attraction among the public. As soon as the Ninth Month and Tenth Month of the lunar calendar had arrived or New Year had passed, everyone would ask for the latest information. People would secretly tell each other in which gully below the village a stage had been erected and tell each other whether the famous female impersonator from a neighboring town who last time was said to be coming but did not show up, was engaged this time and would come. At such a time, people's hearts were secretly filled with a difficult-to-describe joy and anticipation. Some of them even would not be able to eat their dinner at ease because he or she wanted to come up with a way either to deceive the family head or to obtain his permission so as to be able to go as quickly as possible to the place of the performance and to find the best spot for the benches.

As far as the contents of the plays that were performed is concerned, these not only were close to everyone's lives, making people feel directly involved, but those beautiful lyrical poems and those meandering and complicated narrative poems were, for performers and audiences alike, simply speaking their own experiences and adventures; they were their own emotions and illusions.

The daughter of a farmer's family falls in love with her family's young farmhand but there is no way in which she can express her feelings to him in words. She has no interest in feeding the pigs, she becomes too lazy to make shoes, and as she continues to think of him, she cannot come up with any ideas, so she brews a pot of the finest "hair-tip" tea that she has picked herself and takes it to that young fellow in the fields. That stupid fellow has no clue about her intentions, and when he later understands, he is both surprised and happy, but he is also filled with fear. It makes the girl so angry that on the one hand she hates him, but on the other hand she pities him.

A young clerk falls in love with the widowed daughter-in-law of the innkeeper for whom he works. When this affair is discovered by his boss, the clerk is immediately fired. When the clerk is about to leave before the break of dawn, she stuffs some buns and shoes she has made herself into the bundle that her lover is carrying on his back, and she urges him to send word to her as soon as he has found a place to live. The two of them weep and cry, cry and weep, and find it impossible to part. Eventually, the male party takes an oath that he will save all his earnings for the next three years and then will return and marry her.

As for *Married to a Heavenly Immortal*, we locally called it *Seventh Sister Descends to the Mortal World*. This was a complete play, and its performance would last until after midnight and the call of the rooster. Even if you had seen it one hundred times, it would not bore you. Whenever it was performed the hearts onstage and belowstage were interconnected: the pulses jumped to the same beat and the hearts' blood intermingled. This was because what was performed was your own life, and what you watched were your own secret emotions. Onstage they forgot they were performing a play, and belowstage they forgot they were watching a play. The laughter was their own heartfelt laughter, their tears were their own sincere tears, and no one could control oneself. When there was "choral singing," everyone onstage and belowstage would sing with one voice; they became united as one and everyone was swept along. This was an extremely marvelous situation because rather than performing and watching a play, it was declaring and manifesting one's innermost feelings and in the process acquiring a clearer understanding of one's own current situation and the happiness that one so ardently desired. In this way, each member of the audience obtained comfort and support. In days of inexpressible gloom and unutterable bitterness, the audience found strength and once again could energetically continue to live on.

But good things encounter many obstructions. Such a state of intoxication so rich in poetic flavor often could not be enjoyed to the full. Sometimes the leaders of the lineage would send people to disrupt the performance; sometimes the boss of an important performer would come to tell him he had some important job to do the next day, so the performer could only perform half the play. The most frequent problem applied to many people in the audience: at the very moment when they were watching the most brilliant and moving episode, they remembered that so late at night they might find the door closed upon their return, or they thought of the dressing-down they would receive upon coming home so late, so they would reluctantly take up their bench and return home, just like the interruption of Dong Yong and Seventh Sister's beautiful and happy life.

But such a nightmare will not return. The "Huangmei Tune" of my hometown has created quite a stir throughout the nation and overseas, and at present I, a man approaching 50, am sitting here with my daughter in a brightly lit theater in the people's capital, appreciating this play I know so well and love so much: *Seventh Sister Descends to the Mortal World*. Who could have imagined this in the past? Who could have even conceived of this?

I was very satisfied by the ensemble's performance. The actors all had a lovable Anhui accent, especially the two young stars, that Immortal Maiden with her transparent and sincere large eyes and that Dong Yong with his simple and honest face. They both were so smart and sincere, so decent and straight. Yan Fengying and Wang Shaofang were eminently capable of embodying those moving emotions and they performed in a smooth and natural manner. What was most to be praised was that from time to time they exposed their true internal feelings. When Seventh Sister was about to ascend to heaven, Yan Fengying's eyes were filled with big tears, and her singing was filled with sad sentiment, deeply moving and oh so somber. Suddenly feelings and emotions that had been deeply hidden in my heart, that I had forgotten for a long time and that I was unable to give a name, were aroused. It moved me so much that I could not control myself. Thereupon, I once again experienced that limitless and poetic aesthetic enjoyment.

It is my opinion that the rich local atmosphere and the long-established and rich suggestion of the people's daily lives are the vital strength of local theater. We should treasure this, protect this, and properly develop and glorify this. This is at present the urgent task of actors in the local theater companies of our country. To raise the level is essential, but one cannot raise it to such a degree that one leaves its native soil and is left dangling between heaven and earth. The accent should not be changed because otherwise it becomes a "standard" Huangmei Opera and Anhui Huangmei Opera will have disappeared. The long-established and rich suggestion of the people's daily lives is first of all expressed through the local accent of the language. As soon as you abandon the local dialect, the suggestion of the people's daily lives is then easily discarded as well, together with the local atmosphere. Improvement and training in acting skills also cannot be neglected, but the aim should be to give even better expression to the suggestion of the people's daily lives. If you "elevate" the technique but lose the suggestion of real life, you will become a paper flower and you will find it difficult to attract bees and butterflies. I would like to propose to our regional drama actors to be a little bit more careful in this respect. Would that be a proper proposal?

The work of theater reform is not an easy task. *Married to a Heavenly Immortal* still has great seductive power, and this is something very much to be appreciated. But in my one-sided view, I felt that the reworking of some of the dance scenes still merits some consideration. Scenes such as "ordering the silk" and "weaving brocade" to some degree resembled "group gymnastics" and the Red Ribbon Dance, and they seemed not at all to correspond to the atmosphere of the play. As far as the plot and the characters are concerned, I believe it is better not to change them. For example, when Seventh Sister descends to earth, the stipulation that she has to return within three months is originally imposed by the Jade Emperor, on the one hand to reward Dong Yong for his filial piety and on the other hand to punish the Immortal Maiden who had longed for the mortal world. When the karmic bond of the three months is finished, the Immortal Maiden knows that the celestial rules cannot be disobeyed. Even though she cannot let go of her happiness in the human world, in the end she cannot but abandon it and her only option is to return to heaven on her own. In this way, the Immortal Maiden will return to heaven deliberately and on her own initiative. Yet, at the same time, she cannot abandon her husband and the human world, so her inner feelings are contradictory and her character is complicated. Therefore, when she ascends to heaven she is at a loss about what to do and she weeps until she faints. The so-called "karmic bond of one hundred days" only so has a cause, the tragic meaning only so is great, the emotional impact on people only so is effective, the anti-feudal theme only so is even stronger, and the reflection of history and the realities of life only so are to the point. Now, following the revision, the Immortal Maiden secretly descends to the mortal world on her own initiative, and when she ascends to heaven she is repeatedly pressured to do so by a divinity in golden armor who acts on imperial orders. She has been turned into a revolutionary girl who has failed in her resistance and the contradictions are now external. In her thoughts there are no longer any contradictions, and her characterization has been simplified. The "karmic bond of one hundred days" has lost its motivation, the feudal pressure that it manifested has been weakened, the emotive force of the tragedy has been diminished, and the feelings that are transmitted to the audience are no longer so serious. I am of the opinion that all good fairy tales[100] of the old period do not have to be revised; even less should we revise them on the basis of our current way of thinking and our ambitions. I have been told that these changes were made when shooting the movie. It is my opinion that it would be better if in future performances the company can undo these changes.

On the bus on our way back home there were some young men and women who in a deeply moving manner were loudly singing the Huangmei tunes of our hometown. This made me remember how when I was little I would go back home during those dark nights under starry skies with my elder sister, who, despite her young age, lived the life of a widow, and with my aunts, who all experienced tragic circumstances, and how they would be singing while they walked. But their voices would be subdued, and at the same time they would sigh many a sigh and wipe away their tears with the edge of their clothes.

But my daughter next to me was smiling. She had seen the movie *Married to a Heavenly Immortal* twice, and this time she had seen the play. Now she clearly was greatly satisfied. But I was wondering in my heart: How can you truly appreciate *Married to a Heavenly Immortal*? How can you really understand our joy and happiness today when watching Huangmei Opera?

Dong Meikan[101]

From the Revision of *Married to a Heavenly Immortal* to the Problem of the Reception of our Theatrical Heritage[102]

December 3, 1956

The artistic accomplishments of the Huangmei Opera *Married to a Heavenly Immortal* on the silver screen and on the stage have already been praised by many people. Here I would like to discuss the original stage version of *Married to a Heavenly Immortal* (performed for invited theater professionals) and the qualities of the composition and the performance of the revised version (which is being performed publicly right now; even though I have not yet seen it, I have been told that it is not much different from the movie version, so I can still talk about it), because it has given me many insights. Also, as the Cantonese theater world is right now discussing the problem of its theatrical heritage, if I write down these insights, these may serve as reference for the Anhui Provincial Huangmei Opera Company and the comrades in the Cantonese theater world.

The content and the singing, recitation, and action at the performance for invited guests all followed the original. It was very much like the performance by the Wenzhou *Luantan* Troupe that I had seen as a child.[103] The original version was similar to all old plays in that in order to make it easy for illiterate peasants to understand, the story was told [in chronological order] from beginning to end; the scenes were many and short; and the exposition was clear. That is why the revised version took the trouble to "remove the superfluous details." It deleted superfluous scenes and secondary incidents that were not all that important, such as Dong Yong being chased away when borrowing money and Dong Yong selling himself in order to bury his father, and it started right away with Dong Yong on his way to the house of Old Master Fu and running into the Immortal Maiden on the road. Even more, the revised version achieved the task of elevating the ideological content of the work. That is to say, following the instructions of Chairman Mao to "discard the dross and select the essence," this revision of our heritage was from a class standpoint and the result was relatively satisfying. The leading thought of the original version emphasized filial piety, and this was still acceptable. What was unacceptable was that it described the charity and goodness of Old Master Fu, who adopts Dong Yong and Seventh Sister as his adoptive children and in the end even marries off his own daughter as the second wife of Dong Yong. Such treatment covers up the class contradictions. This is truly dross! The editors have removed this, and without a doubt this manifests their talent and ability. But if you only notice this aspect, it is insufficient. The excellence of the editors is that they have given a positive meaning to the main theme, they have highlighted the conflict and contradictions, and in this way they not only have enriched the ideological content of the play but also have achieved a clean structure, emphasizing its excellent artistry and strengthening its emotive power. For instance, when Seventh Sister descends to earth she does so in the original version because the Jade Emperor takes pity on Dong Yong because of his pure filial piety and therefore orders Seventh Sister to become Dong Yong's wife for one hundred days. This is not because Seventh Sister on her own initiative out of love for Dong Yong and at great risk to herself against all orders goes down to marry him. Another instance is that in the original version Old Master Fu is charitable and good, adopting Dong Yong and Seventh Sister and marrying off his own daughter to Dong Yong to take Seventh Sister's place, and it is not the case that Old Master Fu out of cruelty and self-interest subjects Dong Yong and Seventh Sister to all kinds of abuse. In these cases, the editors have revised the play in a proper and correct way. Not only have they enriched the dramatic contradictions and conflicts, they have also conspicuously given shape to Seventh Sister's strong anti-feudal struggle. At the same time, they have not wounded tendons or bones or left the marks of their axe. The comrades in Canton involved in drama writing should modestly study their example.

Of course, there is no work of art that is perfectly beautiful and without any deficiency. *Married to a Heavenly Immortal* is no exception to this rule. The original had some very interesting incidents and songs and recitations that have been cut, and this, one has to say, has done some damage to its vitality. In particular, the song tunes have been changed from rich to simple. The popular tunes that originally were so enjoyed by the people have been removed, and it seems that what is left are only one or two melodies that may better be called Anhui tunes rather than Huangmei tunes. It is my opinion that the Anhui Provincial Huangmei Opera Company should once again reconsider this issue. Theater is art, and it is absolutely necessary to provide the audience with an enjoyment of beauty. If you perform a play for a few hours and you only let your audience hear one or two melodies, your audience will complain that the music is too monotonous. I am from Zhejiang province, but I do not love Shaoxing Opera because its melodies are too limited. As a member of the audience I cannot but make this demand. Of course, this does not mean that more is better, but it does mean that the music should not be too simple. To come back to our topic, *Marriage to a Heavenly Immortal* has a few tunes that are very charming and pleasant, and the comrades who were performing them had a certain skill in singing and recitation. This also merits our praise.

What moved me most was not only the script but most importantly the art of performance. To this very day I am of the opinion that our country's theater is musical theater. It is not "spoken drama," and it is also not the so-called "new opera." It has its own characteristics, it has its own norms, it has it own originality, and most of all it has its own national characteristics. At the same time, great artists of successive generations have created an art of performance that provides people with three-dimensional beauty as they have adapted themselves to the circumstance that the audience was standing on three sides. This is different from spoken drama that is performed on a mirror-frame stage in front of the audience and movies projected on the silver screen that only have to provide people with two-dimensional beauty and that are quite different in their art of performance (this also applies to costumes). Therefore, we cannot do without a suitable staging practice when it comes to performing classical plays. A revision of traditional plays that does not continue the traditional performance techniques will be unable to satisfy our demands. The way in which the performance by the Suzhou *Kunqu* Troupe of *Fifteen Strings of Cash* outdoes the performances by all other troupes is a clear example. In the original version of *Married to a Heavenly Immortal* there is one scene that may serve as an example. That is the performance of "The Separation." Perhaps that scene[104] is not suitable for the movies and it is acceptable to delete it, but onstage it should be preserved. Its excellence is precisely in that it provides people with three-dimensional beauty. These are excellent traditional techniques, and even though it was said that the comrades who were performing it were still young, their training was insufficient, and their "water-hair," "iron plank," "knee-walking," and "hopping"[105] did not yet show a high degree of technique, they still could continue the old norms and perform in a satisfying way. So this was very praiseworthy! There were people who stated that the performance of this scene did not equal the performance of *The Hundred Days Match* in Correct Pronunciation Opera (*Zhengzi xi* 正字戲),[106] but I disagree strongly because these two traditional performance techniques "each have a history of one thousand autumns." Correct Pronunciation Opera is an offshoot of *Kunqu*

Opera and seeks its beauty in grace and charm, whereas Huangmei Opera is an offshoot of *luantan* and stresses simplicity and boldness. The repeated "united fans" of Dong Yong and Seventh Sister display a tragic emotion despite its coarseness; it corresponds to the logic of life and also stirs up people's sad and sympathetic emotions, achieving a tragic beauty. It is said that this was cut after the revision, and I feel that this is a pity. This performance technique is an excellent tradition, and it also belongs to the unique characteristics of Huangmei Opera as a subgenre of *luantan*, which means it cannot be put on one line with movies or spoken drama, so it should be retrieved. I also hope that comrades who are performers will study more with elder artists and will train even harder, with the result that they will be able not only to preserve these old set forms but also will be able to perform each specific movement with force and clarity.

To sum up, of all the brother opera genres that have come to Canton to perform, Huangmei Opera has been the most satisfying. I believe that in composing, directing, and performing it can serve as a mirror for the Cantonese theater world, which is something very enjoyable.

Notes

Chapter 1

1 The imposition of Party/state control over the Chinese film industry was effectively accomplished by the end of 1951, even though formal nationalization of the industry was not completed until 1953. See Laikwan Pang, "Between Will and Negotiation: Film Policy in the First Three Years of the People's Republic of China," in *The Oxford Handbook of Chinese Cinemas*, ed. Carlos Rojas and Eileen Cheng-yin Chow (Oxford: Oxford University Press, 2013), pp. 472–498. This political control adversely affected the quality of the overwhelming majority of movies produced in the early years of the PRC to the extent that in November 1956 (during the Hundred Flowers period) the *Wenhuibao* 文匯報 newspaper began a discussion column entitled "Why Are There So Few Good Chinese Films?" Most participants in the debate blamed the rigid political control for the lack of quality that resulted in the declining audiences. See Yomi Breaster, "A Genealogy of Cinephilia in the Maoist Period," in *The Oxford Handbook of Chinese Cinemas*, pp. 98–115.

2 The event was officially titled the Donghua diqu xiqu guanmo yanhui 東華地區戲曲觀摩演匯 (East China Region Collective Performances of Traditional Drama for Observation and Evaluation).

3 For a more detailed account of the origin and development of the legend of Dong Yong, see Wilt L. Idema, *Filial Piety and Its Divine Rewards: The Legend of Dong Yong and Weaving Maiden, with Related Texts* (Indianapolis: Hackett, 2009), which provides full translations of the most important preserved premodern versions of the legend. The Chinese texts of a number of popular premodern adaptations have been collected in Du Yingtao, ed., *Dong Yong Chenxiang heji* (Shanghai: Gudian wenxue chubanshe, 1957). For a more comprehensive collection of materials on the legend of Dong Yong, see Li Jianye and Dong Yanjin, eds., *Dong Yong yu xiao wenhua* (Ji'nan: Qi Lu shushe, 2003). For Chinese monographs on the origin and development of the legend of Dong Yong, see Ji Yonggui, *Dong Yong yuxian chuanshuo yanjiu* (Hefei: Anhui daxue chubanshe, 2006); Lang Jing, *Dong Yong gushi de zhanyan ji qi wenhua jiegou* (Shanghai: Shanghai guji chubanshe, 2005); and Lang Jing, *Dong Yong chuanshuo* (Beijing: Zhongguo shehui chubanshe, 2008).

4 Zhao Youwen, annot., *Cao Zhi ji jiaozhu* (reprint; Taipei: Mingwen shuju, 1985), p. 327.

5 The Chinese scholartree, also known as the Japanese pagoda tree, is the *Sophora Japonica*. "This ornamental tree … is found all over China. It often attains a great age, and takes the fantastic shapes so dear to the Chinese taste. It is venerated and preserved, the branches being supported by posts, and shrines being placed near the trees." Norman Shaw. *Chinese Forest Trees and Timber Supply* (London: T. F. Unwin, 1914), p. 255.

6 Xie Baogeng, comp., *Zhongguo xiaodao jinghua* (Shanghai: Shanghai shehui kexueyuan chubanshe, 2000), p. 487. For complete translations of the *Twenty Four Exemplars of Filial Piety*, see Ivan Chên, tr., *The Book of Filial Duty* (London: J. Murray, 1908) and Alfred Koehn, *Filial Devotion in China* (Peking: Lotus Court, 1943). David K. Jordan, "Folk Filial Piety in Taiwan: *The Twenty-four Filial Exemplars*," in *The Psycho-Cultural Dynamics of the Confucian Family: Past and Present*, ed. Walter H. Slote (Seoul: International Cultural Society of Korea, 1986), pp. 47–112, provides a full translation preceded by an in-depth analysis.

7 Zhang Chengjian, "Dunhuang faxian de *Dong Yong bianwen* qiantan," *Wenxue yichan*, No. 3 (1988), pp. 27–31 points out that the divine maiden is unambiguously identified as Weaving Maiden for the first time in sources from the early years of the Song dynasty (960–1278). Prior to that period she is basically described as an aspara sent down to earth by Indra.

8 For a survey of the development of the legend of Weaving Maiden and Buffalo Boy, see Idema, *Filial Piety and Its Divine Rewards*, pp. 81–99.

9 Xiaogan prides itself on its association with Dong Yong to this very day and a Dong Yong Park has been established to serve the needs of the tourist industry.

10 Great White is the planet Venus. The Astral God of Great White often appears in popular traditional tales in the guise of an old man who comes to the aid of the hero or heroine of the tale when he or she is in distress. He may be acting on his own initiative, but often he has been dispatched by the Jade Emperor.

11 The person who after having passed the metropolitan examinations, placed first in the palace examinations was called "Top-of-the-List" (*zhuangyuan* 狀元), as his name appeared in first place on the public list of those who had passed the examination. The Top-of-the-List was allowed to parade through the capital for three days to celebrate his success. The title "Top-of-the-List for Presenting Treasure" is an invention of the playwright.

12 [Huang Wenyang and Kang Dong, eds.], *Quhai zongmu tiyao, 46 juan* (Beijing: Renmin wenxue chubanshe, 1959), pp. 1190–1192.

13 One such edition was published by the Kunji shuju 坤記書局 in Anqing, which from the 1920s to the 1950s specialized in woodblock printings of Huangmei Opera materials.

14 Chow Tse-tsung, *The May Fourth Movement: Intellectual Revolution in Modern China* (Cambridge MA: Harvard University Press, 1960), pp. 300–313.

15 Olga Lang, *Chinese Family and Society* (New Haven: Yale University Press, 1950); Susan L. Glosser, *Chinese Visions of Family and State, 1915–1953* (Berkeley: University of California Press, 2003).

16 The "classic" novel on the evils of the traditional family system and its underlying morality is Ba Jin's 巴金 *Family* (*Jia* 家) of 1930. It was translated into English as Pa Chin, *Family*, tr. Sidney Shapiro (Peking: Foreign Languages Press, 1958), and was reprinted in the United States in 1972, with an introduction by Olga Lang. Olga Lang earlier produced a monograph on Ba Jin entitled *Pa Chin and His Writings: Chinese Youth between the Two Revolutions* (Cambridge MA: Harvard University

Press, 1967). One of Shi Hui's first major roles as an actor was that of the unbending patriarch Gao 高 in a stage adaptation of Ba Jin's novel.

17 Haiyan Lee, *Revolution of the Heart: A Genealogy of Love in China, 1900–1950* (Stanford: Stanford University Press, 2007).

18 China's first Western-style operas (*geju* 歌劇) were composed in the 1940s. The most important of these works was *White-Haired Girl* (*Baimao nü* 白毛女), which was written in Yan'an by He Jingzhi 賀敬之 (b. 1924), who signed for the book and lyrics, and Ding Yi 丁毅 (b. 1921), who signed for the music. The first performance of the opera took place in 1944, but thereafter it was continuously revised. *White-Haired Girl* tells the story of a girl who is abused by a local landlord. Living in hiding in a cave, her hair all turns white and her occasional appearances scare the villagers who believe she is a ghost. The arrival of Communist guerrillas in the village results in a happy ending as the local bully is executed, and the white-haired girl's hair turns black again and she is reunited with her original sweetheart. This opera, which was composed on the basis of local tunes in northwest China, was widely performed in the late 1940s and early 1950s. As early as 1950 it was adapted as a movie that enjoyed even greater popularity (the movie incorporated only a few of the arias in the original opera). Later the story was also adapted as a ballet, which was one of the model plays during the Cultural Revolution.

19 State support after 1949 ensured the survival of *Kunqu* as a dramatic genre. The 1956 revision of a seventeenth-century *Kunqu* opera as *Fifteen Strings of Cash* (*Shiwu guan* 十五貫) enjoyed such success that it was said that "a single play has saved a genre!" See Chu Suchen, *Fifteen Strings of Cash: A Kunchu Opera*, rvsd. Chen Sze; tr. Yang Hsien-yi and Gladys Yang (Peking: Foreign Languages Press, 1957). The play was quickly turned into a very successful movie.

20 Pure *banqiang* operas probably do not exist, as each *banqiang* genre also makes use of a limited number of supplementary melodies to increase its musical variety.

21 "Thirty-six" is a round number here. When in 1958 the Bureau of Culture of Anhui province compiled the section on Huangmei Opera for the *Anhuisheng chuantong jumu huibian* 安徽省傳統劇目匯編 (Complete compilation of traditional plays from Anhui province), the ten volumes contained 47 "big plays" and 65 "small plays." See Wang Chang'an, ed., *Zhongguo Huangmeixi* (Hefei: Anhui wenyi chubanshe, 2009), p. 1159.

22 An idyllic description of rural performances of Huangmei Opera in the early twentieth century, which is provided by Wu Zuxiang 吳組緗 in his review of the 1956 performance in Beijing of *Married to a Heavenly Immortal* by the Anhui Provincial Huangmei Opera Company, is reprinted in Wang Chang'an, ed., *Zhongguo Huangmeixi*, pp. 1069–1070 and is translated in this volume.

23 For a brief account of the development of Huangmei Opera, see *Zhongguo xiqu zhi: Anhui juan* (Beijing: Zhongguo ISBN zhongxin, 1993), pp. 98–101. Also see Wang Zhaoqian, "Huangmeixi," in *Zhongguo difang xiqu congtan*, ed. Wang Qiugui (Xinzhu: Guoli Qinghua daxue, Renwen shehui xueyuan sixiang wenhua shi yanjiushi, 1995), pp. 167–204. For a comprehensive encyclopedic account of Huangmei

Opera and its development in the twentieth century, see Wang Chang'an, ed., *Zhongguo Huangmeixi.*

24 Shi Bailin, *Huangmeixi yinyue gailun* (Beijing: Renmin yinyue chubanshe, 1989). Some printed editions of *Married to a Heavenly Immortal* specify the way that each aria should be sung, but other editions do not.

25 For general English-language surveys on the development of Chinese drama (including "spoken drama") in the twentieth century up to the Cultural Revolution, see A.C. Scott, *Literature and the Arts in Twentieth Century China* (London: G. Allen & Unwin, 1965); William Dolby, *A History of Chinese Drama* (London: P. Elek, 1976), pp. 197–257; Colin Mackerras, *The Chinese Theatre in Modern Times: From 1840 to the Present Day* (London: Thames and Hudson, 1975); and idem, *Chinese Drama: A Historical Survey* (Beijing: New World Press, 1990), pp. 96–220.

26 For a fascinating discussion of the many and far-reaching changes affecting Peking Opera in the early decades of the twentieth century, see Joshua Goldstein, *Drama Kings: Players and Publics in the Re-creation of Peking Opera, 1870–1937* (Berkeley: University of California Press, 2007). Many of the changes in performance practices adopted during this period were codified after 1949, also becoming a model for other genres of regional theater. Qi Rushan's writings on the aesthetics of *guoju* continued to be highly influential after 1949, even though his name could not be mentioned for many years after 1949 as he had fled to Taiwan.

27 In his *Talks at the Yan'an Forum on Literature and Art* of 1942, which became the basis of cultural policy after 1949, Mao Zedong 毛澤東 explicitly ordered authors to make use of traditional forms in order to appeal to workers, peasants, and soldiers. See Bonnie S. McDougall, *Mao Zedong's "Talks at the Yan'an Conference on Literature and Art": A Translation of the 1943 Text with Commentary* (Ann Arbor: Center for Chinese Studies, University of Michigan, 1980).

28 "Traditional Drama," in Chang-tai Hung, *War and Popular Culture: Resistance in Modern China, 1937–1945* (Berkeley: University of California Press, 1994), pp. 85–92. The reform of *Yangge* 秧歌 (traditional dances and skits in northern Shaanxi) to become an instrument of revolutionary propaganda under the supervision of the Chinese Communist Party in Yan'an during the period from 1937 to 1945 is the subject of David Holm, *Art and Ideology in Revolutionary China* (Oxford: Clarendon Press, 1991).

29 Tian Han's 1940s revision of the Peking Opera version of the legend of the White Snake enjoyed considerable success and is still performed.

30 Chou Yang, "The Reform and Development of Chinese Opera (a speech delivered at the closing session of the First National Festival of Classical and Folk Drama in Peking)," in Chou Yang, *China's New Literature and Art* (Peking: Foreign Languages Press, 1954), p. 104. Elsewhere in the same talk Zhou Yang demands that drama imbue the people with "the ideals of patriotism and socialism, establishing new social ethics, raising the people's moral qualities and enriching their spiritual life" (p. 106).

31 For a detailed survey of this debate, see Zhu Yinghui, *Dangdai xiqu sishinian*

(Shanghai: Wenhua yishu chubanshe, 1993), pp. 129–140; and Liu Fangzheng, "Guanyu shenhuaju de zhenglun," in *Zhongguo xiju lunbian*, by Tian Benxiang, Song Baozhen, and Liu Fangzheng (Nanchang: Baihuazhou wenyi chubanshe, 2007), Vol. 2, pp. 669–687. For a short English-language summary, see Hong Zicheng, *A History of Contemporary Chinese Literature*, tr. Michael D. Day (Leiden: Brill, 2007), pp. 197–198.

32 Yang Shaoxuan gained fame and status in Yan'an as one of the authors of *Forced to Join the Rebels at Liangshan* (*Bishang Liangshan* 逼上梁山), a modern Peking Opera that had been praised by Mao Zedong.

33 Chou Yang, *China's New Literature and Art*, pp. 126–127. By this time Yang had been relieved of his position at the Bureau for the Reform of Traditional Opera. In 1961 he lost his Party membership and during the Cultural Revolution he was hounded to death.

34 Chou Yang, *China's New Literature and Art*, pp. 115–116. In claiming that a folktale is only a "form" that can be filled with new content, Yang was of course using the language of Mao Zedong, who in his 1942 *Talks at the Yan'an Forum on Literature and Art* had urged writers to present new content in traditional forms so as to facilitate its acceptance by the masses of workers, peasants, and soldiers. Zhou Yang's standpoint appears to more closely reflect the interpretation of folklore in the Soviet Union at the time, following Maksim Gorki's defense of myth and folktales in 1934. See Felix J. Oinas, "The Political Uses and Themes of Folklore in the Soviet Union," *Journal of the Folklore Institute*, Vol. 12, No. 2/3 (1975): 157–175.

35 Fairy tales were positively included in Zhou Yang's large grab bag of "myths and folktales." See Walter J. and Ruth I. Meserve, "Myth and Superstition in Communist China's Drama and Theatre," in *Folklore in the Modern World*, ed. Richard M. Dorson (The Hague: Mouton, 1978), p. 131.

36 On the often ruthless nature of the imposition of total Party control throughout society, see Frank Dikötter, *The Tragedy of Liberation: A History of the Chinese Revolution 1945–57* (London: Bloomsbury, 2013).

37 The state-run companies usually monopolized the best performance venues, creating considerable hardship for the remaining private companies. Qiliang He, *Gilded Voices: Economics, Politics, and Storytelling in the Yangzi Delta since 1949* (Leiden: Brill, 2012) provides a detailed discussion on how this worked out in the case of Shanghai storytellers, both before and after the Cultural Revolution.

38 Wang Anqi highlights this aspect of theater reform in her publications: "'Yanyuan juchang' xiang 'bianju zhongxin' de guodu: Dalu 'xiqu gaige' xiaoying yu dangdai xiqu zhixing zhuanbian zhi guancha," *Zhongguo wenzhe yanjiu jikan*, No. 19 (2001): 251–316; *Dangdai xiqu, fu jubenxuan* (Taipei: Sanmin shuju, 2002). But she also discusses cases in which playwrights adapted their texts to the specific qualities of the individual actors.

39 Twenty-six plays were explicitly banned by the central authorities, but many more plays disappeared from the repertoire because cautious local cadres did not want to make any mistakes. For a detailed discussion of the extent of censorship (resulting

in a severe shortage of performable plays in the early 1950s) and its lasting negative impact on the preservation of traditional performance techniques, see Liu Siyuan, "Theatre Reform as Censorship: Censoring Traditional Theatre in China in the Early 1950s," *Theatre Journal*, Vol. 61, No. 3 (2009): 387–406.

40 Bernd Eberstein, *Das chinesische Theater im 20. Jahrhundert* (Wiesbaden: Otto Harrassowitz, 1983), pp. 250–284 is still the most detailed Western-language survey of the reform of traditional theater in the early 1950s. Chinese scholarship is more detailed, but it tends to heavily emphasize Peking Opera. See, for instance, the following general surveys: Zhao Cong, *Zhongguo dalu de xiqu gaige* (Hong Kong: Chinese University Press, 1969); Zhu Yinghui, *Dangdai xiqu sishinian*; Zhang Geng, ed., *Dangdai Zhongguo xiqu* (Beijing: Dangdai Zhongguo chubanshe, 1995); Fu Jin, *Xin Zhongguo xiju shi, 1949–2000* (Changsha: Hunan meishu chubanshe, 2002); and Yu Cong and Wang Ankui, eds., *Zhongguo dangdai xiqushi* (Beijing: Xueyuan chubanshe, 2005). A brief summary of PRC scholarship on theater reform during the 1949–1966 period is provided in Zhou Tao, *Minjian wenhua yu shiqinian xiqu wenhua* (Guilin: Guangxi shifan daxue chubanshe, 2012), pp.14–23. Zhou concludes that many recent studies too onesidedly emphasize the imposition of a unified political discourse.

For a detailed discussion of how theater reform affected Peking Opera, see Li Ruru, *The Soul of Beijing Opera: Theatrical Creativity and Continuity in the Changing World* (Hong Kong: Hong Kong University Press, 2010), pp. 122–137. Jonathan P. J. Stock, *Huju: Traditional Opera in Modern Shanghai* (Oxford: Oxford University Press, 2003), pp. 161–167 discusses the impact of theater reform on Shanghai Opera (*Huju* 滬劇) in the 1950s; Jin Jiang, *Women Playing Men: Yue Opera and Social Change in Twentieth-Century Shanghai* (Seattle: University of Washington Press, 2009), pp. 173–190 does the same for Shaoxing Opera (*Yueju* 越劇), whereas Gene Cooper provides a short description of the transformation of Jinhua Opera (*Wuju* 婺劇) in his *The Market and Temple Fairs of Rural China: Red Fire* (London: Routledge, 2013), pp. 142–149. Also see Shi-Zheng Chen, "The Tradition, Reformation and Innovation of Huaguxi: Hunan Flower Drum Opera," *TDR*, Vol. 39, No. 1 (1995): 129–136. Hsiao-Mei Hsieh, "Where Have All The Different *Butterfly Lovers* Gone? The Homogenization of Local Theater as a Result of the Theater Reform in China as Seen in *Gezai xi/Xiangju*," *Chinoperl Papers*, Vol. 30, No. 1 (2011): 103–122 stresses the scripted nature of performances and the imposition of directors as elements in the theater reform. The homogenizing impact on local genres of theater is also discussed in Lin Heyi, *Cong xiqu piping dao lilun jiangou* (Taipei: Guojia chubanshe, 2011), pp. 261–307.

41 Zeng lost his position in 1962 because he had allowed Anhui farmers to farm their own piece of land in order to mitigate the disastrous consequences of the Great Leap Forward.

42 Wang Zhaoqian, "*Tianxian pei* he *Nü fuma* de fajue he gaibian," *Huangmeixi yishu*, No. 2 (2002): 19. These changes were very much in tune with the two major mass campaigns of the early 1950s: the land reform campaign (which stressed class

struggle) and the marriage reform campaign (which stressed the freedom of young people to choose their own marriage partners).

43 For the Chinese text of this revised version of *Collecting Pig Fodder*, see Wang Chang'an, ed., *Zhongguo Huangmeixi*, pp. 559–570. In the original version a young woman stealing bamboo shoots is caught in the act by the guard in the bamboo garden. When he accuses her of theft and demands repayment, she accuses him of having stolen a cow. But the couple that sets out by cursing one another ends up courting each other. Wang Xiaoyun, "Minjian kuanghan yishi: Huangmeixi de xiangdui yuanshengtai," in *Xiqu minsu Huiwenhua lunji*, ed. Zhu Wanshu and Bian Li (Hefei: Anhui daxue chubanshe, 2004), pp. 530–544 compares this revised version of *Collecting Pig Fodder* with earlier versions as dictated by older actors and stresses the extent to which the text has been sanitized and bowdlerized: in the edited version instead of stealing bamboo shoots the young woman has only inadvertently damaged some!

44 For a description of these performances and an extensive summary of their coverage in Shanghai newspapers at the time, see Wang Chang'an, ed., *Zhongguo Huangmeixi*, pp. 127–131.

45 Wang Chang'an, ed., *Zhongguo Huangmeixi*, pp. 131–134. On their return home from Korea at the end of the year the Huangmei Opera actors also performed in Beijing. One of these performances (on November 26, 1953) was attended by some of the highest cadres. An informal discussion meeting on the future of Huangmei Opera was chaired by Tian Han on January 7, 1954.

46 Wang Chang'an, ed., *Zhongguo Huangmeixi*, pp. 418–454 provides an edition of *Married to a Heavenly Immortal* said to be based on Hu Yuting's oral version, collated with the printed version put out by the Kunji shuju in the early half of the twentieth century. Hu Yuting was a veteran Huangmei Opera performer, who had trained as a *dan* 旦 (female role) and had performed since the age of 13. He was renowned for his prodigious memory and was said to be able recite from memory all "thirty-six big plays and seventy-two small plays" in the traditional Huangmei Opera repertoire. For a short biographical sketch of Hu Yuting, see Wang Chang'an, ed., *Zhongguo Huangmeixi*, pp. 113–115.

47 Hong Fei, "Guanyu *Tianxian pei*," *Huangmeixi yishu*, No. 3 (1988): 32.

48 See Ban Youshu, "Zhengli hou de Huangmeixi *Tianxian pei*," *Anhui ribao*, November 25, 1953. This article was based on his contribution to a discussion meeting devoted to the play following its performance. The issue that most vexed all concerned was the nature of the ending. The traditional happy ending was ideologically unacceptable, but various alternative happy endings were also rejected during rehearsals or even earlier; the revised version ended more or less by default with "Separating at the Scholartree." See Lu Hongfei, *Huangmeixi yuanliu* (Hefei: Anhui wenyi chubanshe, 1985), p. 332.

49 Megan Evans, "The Emerging Role of the Director in Chinese *Xiqu*," *Asian Theatre Journal*, Vol. 24, No. 2 (2007): 470–504. Many first-generation directors of traditional Chinese opera had a background in "spoken drama." As performances

increasingly moved from outdoors to indoors, one of the other innovations introduced at this time was the use of scenery.

50 Huang Chi, "Jinian Huangmeixi shouwei daoyan Li Liping," *Huangmeixi yishu*, No. 1 (2003): 20–21. Quickly following the successful performances of *Married to a Heavenly Immortal*, Li Liping "unfortunately was listed in a different register for reasons that are well-known to all" and lost his political rights. It is not clear to me whether the author here is referring to the Pan Hannian case of 1955, the campaign against Hu Feng 胡風 (1902–1985),or the 1957 anti-rightist movement.

51 On the career of Qiao Zhiliang, see, for instance, Jin Qi'an, "Cong Jingju laosheng dao Huangmeixi daoyan: Ji sheng zhengxie weiyuan Qiao Zhiliang," *Jiang Huai wenshi*, No. 6 (1997): 52–59; and Wang Chang'an, ed., *Zhongguo Huangmeixi*, pp. 998–1000. Qiao Zhiliang would go on to become a very successful director of Huangmei Opera plays up to the Cultural Revolution. Late in life he dictated his reminiscences of directing *Married to a Heavenly Maiden* to Zhang Chuancai 張傳財 and Yao Yuwen 姚育文. See Qiao Zhiliang, Zhang Chuancai, and Yao Yuwen, "Yi daoyan *Tianxian pei*," *Huangmeixi yishu*, No. 4(1996): 75–94. This article, which is translated in this volume, discusses in considerable detail the staging of each of the play's scenes, highlighting the differences with the traditional play and movie.

52 On Shi Bailin, see Hu Kuisheng, *Huangmeixi renwu* (Hefei: Anhui renmin chubanshe, 2010), pp. 93–115 and Wang Chang'an, ed., *Zhongguo Huangmeixi*, pp. 400–402. On Wang Zhaoqian, see Wang Chang'an, ed., *Zhongguo Huangmeixi*, pp.1005–1007. Wang Zhaoqian later wrote the first script of *The Female Prince-Consort* (*Nü fuma* 女駙馬). The play, which was first performed in 1958, became one of the most popular Huangmei Operas of all time.

53 This scene may well be the most original contribution of Huangmei Opera to the plot in the traditional story of Dong Yong and Seventh Sister.

54 In view of the complicated and long-drawn out process of revision it is perhaps unremarkable that the text of the revised play as printed in 1955 seems to contain some loose ends. For instance, it is clearly suggested that the landlord's son Fu Guanbao 傅官保 will try to seduce Seventh Sister, but this is never followed up upon in the play. Also, although Third Sister promises to keep the Jade Emperor in the dark about Seventh Sister's whereabouts, it is never explained why she fails to do so later in the play. In a later version of the text that incorporated further revisions, these loose ends are resolved.

55 Fang Xiqiu and Shi Xinzhong, "Huangmeixi *Tianxian pei* gaibian de wenhua meixue wenti," *Jiang Huai luntan*, No. 3 (2011): 177–182, 192. They describe the changes in terms of *tezhenghua* 特徵化 (strengthening the characteristics), *wenrenhua* 文人化 (enhancing the appeal to traditional literary sensibilities), and *yahua* 雅化 (increased sophistication). Critics in the mid-1950s were less gushing in their admiration. Some questioned the combination of fairy-tale elements (the story of Dong Yong and Seventh Sister) and the realistic scenes of class struggle (pitting Dong Yong against Landlord Fu). Others, such as Wu Zuxiang, deplored

the simplification of the character of Seventh Sister. See Lu Hongfei, *Huangmeixi yuanliu*, pp. 327–336.

56 This scene no longer appeared in the Shanghai edition of August 1955. Perhaps in reaction to criticism that it was wrong to drop this moving scene, Lu Hongfei stresses in at least one later publication that he took care to preserve it.

57 Tang Fangming, "*Tianxian pei* yuanxing yu gaibianben bijiao," *Kejiao wenhui*, No. 11 (2010): 65.

58 After the Anhui Provincial Huangmei Opera Company performed the play in September and October 1956 in Beijing, it was criticized during a Beijing symposium on October 17 and chaired by Tian Han for its tendency to imitate the movie version. The omission of the scene "Selling Oneself to Bury One's Father" was highlighted in the criticism. See "Huangmeixi zuotanhui," *Zhongguo xiju*, No. 11 (1956): 17. It should be noted that on this and other occasions the company also performed the traditional play for invited specialists so that they could judge the nature of the revisions.

59 *Record of Marvels* (*Xuanguai lu* 玄怪錄) by Niu Sengru 牛僧孺 (780–848) contains a story entitled "Student Cui" (*Cui shusheng* 崔書生), which tells of a young man who marries a mysterious woman who showers him with treasures. After they are separated, he learns she was the Third Daughter of the Queen-Mother. See Niu Sengru, Li Fuyan et al., *Xuanguai lu, Xu xuanguai lu* (Beijing: Zhonghua shuju, 1982), pp. 36–38. In popular literature of the late imperial period it is Fourth Sister who descends to the mortal world to become the wife of a certain Cui Wenrui 崔文瑞, whom she showers with riches. When his wealth attracts the jealousy of outsiders, she forcibly defends her husband, defeating all mortal and celestial troops that are dispatched to arrest her until she is allowed to bring her husband (and his mother) with her to heaven. See Yamamoto Noriko, "Araburu senjo: Zhang Sijie," *Chūgoku gakushi* (2004): 23–41, and Wilt L. Idema, intro. and tr., "Fourth Sister Zhang Creates Havoc in the Eastern Capital," *Chinoperl Papers*, Vol. 31 (2012): 37–112.

60 See Jin Zhi, "Wo yu *Tianxian pei*," *Huangmeixi yishu*, No. 1 (1988): 31–37 for a discussion of the continued rewritings in 1956–1957, when Jin Zhi 金芝 was ordered to "streamline" the text in preparation for a second national theater festival in Beijing that never materialized. He notes that in those years the program notes might credit the text to "Hong Fei, Sang Hu, and Jin Zhi." (Sang Hu signed for the movie script.) Lu Hongfei, *Huangmeixi yuanliu*, pp. 304–310 extensively quotes those critics who faulted the 1955 and 1956 play for being too influenced by the movie and catalogues those elements of the old play and his script that were restored in 1957 and thereafter.

61 Wang Chang'an, ed., *Zhongguo Huangmeixi*, pp. 509–533 also includes "a classic version" of *Married to a Heavenly Immortal*, which is introduced as currently the most commonly performed version. The divine warrior made his stage appearance as early as 1956, as is clear from Wu Zuxiang's review of the 1956 Beijing performance of the play.

62 Kristine Harris, "*The Romance of the Western Chamber* and the Classical Subject Film in 1920s Shanghai," in *Cinema and Urban Culture in Shanghai, 1922–1943*, ed. Yingjin Zhang (Stanford: Stanford University Press, 1999), pp. 51–73.

63 Gao Xiaojian, *Zhongguo xiqu dianying shi* (Beijing: Wenhua yishu chubanshe, 2005). *Marriage to a Heavenly Immortal* is discussed on pp. 128–132.

64 Zhu Yingtai falls in love with her roommate Liang Shanbo, but he is unaware that she is a girl. It is only sometime later when he visits his former roommate at her home that he realizes she is a female and he passionately falls in love with her. But by that time Zhu Yingtai has been promised in marriage to another young man. Liang Shanbo dies in grief, and when Zhu Yingtai's wedding procession passes by his grave, she steps down from her sedan chair and is swallowed up by his grave. In many versions of the legend, the couple is then turned into butterflies. For a survey of the premodern development of this legend and translations of a number of narrative ballads, see Wilt L. Idema, *The Butterfly Lovers: The Legend of Liang Shanbo and Zhu Yingtai—Four Versions, with Related Texts* (Indianapolis: Hackett, 2010).

65 Jiang, *Women Playing Men*.

66 The Sichuan Opera on the same theme that was also performed at the Beijing theater festival is available in an English translation entitled *Love under the Willows: A Szechuan Opera. Liang Shan-po and Chu Yingtai*, tr. Yang Hsien-yi and Gladys Yang (Peking: Foreign Languages Press, 1956).

67 Li Yizhong, "Dangnian pengshi Sang Hu yi: Fuqin Sang Hu yu xin Zhongguo dianying sanxing diyi," *Shanghai caifeng*, No. 1(2011): 64–67. Jin Danyuan, "20 shiji 50 niandai xiqupian yu guzhuangxi yingxiangzhong tuchu 'renminxing' de meixue yiyi," *Wenyi lilun yanjiu*, No. 2 (2011): 129–134 argues that the notion of *renminxing* 人民性 ("popular character," the Chinese translation of the Russian term *narodnost*) helped to create ideological space for this movie and others like it, such as *Married to a Heavenly Immortal*. Stephen Teo, "The Opera Film in Chinese Cinema: Cultural Nationalism and Cinematic Form," in *The Oxford Handbook of Chinese Cinemas*, pp. 209–224 discusses the 1954 movie (and its 1963 remake as *Love Eterne* by the Shaw Brothers in Hong Kong) against the background of pre-1949 experiments by Fei Mu 費穆. On Fei Mu's collaboration with Mei Lanfang, see also David Der-wei Wang, "Fei Mu, Mei Lanfang, and the Polemics of Screening China," in *The Oxford Handbook of Chinese Cinemas*, pp. 62–78.

68 The movie is available on DVD as *Tianxian pei Fairy Couple* from the Guangdong Tianren yingyin chuanbo youxian gongsi (ISRC CN-G03-06-0042-)/V.J9), in Guangzhou. The movie can also be viewed on YouTube and Tudou.

69 Shi Hui and Sang Hu had collaborated before, for instance in the 1947 comedy *Long Live the Missus* (*Taitai wansui* 太太萬歲), which was directed by Sang Hu and in which Shi Hui played an argumentative and miserly old father (the script for this movie was provided by Zhang Ailing 張愛玲).

70 Geremie Barmé, "Shi Hui: A Profile," *Chinese Literature,* No. 8 (1983): 96–104. For a detailed account of Shi Hui's activities in the immediate post-1949 period, see Paul G. Pickowicz, "Acting Like Revolutionaries: Shi Hui, the Wenhua Studio,

and Private-Sector Filmmaking, 1949–52," in *Dilemmas of Victory: The Early Years of the People's Republic of China*, ed. Jeremy Brown and Paul G. Pickowicz (Cambridge MA: Harvard University Press, 2007), pp. 256–287. Shi Hui's finest movie is, by common consensus, *My Life* (*Wo zhe yi beizi* 我這一輩子) of 1950. This movie, based on a story with the same title by Lao She 老舍 (1899–1966), was scripted and directed by Shi Hui, who also played the leading role of a Beijing policeman, whose tragic life story summarizes China's experience during the Republican period. Shi Hui's movies in the immediate post-1949 period received considerable criticism, however, from Party hard-liners, and by 1953 he was effectively sidelined.

71 Shi Hui was to be assisted as director by Li Liping and Qiao Zhiliang, but Li Liping was called back to Hefei before the shooting began. Qiao Zhiliang was retained as director for the dance items.

72 Sang Hu, "Yinmu shang de *Tianxian pei*," *Dazhong dianying*, No. 4 (1956): 8–9. Also see Shi Hui, "*Tianxian pei* daoyan shouji," in *Shi Hui tan yi lu*, ed. Wei Shaochang (Shanghai: Shanghai wenyi chubanshe, 1982), pp. 242–253. Full translations of these two texts are included in this volume. It should be noted that Shi Hui and Sang Hu more precisely characterized the story as a "myth" (*shenhua* 神話) rather than a "fairy tale" (*tonghua* 童話). I have chosen the translation "fairy tale" here as it seems to better correspond to the atmosphere of the play and the movie. Several live action fairy-tale feature films from Eastern Europe were shown in China in the early 1950s, for instance the Russian movie *Mamenny Tsvetok* (The Stone Flower) of 1946, the East German movie *Das kalte Herz* (The Cold Heart) of 1950, and the Czech movie *Pysná Princenza* (The Proud Princess) of 1952. Probably the most popular Russian live action fairy-tale movie in the years following World War II was *Zolushka* (Cinderella) of 1947, a traditional melodrama with melodic songs and entertaining dances, but this movie appears not to have been released in China (Sang Hu may have seen it while studying in the Soviet Union). For a survey of fairy-tale movies from Eastern Europe after World War II, see Jack Zipes, *The Enchanted Screen: The Unknown History of Fairy-Tale Films* (London: Routledge, 2011), ch. 14. Neither Sang Hu nor Shi Hui mentions a specific movie as inspiration for their notion of a "fairy-tale feature film with song and dance."

73 According to Shi Hui, the main theme of the movie was the struggle against heavenly authority, and the secondary theme was the struggle against the landlord classes.

74 I have not seen Sang Hu's original script and do not know whether it survives, but remarks by Shi Hui suggest that it departed far more from the 1954 play than the movie as it was released in 1956. Sang Hu's son, Professor Li Yizhong 李亦中 has informed me in a private communication that he is not aware of the whereabouts of the script and is not sure whether it has been preserved.

75 Dai Zaimin took the studio to task for this omission in his "Cong dianying *Tianxian pei* de piantou tanqi," *Zhongguo dianying*, No. 5 (1957): 5–6. Also see Lu Hongfei, "*Tianxian pei* de lailong qumai," *Huangmeixi yishu*, No. 2(2000): 13. In his 1985 *Huangmeixi yuanliu*, pp. 305–306, Lu Hongfei retaliates against the omission

of his name in the movie credits by not mentioning Sang Hu and Shi Hui in his account of the spectacular success of the movie. In the following pages of his book he also quotes extensively from those critics who valued the play over the movie or who criticized the play and its actors for abandoning the true characteristics of Huangmei Opera in the movie imitation.

76 Sang Hu, "Tantan xiqupian de juben wenti," in *Lun xiqu dianying*, Zhang Junxiang, Sang Hu et al. (Beijing: Zhongguo dianying chubanshe, 1949), p. 41.

77 A number of scenes from the play that originally were scheduled to be cut or very much simplified were eventually retained because of their popularity with the audience.

78 Wang Yue, "Xiqu dianying *Tianxian pei* chuangzuo shoufa shangxi," *Zhongguo xiqu xueyuan xuebao*, No. 4 (2008): 64–67.

79 But this also reinforced the "feminization" of Dong Yong. In traditional popular literature it is Li Sanniang 李三娘, the pregnant wife of Liu Zhiyuan 劉智遠, who is ordered by her evil brothers to push the mill throughout the night after they have evicted her husband, originally a poor farmhand, from the family farm. This story is usually referred to as *Baitu ji* 白兔記 (The White Hare).

80 Wang Yue, "Xiqu dianying *Tianxian pei* chuangzuo shoufa shangxi," 66–67.

81 The importance of doing away with the drum is stressed by Shi Bailin, in his "Shi Hui he dianying *Tianxian pei*," *Xijujie*, No. 2(1987): 9–10. An expert on Huangmei Opera music, Shi Bailin served as consultant when the movie was being made. He claims that the decision to suppress the drum allowed the actors to perform more naturally because their movements were no longer dictated by the rhythm of the drum.

82 *The Opera Quarterly*, Vol. 26, No. 2–3 (2010) is a special issue devoted to "Chinese Opera Film," ed. Paola Iovene and Judith Zeitlin, but most of the articles in this issue deal with movies from 1958 and later. Lydia H. Liu, "A Folksong Immortal and Official Popular Culture in Twentieth-Century China," in *Writing and Materiality in China: Essays in Honor of Patrick Hanan*, ed. Judith T. Zeitlin and Lydia H. Liu (Cambridge MA: Asia Center, Harvard University, 2003), pp. 553–609 discusses the 1961 movie *Liu Sanjie* 劉三姐, which was based on a 1959 Caidiao Opera 彩調劇 from Guangxi. Commenting on this opera, she writes, "The rich ambiguities and polyvalence of the folk legends are thus reduced to a story of class struggle" (p. 579) because in the movie the screenwriter had carefully removed "any remaining hints of ethnic and gender conflict" (p. 580). Lydia Liu further points out that the movie "insists on the motif of romantic love as an instantiation of class struggle" (p. 581). *Liu Sanjie* is also briefly discussed by Paul Clark in his paragraphs devoted to "Musical Films: Nationalized Style" (pp. 107–109) in his survey of post-1949 film genres in the PRC, *Chinese Cinema: Culture and Politics Since 1949* (Cambridge: Cambridge University Press, 1987); the only other example of the genre that he mentions is *The Dream of the Red Chamber* (*Honglou meng* 紅樓夢), a Shaoxing Opera version of the famous eighteenth-century novel produced in 1962. Clark

briefly discusses the debates on cinematic opera adaptations from the 1950s and early 1960s on pp. 68–69.

83 Jan Leyda, *Dianying: An Account of Films and the Film Audience in China* (Cambridge. MA: MIT Press, 1972) does not include *Marriage to a Heavenly Immortal* on its list of "Important Chinese Films Made by Chinese and Foreign Groups from 1897 to 1966" (pp. 392–414). More recently, *Married to a Heavenly Immortal* also failed to make the list in Simon Fowler, *101 Essential Chinese Movies* (Hong Kong: Earnshaw Books, 2010). Leyda's only reference to the film is found in his entry on Sang Hu on p. 371: "Any plan to continue a series of sweet opera and fairy-tale films was discouraged by attacks on *The Fairy Couple* (1955). (However, a poll in 1959 revealed this as one of the three Chinese films with the largest attendance, along with *White-Haired Girl* and *Capture of Mount Hua*)." The entry on "Filmed Stage Performances." in *Encyclopedia of Chinese Film*, ed. Yingjin Zhang (London: Routledge, 1998), pp. 166–167 does not even mention *Married to a Heavenly Immortal*. The movie is not listed in the entry on Sang Hu, and its description in the entry on Shi Hui reads as follows: "*The Heavenly Match*, a filmed stage performance, became a box-office hit in Hong Kong and started a decade-long trend there for opera movies" (p. 304). Paul G. Pickowicz, in his otherwise very detailed survey of Shi Hui's work after 1949 "Acting Like Revolutionaries," only notes in one sentence: "In 1955 he directed an exotic fairy-tale opera titled *Tian xian pei* (A Heavenly Match) that had been written by his old friend Sang Hu" (p. 286). *Married to a Heavenly Immortal* is briefly discussed by Stephen Teo, "The Opera Film in Chinese Cinema," pp. 218–219 (Teo translates the movie's title as *The Heavenly Match*).

84 During the Cultural Revolution Wang Shaofang was made to criticize Zeng Xisheng and Shi Hui. Zeng had allegedly told Wang Shaofang to play Dong Yong as somewhat more of a blockhead, while Shi Hui had allegedly told him to play Dong Yong as more "naïve."

85 Zhang Jing, "Zhengzhi sheguo zhong minjian qinghuai de jingdian yanyi: *Tianxian pei* dujie," in *Zhongguo dianying fenxi*, ed. Rao Shuguang (Beijing: Zhongguo guangbo dianshi chubanshe, 2007), pp. 60–71 does not mention the actors at all in her detailed analysis of the movie. Zhang fully credits the revision of the original play and the imposition of a political message to Lu Hongfei, and praises Shi Hui's superb camera work and creativity in adapting the play. She explains the enormous success of the movie as due to the survival of many popular elements despite the political rewriting and the humorous nature of much of the movie.

86 "The duet 'The Couple Returning Home' from the opera *The Fairy Couple* is known to the whole country." Xiao Yang Zhang, *Shakespeare in China: A Comparative Study of Two Traditions and Cultures* (Newark: University of Delaware Press/ London: Associated University Presses, 1987), p. 162.

87 On the popularity of the movie at that time, see, for example, Xiaoyu Xiao and D. Ray Heisey, "Liberationist Populism in the Chinese Film *Tian Xian Pei*: A Feminist

Critique," *Women's Studies in Communication*, Vol. 19, No. 3 (1996): 321–322. An only very slightly revised version of this article was published by the same authors under the title "Shifting the Performative Characteristics of Opera and the Status Quo for Women in China," in *Intercultural Communication and Creative Practice: Music, Dance, and Women's Cultural Identity*, ed. Laura Lengeld (Westport, CT: Praeger, 2005), pp. 195–210. For a selection of letters from enthusiastic viewers, see Wang Chang'an, ed., *Zhongguo Huangmeixi*, p. 135.

88 See Yan Fengying, "Wo yan Qixiannü," *Zhongguo dianying*, No. 3 (1956): 30–32 for a detailed description of her understanding of the role of Seventh Sister and the differences in characterization and performance techniques between the pre-1949 version of *Married to a Heavenly Immortal* and the revised 1954 version. The same issue of *Zhongguo dianying* (on pp. 33–34) contains a comparable article by her co-star Wang Shaofang, "Wo yan Dong Yong," on his understanding and performance of the role of Dong Yong. Both these articles appear to be based on interviews with the performers in 1956, when, after the movie had made them into national stars, the Anhui Provincial Huangmei Opera Company performed in Beijing in September and October of that year. Full translations of these two texts are included in this volume.

89 Yan Fengying's dramatic experiences provide ample materials for more novelistic treatments of her life, such as Yin Wei and Wang Xiaoying, *Yan Fengying* (Hefei: Huangshan shushe, 1985), and Wang Guanya, *Yan Fengying: Bingfei chuanqi de chuanqi* (Wuhan: Changjiang wenyi chubanshe, 1985). Her life story was also adapted into a fifteen-part television biopic which was aired to great success in 1988. See Xiao and Heisey, "Liberationist Populism in the Chinese Film *Tian Xian Pei*: A Feminist Critique," pp. 326–328. More recently, it also provided materials for a Huangmei Opera entitled *Yan Fengying*.

90 Wang Shaofang's career has been chronicled in great detail by Lu Hongfei in a series of articles. See Hong Fei, "Wang Shaofang de zuihou shinian," *Huangmeixi yishu*, No. 1 (2001): 11–18; Hong Fei, "Wo pei Wang Shaofang zouguo huangtang suiyue," *Huangmeixi yishu*, No. 1 (2001): 20–25; Hong Fei, "Wang Shaofang shengping xinian (1920-1949 nian)," *Huangmeixi yishu*, No. 4 (2001): 7–15; Hong Fei, "Wang Shaofang shengping xinian (1950–1966 nian)," *Huangmeixi yishu*, No. 2 (2002): 12–19.

91 Wang Chang'an, ed., *Zhongguo Huangmeixi*, pp. 136–138. The Anhui Provincial Huangmei Opera Company performed in Beijing in September and October 1956, and later that year in Guangzhou. These performances elicited articles by Wu Zuxiang and Dong Meikan 董每戡 that combined praise with mild criticism. The September 27, 1956 Beijing performance of *Married to a Heavenly Immortal* was attended by Party veteran Kang Sheng 康生 (1898–1975) who, upon his return home, fired off a highly critical letter. For the text of this letter see *Zhongguo xiqu zhi: Anhui juan*, pp. 739–740. The letter may well have been one of the reasons for the convening of a symposium on Huangmei Opera in Beijing in October. The symposium was chaired by Tian Han.

92 Liu, "A Folksong Immortal and Official Popular Culture in Twentieth-Century China," pp. 570–580, discusses the remarkable popularity of "official popular culture" inside and outside of the PRC. Perhaps because she is focused on "official popular culture" in minority regions she does not consider the success of *Married to a Heavenly Immortal.*

93 In the play the heroine dresses as a man and takes the examinations under the name of her imprisoned fiancé; when she passes the examinations with highest honors, she is selected by the emperor as prince-consort for one of his daughters. The two women then convince the emperor to release the imprisoned young man so that the lovers can marry. A suitable groom for the princess is also found. The Chinese text of the adaptation is available in Wang Chang'an, ed., *Zhongguo Huangmeixi,* pp. 534–559. This play is available in an English translation by Qian Ma entitled "The Girl Who Marries a Princess" in her *Women in Traditional Chinese Theater: The Heroine's Play* (Lanham, MD: University Press of America, 2005), pp. 249–302. The translation is said to be based on "a performance." Lu Hongfei also signed for the script of the 1959 movie based on the play. To counter arguments in favor of Wang Zhaoqian's claim to authorship of *The Female Prince-Consort,* Lu details his claims in his "*Tianxian pei* lailong qumai," 15–17.

94 Both movies credited Lu Hongfei as the writer of the scripts. The movies were released outside of the PRC and could not be shown inside the country at the time because of the changed political climate.

95 Wang Chang'an, ed., *Zhongguo Huangmeixi,* pp. 141–142. The movies shot in the PRC were based on existing operas, whereas the Hong Kong productions had original scripts—even though they were often knock-offs of Mainland productions. See Edwin W. Chen, "Musical China, Classical Impression: A Preliminary Study of Shaws' *Huangmei Diao* Film," in *The Shaw Screen: A Preliminary Study,* ed. Wong Ain-ling (Hong Kong: Hong Kong Film Archive, 2003), pp. 51–73. Also see Xiangyang Chen, "Women, Gender Aesthetics, and the Vernacular: Huangmei Opera Films from China to Hong Kong," in *Gender Meets Genre in Postwar Cinemas,* ed. Christine Gledhill (Urbana: University of Illinois Press, 2012), pp. 177–190.

96 Breaster, "A Genealogy of Cinephilia in the Maoist Period," pp. 104–105.

97 Pickowicz, "Acting Like Revolutionaries," pp. 286–287.

98 Yen Chia-ch'i and Kao Kao, *The Ten-Year History of the Cultural Revolution* (Taipei: Institute of Current China Studies, 1988), pp. 266–267. Another victim of the PRC was her dance teacher Liu Huixian, the wife of Qiao Zhiliang.

99 For an evocation of the excitement generated by the showings of the movie during those years, see Qin Yonggui, "30 nianqian kan dianying *Tianxian pei,*" *Longmenzhen,* No. 8 (2009): 37–40. *Married to a Heavenly Immortal* was one of the opera movies which were re-released at this time and once again attracted large crowds to the theaters.

100 Zhang Geng, ed., *Dangdai Zhongguo xiqu,* pp. 679–680.

101 His last movie, a documentary entitled *The Final Years of Cai Yuanpei* (*Cai Yuanpei wannian* 蔡元培晚年), however, was never released during his lifetime.

102 They ultimately lost the lawsuit. See
http://news.163.com/10/0420/15/64NLUC80000146BD.html
http://www.cipnews.com.cn/showArticle.asp?Articleid=28998, accessed January 30, 2014.

103 For a catalogue listing all film and television adaptations, see Xu Gongbing, "Jianguo liushinian lai Huangmeixi dianying dianshiju yaomu," *Huangmeixi yishu*, No. 12 (2010): 52–55.

104 The contemporary Huangmei Opera performer Tan Chunfang 檀春芳, following a 2008 performance of *Tianxian pei* in Macao, once again hails filial piety as the message of *Tianxian pei* in "*Tianxian pei* yiju gengshende hanyi: Wo yan Dong Yong yijiaoer xiangdaode," *Huangmeixi yishu*, No. 3(2010): 70.

105 The Chinese text is included in Wang Anyi, *Yinju de shidai: Wang Anyi zhong duanpian xiaoshuo ji* (Shanghai: Shanghai wenyi chubanshe, 1999), pp. 19–37.

106 For a short discussion of this story, see Ban Wang, "History in a Mythical Key: Temporality, Memory, and Tradition in Wang Anyi's Fiction," *Journal of Contemporary China*, Vol. 12, No. 37 (2003): 618–621. Wang makes no reference to the play or the movie. Also see the analysis of this story by Andrea Riemenschnitter, *Karneval der Götter: Mythologie, Moderne und Nation in Chinas 20. Jahrhundert* (Bern/New York: P. Lang, 2011), pp. 347–351, which relates the story both to the movie of the same title and to the death of Yan Fengying.

Chapter 2

1 Linda Hutcheon, *A Theory of Adaptation* (London: Routledge, 2006); Julie Sanders, *Adaptation and Appropriation* (London: Routledge, 2006).

2 "Introduction," *The Lute: Kao Ming's P'i-p'a chi*, tr. Jean Mulligan (New York: Columbia University Press, 1980), pp. 11–12.

3 Wilt L. Idema, "Emulation through Readaptation in Yüan and Early Ming," *Asia Major*, Third Series, Vol. 3, No. 1(1990): 113–128.

4 We find such "reversal plays" not only among *zaju* but also among *chuanqi* of the Ming. See Wang Liangcheng, "Mingdai de fan'anju ji qi shenmei fengshang shulun," *Yishu baijia*, No. 1(2007): 19–22 and Huo Jianyu, "Lun Mingdai fan'anju xingqi zhi yuanyin," *Nanjing shehui kexue*, No. 4 (2007): 118–122. One motivation for "reversal plays" may be the desire to portray history as it should have been. For instance, whereas early plays on the exploits of the great general Yue Fei 岳飛 (1103–1142) in his campaigns against the Jurchen stress the tragic outcome due to treason, later plays often portray a triumphant Yue Fei who eventually succeeds in recapturing northern China and freeing the captured emperors. See Fu Dixiu, "Yue Fei ticai xiqu liubian kaoshu," *Zhejiang yishu zhiye xueyuan xuebao*, No. 3 (2008): 39–44.

5 As southern plays were expected to conclude with a "Grand Reunion" scene in which all conflicts are resolved, this often called for major revisions of the source materials. For instance, in the (lost) Ming stage adaptations of the legend of Liang Shanbo and Zhu Yingtai as a *chuanqi*, the play would not end with the death of

the two lovers but with their resurrection, so the play could have a happy ending and conclude with their marriage.

6 Tian Yuan Tan, "The Sovereign and the Theater: Reconsidering the Impact of Ming Taizu's Prohibitions," in *Long Live the Emperor! Uses of the Ming Founder across Six Centuries of East Asian History*, ed. Sarah Schneewind (Minneapolis: Society for Ming Studies, 2008), pp. 149–169.

7 Wilt L. Idema, "Why You Never Have Read a Yuan Drama: The Transformation of *Zaju* at the Ming Court," in *Studi in onore di Lionello Lanciotti*, ed. S.M. Carletti, M. Sacchetti, and P. Santangelo (Napoli: Istituto universitario orientale, Dipartimento di studi asiatici, 1996), pp. 765–791.

8 Stephen H. West, "Text and Ideology: Ming Editors and Northern Drama," in *The Song-Yuan-Ming Transition in Chinese History*, ed. Paul Jakov Smith and Richard von Glahn (Cambridge MA: Asia Center, Harvard University, 2003), pp. 329–373.

9 Catherine C. Swatek, *Peony Pavilion Onstage: Four Centuries in the Career of a Chinese Drama* (Ann Arbor: Center for Chinese Studies, University of Michigan, 2002).

10 Wilt L. Idema, "The Ideological Manipulation of Traditional Drama in Ming Times: Some Comments on the Work of Tanaka Issei," in *Norms and the State in China*, ed. Chun-chieh Huang and Erik Zürcher (Leiden: E.J. Brill, 1993), p. 66.

11 For a short introduction to this topic, see Wilt L. Idema, "Performances on a Three-tiered Stage: Court Theatre During the Qianlong Era," in *Ad Seres et Tungusos: Festschrift für Martin Gimm*, ed. Lutz Bieg, Erling von Mende, and Martina Siebert (Wiesbaden: Otto Harrassowitz, 2000), pp. 201–219. The Chinese texts of these palace extravaganzas have been reproduced in the ninth series of *Guben xiqu congkan* 古本戲曲叢刊. For a more general study of court drama of the Qing dynasty see Ye Xiaoqing, *Ascendant Peace in the Four Seas: Drama at the Qing Imperial Court* (Hong Kong: The Chinese University Press, 2012).

12 Andrea S. Goldman discusses how Peking Opera appropriated materials from Kunqu Opera in her *Opera and the City: The Politics of Culture in Beijing, 1770–1900* (Stanford: Stanford University Press, 2012), pp. 145–235.

13 Qitao Guo, *Ritual Opera and Mercantile Lineage: The Confucian Transformation of Popular Culture in Late Imperial Huizhou* (Stanford: Stanford University Press, 2005). The legend of Mulian saving his mother from hell provided the founding myth for the Ghost Festival that is celebrated each year on the fifteenth of the Seventh Lunar Month. Following the death of his parents, Mulian, who as a disciple of the Buddha has become a monk, is surprised to learn that his father is residing in heaven but his mother has been condemned to cruel torture in hell. From the Buddha he learns that this is punishment for her sins while alive, such as refusing to make donations to monks and nuns and breaking her vow to stick to a vegetarian diet. Mulian travels through all eighteen hells and eventually locates his mother in Avici Hell. Empowered by the Buddha, Mulian frees his mother, who is first reborn as a dog and later is allowed to ascend to heaven. The Buddha then teaches Mulian that all those who make donations to the Buddhist clergy

on the occasion of the Ghost Festival will be able to assist their deceased parents, who may be suffering in hell for the sins they committed while alive, to obtain a speedy rebirth in heaven. The story was already widely known in the ninth and tenth centuries, and was performed on stage from the eleventh century onwards. A full performance of a Mulian play, with its many inserted episodes of sin and punishment and suffering and salvation, might last for seven days. The palace version of the Qing dynasty even required ten days for a full performance.

14 Situ Xiuying, *Mingdai jiaohuaju qunguan* (Shanghai: Shanghai guji chubanshe, 2009).

15 Alfred Forke, tr., *Elf chinesische Singspieltexte aus neuerer Zeit: Nebst zwei Dramen in westlicher Manier* (Stuttgart: F. Steiner, 1993), pp. 375–390.

16 For the views of Liang and Chen on the power of theater, see Faye Chunfang Fei, ed. and tr., *Chinese Theories of Theater and Performance from Confucius to the Present* (Ann Arbor: University of Michigan Press, 1999), pp. 109–111, 117–120. The only Western opera that directly instigated a rebellion was *La muette de Portici*, which deals with a seventeenth-century uprising in Naples against the Spanish. Its performance on August 25, 1830 in Brussels led to riots that eventually resulted in Belgium's independence from the Netherlands.

17 Shiamin Kwa and Wilt L. Idema, *Mulan: Five Versions of a Classic Chinese Legend, with Related Texts* (Indianapolis: Hackett, 2010), pp. 9–30.

18 Ibid., pp. 31–51.

19 Joshua Goldstein, *Drama Kings: Players and Publics in the Re-Creation of Peking Opera, 1870–1937* (Berkeley: University of California Press, 2007), pp. 89–133. See also Li Xiaoti, *Qingmo de xiaceng shehui qimeng yundong*, 1901–1911 (Taipei: Academia Sinica, 1992), pp. 149–210. For a detailed study of the continuing attempts throughout the twentieth century to deal with contemporary issues (involving contemporary costume and scenery) in the many genres of traditional Chinese theater, see Gao Yilong and Li Xiao, eds., *Zhongguo xiqu xiandaixi shi* (Shanghai: Shanghai wenhua chubanshe, 1999).

20 While doing so, many of them would condemn traditional Chinese theater as utterly backwards in all respects. See Bernd Eberstein, *Das chinesische Theater im 20. Jahrhundert* (Wiesbaden: Otto Harrassowitz, 1983), pp. 35–42; Bernd Eberstein, "Introduction: Thespis in the Pear Garden," in *A Selective Guide to Chinese Literature 1900–1949*. Vol. 4: *The Drama*, ed. Bernd Eberstein (Leiden: E.J. Brill, 1990), pp. 17–19.

21 Li Jin, "Theater of Pathos: Sentimental Melodramas in the New Drama Legacy," *Modern Chinese Literature and Culture*, Vol. 24, No. 2 (2012): 94–128 notes the predominance of sentimental melodramas, often adapted from contemporary sentimental fiction, in the new drama of the 1910s.

22 Eberstein, "Introduction: Thespis in the Pear Garden," pp. 1–45; Chen Xiaomei, "Twentieth-Century Spoken Drama," in *The Columbia History of Chinese Literature*, ed. Victor H. Mair (New York: Columbia University Press, 2001), pp. 848–877.

23 Yu Cong and Wang Ankui, eds., *Zhongguo dangdai xiqu shi* (Beijing: Xueyuan chubanshe, 2006), pp. 126–155.

24 For a comprehensive study of these changes as exemplified by the changes in Peking Opera, see Goldstein, *Drama Kings*. On the rise of the star system, see Catherine Vance Yeh, "Where is the Center of Cultural Production? The Rise of the Actor to National Stardom and the Beijing/Shanghai Challenge (1860s–1910s)," *Late Imperial China*, Vol. 25, No. 2 (2004): 74–118.

25 Goldstein, *Drama Kings*, pp. 150–171.

26 On Mei Lanfang's American tour, see ibid., pp. 264–289. Also see Mei Shaowu, "Mei Lanfang as Seen by His Foreign Audiences and Critics," in *Peking Opera and Mei Lanfang: A Guide to China's Traditional Theatre and the Art of Its Great Master*, ed. Wu Zuguang, Huang Zuolin, and Mei Shaowu (Beijing: New World Press, 1981), pp. 46–65; and Catherine Vance Yeh, "Politics, Art, and Eroticism: The Female Impersonator as the National Cultural Symbol of Republican China," in *Performing "Nation": Gender Politics in Literature, Theater, and the Visual Arts of China and Japan, 1880–1940*, ed. Doris Croissant, Catherine Vance Yeh, and Joshua S. Mostow (Leiden: Brill, 2008), pp. 205–239.

27 Ellen R. Judd, "Revolutionary Drama and Song in the Jiangxi Soviet," *Modern China*, Vol. 9, No. 1 (1983): 127–160. Zuo Lai and Liang Huaqun, *Suqu "hongse xiju" shihua* (Beijing: Wenhua yishu chubanshe, 1987) stress that this period also saw the creation of a number of important full-length *huaju*.

28 On the gap separating urban intellectuals and local folk artists (actors and storytellers) as well as the successful cases of cooperation, see Ellen T. Judd, "Cultural Articulation in the Chinese Countryside," *Modern China*, Vol. 16, No. 3 (1990): 269–308.

29 In other parts of China, Yangge might refer to more developed plays. The Yangge plays of Dingxian in Hebei were collected by social activists who were working there in the 1920s and 1930s, and are available in English translation in Sidney D. Gamble, ed., *Chinese Village Plays from the Ting Hsien Region (Yang Ke Hsüan): A Collection of Forty-Eight Chinese Rural Plays as Staged by Villagers from Ting Hsien in Northern China* (Amsterdam: Philo Press, 1970). For studies of these plays, see David R. Arkush, "Love and Marriage in North China Peasant Operas," in *Unofficial China: Popular Culture and Thought in the People's Republic*, ed. Perry Link, Richard Madsen, and Paul G. Pickowicz (Boulder: Westview Press, 1989), pp. 72–87; and David R. Arkush, "The Moral World of Hebei Village Opera," in *Ideas across Cultures: Essays on Chinese Thought in Honor of Benjamin I. Schwartz*, ed. Paul A. Cohen and Merle Goldman (Cambridge, MA: Harvard University Press, 1990), pp. 87–107. For a detailed study of how the local Yangge plays in Shanxi were affected by regional and national politics over the course of the twentieth century, see Han Xiaoli, *Bei gaizao de minjian xiqu: Yi 20 shiji Shanxi Yangge xiaoxi wei zhongxin de shehuishi kaocha* (Beijing: Beijing daxue chubanshe, 2012).

30 For an introduction to the rewritten Yangge plays, see Jaroslav Průšek, *Die*

Literatur des befreiten China und ihre Volkstraditionen, tr. Pavel Eisner and Wilhelm Gampert (Prag: Artia, 1955), pp. 359–387. The most detailed description of traditional Shaanxi Yangge dances and skits is provided in David L. Holm, *Art and Ideology in Revolutionary China* (Oxford: Oxford University Press, 1991). Florence Graezer Bideau, *La danse du Yangge: Culture et politique dans la Chine du XXe siècle* (Paris: Découverte, 2012) focuses especially on the revival of Yangge dances after the Cultural Revolution.

31 For a description of village amateur theatricals in southern Anhui in the years from 1949 to 1953, see Wang Chang'an, ed., *Zhongguo Huangmeixi* (Hefei: Anhui wenyi chubanshe, 2009), pp. 120–124. For a detailed study of village amateur theatricals in the neighboring province of Hubei, see Brian DeMare, "Local Actors and National Politics: Rural Amateur Drama Troupes and Mass Campaigns in Hubei Province, 1949–1953," *Modern Chinese Literature and Culture*, Vol. 24, No. 2 (2012): 129–178. In Hubei too cultural workers organized local theater groups at the village level to perform short revolutionary plays, preferably based on local incidents but in traditional styles. The quick success of this movement shows that in many cases these "amateur troupes" were based on pre-existing (semi-) professional troupes that often used their new status to improve their economic position. Once these village troupes had served their purpose in supporting the land reform movement, the troupes underwent a rectification. This rectification covered both the class status of the personnel as well the content of the plays. Shows that were strongly criticized included those "that portrayed landlords as scholars, peasants as clowns, and cadres as wearing green kerchiefs (symbolizing that they had been cuckolded)" (p. 165).

32 *Renmin ribao*, May 7, 1951.

33 Průšek, *Die Literatur des befreiten Chinas*, pp. 352–356.

34 An English translation of this letter can be found in Fei, *Chinese Theories of Theater and Performance*, p. 142.

35 Chang-tai Hung, *War and Popular Culture: Resistance in Modern China* (Berkeley: University of California Press, 1994), pp. 85–92.

36 Carolyn Fitzgerald, "Mandarin Ducks at the Battlefield: Ouyang Yuqian's Shifting Reconfigurations of Nora and Mulan," *Chinoperl Papers*, Vol. 29, No. 1 (2010): 45–104; Kwa and Idema, eds. and trs., *Mulan*, pp. 53–102, 114–117.

37 Yu Cong and Wang Ankui, eds., *Zhongguo dangdai xiqu shi*, pp. 61–66. The contribution of the famous director Li Zigui 李紫貴 to its continuous revision and eventual success is discussed in ibid., pp. 140–145. For English translations of the final version of the rewritten play, see Tien Han, *The White Snake: A Peking Opera*. tr. Yang Hsien-yi and Gladys Yang (Peking: Foreign Languages Press, 1957), and Tyan Han, "The White Snake," tr. Donald Chang and English verse adaptation by William Packard, in *The Red Pear Garden: Three Great Dramas of Revolutionary China*, ed. John D. Mitchell (Boston: David R. Godine, 1973), pp. 49–120. For a survey of the development of the legend of the White Snake from the Ming dynasty to modern times, see Richard Strassberg, "Introduction," in

ibid., pp. 20–27; and Wilt L. Idema, *The White Snake and her Son: A Translation of The Precious Scroll of Thunder Peak with Related Texts* (Indianapolis: Hackett, 2009), pp. xi–xxiv. In the Ming dynasty versions of the tale the White Snake is imprisoned below Hangzhou's Thunder Peak Pagoda for all eternity, but in the Qing dynasty versions she is freed by her filial son after he passes the government examinations. In Tian Han's version, she is freed from prison by her maid servant, the Blue Snake, and the united masses of watery creatures.

38 Liu Siyuan, "Theater Reform as Censorship: Censoring Traditional Theatre in China in the Early 1950s," *Theatre Journal*, Vol. 61, No. 3 (2009), pp. 389–393.

39 *Renmin ribao*, May 7, 1951.

40 Yu Cong and Wang Ankui, eds., *Zhongguo dangdai xiqu shi*, pp. 40–45. For a survey of the most successful revisions of the early 1950s, see ibid., pp. 45–67. Western studies of adaptations usually treat political reinterpretations as the individual choice of the person responsible for the adaptation. See Hutcheon, *A Theory of Adaptation*, pp. 92–95.

41 Shi-Zheng Chen, "The Tradition, Reformation, and Innovation of Huaguxi: Hunan Flower Drum Opera," *TD*, Vol. 39, No. 1 (1995): 135–137.

42 The fate of Peking Opera on Taiwan in the 1950s and early 1960s in many ways paralleled developments in mainland China. Peking Opera was performed in Western-style theaters by state-sponsored companies and the repertoire was subject to strict ideological controls. See Irmgard Johnson, "The Reform of Peking Opera in Taiwan," *China Quarterly*, No. 57 (1974): 140–145; Nancy Guy, *Peking Opera and Politics in Taiwan* (Urbana: University of Illinois Press, 2005).

43 Derk Bodde, *Peking Diary: 1948–1949 a Year of Revolution* (reprint; Greenwich, CT: Fawcett, 1967), pp. 232–234.

44 Zhu Yinghui, *Dangdai xiqu sishinian* (Beijing: Wenhua yishu chubanshe, 1993), p. 132.

45 "The Foolish Old Man Who Removed the Mountains" is the title of Mao Zedong's concluding speech on June 11, 1945 at the Seventh National Congress of the Chinese Communist Party. In this speech Mao retells the ancient fable of the Foolish Old Man who sets out to remove two mountains that block his view. When ridiculed that he would not live long enough to see the results of his labor, he replies that his sons will continue his task, and his sons will be replaced by their sons, and so on, until the mountains will have been leveled. Moved by his determination, the gods then remove the mountains. The two mountains, Mao explained, were imperialism and feudalism that blocked the progress of the Chinese people, so the Chinese Communist Party would have to continue its struggle until it had achieved victory. This short speech was one of Mao's most widely read essays during the Cultural Revolution.

46 Jon Kowallis, *The Lyrical Lu Xun: A Study of his Classical-Style Verse* (Honolulu: University of Hawai'i Press, 1996), pp. 202–208. The couplet is found in Lu Xun's October 12, 1932 poem "Laughing at My Own Predicament" (*Zichao* 自嘲). The couplet became sacrosanct when Mao Zedong quoted it in his *Talks at the Yan'an*

Forum on Literature and Art. According to Mao's interpretation, the "thousand pointing fingers" referred to "our enemies," and "the children" symbolized the Party and the masses.

47 Zhu Yinghui, *Dangdai xiqu sishinian*, pp. 134–135.

48 Fu Jin, *Xin Zhongguo xijushi, 1949–2000* (Changsha: Hunan meishu chubanshe, 2002), pp. 26–27. Yang Shaoxuan was relieved of his position as a deputy director in the summer of 1952. He was expelled from the Communist Party in 1961 and hounded to death during the Cultural Revolution.

49 See the section on theater reform in Chapter 1 of this volume.

50 In 1953 yet another adaptation of the legend of Buffalo Boy and Weaving Maiden, this time from Guangxi, was criticized for "failing to express the one truth that the world is created through labor." Walter J. Meserve and Ruth I. Meserve, "Myth and Superstition in Communist China's Drama and Theater," in *Folklore in the Modern World*, ed. Richard M. Dorson (The Hague: Mouton, 1978), pp. 132–133.

51 Sanders, *Adaptation and Appropriation*, p. 84; Zeng Yongyi, *Suwenxue gailun* (Taipei: Sanmin shuju, 2003), pp. 409–599, identifies a number of traditional Chinese stories as "national stories" (*minzu gushi* 民族故事) because of their enduring and nationwide popularity with storytellers and playwrights and traces their transformation over the centuries. Zeng Yongyi includes a discussion of the premodern adaptations of the tale of Dong Yong (pp. 438–443) in the section devoted to the legend of Buffalo Boy and Weaving Maiden (pp. 428–449). Andrea Riemenschnitter, *Karneval der Götter: Mythologie, Moderne und Nation in China's 20. Jahrhunderdt* (Bern/New York: P. Lang, 2011) stresses that the adaptations of popular premodern Chinese tales allowed Chinese authors throughout the twentieth century to analyze new and/or foreign values and attitudes without having to question the continuity of Chinese culture.

52 For a full translation of this ballad, see Wilt L. Idema, ed. and tr., *Filial Piety and Its Divine Rewards: The Legend of Dong Yong and Weaving Maiden with Related Texts* (Indianapolis: Hackett, 2009), pp. 1–7.

53 For a full translation of this set of songs, see ibid., pp. 9–13. For the Chinese text, see, for instance, Li Jianye and Dong Jinyan, eds., *Dong Yong yu xiao wenhua* (Ji'nan: Qi Lu shushe, 2003), pp. 529–530.

54 For convenient typeset editions of these scenes, see ibid., pp. 531–572.

55 For a full translation of this scene as included in *Newly Printed Currently Popular Songs and Arias from North and South: A Comprehensive Selection of a Myriad of Tunes* (*Xinjuan Nanbei shishang yuefu yadiao Wanqu hexuan* 新鐫南北時尚樂府雅調萬曲合選), see Idema, ed. and tr., *Filial Piety and Its Divine Rewards*, pp. 29–40.

56 The roles of the landlord's son and the bandit chief most likely were invented in order to provide parts for a typical *chuanqi* company's *chou* (clown) and *wusheng* 武生 ("martial male," heavy).

57 For examples, see Li Jianye and Dong Jinyan, eds., *Dong Yong yu xiao wenhua*, pp. 597–660. The story was also widely popular in prosimetric literature of the Qing dynasty.

58 Liu Chunjiang and Chen Jianjun, *Hukou Qingyangqiang* (Nanchang: Jiangxi renmin chubanshe, 2008), p. 12.

59 Ban Youshu, "Ye tan Tianxian pei de lailong qumai: Cong Qingyangqiang dao Huangmeixi, meiyou juedui de zuozhe," *Huangmeixi yishu*, No. 3 (2000): 10. Ban mistakenly states that the *Hukou Qingyangqiang* version of the play on Dong Yong and Seventh Sister was completely lost during the Cultural Revolution.

60 Hong Fei, "Tan *Tianxian pei* de gaibian," *Anhui ribao*, December 10, 1954.

61 Li Jianye and Dong Jinyan, eds., *Dong Yong yu xiao wenhua*, pp. 57–73.

62 Keith Nathaniel Knapp, *Selfless Offspring: Filial Children and Social Order in Early Medieval China* (Honolulu: University of Hawai'i Press, 2005), pp. 27–45.

63 Wu Hung, *The Wu Liang Shrine: The Ideology of Early Chinese Pictorial Art* (Stanford: Stanford University Press, 1989), pp. 289–291. Later texts add that it was a deer-drawn cart.

64 Ji Yonggui, *Dong Yong yuxian chuanshuo yanjiu* (Hefei: Anhui daxue chubanshe, 2006), pp. 170–178. Gaochang was a district in Qiansheng commandery, which in the earliest sources is given as the birthplace of Dong Yong.

65 Haiyan Lee, "Tears that Crumbled the Great Wall: The Archaeology of Feeling in the May Fourth Folklore Movement," *Journal of Asian Studies*, Vol. 64, No. 1 (2005): 35–65 analyzes the way in which the pioneer scholar of folklore, Gu Jiegang 顧頡剛 (1893–1980), imposed a new meaning on the legend of Meng Jiangnü 孟姜女 by turning this traditional exemplar of wifely chastity and fidelity into an embodiment of true passion who freely expressed her emotions of love and resistance. See also Wilt L. Idema, "Old Tales for New Times: Some Comments on the Cultural Translation of China's Four Great Folktales in the Twentieth Century," *Taiwan Journal of East Asian Studies*, Vol. 9, No. 1 (2012): 25–46. The story of Liang Shanbo and Zhu Yingtai was easily reinterpreted as a tale of young people's desire for free love and of women's desire for higher education in premodern society. We have already encountered examples of the reinterpretation of the tale of Mulan and of the legend of the White Snake.

66 Several premodern versions of this tale are reprinted in Du Yingtao, ed., *Dong Yong Chenxiang heji* (Shanghai: Gudian wenxue, 1957), pp. 167–350. A translation of the *Chenxiang baojuan* 沉香寶卷 by Wilt L. Idema as *The Precious Scroll of Chenxiang* is included in *The Columbia Anthology of Chinese Folk and Popular Literature*, ed. Victor H. Mair and Mark Bender (New York: Columbia University Press, 2011), pp. 380–406. For a study of this legend, see Glen Dudbridge, "The Goddess Hua-yüeh San-niang and the Cantonese Ballad Ch'en-hsiang t'ai-tzu," *Hanxue yanjiu*, Vol. 8, No. 1 (1990): 627–646. In 1957 the legend of Huayue Sanniang and her son Chenxiang 沉香, which was adapted as a narrative ballet/dance drama entitled Precious Lotus Lantern (*Bao liandeng* 寶蓮燈), created quite a stir.

67 The description of heaven as a prison reminds one of Nora's rejection of her comfortable upper-class life in Ibsen's *A Doll's House*, which exerted a tremendous influence on Chinese literature in the 1920s and beyond. Haiyan Lee, *Revolution*

of the Heart: A Genealogy of Love in China, 1900–1959 (Stanford: Stanford University Press, 2007), pp. 111–112.

68 Gamble, ed., *Chinese Village Plays*, pp. 635–641, contains a little skit in which Zhang Sijie's lover is a poor woodcutter. The skit is very similar to "Meeting on the Road." In the skit Zhang Sijie claims that all her sisters have had mortal lovers.

69 See Wilt L. Idema, intro. and tr., "Fourth Sister Zhang Creates Havoc in the Eastern Capital," *Chinoperl Papers*, Vol. 31, No. 1 (2012): 37–112; Yamamoto Noriko, "Araburu senjo: Zhang Sijie," *Chūgoku gakushi* (2004): 23–41.

70 Lu Hongfei, "Tianxian pei de lailong qumai," *Huangmei yishu*, No. 2 (2000): 10–14.

71 Ibid., p. 14.

72 Ibid., p. 13.

73 The issue of Lu Hongfei's authorship of the revised version *Married to a Heavenly Immortal* is further complicated by the controversy surrounding his contribution to *The Female Prince-Consort* 女駙馬, yet another enduring Huangmei Opera stage favorite that originally was revised by Wang Zhaoqian.

74 For the resurgence of professional theater in Anqing after 1949, see Wang Chang'an, ed., *Zhongguo Huangmeixi*, pp. 124–127.

75 Ban Youshu, "Ye tan *Tianxian pei* de lailong qumai," p. 12.

76 Ibid.

77 Ibid.

78 For a biographical sketch of Pan Jingli, see Wang Chang'an, ed., *Zhongguo Huangmeixi*, pp. 969–972.

79 Wang Zhaoqian, "*Tianxian pei* he *Nü fuma* de fajue he gaibian: Da Chen Rongsheng tongzhi," *Huangmeixi yishu*, No. 2 (2000): 19. But Wang Zhaoqian, ed., *Huangmeixi yinyue* (Hefei: Anhui renmin chubanshe, 1957), pp. 348–373 does not mention Ban Youshu.

80 Zheng Lisong, "Dui *Tianxian pei* de yixie huiyi," *Huangmei yishu*, No. 3 (2000): 20.

81 The pre-1949 versions at our disposal stress even more strongly the Jade Emperor's order. But traditional performers worked without texts and enjoyed great liberty to change the texts at will.

82 Zheng Lisong, "Dui *Tianxian pei* de yixie huiyi," p. 21.

83 Fatalism in the jargon of the time refers to meek acceptance of one's position in society and strict obedience to one's superiors.

84 We will never know whether Pan Jingli deliberately omitted the opening lines of the aria or simply forgot them on this occasion.

85 Zheng Lisong, "Dui *Tianxian pei* de yixie huiyi," p. 21.

86 Wang Shaofang, "Wo yan Dong Yong," *Zhongguo dianying*, No. 3 (1956): 33–34.

87 Newspaper comments on the 1952 Shanghai performances are collected in Lu Hongfei, *Huangmeixi yuanliu* (Hefei: Anhui wenyi chubanshe, 1985), pp. 287–294.

88 Wang Zhaoqian, ed., *Huangmeixi yinyue*, pp. 348–351.

89 In its second issue of 1953 the national theater journal *Juben* 劇本 published a revised version of the separation scene in the Hubei Opera (*Chuju* 楚劇) version of the legend of Dong Yong and Seventh Sister, entitled "Bairi yuan: Chuju"

(pp. 55–59), confirming the political acceptability of the theme. One of the plays performed at the theater festival in Guangzhou in November 1954 was an adaptation of the legend of Dong Yong and Seventh Sister.

90 Ban Youshu, "Ye tan *Tianxian pei* de lailong qumai," p. 13. Ban suggests that Lu still might have his draft.

91 Ibid.

92 See ibid., which questions the objectivity of the 1963 investigation into the authorship of *Married to a Heavenly Immortal.*

93 Ibid., p. 14.

94 Ibid.

95 Lu Hongfei, "*Tianxian pei* de lailong qumai," p. 10.

96 Du Yingtao, ed., *Dong Yong Chenxiang heji*, pp. 135–154. The text is also reprinted in Li Jianye and Dong Jinyan, eds., *Dong Yong yu xiao wenhua*, pp. 573–596.

97 Chinese gods are expected to be free from all sexual desire and the tiniest inkling of carnal passion is enough reason to be banished from heaven. Once the banished deity has transcended passion by experiencing its sufferings on earth, he or she may be allowed to return to heaven and assume his or her original position.

98 Wang Chang'an, ed., *Zhongguo Huangmeixi*, pp. 418–454.

99 Ibid., pp. 439–446.

100 Ban Youshu, "Zhengli hou de Huangmeixi *Tianxian pei*," *Anhui ribao*, November 25, 1953 stresses that this vision of a happy life in which husband and wife have clearly demarcated spheres of activity was not a contemporary ideal, but an ideal in traditional premodern peasant society.

101 In the 1953 Chuju version of this scene Seventh Sister complains about her father's order to return to heaven ("How I hate that order of my father the king that rips these mandarin ducks apart"), but it is not clear whether this refers to the original order of the Jade Emperor sending her down to earth or to a later order.

102 In the 1955 printing of the play, this scene opens with the famous love duet of Dong Yong and Seventh Sister. Seventh Sister then sends Dong Yong off to say goodbye to some fellow workers. This then clears the stage so she can be summoned back to heaven without Dong Yong being present onstage.

103 The printed version of the traditional version has no voice from heaven in this scene, but in the version as dictated by Hu Yuting, a backstage voice orders Seventh Sister to return when the third quarter of the hour of noon has arrived.

104 The same shift can be observed in the 1953 Chuju version of this scene. When Seventh Sister asks Dong Yong about his former master, Dong Yong complains that his master had worked him to the bone and did not treat him to a farewell dinner as promised, but his fellow workers had arranged a farewell dinner.

105 It should also be pointed out that Lu Hongfei simplified the language of the arias by doing away with almost all of the historical allusions that are found in the texts of the traditional play.

106 Ban Youshu, "Zhengli hou de Huangmeixi *Tianxian pei*." In the October 1953 performances, the role of Seventh Sister was performed by Chen Yuehuan 陳月環 (Yan Fengying was pregnant at the time), and the role of Dong Yong was

performed by Zha Ruihe 查瑞和 (Wang Shaofang had not yet joined the Anhui Provincial Huangmei Opera Company and was on tour in Korea).

107 In the rehearsals during the spring of 1954 Yan Fengying played Seventh Sister opposite Zha Ruihe as Dong Yong. When in the summer of 1954 the decision was made to have the play performed at the East China Theater Festival in the fall, Wang Shaofang, who in the meantime had returned to Anqing, was reassigned, along with many other leading actors and actresses, to the provincial company in order to make the best possible showing. One consideration in bringing Wang Shaofang to Hefei was that he had already been playing Dong Yong with great success for two years in "Meeting on the Road" as revised by Ban Youshu.

108 Hu Yuting and Lu Hongfei, "Tianxian pei," *Huadongqu xiqu guanmo yanchu dahui*, Vol. 2: *Anhuisheng daibiaotuan yanchu juben xuanji* (Shanghai: Huadongqu xiqu guanmo yanchu dahui, 1954), pp. 1–34.

109 Lu Hongfei, "*Tianxian pei* de lailong qumai," p. 13. One reason to reject such a triumphant ending may have been that it smacked too much of the 1950 and 1951 plays that had been condemned for their "antihistoricism," "formulism," and "sloganeering." Wang Chang'an, ed., *Zhongguo Huangmeixi*, p. 148 credits this suggestion to Provincial Party Secretary Zeng Xisheng.

110 Li Liping, "*Tianxian pei* wutaiju de paiyan," *Huangmeixi yishu*, No. 1 (1981), pp. 159–160, claims that he had already realized in 1953 that it would be wrong to add such a "brilliant tail" to the play because it was a tragedy, but still it was included in the spring 1954 tryouts. Wang Chang'an, ed., *Zhongguo Huangmeixi*, p. 148.

111 Zheng Lisong, "Dui *Tianxian pei* de yixie huiyi," p. 20.

112 Li Liping, "*Tianxian pei* wutaiju de paiyan," pp. 157–161.

113 Li Liping, "Sishiqi nian qiande wangshi: Yan Fengying qishi danchen yijiu," *Huangmeixi yishu*, No. 4 (2000): 37–41.

114 Qiao Zhiliang, Zhang Chuancai, and Yao Yuwen, "Yi daoyan *Tianxian pei*," *Huangmeixi yishu*, No. 4 (1996): 75–94.

115 Tai Yih-jian, "Stanislavsky and the Chinese Theatre," *Journal of Oriental Studies*, Vol. 16, No. 1–2 (1978): 49–62.

116 Hong Fei, "Tan Tianxian pei de gaibian."

117 Ye Yiqun's Party career was cut short in 1955 when Pan Hannian 潘漢年 (1906–1977), the deputy mayor of Shanghai, was accused of collaboration with the Japanese and with the Wang Jingwei regime during the war years (1937–1945) when he was in charge of the Party's secret service in the occupied areas. Ye Yiqun's role during the Occupation Period was also "under investigation" for many years, but he died in 1966 as a victim of the Cultural Revolution. Pan Hannian died in prison in 1977, but was later rehabilitated.

118 Yi Qun, "Huadong xiqu guanmo yinxiang zaji," *Jiefang ribao*, November 5, 1954.

119 Ibid.

120 Hu Yuting, ed., *Tianxian pei: Huangmeixi* (Shanghai: Shanghai wenhua chubanshe, 1955).

121 Hu Yuting and Lu Hongfei, "Tianxian pei," Vol. 2, pp. 6–7.

122 See, for instance, Idema, ed. and tr., *Filial Piety and Its Divine Rewards*, pp. 63–68.

123 This lesser emphasis on the evils of the landlord class in the 1955 edition of *Married to a Heavenly Immortal* also corresponds to a change in the political climate. Following the period of Land Reform (1949–1953) with its heavy emphasis on rural class struggle, emphasis in rural policy shifted to the formation of cooperatives.

124 Writing in 2000 Li Liping complained that Shi Hui replaced the episode of Seventh Sister writing a letter to Dong Yong with her own blood with an episode of her carving her letter in the bark of the scholartree, thus robbing her of a great acting scene. Li Liping, "Sishiqi nian qiande wangshi," p. 40. Shi Hui's change may have been inspired by a desire to enhance the role of the scholartree in the play, but the letter written in blood may also have been objectionable because of its association with Buddhist practices of blood-writing.

125 Wang Chang'an, ed., *Zhongguo Huangmeixi*, pp. 136–138.

126 Jin Zhi, "Wo yu *Tianxian pei*," *Huangmeixi yishu*, No. 1 (1988): 31–37.

127 Reproduced in *Zhongguo xiqu zhi: Anhui juan* (Beijing: Zhongguo ISBN zhongxin, 1993), pp. 739–740.

128 Wang Chang'an, ed., *Zhongguo Huangmeixi*, pp. 146, 1069–1070. Xu Yaoqing, writing in *Guangming ribao* on November 3, 1956 (quoted in Wang Chang'an, ed., *Zhongguo Huangmeixi*, p. 146) countered by praising the treatment of Seventh Sister in the revised version.

129 Wang Chang'an, ed., *Zhongguo Huangmeixi*, pp. 1071–1072.

130 These criticisms are quoted in great detail by Lu Hongfei in his *Huangmeixi yuanliu*, pp. 304–310.

131 Quoted by Hong Fei, "Guanyu *Tianxian pei*," *Huangmeixi yishu*, No. 3 (1988): 34.

132 *The caidan* 采旦 specializes in playing lively female roles.

133 Quoted in Wang Chang'an, ed., *Zhongguo Huangmeixi*, p. 138.

134 Hu Yuting and Lu Hongfei, "Tianxian pei," *Anhui xiqu xuanji* (Hefei: Anhui renmin chubanshe, 1959), reprinted in Li Jianye and Dong Jinyan, eds., *Dong Yong yu xiao wenhua*, pp. 661–716.

135 Most recently the text of *Married to a Heavenly Immortal* was reprinted in Lin Lu and Lu Lin, eds., *Lu Hongfei Lin Qing Huangmeixi juzuo quanji* (Hefei: Anhui wenyi chubanshe, 2012), pp. 3–35. The only information provided about the text is that it is the "performance script of the Anhui Provincial Huangmei Opera Company"; Lu Hongfei is listed as the editor (*gaibian* 改編) of the text.

Chapter 3

1 Du Yingtao, ed., *Dong Yong Chenxiang heji* (Shanghai: Gudian wenxue chubanshe, 1957), pp.135–154. The text has also been reproduced in Li Jianye and Dong Jinyan, eds., *Dong Yong yu xiao wenhua* (Ji'nan: Qi Lu shushe, 2003), pp. 573–596.

2 Wang Chang'an, ed., *Zhongguo Huangmeixi* (Hefei: Anhui wenyi chubanshe, 2009), pp. 418–454.

3 Ibid., pp. 439–445.

4 The Chinese text only reads "the *xiaosheng* 小生 enters." I have identified the character performed by the *xiaosheng* for ease of reading. I have also done so in the case of the other role-types.

5 These two lines make it clear that Dong Yong, despite his poverty, is not a peasant but a student who is preparing for government service by studying the Classics. His high status makes the decision to sell himself all the more remarkable. When he first visits the Fu Mansion, he is treated with the respect his status calls for.

6 The Four Treasures of the Scholar's Study are brush, paper, inkstone, and ink.

7 In traditional China the color of mourning is white.

8 Guanbao is the personal name of the Young Master, the son of Old Master Fu.

9 Jasper Pond is the location where the Queen-Mother of the West, the ruler of all female immortals, treats the divine immortals to the peaches of immortality, which ripen only once every three thousand years.

10 Buffalo Boy (Altair) and Weaving Maiden (Vega) are stars on opposite sides of the Heavenly River (the Milky Way). According to legend, they are a couple. After their marriage they became infatuated with each other and neglected their duties, so they were separated by the Jade Emperor, who allowed them to meet only once each year on the night of the seventh of the Seventh Lunar Month, when magpies form a bridge across the Heavenly River. For a more detailed discussion of the origin and development of this legend, see Wilt L. Idema, "Weaving Maiden and Buffalo Boy in Myth and Fairy Tale," in Wilt L. Idema, *Filial Piety and Its Divine Rewards: The Legend of Dong Yong and Weaving Maiden with Related Texts* (Indianapolis: Hackett, 2009), pp. 79–99.

11 The Palace of Dipper and Buffalo refers to the heavenly palaces. The Dipper is the Chinese name for Ursa Maior; Buffalo is the Chinese name for Altair.

12 In this play Magpie Bridge is treated as a permanent feature of the topography of heaven.

13 These four lines probably are intended to suggest the numinous powers and divine inhabitants of heaven. Mt. Emei, in western Sichuan, is a famous holy mountain that became increasingly prominent in late-imperial popular literature as the home of the gods. See James M. Hargett, *Stairway to Heaven: A Journey to the Summit of Mount Emei* (Albany: State University of New York Press, 2006). The Eight Immortals are a widely venerated group of immortals since the twelfth century. Old Gardener Zhang (Zhang Guolao 張果老) is one of the Eight Immortals. In his old age Jiang Ziya 姜子牙, who is also known by a host of other names, served King Wen and King Wu during the founding of the Zhou dynasty (eleventh century BCE–256 BCE). In later ages he was venerated as god of war.

14 The word translated as "to characterize" is *zan* 贊, which in dictionaries is often translated as "to extol, to praise," but in traditional storytelling it is used to designate set descriptions.

15 The Imperial Poster refers to the government announcement of the upcoming round of the metropolitan examinations or to the poster announcing the result of the examinations.

16 The Top-of-the-List is the student who places first in the palace examinations that follow the metropolitan examinations.

17 In traditional Chinese mythology, the world of gods and immortals is one of purity. The slightest sign of sexual desire is sufficient reason to be banished from the heavenly realm. Those who are banished from heaven in this way will experience all the sufferings of passion in the mortal world and thus will learn to transcend passion, whereupon they may be recalled to heaven.

18 The pronunciation of the word "orchid" (*lan* 蘭) is in many Chinese dialects indistinguishable from the word "difficult, hard; problem, trouble, disaster" (*nan* 難).

19 The Yellow Springs refer to the underworld, the realm of the dead.

20 That is, the ancestral tablet in which his father's soul resides.

21 The light of the moon resembles silver.

22 Chang'e 嫦娥 is the beautiful goddess of the moon. Here, the term is used more generally to refer to an immortal maiden.

23 Maitreya is the Buddha of the future. Dong Yong here imitates the behavior of pious pilgrims who recite the name of the Buddha while traveling.

24 Yan Hui 顏回 was the favorite disciple of Confucius (551–479 BCE). When Yan died at a relatively early age, the Master wept excessively (*Analects* XI, 9). Zi Lu 子路 was one of Confucius's other disciples. The collective biography of Confucius's disciples in Sima Qian's 司馬遷 *Shiji* 史記 notes the distress of the Master upon learning of Zi Lu's death in battle in 480 BCE.

25 Cao Cao 曹操 (155–220), Sun Quan 孫權 (182–252), and Liu Bei 劉備 (161–223) were three of the major warlords during the final decades of the Eastern Han dynasty (25–220). Cao Cao eventually controlled northern China; Sun Quan was based in the southeast; and Liu Bei dominated central China (he later also occupied Sichuan). Sun Quan's chief-of-staff was Zhou Yu 周瑜 (Gongjin 公瑾; 175–210), while Liu Bei's chief-of-staff was Zhuge Liang 諸葛亮 (Kongming 孔明; 181–234). In 208 when Cao Cao invaded the south, Liu Bei and Sun Quan, despite their mutual suspicions, decided to collaborate, and Zhuge Liang and Zhou Yu inflicted a massive defeat on Cao Cao's fleet at Red Cliff, whereupon Cao Cao fled back to the north. Zhou Yu, repeatedly outwitted by Zhuge Liang, died of frustration several years later. Lord Guan is Guan Yu 關羽 (d. 219), one of the sworn brothers of Liu Bei. The wars of the final decades of the Eastern Han dynasty, resulting in the establishment of the "Three Kingdoms" of Wei, Wu, and Su-Han, have been immortalized in the *Romance of the Three Kingdoms* (*Sanguo zhi yanyi* 三國志演義), one of China's most popular traditional novels.

26 Chinese goldthread (*Coptis chinensis*) has a bitter-tasting stem and root, which is used in Chinese medicine. The bark of the Amur cork tree (*Phellodendron amurense*) likewise is used in Chinese medicine and is known for its bitter taste.

27 As emperors are dragons, future emperors down on their luck are often compared to dragons outside their natural element. Dong Yong is never described as an emperor, so the two lines here only indicate his future rise in status.

28 Great White is the Chinese name for the planet Venus, one of the "moving stars." In the scheme of the Five Elements (metal, wood, water, fire, and earth) Venus is associated with the element metal. As a result, the god of the planet Venus is designated as the Metal Star. In traditional Chinese legends he often appears on earth in the guise of a friendly old man to help out those in need.

29 Seventh Sister is claiming she eloped with Dong Yong after he promised to marry her.

30 With the exception of the tone for *bai*, *bairi* 百日 (one hundred days) has the same pronunciation as *bairi* 白日 (a clear day, daytime, broad daylight).

31 The "mouth" of a knife is its cutting edge.

32 Luck (*fu* 福) has the same pronunciation as "wife" (*fu* 婦). "Longevity" (*shou* 壽) rhymes with "follows" (*hou* 後).

33 This name is an allusion to Venus as the Morning Star. The surname Jin 金 is written with the character used for "metal, bronze, gold," and the two characters used to write *ri* 日 and *sheng* 生 when put together form the character *xing* 星 (star).

34 Penglai is one of the floating isles of the immortals in the Eastern Ocean.

35 Fish and water are a conventional image for a harmonious relationship (and happy sex).

36 In traditional China the night was divided into five watches of equal length, and each watch was divided into five "fifths."

37 See note 36.

38 The following set of five songs was originally a set of love songs, sung to one of the many tunes entitled "Five Watches." In premodern China, lovers often addressed each other as "brother" and "sister."

39 The Golden Rooster is the heavenly bird that each morning announces dawn. His call is echoed by all roosters on earth.

40 "Red dust" is a common metaphor for the mortal world.

41 This is probably a reference to her bound feet.

42 "Up above" is a cliché to address one's superiors who are "up above" because they will be seated in the hall on a raised platform, while the speaker will stand in the courtyard below. Dong Yong does not realize that Seventh Sister's parents are really "up above" as they are eternal gods living in heaven.

43 The words for "heaven" (*tian* 天) and for "to add, to increase" (*tian* 添) have the same pronunciation.

44 The last sentence probably means that Dong Yong is threatening to give Seventh Sister a beating.

45 Mandarin ducks mate for life, thus they are an emblem of conjugal love.

46 Changgeng is another name for the planet Venus as the Evening Star.

47 Dong Zhongshu 董仲舒 (179–104 BCE) was a major philosopher in the second part of the second century BCE.

48 In the version of the play recited from memory by Hu Yuting, Dong Yong becomes the adopted son of Mr. Fu following the miracle of Seventh Sister weaving ten bolts of silk in a single night.

49 When a poster is posted seeking a person of extraordinary abilities, the person who believes he qualifies will take away the poster and present himself at the gate.
50 Xiaogan 孝感 can be translated as the "Filial Piety Miracle."
51 The Gate of Yu refers to the rapids in the Yellow River. Carp that were able to cross these rapids were said to have turned into dragons. Passing the examinations is often compared to passing the Gate of Yu. Therefore, this line suggests that in the past Dong Yong had three times unsuccessfully participated in the examinations.
52 The Three Stars refer to the sun, the moon, and the planets.
53 The gauze cap and crimson gown of an official.
54 His adoptive father, Old Master Fu.
55 A green hat is the prescribed headgear for pimps.
56 The Five Thunders are a powerful exorcist technique that enjoyed great popularity throughout the last millennium.
57 These two lines each have ten syllables. Such ten-syllable lines usually have a clear tripartite structure as they are subdivided into three, three, and four syllables. The typography tries to suggest this tripartite structure of the lines.
58 Confucius.
59 In this poem Dong Yong expresses his joy at being able to resume his studies. The Si 泗 is a river in Shandong, and Confucius is said to have taught his pupils "on the banks of the Si."
60 King Yama, the highest god in the courts of the underworld, impartially judges the souls of the deceased.
61 The thunder gods are depicted as men with fleshy wings, a bird's beak, and bird's legs. They carry a hammer as a weapon.
62 The middle of the Seventh Month, also known as Middle Prime, is the date of the Ghost Festival, when the souls of the deceased are allowed to return to their original homes and partake of the offerings of their descendants.
63 As an offering to the dead.

Chapter 4

1 Hu Yuting and Lu Hongfei, "Tianxian pei," in *Huadongqu xiqu guanmo yanchu dahui*. Vol. 2: *Anhuisheng daibiaotuan yanchu juben xuanji* (Shanghai: Huadongqu xiqu guanmo yanchu dahui, 1954), pp. 1–34.
2 Hu Yuting and Hong Fei ed., *Tianxian pei: Huangmeixi* (Shanghai: Shanghai wenhua chubanshe, 1955).
3 "Tianxian pei (Huangmeixi)," in *Zhongguo difang xiqu jicheng: Anhuisheng juan,* Zhongguo xijujia xiehui and Anhuisheng wenhuaju, 2 vols. (Beijing: Zhongguo xiju chubanshe, 1959), pp. 129–193.
4 Li Jianye and Dong Jinyan, eds., *Dong Yong yu xiao wenhua* (Ji'nan: Qi Lu shushe, 2003), pp. 661–716.
5 Hong Fei 洪非 was the literary pseudonym of Lu Hongfei.
6 The golden plaque refers to the list of those who have passed the metropolitan examintions and the following palace examinations.
7 Most likely the author intended to refer to Chinese goldthread (*Coptis sinensis*)

a herbaceous perennial known for its bitter roots and stems that are used in traditional Chinese medicine.

8 For "heavenly beauty," the text writes "Chang'e from the moon."

9 Marriage.

10 Buffalo Boy (Altair) and Weaving Maiden (Vega) are placed on opposite banks of the Heavenly River (also known as the Silver River; the Milky Way) after they have neglected their duties following their marriage. Once every year, in the night of the seventh of the Seventh Month, magpies form a bridge across the Heavenly River so the couple may meet.

11 When the Chinese envoy Su Wu 蘇武 (d. 60 BCE) was detained by the northern Xiongnu, he informed the emperor of his situation by attaching a letter to the leg of a goose. When the emperor shot down the bird on its southward migration, he discovered the letter.

12 The Chinese word for date is *zaozi* 棗子. This expression can also be understood as 早子 (*zaozi*, an early son).

13 This is obviously a misprint for "ocean."

14 "Heaven" (*tian* 天) and "to add" (*tian* 添) have the same pronunciation.

15 Chang'e is the beautiful goddess of the moon. The final line may also be translated as "About to leave her mortal man." It is this second meaning which is intended by Seventh Sister, but the other translation would be the first to come to mind for any unsuspecting reader or listener.

Chapter 5

1 Ban Youshu, "Zhengli hou de Huangmeixi *Tianxian pei*," *Anhui ribao*, November 25, 1953.

2 In Chinese Marxist literary theory a work is said to have *renminxing* (a translation of the Russian *narodnost'*) if it is not only widely popular among the people but, most importantly, also reflects the revolutionary aspirations of the people (as determined by the Party).

3 Ban systematically writes Dong Yong as Dong Yun 董允.

4 The *caidan* ("brightly-colored female") is a role-type specializing in the performance of mischievous, frivolous, and adulterous female characters. This change of role-type was later criticized at the 1956 Beijing symposium on Huangmei Opera. According to Tang Shi, "*Tianxian pei* zhong Yan Fengying de biaoyan," *Zhongguo xiju*, No. 11 (1956): 17, the role of Eldest Sister was once again performed by a *caidan* during the performances at the 1954 East China Theater Festival.

5 "Abstract generalization" and "formalism" were highlighted by Zhou Yang in September 1953 as mistakes to be avoided in literary works. See D. W. Fokkema, *Literary Doctrine in China and Soviet Influence 1956–1960* (The Hague: Mouton, 1965), pp. 41–42.

6 The Chinese has *shenhua ju* 神話劇 which more precisely should be translated as a "myth play."

7 Hong Fei, "Tan *Tianxian pei* de gaibian," *Anhui ribao*, December 10, 1954.

8 Here and elsewhere the Chinese term actually used is "myth" (*shenhua*).

9 [Gan Bao], *In Search of the Supernatural: The Written Record*, tr. Kenneth J. DeWoskin and J.I. Crump, Jr. (Stanford: Stanford University Press, 1996), p. 14. In view of the transmission history of *Soushen ji* one cannot be sure that items included in the modern editions of the text indeed date from the fourth century.

10 Zhongguo lishi yanjiu hui, comp., *Zhongguo tongshi jianbian* (Shanghai: Xinhua shudian, 1950), p. 159. The first edition of this work was published in Yan'an in 1941.

11 Wilt L. Idema, ed. and tr., *Filial Piety and Its Divine Rewards: The Legend of Dong Yong and Weaving Maiden with Related Texts* (Indianapolis: Hackett, 2009), pp. 3–7 presents a full translation of this ballad.

12 This is one of the sections of the *Stories from the Pure Level Mountain Hall* (*Qingping shantang huaben* 清平山堂話本), a collection of vernacular stories published in the mid-sixteenth century. For a full translation of the story, see ibid., pp. 15–27.

13 A translation of this summary is provided in the Introduction to this volume.

14 *Qiuye yue* is one of the seven late-Ming drama anthologies that contains the text of this scene. For a translation (based on one of the other anthologies), see Idema, *Filial Piety and Its Divine Rewards*, pp. 29–43.

15 Wang Chang'an, ed., *Zhongguo Huangmeixi* (Hefei: Anhui wenyi chubanshe, 2009), pp. 432–433.

16 These lines have no counterpart in the printed version of the traditional play but they are included in the stage version of the play as dictated by Hu Yuting. "Impermanence" is the personification of death. The Hegemon King is Xiang Yu 項羽 (232–202 BCE), one of the contenders for the throne after the collapse of the Qin dynasty (221–208 BCE). Hot-tempered by character, he was abandoned by his advisers and was eventually defeated by Liu Bang 劉邦 (d. 195 BCE), the first emperor of the Western Han dynasty (206 BCE–8 CE). Han Xin 韓信 (d. 196 BCE), one of the most effective generals in the service of Liu Bang, played a central role in the defeat of Xiang Yu, but following the end of the warfare Liu Bang grew suspicious of him and had him murdered. These lines were condemned by Lu Hongfei because in them Dong Yong relativizes his fate and betrays a fatalistic attitude.

17 The "fatalistic arrangement" refers to the fact that in the traditional play Seventh Sister is fully aware that her relationship with Dong Yong will last for only one hundred days, and obeying the orders of her superiors, in this case her father, the Jade Emperor, she leaves him on her own initiative when the term is up.

18 The notes on Dong Yong from the local gazetteers collected by Li Jianye and Dong Jinyan, eds., *Dong Yong yu xiao wenhua* (Ji'nan: Qi Lu shushe, 2003), pp. 57–73 lack detailed descriptions of how Dong Yong was abused. Perhaps the author of the article is thinking of the following episode found in the Xiaogan local gazetteer:

> When his father died, [Dong Yong] was unable to bury him. He borrowed the money from a local rich man surnamed Pei 裴 and contractually promised to become his slave to repay him. Following the funeral, he set out for the Pei

family to serve as their slave. While on the road he met a woman who wanted to become his wife. Astonished, Master Pei said, "We agreed on the sale of a single person, and now you add a second person? What can this woman do? I really cannot feed you during this famine." Dong replied, "My wife can weave." In order to set an impossible condition, Master Pei said, "If she can weave three hundred bolts in one month, I will free you from your bondage. If not, I will have to send your wife away." The woman said, "I can do that."

19 See Tai Yih-jian, "Stanislavsky and the Chinese Theatre," *Journal of Oriental Studies*, Vol. 16, No. 1–2 (1978): 49–62. Also see Tian Benxiang, Song Baozhen, and Liu Fangzheng, *Zhongguo xiju lunbian* (Nanchang: Baihuazhou wenyi chubanshe, 2007), Vol. 1, pp. 274–287 and 342–377 for the rise, fall, and resurrection of the Stanislavsky system in China.

20 Yan Fengying, "Wo yan Qixiannü," *Zhongguo dianying*, No. 3 (1956): 30–32.

21 This describes the parting of the lovers Hu Ernü 胡二女 and Cai Mingfeng 蔡鳴鳳. Cai Mingfeng had been staying at an inn that was operated by Hu Ernü. The two become lovers even though they both are married; eventually Cai Mingfeng decides to return home. During the Cultural Revolution Yan Fengying was fiercely criticized for her performance in this little play on adultery.

22 This play is devoted to the love affair between the student Hong Lianbao 洪連寶 and the young lady Fang Xiuying 方秀英. Hong Lianbao disguises himself as a maid so he can be sold to the Fang Mansion and be together with his beloved Xiuying.

23 When the two lovers Wei Langbao 韋郎保 and Jia Yuzhen 賈玉珍 meet each other again after a long separation, they agree to meet at midnight below the bridge across Indigo River in order to elope. While Jia Yuzhen is detained by her mistress, Wei Langbao is drowned by a flash flood. When Yuzhen discovers her lover has died, she commits suicide by jumping into the river.

24 A *dan* refers to a (male or female) performer who by training specializes in playing female roles. A *huadan* ("painted female") specializes in playing young and vivacious female characters. It would make more sense to have a *huadan* perform the role of Seventh Sister in "Meeting on the Road" than in "The Separation." That this is actually what occurred is suggested later in this piece. According to Tang Shi, "*Tianxian pei* zhong Yan Fengying de biaoyan," *Zhongguo xiju*, No. 11 (1956): 17, in the traditional play the role of Seventh Sister in "Meeting on the Road" was performed by a *huadan*, whereas her role in "The Separation" was performed by a *wudan* 武旦, or a "martial female," because of the physically demanding nature of the role in that scene.

25 That is to say, a son in mourning and dressed accordingly.

26 Yang Siya in *Shazigang* is a young daughter-in-law who is abused by her cruel mother-in-law until the latter is punished by her elder brother Yang Sanya.

27 Jia Baoyu and Lin Daiyu, the two central (upper-class) characters in the famous eighteenth-century novel *Dream of the Red Chamber* (*Honglou meng* 紅樓夢; also translated as *Story of the Stone*), are incapable of declaring themselves to each other even though they are deeply in love.

28 This small Huangmei Opera was created in 1953 by Wang Shaofang on the basis of an item in the traditional repertoire. It describes a husband and wife watching the lanterns on First Night. A performance of the play starring Wang Shaofang and Yan Fengying was filmed in 1956.

29 Xun Huisheng (1900–1968) was one of Peking Opera's "Four Great Female Impersonators" during the Republican era, and *Reddy* was one of his original plays. The play is named after its main character, the wily maid Hongniang 紅娘 (Reddy) from *Romance of the Western Chamber* (*Xixiang ji* 西廂記), China's most famous love comedy.

30 Bai Yunsheng (1902–1972) was originally trained as a *Kunqu dan*, but he later played male roles. In the 1930s he performed as a Peking Opera actor. After 1949 he was active primarily as a teacher and a coach.

31 Wang Shaofang, "Wo yan Dong Yong," *Zhongguo dianying*, No. 3 (1956): 33–34.

32 Professional actors were considered lowclass in traditional China.

33 Student Zhang is the male protagonist in *Romance of the Western Chamber*, China's most famous love comedy. The play was first adapted for the stage in the late thirteenth century by Wang Shifu 王實甫. In later centuries it belonged to the repertoire of basically every genre of regional opera.

34 Liang Shanbo is the male protagonist in the romance of Liang Shanbo and Zhu Yingtai. Plays based on this romance are found in almost every genre of regional opera.

35 Xu Xian, an apprentice in an apothecary, is the name of the male protagonist in the legend of the White Snake.

36 Wei Kuiyuan is another name for Wei Langbao.

37 In this play the young maiden Zhao Cuihua 趙翠花 falls in love with the student Hu 胡 (Wu) Sanbao during a spring outing. She picks up a fan he has dropped and once she returns home, she becomes ill in longing for love. The *xiaosheng* is a role-type specializing in the portrayal of upper-class young men, such as students who are preparing for the state examinations.

38 The biographical notes on Dong Yong in the Xiaogan local gazetteers are quoted in Li Jianye and Dong Jinyan, eds., *Dong Yong yu xiao wenhua* (Ji'nan: Qi Lu shushe, 2003), pp. 67–73. Although these materials stress his poverty, they do not mention his status.

39 Even when she proposes marriage to him, Liang Shanbo does not realize that his best friend Zhu Yingtai is actually a girl disguised as a boy.

40 Thinking that his beloved Yingying 鶯鶯 has invited him for a night rendezvous, Student Zhang climbs over the wall around the courtyard where she is staying.

41 *Hunting the Tiger* is a Peking Opera in which two peasants are ordered to catch a ferocious tiger. *Wusheng* is the designation of a role-type specializing in the portrayal of martial heroes.

42 Li Liping, "*Tianxian pei* wutaiju de paiyan," *Huangmeixi yishu*, No. 1 (1981): 157–161.

43 This is a tentative translation.

44 Water-sleeves (*shuixiu* 水袖) are 1–1.5 meter extensions to long-sleeved costumes for female roles in a variety of traditional Chinese opera genres.

45 The wig comes with a long queue that is shaked and swirled by the actor or actress to express extreme emotion. Handling the queue well requires considerable skill and stamina.

46 The Chinese text actually says "water colors" but that does not make sense to me.

47 When falling forward the performer first touches the ground with his or her left shoulder and then makes a roll before rising. It is one of the basic techniques in fighting scenes.

48 Qiao Zhiliang, Zhang Chuancai, and Yao Yuwen, "Yi daoyan *Tianxian pei*," *Huangmeixi yishu*, No. 4 (1996): 75–94. This article was translated by Tarryn Li-min Chun.

49 The word used is actually *shenhua* (myth).

50 The cloud broom looks very much like a fly whisk. On stage it is a typical attribute of monks and priests, gods and immortals.

51 Imitation though stylized acting.

52 I.e., in the style of *Huangmei*—Yellow Plum—Opera.

53 That is, the incense Seventh Sister can burn to summon her sisters whenever she finds herself in trouble in the world below.

54 The "Four Skills and Five Canons" (*sigong wufa* 四功五法) are the fundamental tenets of Peking Opera. Typically, the four skills are singing (*chang* 唱), recitation (*nian* 念), gesture (*zuo* 作), and combat (*da* 打), and the five canons cover the mouth (*kou* 口), hands (*shou* 手), body (*shen* 身), eyes (*yan* 眼), and steps (*bu* 步), although there are some differences in interpretation of the phrase "Four Skills and Five Canons" among acting schools. For a discussion of these tenets in actor training, see "Training a Total Performer: Four Skills and Five Canons," in Li Ruru, *The Soul of Beijing Opera: Theatrical Creativity and Continuity in the Changing World* (Hong Kong: Hong Kong University Press, 2010), ch. 2, pp. 57–58.

55 Typically, the entrance of a character in Peking Opera would be accompanied by certain footstep patterns and poses that served to introduce the character, followed by a self-introductory speech. In this case, the audience has already been introduced to Dong Yong through the gaze of Seventh Sister, thus eliminating the need for these specific conventions.

56 "Four-directions Step" (*sifangbu* 四方步), or "Eight-character Step" (*bazibu* 八字步), is a walking pattern used by the *laosheng* 老生 role-type in Peking Opera. It involves coordination among all four limbs, with the legs lifting high enough to reveal the actor's boots and pivoting at the waist while walking in a slow, stately fashion.

57 The bodhisattva Guanyin 觀音 is widely venerated in China. Since the tenth century Guanyin is often depicted in female shape and considered an exemplar of female beauty.

58 When Guanbao first appears on the scene in the 1954 text of the revised edition, in order to stress his stupidity he recites a poem that discloses his inability to

recognize the difference between the two very common characters "great" (*da* 大) and "grand" (*tai* 太). When his father corrects him from backstage, the unfilial son Guanbao curses his father under his breath. This little scene has no counterpart in either the printed version of the traditional play or in the version dictated by Hu Yuting.

59 In this play, performed by Mei Lanfang, Hemp Maiden visits the Queen-Mother of the West on the occasion of her birthday and offers her gifts with dance and song.

60 This Peking Opera is based on ch. 72 and ch. 73 of the late-sixteenth-century novel *Journey to the West* (*Xiyou ji* 西遊記), in which the spider demon, in the guise of a peasant girl, seduces the pilgrim Xuanzang 玄臧, who thereupon has to be freed by his servant Monkey (Sun Wukong).

61 The Red Ribbon Dance (*Hongchouwu* 紅綢舞) was a popular group dance that was revised and performed with considerable success in the 1950s. It won first prize at the first World Youth Festival.

62 A reference to the September 27, 1956 letter by Kang Sheng. The criticism was echoed by Wu Zuxiang.

63 The revival here refers to the version edited by Jin Zhi in 1956 and performed in Beijing and elsewhere.

64 That is, the specific "Five Watches Tune" that is used in the play is specific to Huangmei Opera. Throughout China many different tunes are named after the five watches of the night.

65 *Pingtan* 評彈 refers to the style of singing that was employed in Suzhou narrative ballads.

66 "Kneeling steps" refers to the technique of moving forward quickly on one's knees with an erect body.

67 For a collection of articles expressing different opinions on this issue, see Zhang Junxiang, Sang Hu, et al., *Lun xiqu dianying* (Beijing: Zhongguo dianying chubanshe, 1959). For a survey of these debates, see Gao Xiaojian, *Zhongguo xiqu dianying shi* (Beijing: Wenhua yishu chubanshe, 2005), pp. 174–189.

68 Sang Hu, "Yinmu shangde *Tianxian pei*," *Dazhong dianying*, No. 4 (1956): 8–9.

69 Here Sang Hu is referring to the performances of Huangmei Opera in Shanghai in the fall of 1952.

70 The Chinese term used here is *shenhua*, which is usually translated as "myth." However, "fairy tale" seems to better convey the intended meaning of the author.

71 The movie's director was Shi Hui.

72 Shi Hui, "*Tianxian pei* daoyan shouji," *Dianying yishu*, No. 5 (1957): 24–27; also reprinted in Wei Shaochang, ed., *Shi Hui tan yi lu* (Shanghai: Shanghai wenyi chubanshe, 1982), pp. 242–253. An earlier version of this translation was published in a special issue of *The Opera Quarterly* dedicated to Chinese opera movies and edited by Paola Iovene and Judith T. Zeitlin, as Shi Hui, "Notes about Directing *Married to a Heavenly Immortal*," tr. Wilt L. Idema, *The Opera Quarterly*, Vol. 26, No. 2–3 (2010): 435–445.

73 The Chinese text systematically speaks about a "myth-movie" (*shenhua pian*), but

"fairy-tale movie" probably better conveys the intention of the author.

74 The Southern Gate of Heaven guards the connection between heaven and earth.

75 The "set forms" refer primarily to the acting conventions of traditional theater, such as Peking Opera.

76 Presumably the scriptwriter, i.e., Sang Hu.

77 White Snake and Zhu Yingtai are the heroines of two well-known popular legends, often adapted for the stage. Zhu Yingtai is a young girl who dresses as a boy in order to be able to study at an academy away from home. There she falls in love with her roommate Liang Shanbo. The latter is at first suspicious she may be a girl, but later becomes so convinced that she is a boy that he misses her hints that she wants him to marry her. When she returns home, her parents engage her to a son of the Ma 馬 family. Liang learns of this during a visit, and he falls ill as soon as he arrives back home; he soon dies. When Zhu Yingtai's wedding procession passes by his grave, she steps down from her sedan chair and jumps into the open grave in order to join Liang Shanbo. White Snake is the human transformation of a thousand year old white snake, who takes on the shape of a young widow dressed in white (the Chinese mourning color). She falls in love with the poor and handsome Xu Xian, whom she showers with gifts, which turn out to be stolen goods. When Xu Xian is banished from Hangzhou to Suzhou, she follows him there, and when he later is banished to Zhenjiang, she follows him there as well. When Xu Xian learns her true nature from the abbot Fahai 法海, he returns to Hangzhou, but she follows him once again. Eventually she is imprisoned by abbot Fahai below the Thunder Peak Pagoda on the southern banks of Hangzhou's West Lake.

78 Walking in a circle is a stage convention to indicate that the performer has moved from one locality to the next in the story.

79 The "leadership" included the director-in-chief of the studio and the studio's Party committee.

80 I have been unable to locate this term in any reference work, but I believe that it may refer to a breathing technique.

81 This refers to the stage technique of falling backward fully stretched out, for instance, when fainting or dying, in the manner of a rigid corpse.

82 The horsewhip is used to symbolize riding a horse.

83 The Peking Opera stage tends to be bare except for a small table and two chairs, which may be used to symbolize various objects, such as walls and towers.

84 This is a specific rhythm beaten out on the gong to underscore violent passion, whether joy, rage, sadness, or frustration.

85 This is a particular rhythm beaten out on a gong when one of the performers is weeping.

86 Four loud strokes on the large gong and the small gong, accompanying the entrances, exits, and frozen poses.

87 In 1956 Han Shangyi criticized the movie for going too far in the realism of its settings. See Han Shangyi, "The Design and Style of Opera Films," tr. Jessica Ka Yee

Chan and Judith T. Zeitlin, with notes by Anne Rebull, *The Opera Quarterly*, Vol. 26, No. 2–3 (2010): 448.

88 This movie was released in 1954. It was directed by Huang Zuolin 黃佐臨, a close collaborator of Shi Hui and Sang Hu in the immediate post–1949 years.

89 Galina Ulanova was the most famous ballerina in the Soviet Union during the 1940s and 1950s. The music for the ballet *Romeo and Juliet* was composed in 1935 by Sergey Prokofiev, and the ballet was first performed in 1940 by the Kirov Ballet in Leningrad (now St. Petersburg). A film of the performance of the ballet by the Bolshoi Ballet, starring Ulanova, was released in 1954. The movie was introduced to Chinese audiences by Xiao Qian, "Yibu gesong qingchun, zhouzu fuxiu shili de wujupian: Jieshao *Luomi'ou yu Zhuliye*," *Dazhong dianying*, No. 3 (1956): 24–25.

90 When the monkey king Sun Wukong has been ennobled as a Great Sage Equal to Heaven but is not invited to a banquet hosted by the Queen Mother of the West, he steals her peaches of immortality, eats Laozi's elixir of longevity, and returns to his original abode on Flower-Fruit Mountain. When the Jade Emperor dispatches his troops against Sun Wukong, they are soundly defeated. This Peking Opera is the signature item of Yang Xiaolou 楊小樓.

91 Great Sage is one of the titles of Sun Wukong.

92 The translation omits a concrete musical example.

93 Handiao, Huidiao, Xipi, Erhuang, and Qinqiang are all names of basic melodies, named after their place of origin, that became the basis of elaborate tune systems and exerted a large influence on the music of regional opera in the late-imperial period and beyond.

94 The November 1956 issue of *Zhongguo xiju*, which on pp. 16–17 printed a brief report on this symposium, also contains an article by Tang Shi, entitled "*Tianxian pei* zhong Yan Fengying de biaoyan," which elaborates on some of the issues noted in that report. Tang compares at length Yan Fengying's performance at the 1954 East China Theater Festival with her 1956 performance in Beijing, criticizing her for having lost much of her original vivaciousness.

95 Kang Sheng is one of the most demonic (and demonized) figures in the history of the Chinese Communist Party. Following years of study in the Soviet Union he returned to Yan'an to become Mao's henchman in the execution of the 1942 Rectification Campaign. He then rose to become one of the highest-ranking members in the Party hierarchy. He was not active for a number of years because of an unspecified illness, but he reemerged in the national spotlight early in 1956. From his youth he had been an ardent lover of the theater. During the 1956–1962 period he manifested himself as an outspoken supporter of the unrevised repertoire of traditional theater and "vigorously defended the bawdy and superstitious plays of the past" (John Byron and Robert Pack, *The Claws of the Dragon: Kang Sheng, The Evil Genius Behind Mao and His Legacy of Terror in People's China* [New York: Simon and Schuster, 1992], p. 261). He would change his attitudes after 1962 and during the Cultural Revolution he became closely associated with Jiang Qing.

96 "Kang Sheng kan *Tianxian pei* houde yifeng xin," in *Zhongguo xiqu zhi: Anhui juan* (Beijing: Zhongguo ISBN zhongxin, 1993), pp. 739–740.

97 "Huangmeixi zuotanhui," *Zhongguo xiju*, No. 11 (1956), p. 17.

98 Wu Zuxiang 吳組緗 (1908–1994) hailed from Jingxian in Anhui. From 1930 to 1935 he studied at Qinghua University, first in the Department of Economics, and later in the Department of Chinese. During these years, he established a reputation as a writer of rural fiction. He stopped writing fiction after 1943. Beginning in 1952 he taught at Peking University as a specialist in traditional Chinese vernacular fiction. His scholarly life was interrupted by the Cultural Revolution, when he suffered persecution.

99 Wu Zuxiang, "Kan *Tianxian pei.*" This essay was first published in *Beijing ribao*, 北京日報 October 3 and 4, 1956. The translation is based on the text provided in Wang Chang'an, ed., *Zhongguo Huangmeixi* (Hefei: Anhui wenyi chubanshe, 2009), pp. 1069–1070.

100 The text actually writes "myth."

101 Dong Meikan 董每戡 (1907–1980) hailed from Wenzhou in Zhejiang province. Following study in Shanghai, he joined the Chinese Communist Party in 1927. In the 1930s he was active as a playwright of "spoken drama." By 1943 he was primarily active as a university teacher, specializing in traditional Chinese theater. In 1953 he joined the faculty of Zhongshan University in Guangzhou, but in 1957 he and his wife were declared "rightist elements" and as a result the family lived a life of poverty and persecution for the next twenty years. Their situation became worse during the Cultural Revolution, when Dong's books were confiscated and many of his unpublished writings were destroyed. Dong and his wife were rehabilitated in 1979, but he died soon thereafter.

102 Dong Meikan, "Cong *Tianxian pei* de gaibian tandao jieshou xiju yichan wenti." This piece was first published in *Nanfang ribao*, December 20, 1956. The translation is based on the text as reproduced in Wang Chang'an, ed., *Zhongguo Huangmeixi* (Hefei: Anhui wenyi chubanshe, 2009), pp. 1071–1072.

103 *Luantan* is a general designation of those genres of regional opera that rely on "matrix melody" (*banqiang*) music. The term has been in use since the eighteenth century.

104 That is, some traditional performance techniques in this scene.

105 These four terms refer to traditional bodily techniques to express intense emotions. "Water-hair" refers to long artificial hair attached to a male actor's cap that can be shaken and swirled by movements of the head. "Iron plank" here probably refers to the technique of falling down with the body fully stretched. The names of the other two techniques are more or less self-explanatory.

106 Correct Pronunciation Opera is a local Cantonese genre of regional drama. At the 1956 Guangzhou Theater Festival it performed its own version of the legend of Dong Yong and Seventh Sister.

Bibliography

Arkush, David R. "Love and Marriage in North China Peasant Operas," in Perry Link, Richard Madsen, and Paul G. Pickowicz, eds. *Unofficial China: Popular Culture and Thought in the People's Republic*. Boulder: Westview Press, 1989, pp. 72–87.

Arkush, David R. "The Moral World of Hebei Village Opera," in Paul A. Cohen and Merle Goldman, eds. *Ideas across Cultures: Essays on Chinese Thought in Honor of Benjamin I. Schwartz*. Cambridge, MA: Harvard University Press, 1990, pp. 87–107.

Bai Longju 柏龍駒. "Huangmeixi de mei kai san du" 黃梅戲的梅開三度 [Three new beginnings for Huangmei Opera], in Ye Bingnan 葉炳南, ed. *Xin Zhongguo difang xiju gaige jishi* 新中國地方戲劇改革紀實 [Records of the reform of local opera in new China]. Beijing: Zhongguo wenshi chubanshe, 2000, pp. 505–514.

"Bairi yuan: Chuju" 百日緣：楚劇 [The hundred-day marriage: A Hubei Opera]. *Juben*, No. 2 (1953): 55–59.

Ban Youshu 班友書. *Huangmeixi gujin zongheng* 黃梅戲古今縱橫 [Sundry essays on Huangmei Opera in past and present]. Hefei: Anhui wenyi chubanshe, 2000.

Ban Youshu. "Ye tan *Tianxian pei* de lailong qumai: Cong Qingyangqiang dao Huangmeixi meiyou juedui de zuozhe" 也談天仙配的來龍去脈：從青陽腔到黃梅戲沒有絕對的作者 [My opinion about the convoluted development of *Married to a Heavenly Immortal*: From Qiangyang Opera to Huangmei Opera there has never been one absolute author]. *Huangmeixi yishu*, No. 3 (2000): 10–14.

Ban Youshu. "Zhengli hou de Huangmeixi *Tianxian pei*" 整理後的黃梅戲天仙配 [The revised Huangmei Opera *Married to a Heavenly Immortal*]. *Anhui ribao*, November 25, 1953.

Barmé, Geremie. "Shi Hui: A Profile." *Chinese Literature*, No. 8 (1983): 96–104.

Bideau, Florence Graezer. *La danse du yangge: Culture et politique dans la Chine du XXe siècle* [Yangge dance: Culture and politics in twentieth-century China]. Paris: Découverte, 2012.

Bodde, Derk. *Peking Diary: 1948–1949 a Year of Revolution*. Reprint; Greenwich, CT: Fawcett, 1967.

Breaster, Yomi. "A Genealogy of Cinephilia in the Maoist Period," in Carlos Rojas and Eileen Cheng-yin Chow, eds. *The Oxford Handbook of Chinese Cinemas*. Oxford: Oxford University Press, 2013, pp. 98–115.

Byron, John and Robert Pack. *The Claws of the Dragon: Kang Sheng, The Evil Genius*

Behind Mao and His Legacy of Terror in People's China. New York: Simon and Schuster, 1992.

Chen, Edwin W. "Musical China, Classical Impression: A Preliminary Study of Shaws' *Huangmei Diao* Film," in Wong Ain-ling, ed. *The Shaw Screen: A Preliminary Study*. Hong Kong: Hong Kong Film Archive, 2003, pp. 51–73.

Chên, Ivan, tr. *The Book of Filial Duty*. London: J. Murray, 1908.

Chen, Shi-Zheng. "The Tradition, Reformation and Innovation of Huaguxi: Hunan Flower Drum Opera." *TDR*, Vol. 39, No. 1 (1995): 129–149.

Chen, Xiangyang. "Women, Generic Aesthetics, and the Vernacular: Huangmei Opera Films from China to Hong Kong," in Christine Gledhill, ed. *Gender Meets Genre in Postwar Cinemas*. Urbana: University of Illinois Press, 2012, pp. 177–190.

Chen, Xiaomei. "Twentieth-Century Spoken Drama," in Victor H. Mair, ed. *The Columbia History of Chinese Literature*. New York: Columbia University Press, 2001, pp. 848–877.

Chou, Yang. *China's New Literature and Art: Essays and Addresses*. Peking: Foreign Languages Press, 1954.

Chow, Tse-tsung. *The May Fourth Movement: Intellectual Revolution in Modern China*. Cambridge, MA: Harvard University Press, 1960.

Chu Su-chen. *Fifteen Strings of Cash: A Kunchu Opera*, rvsd. Chen Sze; tr. Yang Hsien-yi and Gladys Yang. Peking: Foreign Languages Press, 1957.

Clark, Paul. *Chinese Cinema: Culture and Politics since 1949*. Cambridge: Cambridge University Press, 1987.

Cooper, Gene. *The Market and Temple Fairs of Rural China: Red Fire*. London: Routledge, 2013.

Dai Zaimin 戴再民. "Cong dianying *Tianxian pei* de piantou tanqi" 從電影天仙配的片頭談起 [The credits in the movie *Married to a Heavenly Immortal*]. *Zhongguo dianying*, No. 5 (1957): 5–6.

DeMare, Brian. "Local Actors and National Politics: Rural Amateur Drama Troupes and Mass Campaigns in Hubei Province, 1949–1953." *Modern Chinese Literature and Culture*, Vol. 24, No. 2 (2012): 129–178.

Dikötter, Frank. *The Tragedy of Liberation: A History of the Chinese Revolution 1945–57*. London: Bloomsbury, 2013.

Ding Junmei 丁俊美. "Wang Shaofang dui Huangmeixi de zhuoyue gongxian" 王少舫對黃梅戲的卓越貢獻 [The extraordinary contributions of Wang Shaofang to Huangmei Opera]. *Zhonghua yishu luncong*, No. 6 (2006): 203–206.

Dolby, William. *A History of Chinese Drama*. London: P. Elek, 1976.

Dong Meikan 董每戡. "Cong *Tianxian pei* de gaibian tandao jieshou xiju yichan wenti" 從天仙配的改編談到接受戲劇遺產問題 [From the revision of *Married to a Heavenly Immortal* to the problem of the reception of our theatrical heritage], in Wang Chang'an 王長安, ed. *Zhongguo Huangmeixi* 中國黃梅戲 [China's Huangmei Opera]. Hefei: Anhui wenyi chubanshe, 2009, pp. 1071–1072.

Du Yingtao 杜穎陶, ed. *Dong Yong Chenxiang heji* 董永沉香合集 [The combined collection of Dong Yong and Chenxiang]. Shanghai: Gudian wenxue chubanshe, 1957.

Dudbridge, Glen. "The Goddess Hua-yüeh San-niang and the Cantonese Ballad *Ch'en-hsiang t'ai-tzu.*" *Hanxue yanjiu*, Vol. 8, No. 1 (1990): 627–646.

Eberstein, Bernd. *Das chinesische Theater im 20. Jahrhundert* [Chinese theater in the twentieth century]. Wiesbaden: Otto Harrassowitz, 1983.

Eberstein, Bernd. "Introduction: Thespis in the Pear Garden," in Bernd Eberstein, ed. *A Selective Guide to Chinese Literature 1900–1949*. Vol. 4: *The Drama*. Leiden: E.J. Brill, 1990, pp. 1–45.

Evans, Megan. "The Emerging Role of the Director in Chinese *Xiqu*." *Asian Theatre Journal*, Vol. 24, No. 2 (2007): 470–504.

Fang Xiqiu 方錫球 and Shi Xinzhong 時新中 . "Huangmeixi *Tianxian pei* gaibian de wenhua meixue wenti" 黃梅戲《天仙配》改編的文化美學問題 [Cultural and aesthetic issues in the revision of the Huangmei Opera *Married to a Heavenly Immortal*]. *Jiang Huai luntan*, No. 3 (2011): 177–182, 192.

Fei, Faye Chunfang, ed. and tr. *Chinese Theories of Theater and Performance from Confucius to the Present*. Ann Arbor: University of Michigan Press, 1999.

Fitzgerald, Carolyn. "Mandarin Ducks at the Battlefield: Ouyang Yuqian's Shifting Reconfigurations of Nora and Mulan." *Chinoperl Papers*, Vol. 29 (2010): 45–104.

Fokkema, D.W. *Literary Doctrine in China and Soviet Influence 1956–1960*. The Hague: Mouton, 1965.

Forke, Alfred, tr. *Elf chinesische Singspieltexte aus neuerer Zeit: Nebst zwei Dramen in westlicher Manier* [Eleven Chinese operas from recent times, together with two Western-style plays]. Stuttgart: F. Steiner, 1993.

Fowler, Simon. *101 Essential Chinese Movies*. Hong Kong: Earnshaw Books, 2010.

Fu Dixiu 伏滌修. "Yue Fei ticai xiqu liubian kaoshu" 岳飛題材戲曲流變考述 [A critical survey of the development of the plays on Yue Fei]. *Zhejiang yishu zhiye xueyuan xuebao*, No. 3 (2008): 39–44.

Fu Jin 傅謹 . *Xin Zhongguo xiju shi, 1949–2000* 新中國戲劇史, 1949–2000 [A history of Chinese drama, 1949–2000]. Changsha: Hunan meishu chubanshe, 2002.

Gamble, Sidney D., ed. *Chinese Village Plays from the Ting Hsien Region (Yang Ke Hsüan): A Collection of Forty-Eight Chinese Rural Plays as Staged by Villagers from Ting Hsien in Northern China*. Amsterdam: Philo Press, 1970.

[Gan Bao]. *In Search of the Supernatural: The Written Record*, tr. Kenneth J. DeWoskin and J.I. Crump, Jr. Stanford: Stanford University Press, 1996.

Gao Xiaojian 高小健. *Zhongguo xiqu dianying shi* 中國戲曲電影史 [A history of Chinese operatic films]. Beijing: Wenhua yishu chubanshe, 2005.

Gao Yilong 高義龍 and Li Xiao 李曉, eds. *Zhongguo xiqu xiandaixi shi* 中國戲曲現代戲史 [A history of plays on contemporary themes in traditional Chinese opera]. Shanghai: Shanghai wenhua chubanshe, 1999.

Ge Guang 葛光 . "Beiju rensheng Yan Fengying" 悲劇人生嚴鳳英 [The tragic life of Yan Fengying]. *Wenhua yuekan*, No. 6 (1997): 19–23.

Glosser, Susan L. *Chinese Visions of Family and State, 1915–1953*. Berkeley: University of California Press, 2003.

Goldman, Andrea S. *Opera and the City: The Politics of Culture in Beijing, 1770–1900*. Stanford: Stanford University Press, 2012.

Goldstein, Joshua. *Drama Kings: Players and Publics in the Re-Creation of Peking Opera, 1870–1937*. Berkeley: University of California Press, 2007.

Guo, Qitao. *Ritual Opera and Mercantile Lineage: The Confucian Transformation of Popular Culture in Late Imperial Huizhou*. Stanford: Stanford University Press, 2005.

Guy, Nancy. *Peking Opera and Politics in Taiwan*. Urbana: University of Illinois Press, 2005.

Han, Shangyi. "The Design and Style of Opera Films," tr. Jessica Ka Yee Chan and Judith T. Zeitlin, with notes by Anne Rebull. *The Opera Quarterly*, Vol. 26, No. 2–3 (2010): 446–454.

Han Xiaoli 韓曉莉. *Bei gaizao de minjian xiqu: Yi 20 shiji Shanxi yangge xiaoxi wei zhongxin de shehuishi kaocha* 被改造的民間戲曲：以20世紀山西秧歌小戲為中心的社會史考察 [Transformed popular drama: A social history of Shanxi Yangge plays in the twentieth century]. Beijing: Beijing daxue chubanshe, 2012.

Hargett, James M. *Stairway to Heaven: A Journey to the Summit of Mount Emei*. Albany: State University of New York Press, 2006.

Harris, Kristine. "*The Romance of the Western Chamber* and the Classical Subject Film in 1920s Shanghai," in Yingjin Zhang, ed. *Cinema and Urban Culture in Shanghai, 1922–1943*. Stanford: Stanford University Press, 1999, pp. 51–73.

He, Qiliang. *Gilded Voices: Economics, Politics, and Storytelling in the Yangzi Delta since 1949*. Leiden: Brill, 2012.

Holm, David. *Art and Ideology in Revolutionary China*. Oxford: Clarendon Press, 1991.

Hong Fei: also see Lu Hongfei.

Hong Fei 洪非. "Guanyu *Tianxian pei*" 關於天仙配 [About *Married to a Heavenly Immortal*]. *Huangmeixi yishu*, No. 3 (1988): 31–40.

Hong Fei. "Tan *Tianxian pei* de gaibian" 談天仙配的改編 [On the revision of *Married to a Heavenly Immortal*]. *Anhui ribao*, December 10, 1954.

Hong Fei. "Tian Han yu Huangmeixi ji qita" 田漢與黃梅戲及其他 [Tian Han, Huangmei Opera, and more]. *Huangmeixi yishu*, No. 1 (1999): 5–10.

Hong Fei. "Wang Shaofang de zuihou shinian" 王少舫的最後十年 [Wang Shaofang's last ten years]. *Huangmeixi yishu*, No. 1 (2000): 11–18.

Hong Fei. "Wang Shaofang shengping xinian (1920–1949 nian)" 王少舫生平系年（1920–1949年）[A chronology of the life of Wang Shaofang (1920–1949)]. *Huangmeixi yishu*, No. 4 (2001): 7–15.

Hong Fei. "Wang Shaofang shengping xinian (1950–1966)" 王少舫生平系年（1950–1966年）[A chronology of the life of Wang Shaofang (1950–1966)]. *Huangmeixi yishu*, No. 2 (2002): 12–19.

Hong Fei. "Wo pei Wang Shaofang zouguo huangtang suiyue" 我陪王少舫走過荒唐歲月 [Those absurd years that I lived through with Wang Shaofang]. *Huangmeixi yishu*, No. 1 (2001): 20–25.

Hong Zhongwei 洪中為. "Lu Hongfei zhuan" 陸洪非傳 [The life of Lu Hongfei]. *Huangmeixi yishu*, No. 1 (2003): 16–19; No. 2 (2003): 19–24; No. 3 (2003): 38–42; No. 2 (2004): 18–21; No. 3 (2004): 45–48.

Hong, Zicheng. *A History of Contemporary Chinese Literature*, tr. Michael M. Day. Leiden: Brill, 2007.

Hsieh, Hsiao-Mei. "Where Have All the Different *Butterfly Lovers* Gone? The Homogenization of Local Theater as a Result of the Theater Reform in China as Seen in *Gezai Xi/Xiangju*." *Chinoperl Papers*, Vol. 30 (2011): 103–122.

Hu Kuisheng 胡虧生. *Huangmeixi fengmao* 黃梅戲風貌 [The many faces of Huangmei Opera]. Hefei: Anhui renmin chubanshe, 2008.

Hu Kuisheng. *Huangmeixi renwu* 黃梅戲人物 [The personalities of Huangmei Opera]. Hefei: Anhui renmin chubanshe, 2010.

Hu Yuting 胡玉庭 and Hong Fei 洪非. *Tianxian pei: Huangmeixi* 天仙配黃梅戲 [*Married to a Heavenly Immortal*: A Huangmei Opera]. Shanghai: Shanghai wenhua chubanshe, 1955.

Hu Yuting and Lu Hongfei. "Tianxian pei" 天仙配 [Married to a Heavenly Immortal]. *Huadongqu xiqu guanmo yanchu dahui* 華東區戲曲觀摩演出大會 [Opera Theater Festival of the East China Region], Vol. 2: *Anhuisheng daibiaotuan yanchu juben xuanji* 安徽省代表團演出劇本選集 [Selected scripts of the representative companies of Anhui province]. Shanghai: Huadongqu xiqu guanmo yanchu dahui, 1954, pp. 1–34.

Huang Chi 黃痴. "Jinian Huangmeixi shouwei daoyan: Li Liping" 紀念黃梅戲首位導演：李力平 [In memory of Li Liping, the first director of Huangmei Opera]. *Huangmeixi yishu*, No. 1 (2003): 20–21.

[Huang Wenyang 黃文暘 and Kang Dong 康董 , eds.]. *Quhai zongmu tiyao* [46 juan] 曲海總目提要 [46 卷] [A comprehensive catalogue with content abstracts of the Sea of Songs (46 volumes)]. Beijing: Renmin wenxue chubanshe, 1959.

"Huangmeixi zuotanhui" 黃梅戲座談會 [A symposium on Huangmei Opera]. *Zhongguo xiju*, No. 11 (1956): 17.

Hung, Chang-tai. *War and Popular Culture: Resistance in Modern China, 1937–1945*. Berkeley: University of California Press, 1994.

Huo Jianyu 霍建瑜. "Lun Mingdai fan'anju xingqi zhi yuanyin" 論明代翻案劇興起之原因 [On the reasons for the rise of "reversal plays" in the Ming dynasty]. *Nanjing shehui kexue*, No. 4 (2007): 118–122.

Hutcheon, Linda. *A Theory of Adaptation*. London: Routledge, 2006.

Idema, Wilt L., *The Butterfly Lovers: The Legend of Liang Shanbo and Zhu Yingtai—Four Versions, with Related Texts*. Indianapolis: Hackett, 2010.

Idema, Wilt L. "Emulation through Readaptation in Yüan and Early Ming." *Asia Major*, Third Series, Vol. 3, No. 1 (1990): 113–128.

Idema, Wilt L. *Filial Piety and Its Divine Rewards: The Legend of Dong Yong and Weaving Maiden with Related Texts*. Indianapolis: Hackett, 2009.

Idema, Wilt L., intro. and tr. "Fourth Sister Zhang Creates Havoc in the Eastern Capital." *Chinoperl Papers*, Vol. 31 (2012): 37–112.

Idema, Wilt L. "The Ideological Manipulation of Traditional Drama in Ming Times: Some Comments on the Work of Tanaka Issei," in Chun-chieh Huang and Erik Zürcher, eds. *Norms and the State in China*. Leiden: E.J. Brill, 1993, pp. 50–70.

Idema, Wilt L. "Old Tales for New Times: Some Comments on the Cultural Translation of China's Four Great Folktales in the Twentieth Century." *Taiwan Journal of East Asian Studies*, Vol. 9, No. 1 (2012): 25–46.

Idema, Wilt L. "Performances on a Three-tiered Stage: Court Theatre During the Qianlong Era," in Lutz Bieg, Erling von Mende, and Martina Siebert, eds. *Ad Seres et Tungusos: Festschrift für Martin Gimm* [Ad Seres et Tungusos: Studies in honor of Martin Gimm]. Wiesbaden: Otto Harrassowitz, 2000, pp. 201–219.

Idema, Wilt L. "Weaving Maiden and Buffalo Boy in Myth and Fairy Tale," in *Filial Piety and Its Divine Rewards: The Legend of Dong Yong and Weaving Maiden with Related Texts*. Indianapolis: Hackett, 2009.

Idema, Wilt L. *The White Snake and her Son: A Translation of* The Precious Scroll of Thunder Peak, *with Related Texts*. Indianapolis: Hackett, 2009.

Idema, Wilt L. "Why You Never Have Read a Yuan Drama: The Transformation of *Zaju* at the Ming Court," in S.M. Carletti, M. Sacchetti, and P. Santagelo, eds. *Studi in onore di Lionello Lanciotti* [Studies in honor of Lanciello Lanciotti]. Napoli: Istituto universitario orientale, Dipartimento di studi asiatici, 1996, pp. 765–791.

Iovene, Paola. "Chinese Operas on Stage and Screen: A Short Introduction." *The Opera Quarterly*, Vol. 26, No. 2–3 (2010): 181–199.

Ji Yonggui 紀永貴. *Dong Yong yuxian chuanshuo yanjiu* 董永遇仙傳說研究 [A study of the legend of Dong Yong meeting an immortal]. Hefei: Anhui daxue chubanshe, 2006.

Ji Yonggui. "Huangmeixi *Tianxian pei* de gaibian yu yingxiang" 黃梅戲天仙配的改編與影響 [The revision and impact of the Huangmei Opera *Married to a Heavenly Immortal*]. *Zhonghua wenyi luncong*, No. 6 (2006): 42–65.

Jiang, Jin. *Women Playing Men: Yue Opera and Social Change in Twentieth-Century Shanghai*. Seattle: University of Washington Press, 2009.

Jiang Xingyu 蔣星煜. "*Tianxian pei* gushi de lishi dili kaocha" 天仙配故事的歷史地理考察 [An inquiry into the historical geography of the story *Married to a Heavenly Immortal*], in his *Zhongguo xiqu shi gouchen* 中國戲曲史鈎沉 [Studies on the history of Chinese drama]. Shanghai: Shanghai renmin chubanshe, 2010, pp. 819–826.

Jin Danyuan 金丹元. "20 shiji 50 niandai xiqupian yu guzhuangxi yingxiangzhong tuchu "renminxing" de meixue yiyi" 20世紀50年代戲曲片與古裝戲影像中突出「人民性」的美學意義 [The aesthetic meaning of the prominent popular nature in the images of the operatic movies and the ancient-costume dramas of the 1950s of the 20th century]. *Wenyi lilun yanjiu*, No. 2 (2011):129–134.

Jin Qi'an 金其安. "Cong Jingju laosheng dao Huangmeixi daoyan: Ji sheng zhengxie weiyuan Qiao Zhiliang" 從京劇老生到黃梅戲導演：記省政協委員喬志良 [From Peking Opera *laosheng* to Huangmei Opera director: In memory of Qiao

Zhiliang, member of the provincial political consultative conference]. *Jiang Huai wenshi*, No. 6 (1997): 52–59.

Jin Zhi 金芝. "Wo yu *Tianxian pei*" 我與天仙配 [My relation with *Married to a Heavenly Immortal*]. *Huangmeixi yishu*, No. 1 (1988): 31–37.

Johnson, Irmgard. "The Reform of Peking Opera in Taiwan." *China Quarterly*, No. 57 (1974): 140–145.

Jordan, David K. "Folk Filial Piety in Taiwan: *The Twenty-four Filial Exemplars*," in Walter H. Slote, ed. *The Psycho-Cultural Dynamics of the Confucian Family: Past and Present*. Seoul: International Cultural Society of Korea, 1986, pp. 47–106.

Judd, Ellen R. "Cultural Articulation in the Chinese Countryside, 1937–1947." *Modern China*, Vol. 16, No. 3 (1990): 269–308.

Judd, Ellen R. "Revolutionary Drama and Song in the Jiangxi Soviet." *Modern China*, Vol. 9, No. 1 (1983): 127–160.

Kang Sheng 康生. "Kang Sheng Kan *Tianxian pei* houde yifeng xin" 康生看天仙配後的一封信 [Kang Sheng's letter after watching *Married to a Heavenly Immortal*], in *Zhongguo xiqu zhi: Anhui juan* 中國戲曲志：安徽卷. Beijing: Zhongguo ISBN zhongxin, 1993, pp. 739–740.

Knapp, Keith Nathaniel. *Selfless Offspring: Filial Children and Social Order in Early Medieval China*. Honolulu: University of Hawai'i Press, 2005.

Koehn, Alfred. *Filial Devotion in China*. Peking: Lotus Court, 1943.

Kowallis, Jon. *The Lyrical Lu Xun: A Study of his Classical-Style Verse*. Honolulu: University of Hawai'i Press, 1996.

Kwa, Shiamin and Wilt L. Idema. *Mulan: Five Versions of a Classic Chinese Legend, with Related Texts*. Indianapolis: Hackett, 2010.

Lang Jing 郎淨. *Dong Yong chuanshuo* 董永傳説 [The legend of Dong Yong]. Beijing: Zhongguo shehui chubanshe, 2008.

Lang Jing. *Dong Yong gushi de zhanyan ji qi wenhua jiegou* 董永故事的展演及其文化結構 [The development of the story of Dong Yong and its cultural structure]. Shanghai: Shanghai guji chubanshe, 2005.

Lang, Olga. *Chinese Family and Society.* New Haven: Yale University Press, 1950.

Lang, Olga. *Pa Chin and his Writings: Chinese Youth Between the Two Revolutions*. Cambridge, MA: Harvard University Press, 1967.

Lee, Haiyan. *Revolution of the Heart: A Genealogy of Love in China, 1900–1950*. Stanford: Stanford University Press, 2007.

Lee, Haiyan. "Tears that Crumbled the Great Wall: The Archaeology of Feeling in the May Fourth Folklore Movement." *Journal of Asian Studies*, Vol. 64, No. 1 (2005): 35–65.

Leyda, Jan. *Dianying: An Account of Films and the Film Audience in China*. Cambridge, MA: MIT Press, 1972.

Li Jianye 李建業 and Dong Jinyan 董金艷 , eds. *Dong Yong yu xiao wenhua* 董永與孝文化 [Dong Yong and the culture of filial piety]. Ji'nan: Qi Lu shushe, 2003.

Li Jin. "Theater of Pathos: Sentimental Melodramas in the New Drama Legacy." *Modern Chinese Literature and Culture*, Vol. 24, No. 2 (2012): 94–128.

Li Liping 李力平. "Sishiqi nian qiande wangshi: Yan Fengying qishi danchen yijiu" 四十七年前的往事：嚴鳳英七十誕晨憶舊 [Events of forty-seven years ago: Memories on the seventieth birthday of Yan Fengying]. *Huangmeixi yishu*, No. 4 (2000): 37–41.

Li Liping. "*Tianxian pei* wutaiju de paiyan"《天仙配》舞台劇的排演 [The production of the stage version of *Married to a Heavenly Immortal*]. *Huangmeixi yishu*, No. 1 (1981): 157–161.

Li Liping. "Yige zhenzheng de yishujia: Huiyi he Wang Shaofang tongzhi jici hezuo" 一個真正的藝術家回憶和王少舫同志幾次合作 [A true artist: Memories of my cooperation with comrade Wang Shaofang on several occasions]. *Huangmeixi yishu*, No.1 (1987): 80–85.

Li Ruru. *The Soul of Beijing Opera: Theatrical Creativity and Continuity in the Changing World*. Hong Kong: Hong Kong University Press, 2010.

Li Xiaoti 李孝悌. *Qingmo de xiaceng shehui qimeng yundong*, 1901–1911 清末的下層社會啟蒙運動，1901–1911 [The movement for popular enlightenment at the end of the Qing, 1901–1911]. Taipei: Academia Sinica, 1992.

Li Yizhong 李亦中. "Dangnian pengshi Sang Hu yi: Fuqin Sang Hu yu xin Zhongguo dianying sanxiang diyi" 當年蓬矢桑弧意：父親桑弧與新中國電影三項第一 [The original meaning of the reed arrow and mulberry-wood bow: My father Sang Hu and the three "firsts" in the cinema of new China]. *Shanghai caifeng*, No. 1 (2011): 64–67.

Lin Heyi 林鶴宜. *Cong xiqu piping dao lilun jiangou* 從戲曲批評到理論建構 [From drama criticism to theory construction]. Taipei: Guojia chubanshe, 2011.

Lin Lu 林陸 and Lu Lin 陸林, eds. *Lu Hongfei Lin Qing Huangmeixi juzuo quanji* 陸洪非林青黃梅戲劇作全集 [The collected Huangmei Opera scripts by Lu Hongfei and Lin Qing]. Hefei: Anhui wenyi chubanshe, 2012.

Liu Chunjiang 劉春江 and Chen Jianjun 陳建軍. *Hukou Qingyangqiang* 湖口青陽腔 [Qingyangqiang Opera from Hukou]. Nanchang: Jiangxi renmin chubanshe, 2008.

Liu Fangzheng 劉方正. "Guanyu shenhuaju de lunzheng" 關於神話劇的論爭 [The debate on fairy-tale plays], in Tian Benxiang 田本相, Song Baozhen 宋寶珍, and Liu Fangzheng 劉方正. *Zhongguo xiju lunbian* 中國戲劇論辨 [Discussions on Chinese drama]. Nanchang: Baihuazhou wenyi chubanshe, 2007, Vol. 2, pp. 669–687.

Liu, Lydia H. "A Folksong Immortal and Official Popular Culture in Twentieth-Century China," in Judith T. Zeitlin and Lydia H. Liu, eds. *Writing and Materiality in China: Essays in Honor of Patrick Hanan*. Cambridge, MA: Asia Center, Harvard University, 2003, pp. 553–609.

Liu, Siyuan. "Theatre Reform as Censorship: Censoring Traditional Theatre in China in the Early 1950s." *Theatre Journal*, Vol. 61, No. 3 (2009): 387–406.

Love under the Willows: A Szechuan Opera. Liang Shan-po and Chu Ying-tai, tr. Yang Hsien-yi and Gladys Yang. Peking: Foreign Languages Press, 1956.

Lu Hongfei: also see Hong Fei.

Lu Hongfei 陸洪非. *Huangmeixi yuanliu* 黃梅戲源流 [The origin and development of Huangmei Opera]. Hefei: Anhui wenyi chubanshe, 1985.

Lu Hongfei. "*Tianxian pei* de lailong qumai" 天仙配的來龍去脈 [The convoluted development of *Married to a Heavenly Immortal*]. *Huangmei yishu*, No. 2 (2000): 10–17.

Lu Hongfei. "Wu huan xing yi ji du qiu: Huangmeixi *Tianxian pei* de yanbian" 物換星移幾度秋：黃梅戲天仙配的演變 [Things change and stars move over many years: The changes in the Huangmei Opera *Married to a Heavenly Immortal*], in Chang Danqi 常丹琦, ed. *Mingjia lun mingju* 名家論名劇. Beijing: Shoudu shifan daxue chubanshe, 1994, pp. 299–318.

Ma, Qian, annot. and tr. *Women in Traditional Chinese Theater: The Heroine's Play*. Lanham, MD: University Press of America, 2005.

Mackerras, Colin. *Chinese Drama: A Historical Survey*. Beijing: New World Press, 1990.

Mackerras, Colin. *The Chinese Theatre in Modern Times: From 1840 to the Present Day*. London: Thames and Hudson, 1975.

Mair, Victor H. and Mark Bender, eds. *The Columbia Anthology of Chinese Folk and Popular Literature*. New York: Columbia University Press, 2011.

McDougall, Bonnie S. *Mao Zedong's "Talks at the Yan'an Conference on Literature and Art": A Translation of the 1943 Text with Commentary*. Ann Arbor: Center for Chinese Studies, University of Michigan, 1980.

Mei, Shaowu. "Mei Lanfang as Seen by his Foreign Audiences and Critics," in Wu Zuguang, Huang Zuolin, and Mei Shaowu. *Peking Opera and Mei Lanfang: A Guide to China's Traditional Theatre and the Art of Its Great Master*. Beijing: New World Press, 1981, pp. 46–65.

Meng Liye 孟犁野. *Xin Zhongguo dianying yishu shigao, 1949–1959* 新中國電影藝術史稿, 1949–1959 [A draft history of cinematic art in new China, 1949–1959]. Beijing: Zhongguo dianying chubanshe, 2002.

Meserve, Walter J. and Ruth I. Meserve. "Myth and Superstition in Communist China's Drama and Theatre," in Richard M. Dorson, ed. *Folklore in the Modern World*. The Hague: Mouton, 1978, pp. 125–143.

Mulligan, Jean, tr. *The Lute: Kao Ming's* P'i-p'a chi. New York: Columbia University Press, 1980.

Niu Sengru 牛僧孺, Li Fuyan 李復言. *Xuanguai lu, Xu xuanguai lu* 玄怪錄續玄怪錄 [Record of marvels, Continued record of marvels]. Beijing: Zhonghua shuju, 1982.

Oinas, Felix J. "The Political Uses and Themes of Folklore in the Soviet Union." *Journal of the Folklore Institute*, Vol. 12, No. 2/3 (1975): 157–175.

Pa, Chin. *Family*, intro. Olga Lang. Garden City, NY: Doubleday Anchor Books, 1972; reprint; Boston: Cheng and Tsui, 1999.

Pa, Chin. *The Family*, tr. Sidney Shapiro. Peking: Foreign Languages Press, 1958.

Pang, Laikwan. "Between Will and Negotiation: Film Policy in the First Three Years of the People's Republic of China," in Carlos Rojas and Eileen Cheng-yin Chow, eds. *The Oxford Handbook of Chinese Cinemas*. Oxford: Oxford University Press, 2013, pp. 472–498.

Pi chou Tianxian pei 批臭天仙配 [A critique of that stinking *Married to a Heavenly Immortal*]. Hefei: Anhuisheng Huangmei jutuan geming da pipan zu, 1970.

Pickowicz, Paul G. "Acting Like Revolutionaries: Shi Hui, the Wenhua Studio, and Private-Sector Filmmaking, 1949–52," in Jeremy Brown and Paul G. Pickowicz, eds. *Dilemmas of Victory: The Early Years of the People's Republic of China*. Cambridge, MA: Harvard University Press, 2007, pp. 256–287.

Průšek, Jaroslav. *Die Literatur des befreiten China und ihre Volkstraditionen* [The literature of liberated China and its folk traditions], tr. Pavel Eisner and Wilhelm Gampert. Prag: Artia, 1955.

Qiao Zhiliang 喬志良, Zhang Chuancai 張傳才, and Yao Yuwen 姚育文. "Yi daoyan *Tianxian pei*" 憶導演《天仙配》[Memories of directing *Married to a Heavenly Immortal*]. *Huangmeixi yishu*, No. 4 (1996): 75–94.

Qin Yonggui 秦永貴. "30 nianqian kan dianying *Tianxian pei*" 30年前看電影天仙配 [Watching the movie *Married to a Heavenly Immortal* thirty years ago]. *Longmenzhen*, No. 8 (2009): 37–40.

Riemenschnitter, Andrea. *Karneval der Götter: Mythologie, Moderne und Nation in China's 20. Jahrhunderdt* [Carnival of the gods: Mythology, modern authors, and the nation in China's twentieth century]. Bern/New York: P. Lang, 2011.

Rojas, Carlos and Eileen Cheng-yin Chow, eds. *The Oxford Handbook of Chinese Cinemas*. Oxford: Oxford University Press, 2013.

Sanders, Julie. *Adaptation and Appropriation*. London: Routledge, 2006.

Sang Hu 桑弧. "Tantan xiqupian de juben wenti" 談談戲曲片的劇本問題 [Some remarks about the script of operatic movies], in Zhang Junxiang 張駿祥, Sang Hu, et al. *Lun xiqu dianying* 論戲曲電影 [On operatic movies]. Beijing: Zhongguo dianying chubanshe, 1959, pp. 35–48.

Sang Hu. "Yinmu shang de *Tianxian pei*" 銀幕上的天仙配 [*Married to a Heavenly Immortal* on the silver screen]. *Dazhong dianying*, No. 4 (1956): 8–9.

Scott, A.C. *Literature and the Arts in Twentieth Century China*. London: G. Allen & Unwin, 1965.

Shaw, Norman. *Chinese Forest Trees and Timber Supply*. London: T. F. Unwin, 1914.

Shi Bailin 時白林. *Huangmeixi yinyue gailun* 黃梅戲音樂概論 [An outline of the music of Huangmei Opera]. Beijing: Renmin yinyue chubanshe, 1989.

Shi Bailin. *Shi Bailin zixuan wenji* 時白林自選文集 [Shi Bailin's own choice of articles]. Hefei: Anhui wenyi chubanshe, 2007.

Shi Bailin. "Shi Hui he dianying *Tianxian pei*" 石揮和電影天仙配 [Shi Hui and the movie *Married to a Heavenly Immortal*]. *Xijujie*, No. 2 (1987): 9–10.

Shi, Hui 石揮. "Notes about Directing *Married to a Heavenly Immortal*," tr. Wilt L. Idema. *The Opera Quarterly*, Vol. 26, No. 2–3 (2010): 435–445.

Shi Hui. "*Tianxian pei* daoyan shouji" 天仙配導演手記 [Notes about directing *Married to a Heavenly Immortal*]. *Dianying yishu*, No. 5 (1957): 24–27.

Situ Xiuying 司徒秀英. *Mingdai jiaohuaju qunguan* 明代教化劇群觀 [A

comprehensive survey of moralistic plays of the Ming dynasty]. Shanghai: Shanghai guji chubanshe, 2009.

Stock, Jonathan P.J. *Huju: Traditional Opera in Modern Shanghai*. Oxford: Oxford University Press, 2003.

Strassberg, Richard E. "Introduction," in John D. Mitchell, ed. *The Red Pear Garden: Three Great Dramas of Revolutionary China*. Boston: David R. Godine, 1973, pp. 11–38.

Swatek, Catherine C. *Peony Pavilion Onstage: Four Centuries in the Career of a Chinese Drama*. Ann Arbor: Center for Chinese Studies, University of Michigan, 2002.

Tai, Yih-jian. "Stanislavsky and the Chinese Theater." *Journal of Oriental Studies*, Vol. 16, No. 1–2 (1978): 49–62.

Tan Chunfang 檀春芳. "*Tianxian pei* yiju gengshende hanyi: Wo yan Dong Yong yijiao er xiangdaode" 天仙配一劇更深的含義：我演董永一角而想到的 [An even deeper meaning of the play *Married to a Heavenly Immortal*: What I realized while performing the role of Dong Yong]. *Huangmeixi yishu*, No. 3 (2010): 70.

Tan, Tian Yuan. "The Sovereign and the Theatre: Reconsidering the Impact of Ming Taizu's Prohibition," in Sarah Schneewind, ed. *Long Live the Emperor! Uses of the Ming Founder across Six Centuries of East Asian History*. Minneapolis: Society for Ming Studies, 2008, pp. 149–169.

Tang Fangming 唐芳明. "*Tianxian pei* yuanxing yu gaibianben bijiao" 天仙配原形與改編本比較 [A comparison of the original *Married to a Heavenly Immortal* and its revised version]. *Kejiao wenhui*, No. 11 (2010): 64–65.

Tang Shi 唐湜. "*Tianxian pei* zhong Yan Fengying de biaoyan" 天仙配中嚴鳳英的表演 [The performance of Yan Fengying in *Married to a Heavenly Immortal*]. *Zhongguo xiju*, No. 11 (1956):16–17.

Tang Yahong 湯雅洪. "*Tianxian pei* zhong xiannü jin hezai?" 天仙配眾仙女今何在？ [Where are those Immortal Maidens of *Married to a Heavenly Immortal* now?]. *Huaren shikan*, No. 2 (2001): 48–50.

Teo, Stephen. "The Opera Film in Chinese Cinema: Cultural Nationalism and Cinematic Form," in Carlos Rojas and Eileen Cheng-yin Chow, eds. *The Oxford Handbook of Chinese Cinemas*. Oxford: Oxford University Press, 2013, pp. 209–224.

Tian Benxiang 田本相, Song Baozhen 宋寶珍, and Liu Fangzheng 劉方正. *Zhongguo xiju lunbian* 中國戲劇論辨 [Discussions on Chinese drama], Vol. 1. Nanchang: Baihuazhou wenyi chubanshe, 2007.

"Tianxian pei (Huangmeixi)" 天仙配黃梅戲 [*Married to a Heavenly Immortal* (A Huangmei Opera)], in Zhongguo xijujia xiehui and Anhuisheng wenhuaju 中國戲劇家協會，安徽省文化局, *Zhongguo difang xiqu jicheng: Anhuisheng juan* 中國地方戲曲集成：安徽省卷. 2 vols. Beijing: Zhongguo xiju chubanshe, 1959, pp. 129–193.

T'ien, Han. *The White Snake: A Peking Opera*, tr. Yang Hsien-yi and Gladys Yang. Peking: Foreign Languages Press, 1957.

Tyan, Han (Tian Han). "The White Snake," tr. Donald Chang; English verse adaptation by William Packard, in John D. Mitchell, ed. *The Red Pear Garden: Three Great Dramas of Revolutionary China*. Boston: David R. Godine, 1973, pp. 49–120.

Wang Anqi 王安祈. *Dangdai xiqu, fu jubenxuan* 當代戲曲附劇本選 [Contemporary drama, with a selection of scripts]. Taipei: Sanmin shuju, 2002.

Wang Anqi. "'Yanyuan juchang' xiang 'bianju zhongxin' de guodu: Dalu 'xiqu gaige' xiaoying yu dangdai xiqu zhixing zhuanbian zhi guancha" 演員劇場向編劇中心的過渡：大陸戲曲改革效應與當代戲曲質性轉變之觀察 [The transition from "the actors' stage" to "the centrality of playwriting": An inquiry into the effects of the "theater reform" on the mainland and the change in character of contemporary drama]. *Zhongguo wenzhe yanjiu jikan*, No. 19 (2001): 251–316.

Wang Anyi 王安憶. *Yinju de shidai: Wang Anyi zhong duanpian xiaoshuo ji* 隱居的時代：王安憶中短篇小說集 [Living in hiding: Novellas and short stories by Wang Anyi]. Shanghai: Shanghai wenyi chubanshe, 1999.

Wang, Ban. "History in a Mythical Key: Temporality, Memory, and Tradition in Wang Anyi's Fiction." *Journal of Contemporary China*, Vol. 12, No. 37 (2003): 607–621.

Wang Chang'an 王長安, ed. *Zhongguo Huangmeixi* 中國黃梅戲 [China's Huangmei Opera]. Hefei: Anhui wenyi chubanshe, 2009.

Wang, David Der-wei. "Fei Mu, Mei Lanfang, and the Polemics of Screening China," in Carlos Rojas and Eileen Cheng-yin Chow, eds. *The Oxford Handbook of Chinese Cinemas*. Oxford: Oxford University Press, 2013, pp. 62–78.

Wang Guanya 王冠亞. *Yan Fengying: Bingfei chuanqi de chuanqi* 嚴鳳英：並非傳奇的傳奇 [The not so romantic romance of Yan Fengying]. Wuhan: Changjiang wenyi chubanshe, 1985.

Wang Liangcheng 王良成. "Mingdai de fan'anju ji qi shenmei fengshang shulun" 明代的翻案劇及其審美風尚述論 [A survey of Ming dynasty "reversal plays" and their aesthetic fashion]. *Yishu baijia*, No. 1 (2007): 19–22.

Wang Senran 王森然. *Zhongguo jumu cidian* 中國劇目辭典 [A dictionary of Chinese play titles]. Shijiazhuang: Hebei jiaoyu chubanshe, 1997.

Wang Shaofang 王少舫. "Wo yan Dong Yong" 我演董永 [How I perform Dong Yong]. *Zhongguo dianying*, No. 3 (1956): 33–34.

Wang Xiaoyun 汪曉雲. "Minjian kuanghuan yishi: Huangmeixi de xiangdui yuanshengtai" 民間狂歡儀式：黃梅戲的相對原生態 [Popular carnival rituals: The relatively original shape of Huangmei Opera], in Zhu Wanshu 朱萬曙 and Bian Li 卞利, eds. *Xiqu minsu Hui wenhua lunji* 戲曲民俗徽文化論集 [Articles on traditional opera, popular custom, and Huizhou culture]. Hefei: Anhui daxue chubanshe, 2004, pp. 530–544.

Wang Yue 汪粵. "Xiqu dianying *Tianxian pei* chuangzuo shoufa shangxi" 戲曲電影天仙配創作手法賞析 [An appreciation of the creative method of the operatic movie *Married to a Heavenly Immortal*]. *Zhongguo xiqu xueyuan xuebao*, No. 4 (2008): 64–67.

Wang Zhaoqian 王兆乾. "Huangmeixi" 黃梅戲 [Huangmei Opera], in Wang Qiugui 王秋桂, ed. *Zhongguo difang xiqu congtan* 中國地方戲曲叢談 [Essays on

China's regional operas]. Xinzhu: Guoli Qinghua daxue, Renwen shehui xueyuan, Sixiang wenhuashi yanjiushi, 1995, pp. 167–204.

Wang Zhaoqian, ed. *Huangmeixi yinyue* 黃梅戲音樂 [The music of Huangmei Opera]. Hefei: Anhui renmin chubanshe, 1957.

Wang Zhaoqian. "*Tianxian pei* he *Nü fuma* de fajue he gaibian: Da Chen Rongsheng tongzhi" 天仙配和女駙馬的發掘和改編：答陳榮升同志 [The discovery and revision of *Married to a Heavenly Immortal* and *The Female Prince-Consort*: A reply to comrade Chen Rongsheng]. *Huangmeixi yishu*, No. 2 (2000): 18–23.

Wei Shaochang 魏紹昌, ed. *Shi Hui tan yi lu* 石揮談藝錄 [Shi Hui on art]. Shanghai: Shanghai wenyi chubanshe, 1982.

West, Stephen H. "Text and Ideology: Ming Editors and Northern Drama," in Paul Jakov Smith and Richard von Glahn, eds. *The Song-Yuan-Ming Transition in Chinese History*. Cambridge, MA: Asia Center, Harvard University, 2003, pp. 329–373.

Williams, Philip F. *Village Echoes: The Fiction of Wu Zuxiang*. Boulder: Westview Press, 1993.

Wu Baohe 吳保和. "Hua Mulan, yige Zhongguo wenhua fuhao de yanbian yu chuanbo—cong Mulan xiju dao Mulan dianying" 花木蘭，一個中國文化符號的傳播——從木蘭戲劇到木蘭電影, in Ni Zhen 倪震 and Li Zhenlin 厲震林, eds. *Shuanglun meixue: Zhongguo xiju yu Zhongguo dianying hudong fazhan yanjiu* 雙輪美學：中國戲劇與中國電影互動發展研究 [Two-sided esthetics: A study of the mutual influences in the development of Chinese drama and Chinese film]. Beijing: Zhongguo dianying chubanshe, 2011, pp. 214–227.

Wu Hung. *The Wu Liang Shrine: The Ideology of Early Chinese Pictorial Art*. Stanford: Stanford University Press, 1989.

Wu Zuxiang 吳組緗. "Kan *Tianxian pei*" 看天仙配 [Watching *Married to a Heavenly Immortal*], in Wang Chang'an, ed. *Zhongguo Huangmeixi*. Hefei: Anhui wenyi chubanshe, 2009, pp. 1069–1070.

Xiao Qian 蕭乾. "Yibu gesong qingchun, zhouzu fuxiu shili de wujupian: Jieshao *Luomi'ou yu Zhuliye*" 一部歌頌青春咒詛腐朽勢力的舞劇片：介紹羅密歐與朱麗葉 [A ballet movie that sings the praise of youth and curses corrupt powers: Introducing *Romeo and Juliet*]. *Dazhong dianying*, No. 3 (1956): 24–25.

Xiao, Xiaoyu and D. Ray Heisey. "Liberationist Populism in the Chinese Film *Tian Xian Pei*: A Feminist Critique." *Women's Studies in Communication*, Vol. 19, No. 3 (1996): 313–333.

Xiao, Xiaoyu and D. Ray Heisey. "Shifting the Performative Characteristics of Opera and the Status Quo for Women in China," in Laura Lengel, ed. *Intercultural Communication and Cultural Practice: Music, Dance, and Women's Cultural Identity*. Westport, CT: Praeger, 2005, pp. 195–210.

Xie Baogeng 謝寶耿, comp. *Zhongguo xiaodao jinghua* 中國孝道精華 [The essence of China's filial piety]. Shanghai: Shanghai shehui kexueyuan chubanshe, 2000.

Xu Gongbing 許公炳. "Jianguo liushinian lai Huangmeixi dianying dianshiju yaomu" 建國六十年來黃梅戲電影電視劇要目 [A short catalogue of Huangmei Opera movies and Huangmei Opera television dramas during the sixty years since the establishment of the People's Republic]. *Huangmeixi yishu*, No. 2 (2010): 52–55.

Xu Yaoqing 許耀卿. "*Tianxian pei* xuyao gaihuilai ma?" 天仙配需要改回來嗎？[Do we need to restore *Married to a Heavenly Immortal* to its original shape?]. *Guangming ribao*, November 3, 1956.

Yamamoto Noriko 山本範子. "Araburu senjo: Zhang Sijie" 荒ぶる仙女：張四姐 [An Immortal Maiden gone wild: Zhang Sijie]. *Chūgoku gakushi* (2004): 23–41.

Yan Fengying 嚴鳳英. "Wo yan Qixiannü" 我演七仙女 [How I perform Seventh Sister]. *Zhongguo dianying*, No. 3 (1956): 30–32.

Yang Jie 楊杰. "Yan Fengying yu Huangmeixi" 嚴鳳英與黃梅戲 [Yan Fengying and Huangmei Opera], in Ye Bingnan, ed. *Xin Zhongguo difang xiju gaige jishi* 新中國地方戲劇改革紀實 [Records of the reform of local theater in new China]. Beijing: Zhongguo wenshi chubanshe, 2000, pp. 515–530.

Yang Ming 楊明. "Changqiang, xiqu zuopin yu xiqu dianying zuopin de zhuzuoquan wenti: You *Tianxian pei* an yinfa de sikao" 唱腔戲曲作品與戲曲電影作品的著作權問題：由天仙配案引發的思考 [The problem of copyright in the case of performed operas and operatic movies: From the example of *Married to a Heavenly Immortal*]. *Zhishi chanquan,* No. 1 (2007): 58–61.

Ye Bingnan 葉炳南, ed. *Xin Zhongguo difang xiju gaige jishi* 新中國地方戲劇改革紀實 [Records of the reform of local theater in new China]. Beijing: Zhongguo wenshi chubanshe, 2000.

Yeh, Catherine Vance. "Politics, Art, and Eroticism: The Female Impersonator as the National Cultural Symbol of Republican China," in Doris Croissant, Catherine Vance Yeh, and Joshua S. Mostow, eds. *Performing "Nation": Gender Politics in Literature, Theater, and the Visual Arts of China and Japan, 1880–1940*. Leiden: E.J. Brill, 2008, pp. 205–239.

Yeh, Catherine Vance. "Where is the Center of Cultural Production? The Rise of the Actor to National Stardom and the Beijing/Shanghai Challenge (1860s–1910s)." *Late Imperial China*, Vol. 25, No. 2 (2004): 74–118.

Ye Xiaoqing. *Ascendant Peace in the Four Seas: Drama at the Qing Imperial Court*. Hong Kong: The Chinese University Press, 2012.

Yen Chia-ch'i and Kao Kao. *The Ten-Year History of the Cultural Revolution*. Taipei: Institute of Current China Studies, 1988.

Yi Qun 以群. "Huadong xiqu guanmo yinxiang zaji" 華東戲曲觀摩印象雜記 [Notes on my impressions of the East China Theater Festival]. *Jiefang ribao*, November 5, 1954.

Yin Wei 殷偉 and Wang Xiaoying 王小英. *Yan Fengying* 嚴鳳英 [Yan Fengying]. Hefei: Huangshan shushe, 1985.

Yu Cong 余從 and Wang Ankui 王安葵, eds. *Zhongguo dangdai xiqu shi* 中國當代戲曲史 [A history of contemporary Chinese traditional opera]. Beijing: Xueyuan chubanshe, 2005.

Yu Zhi 余之. "Shi Hui yu Tong Baoling" 石揮與童葆苓 [Shi Hui and Tong Baoling]. *Haipai yiyuan*, No. 6 (2007): 74–77.

Zeng Yongyi 曾永義. *Suwenxue gailun* 俗文學概論 [A general treatise on popular literature]. Taipei: Sanmin shuju, 2003.

Zeng Yongyi and Shi Deyu 施德玉. *Difang xiqu gailun* 地方戲曲概論 [A general treatise on regional opera]. 2 vols. Taipei: Sanmin shuju, 2011.

Zhang Chengjian 張乘健. "Dunhuang faxian de *Dong Yong bianwen* qiantan" 敦煌發現的《董永變文》淺探 [A preliminary discussion of the "transformation text on Dong Yong" discovered at Dunhuang]. *Wenxue yichan*, No. 3 (1988), pp. 26–36.

Zhang Geng 張庚, ed. *Dangdai Zhongguo xiqu* 當代中國戲曲 [Contemporary traditional Chinese opera]. Beijing: Dangdai Zhongguo chubanshe, 1994.

Zhang Jing 張靜. "Zhengzhi shiyu zhong minjian qinghuai de jingdian yanyi: *Tianxian pei* dujie" 政治視閾中民間情懷的經典演繹：《天仙配》讀解 [The emergence of a classic of Chinese popular sentiment under the supervision of politics: An interpretation of *Married to a Heavenly Immortal*], in Rao Shuguang 饒曙光, ed. *Zhongguo dianying fenxi* 中國電影分析 [Analyses of Chinese films]. Beijing: Zhongguo guangbo dianshi chubanshe, 2007, pp. 60–71.

Zhang Junxiang 張駿祥, Sang Hu, et al. *Lun xiqu dianying* 論戲曲電影 [On operatic movies]. Beijing: Zhongguo dianying chubanshe, 1959.

Zhang, Xiao Yang. *Shakespeare in China: A Comparative Study of Two Traditions and Cultures*. Newark: University of Delaware Press/London: Associated University Presses, 1996.

Zhang, Yingjin, ed. *Encyclopedia of Chinese Film*. London: Routledge, 1998.

Zhao Cong 趙聰. *Zhongguo dalu de xiqu gaige 1942–1967* 中國大陸的戲曲改革一九四二——九六七 [Drama reform in mainland China 1942–1967]. Hong Kong: Chinese University Press, 1969.

Zhao Youwen 趙幼文, annot. *Cao Zhi ji jiaozhu* 曹植集校注 [A critical and annotated edition of the collected works of Cao Zhi]. Reprint; Taipei: Mingwen shuju, 1985.

Zheng Lisong 鄭立松. "Dui *Tianxian pei* de yixie huiyi" 對天仙配的一些回憶 [Some memories about *Married to a Heavenly Immortal*]. *Huangmeixi yishu*, No. 3 (2000): 20–21, 19.

Zhongguo lishi yanjiu hui 中國歷史研究會, comp. *Zhongguo tongshi jianbian* 中國通史簡編 [General simplified history of China]. Shanghai: Xinhua shudian, 1950.

Zhongguo xiqu zhi: Anhui juan 中國戲曲志：安徽卷 [Gazetteer of traditional Chinese opera: Anhui province]. Beijing: Zhongguo ISBN zhongxin, 1993.

Zhou Chunyang 周春陽. "Wo suo renshi de Lu Hongfei xiansheng" 我所認識的陸洪非先生 [Mr. Lu Hongfei as I knew him]. *Huangmeixi yishu*, No. 4 (2007): 27, 29.

Zhou Tao 周濤. *Minjian wenhua yu "shiqi nian" xiqu gaibian* 民間文化與十七年戲曲改編 [Popular culture and the rewriting of drama during the "seventeen years"]. Guilin: Guangxi shifan daxue chubanshe, 2012.

Zhu Yinghui 朱穎輝. *Dangdai xiqu sishinian* 當代戲曲四十年 [Forty years of contemporary drama]. Beijing: Wenhua yishu chubanshe, 1993.

Zipes, Jack. *The Enchanted Screen: The Unknown History of Fairy-Tale Films*. New York/London: Routledge, 2011.

Zuo Lai 左萊 and Liang Huaqun 梁化群. *Suqu "hongse xiju" shihua* 蘇區「紅色戲劇」史話 [A history of the "red plays" in the soviet areas]. Beijing: Wenhua yishu chubanshe, 1987.

Index